India, Climate Change, and
The Global Commons

India, Climate Change, and The Global Commons

Second Edition

A. DAMODARAN

OXFORD
UNIVERSITY PRESS

OXFORD
UNIVERSITY PRESS

Great Clarendon Street, Oxford, OX2 6DP,
United Kingdom

Oxford University Press is a department of the University of Oxford.
It furthers the University's objective of excellence in research, scholarship,
and education by publishing worldwide. Oxford is a registered trade mark of
Oxford University Press in the UK and in certain other countries

© A. Damodaran 2024

The moral rights of the author have been asserted

First Edition published in 2010
Second Edition published in 2024

Published in the United States of America by Oxford University Press
198 Madison Avenue, New York, NY 10016, United States of America

British Library Cataloguing in Publication Data

Data available

Library of Congress Control Number: 2023931905

ISBN 978–0–19–289982–8

DOI: 10.1093/oso/9780192899828.001.0001

Printed and bound in India by
Replika Press Pvt. Ltd.

Preface

The world has changed remarkably since the initial version of this book was published twelve years ago. Since then the international community has inched closer to securing major game-changing agreements and programmes of immense importance to global commons. This list includes the Sustainable Development Goals (SDGs) of the United Nations, the Paris Agreement on Climate Change, and the Aichi Biodiversity Targets adopted by the Convention on Biological Diversity. Until 2019, no policy analyst would have imagined a pandemic to be a global common. The advent of the coronavirus (or the COVID-19) pandemic at the end of the previous decade has changed our lives and has made us think differently on how to view and manage global commons. In terms of its geographical spread, COVID-19 rivals the infamous Spanish Flu of 1918. While the Spanish flu virus travelled from the West to the East, the coronavirus has originated and travelled in the reverse direction. While the spread of the Spanish Flu was enabled by inter-continental movement of troops during the First World War, the coronavirus flu rapidly scaled nation-state borders taking advantage of the forces of globalization. By mid-2020, the pandemic had destroyed the world economy. What compounded the problem has been our inability to correctly read the epidemiology and immunology of COVID-19.

During 2014, I launched an Elective Course at IIM Bangalore to cover the theme of global commons flowing from the initial version of the book. But as I grew wiser by the year, I started expanding the scope of the course to incorporate two new dimensions of global commons that were not present in the previous decade. In the year 2015, I commenced researching on blockchains and cryptocurrencies, two major developments in the digital technology field that made their advent in 2008 in the wake of the world economic crisis. This opened my horizons to the idea of a new form of global commons that had international impacts. Bitcoins and other cryptocurrencies that came into existence after 2009 were not designed to obey national boundaries or existing international and national institutions. Further, due to their bottom-up approach towards economic and financial institutions, they promised to usher a different kind of global commons with considerable impacts at local levels. My present position at the Indian Council for Research on International Economic Relations (ICRIER) has extended my interests in the evolving field of metaverse and Web 3.0. The second major 'global commons' that made its advent since 2010 has been the COVID-19 pandemic. While the causal factors of the pandemic had major implications on global environmental conventions/protocols pertaining to the CITES and the CBD, the issue of inequitable distribution of COVID-19 vaccines across the world has raised a major global commons concern of access to life-support systems that has strong implications on the maxim of equity.

Thus, in the revised version of this book, I situate the issue of global commons against the backdrop of the globalization process, nation-states, Information and Communication Technology (ICT) and blockchains, rurality, civic communities, national environmental policies, and finally pandemics. I have also substantially updated topics discussed in the initial version of the book, namely climate change, biodiversity, and related multilateral environmental agreements.

Nation-states fight battles with environmental problems that have a major bearing on global commons and the rules of international demeanour. It is also about a world characterized by funny contradictions! The same world that grapples with economic development, cultural globalization, pandemics, and terrorism also talks about climate change. These signs of diversity, however, run the danger of getting securitized and wired through extreme instrumentalism. The need is to de-instrumentalize the global environmental agenda, which currently does not make sense to large swathes of local spaces in the world, that stick to their own methods of upkeep. The central theme of the book is that plurality and diversity lie at the root of ensuring that a globalized world offers happiness to its citizens. Local communities and nation-states have for long resisted the tendency of a centralized global order to regiment and standardize ways of life across territories and people. Global institutions, nation-states, and local communities are partners in the fight for global commons. Global public goods are important to local communities as they (the local communities) benefit from their preservation. At the same time, for many local communities, global public goods are alien resources as it is sought to be governed in an 'instrumental' manner. For global conventions dealing with climate change, biodiversity, and desertification to acquire local roots, it is important that they are viewed as an extension of national or local commons and not as a resource that is separate from these rooted resources. The movement for conserving global commons can be effective and resilient only if it is linked to the fight for local commons.

The first chapter, titled 'The New International Environment: Changing the Unchanged', surveys the changing world environment brought in by globalization. The impact of globalization on the notion of the Westphalian state is discussed in this chapter. The point made here is that both terrorism and global capital have an inherent bias against the Westphalian order, though one is opposed to the other. The role of epistemic and distributed communities in promoting local identities is discussed here. The advent of global environmental problems of climate change, biodiversity, and desertification is discussed in terms of their varying features. While climate change deals with a global public good that transcends nation-state boundaries, the Conventions of Biodiversity and Hazardous Wastes Movements deal with global public goods that are confined within the boundaries of the nation-state.

The second chapter, 'Stereotypes on Development', deals with development issues confronting India and the world and the implications of this in promoting plural approaches in a globalized world order. Despite the birth of the unipolar world centred around the United States, efforts of nation-states such as Russia, China, and India have been to stay in the Westphalian mode while also availing the benefits of the globalized economic order. The chapter proceeds to discuss the climate change convention and the World Trade Organization (WTO) Agreement in relation to policies of the United States and developing countries. India has emerged as an economic power by going in for an unbalanced growth approach that focuses on certain growth poles to provide its economic push. Further, the country has also approached development in recent years by promoting ICT and modern digital technologies, which is postmodern in terms of its immense potential to produce global, national, and local impacts of far-reaching significance. It is further stated that despite the success of unbalanced growth strategy based on ICT, India could advance in the direction of the traditional as well by tapping the immense potential of its traditional knowledge. The rapid economic growth of countries such as India and China have created their own dynamics for markets, trade, and development. The spirit of sacrifice implicit in the Rio Agreements requires developing countries to change their industrial development paths, fashioned in the 1950s and 1960s. In the case of the WTO, developing countries seek to access global markets for furthering economic development. The WTO offers opportunities to developing countries to pursue their aspirations of making their presence in the global arena. However during the four years of the Trump Presidency in the United States, global trade has lost its momentum. Hopefully the world trade order improves with the Biden Presidency.

Thanks to Millennium Development Goals (MDGs) earlier and Sustainable Development Goals (SDGs) now, there is a greater focus in developing countries towards empowerment of women. Emphasis has been laid on empowerment of women in promoting sanitation, agriculture, sustainable natural resource management, and markets.

The third chapter, 'Challenges of Global Governance: Opinions and Formulations', focuses on how international statesmen like Tony Blair and international organizations such as the United Nations (UN) and the World Bank have perceived the challenges of globalization. It is noted that Blair and many other statesmen from the North have shifted their perception about globalization from that of governance systems to the issue of building capacities. International organizations such as the UN and the World Bank too have shifted their priorities from countries and international disputes to more fundamental matters like human rights, norms of governance, and transnational issues. Today many nation-states and local communities in the world have demonstrated that with quality governance that focuses on human rights and empowerment, it is possible to ensure that people are in a better position to withstand the economic threats of globalization. In many countries the focus is on development policies that enable development of social capital generated by local communities. Indeed social capital forms insular mechanisms that help local communities shield themselves from the adverse effects of globalization. It is argued that robust decentralized governance systems help states to optimize returns from a globalized economy.

The chapter titled 'India: The Multi-Faceted Nation-State', deals with India's multi-faceted nationhood. This chapter argues that despite its problems with the globalized order, the nation-state is still on the ascent. The signs of neo-nationalism have gone well with economic boom in countries such as India. Indeed, dynamic democracies such as India do not resist globalization—rather they co-opt with it through a postmodern process. India's Information Technology hubs like Bengaluru mirror postmodern space within a country that is caught between the forces of tradition and modernity. In the years to come, India has the makings to evolve as a postmodern state that seeks to combine traditionalism with modernity to provide plural responses to forces of globalization.

The fifth chapter, 'India's Rurality and Its Different Faces', takes the reader through India's rural scenario against the backdrop of the MDGs and the SDGs. It is stated that the diversity of India's rural scene has many manifestations. The prosperous fringe of rural India seeks greater liberalization of world trade in agricultural goods, while the not-so-prosperous fringe is reportedly seeking greater protectionism from imports. Drawing upon the experience of the arid state of Rajasthan in India, it is argued that despite best efforts at diversifying the income base of the rural population, the state has not been able to address the issue of redistribution of benefits from economic growth. Further, environmental degradation, that has been contributed by induced 'diversification', adds to the depletion of public goods in Rajasthan. Diversification is not diversity. The richness of diversity comes from the country's rich socioeconomic and cultural essence. The WTO Agreements have provided opportunities to sections of Indian agriculture. However, there is no effort to utilize our advantages in the realm of environmental sustainability to improve global market access. The exception is the unique case of Darjeeling Tea, a brand that combines the virtues of organic agriculture, geographic indications, and brand equity with traditionalism. This has further strengthened the position of this tea brand in the global market. However, when it comes to products like silk, it is seen that traditionalism has not been reinvented as a market-access tool. This may have been due to the absence of local initiatives that could have changed marketing systems. Externally-aided projects in India too have failed to contribute to sustainability on account of their instrumentalism. However, the potential that India's ICT prowess offers to its agricultural sector through disintermediation can be immense. The role of ICT in promoting future trading for agricultural commodities is highlighted as a complementary step that could link India's agricultural sector to the world markets. The price-risk management tools associated with futures trading can help integrate local farmer communities with the global world since it removes the major inhibition these sections have in tapping global markets. Stable prices in turn can create conditions for sustainable agriculture.

Chapter 6, 'Adapting to Globalization or Fighting It?' deals in greater detail with the possibilities of local resistance to discourses of globalization and its associated free trade principle. Local resistance is a symbol of plurality. It also creates possibilities of enabling diversity so essential to survive for poorer sections to survive in a globalized world. The role of ICT in promoting traditional knowledge and compensating them through non-intellectual property rights draws its inspiration from the second enclosure movement. The implicit point made in this chapter is that diversity and local identities can be useful in preventing standardization and instrumentalism in the world.

The environmental processes in the world commencing from the Stockholm Summit of 1972, the Rio Summit of 1992 and the conventions of ozone depletion, climate change, the Basel Convention, biodiversity, and the persistent organic pollutants hold many lessons on how global goods can be crafted and managed.

The significant aspect of the seventh chapter, 'Environmentalism in the World', is its critique of the local impact of these conventions and its communication systems. The chapter considers climate change in relation to WTO and explores the problem of upscaling local environmental success in order to obtain global environmental benefits. The underlying message is that the global environmental conventions (with their implicit instrumentalism) do not have intrinsic synergy with the local milieu, thus preventing possibilities of co-option and plural responses as was noticed in the case of Darjeeling Tea and other unique products.

The eighth chapter, 'Policies for the Environment: The Story of India', goes through the story of evolution of India's environmental policy and legislation. Commencing from the 1970s, India has put in place a variety of legislation and policy statements that address conservation and environmental protection. It is noted that India's environmental legislations have addressed key environmental concerns affecting the country reasonably well. There has also been a trend towards decentralized management of natural resources in India, that is best expressed through the joint forest management programme. However, the implementation of decentralization programmes has been patchy. Nevertheless, with its many limitations it is true that India's policy framework on environmental protection provides enough scope for promoting diverse and local-based approaches to global environmental issues.

The ninth chapter, 'Leaders, Markets, and Values', addresses the role of leaders, markets, and values. After critically surveying the scenario of markets in various parts of the world and the initiatives taken by locally rooted leaders and communities from the South, the chapter concludes that neither leaders nor markets can give a push to sustainable development. It is argued that this task is best left to nation-states and civil societies.

The issue of compensating ecological services is discussed in Chapter 10, titled 'Compensating for Lost Resources: Does It Work?'. After examining various schemes for payment of ecosystem services, the chapter brings out the argument that the most important challenge is to improve valuation of ecosystem services, from the viewpoint of local communities that conserve services. It is also argued that the concept of collective action can be fruitfully employed to establish property rights over natural resources, which, in turn can form the basis for determining the value of ecosystem services.

In Chapter 11, 'The Local Impacts of Multilateral Environmental Agreements: The UNFCCC, CBD, and The Basel Convention', the focus is on the perils of instrumentalism that have affected global environmental management regimes. The chapter considers instrumentalism as a phenomenon which obscures the basic purpose or the mission for which a measure has been conceived. It is argued that the elaborate systems of monitoring and verification associated with multilateral environmental agreements displaces the objectives for which the Agreements have been created. Instrumentalism displaces equity and fairness and focuses on process and procedures, as they focus more on technical efficiency. The chapter highlights instrumentalist features of the climate change convention (including the Paris Agreement on Climate Change of 2015–16), the Basel Convention, the Biodiversity Convention, the Biosafety Protocol, and surveys how Global Environmental Facility (GEF) projects also suffer from the disease. The chapter also surveys instrumentalism that affects projects and schemes in the sectors of water and forests. The grip of instrumentalism on societal risks assessment exercises is also explored.

Chapter 12, titled 'Environment and Trade: The Role of Stakeholders', takes a look at the role of civil societies and nongovernmental organizations (NGOs) in promoting the cause of global public goods like action against climate change, biodiversity conservation, movement of hazardous substances from developed countries to developing countries and trade and environment conflicts. It is stated that civil society groups themselves are not able to cope with the multiple global goods concerns and that there is an urgent need to address cross-cutting issues in order to ensure that the goal of sustainable development is attained in an integrated sense. For this, it is important that capacity promotion of civil society groups takes place. Cross-cutting issues can promote non-instrumental approaches that stress on respecting diversity.

Chapter 13, which is titled 'COVID-19 as Global Commons: Issues of Equity, Sustainability, and Instrumentalism', discusses the principal issues of sustainability and equity involved in the origins, transmission, and management of the COVID-19 pandemic. Besides pointing to the limitations of the CITES, the CBD, and the WTO-SPS in preventing pandemics of zoonotic origins, the chapter touches upon the causes and consequences of the failure of COVAX multilateral facility in providing vaccines to the needy countries in the world.

Chapter 14, titled 'Restructuring Regimes for Sustainable Development', addresses the topic of restructuring international regimes for global sustainable development. After examining the idea of a 'supra-nation-state' entity, such as the World Environment Organization (WEO), against the backdrop of existing institutions, namely, the United Nations Environment Programme (UNEP) and GEF, the chapter comes to the point that the real priority is to have a global governance system which is free from instrumentalism. It is argued that Global Environmental Organizations which are free from instrumentalism would pay attention to national and local aspirations and come out with strategies to ensure that the cause of conserving the global commons is accepted by all.

The final chapter which is titled 'The Diversity Principle, Blockchains, and the Future of Global Commons', underscores the importance of de-instrumentalized approaches to managing the global commons, in the larger interests of upholding social and environmental justice. Here I introduce the concept of distributed network technologies like the blockchain and seek to delve on its possible applications in the realms of improving the performance of Multilateral Environmental Agreements and pandemic management.

Contents

Abbreviations

ABLE	Association of Biotechnology Enterprises
ABS	Access and Benefit Sharing
AIA	Advanced Informed Agreement
ABT	Aichi Biodiversity Targets
AIDS	Acquired Immuno-Deficiency Syndrome
ANPED	The Northern Alliance for Sustainability
ASEAN	Association of South East Asian Nations
BREXIT	Britain and Exit
Bt	*Bacillus thuringiensis*
CAP	Common Agriculture Policy/Corporate Advocacy Priorities
CBAM	Carbon Border Adjustment Mechanism
CBD	Convention on Biological Diversity
CBI	Climate Bonds Initiative
CDM	Clean Development Mechanism
CERs	Certified Emission Reductions
CGIAR	Consultative Group on International Agriculture Research
CITES	Convention on International Trade in Endangered Species
CEPI	Coalition for Epidemic Preparedness Innovations
CFC	Chlorofluorocarbons
CITES	Convention on International Trade in Endangered Species
COP	Conference of Parties
COVAX	COVID-19 Vaccines Global Access
COVAX-AMC	COVID-19 Vaccines Global Access Advance Market Commitment
COVID 19	Coronavirus Disease 2019
CPCB	Central Pollution Control Board
CPI(M)	Communist Party of India (Marxist)
CSD	Commission on Sustainable Development
CSE	Centre for Science and Environment
CTM	Community Trademark
CUTS	Consumer Unity and Trust Society
DDT	Dichlorodiphenyltrichloroethane
DNA	Deoxyribonucleic Acid
ECOSOC	UN Economic and Social Council

EIA	Environmental Impact Assessment
EIB	European Investment Bank
ELCI	Environmental License Center International
EPA	Environment Protection Agency
EPR	Extended Producer Responsibility
ESP	Environmental Service Programme
EST	Environmentally Sound Technologies
FAO	Food and Agriculture Organization
FCCC	Framework Convention on Climate Change
FIFRA	Federal Insecticide Fungicide and Rodenticide Act
FIPB	Foreign Investment Promotion Board
GAIA	Global Anti-Incinerator Alliance
GATS	General Agreement on Trade in Services
GATT	General Agreement on Tariffs and Trade
GBF	Global Biodiversity Framework
GCNBNT	Global Commons Negotiations and Business in Network Technologies
GCF	Green Climate Fund
GEF	Global Environment Facility
GEM	Global Environment Mechanism
GEO	Global Environmental Organization
GHG	Green House Gas
GI	Geographical Indication
GIS	Geographical Information Systems
GMEF	Global Ministerial Environmental Forum
GMO	Genetically Modified Organism
GPG	Global Public Goods
GPL	General Public Licence
GSDP	Gross State Domestic Product
GTZ	Deutsche Gesellschaft für Technische Zusammenarbeit
HFCs	Hydrofluorocarbons
HLP 1	High Level Panel 1 on Biodiversity Financing
IAEA	International Atomic Energy Agency
IARI	Indian Agricultural Research Institute
IBM	International Business Machines
IBRD	International Bank for Reconstruction and Development
ICAR	Indian Council for Agriculture Research
ICT	Information and Communication Technology
IFC	International Finance Corporation
IMF	International Monetary Fund
IMO	International Maritime Organization
INC	Indian National Congress

IP	Intellectual Property
IPCC	Inter-governmental Panel on Climate Change
IPEN	International POPS Elimination Network
IPRs	Intellectual Property Rights
ISO	International Organization for Standardization
IT	Information Technology
ITC	International Tobacco Corporation
ITES	Information Technology Enabling Services
IUCN	International Union for Conservation of Nature
JBIC	Japan Bank for International Cooperation
JETPs	Just Energy Transition Partnerships
JFM	Joint Forest Management
LMO	Living Modified Organism
MDGs	Millennium Development Goals
MEA	Multilateral Environmental Agreement
MERS-CoV	Middle East Respiratory Syndrome—Corona Virus
MoEF	Ministry of Environment and Forests
MRV	Monitoring, Reporting, and Verification
MSP	Minimum Support Price
NAFTA	North American Free Trade Agreement
NAMA	Non-agriculture Market Access
NATO	North Atlantic Treaty Organization
NCSA	National Capacity Building for Self-Assessment
NDC	Nationally Determined Contributions
NTBs	Non-tariff Barriers
OBOR	One Belt, One Road (of China)
ODA	Official Development Assistance
ODS	Ozone Depleting Substances
OECD	Organization for Economic Co-operation and Development
OMGE	Overall Mitigation in Global Emissions
OPEC+	Organization of the Petroleum Exporting Countries Plus
PCBs	Polychlorinated Biphenyls
PCF	Prototype Carbon Fund
PHEIC	Public Health Emergency of International Concern
PIC	Prior Informed Consent
POPS	Persistent Organic Pollutants
PPMs	Process and Production Methods
PRI	Panchayati Raj Institution
PSNR	Permanent Sovereignty over Natural Resources
PSU	Public Sector Undertaking
RAFI	Rural Advancement Foundation International

RSPB	The Royal Society for the Protection of Birds
SARD	Sustainable Agriculture and Rural Development
SARS-CoV-1	Severe Acute Respiratory Syndrome—Corona Virus 1
SARS-CoV-2	Severe Acute Respiratory Syndrome—Corona Virus 2
SBSTA	Subsidiary Body for Scientific and Technological Advice
SDC	Swiss Agency for Development and Corporation
SDG	Sustainable Development Goals
SDIN	Sustainable Development Issues Network
SPS	Sanitary and Phytosanitary Measures
TEEB	The Economics of Ecosystems and Biodiversity
TFAP	Tropical Forest Action Plan
TRIPs	Trade Related Intellectual Property Rights
TSCA	Toxic Substances Control Act
TWN	Third World Network
UNCC	United Nations Compensation Commission
UNCCD	United Nations Convention to Combat Desertification
UNCED	United Nations Conference on Environment and Development
UNCOD	United Nations Conference on Desertification
UNEO	United Nations Environment Organization
UNFCCC	United Nations Framework Convention on Climate Change
UNHCR	United Nations High Commission of the Refugees
WAVES	Wealth Accounting and Valuation of Ecosystem Services
WCED	World Commission on Environment and Development
WCS	World Conservation Strategy
WHO	World Health Organization
WIM	Warsaw International Mechanism
WIPO	World Intellectual Property Organization
WMO	World Meteorological Organization
WWF	World Wide Fund for Nature
WRI	World Resources Institute

1

The New International Environment

Changing the Unchanged

The onset of the devastating coronavirus pandemic in 2020 has altered the foundations of how we see global commons. Until the advent of the pandemic, the forces of economic globalization and global environmental movements formed the faces of global commons. In the aftermath of the pandemic, a new, unwelcome global common has emerged which has yanked global economies down while raising glaring questions regarding the working of international bio conservation regulations and the ability of the world to limit the rise in global temperatures within the range of 1.5°C as compared to pre-industrial levels.

International environmental movements have for a long time questioned the role of economic globalization in wreaking havoc on the quality of environment in developing countries. In recent years, many civil society movements have talked about the desirability of worldwide action to conserve global public goods. Despite its major ideological victory over Communism and other closed political systems in the early 1990s, the economic face of globalization has not been free from its critics. As a matter of fact, protests against the economic order brought in by globalization have only grown louder.

A related issue is about the linkages between the forces of globalization on the one hand and global environmental movements, on the other. While some global environmental movements attribute the ethos of globalization as being responsible for global environmental problems, others argue that the forces of globalization stand in the way of biodiversity conservation and action against climate change.

One of the essential issues which has affected today's world has been the impact of globalization on the Westphalian system of nation-states. The Westphalian system, which is based on the 'Westphalian Treaty' of

India, Climate Change, and The Global Commons. A. Damodaran, Oxford University Press. © A. Damodaran 2024.
DOI: 10.1093/oso/9780192899828.003.0001

the seventeenth century, gave primacy to the idea and practice of the sovereign state. The advent of globalization in the 1990s weakened state sovereignty. This casualty was in no small measure due to the creation of network communities that came into existence with the advent of the Internet. The decline of the Westphalian system marked the emergence of global environmental movements that transcended national boundaries. The spread of terrorism also sought to overturn the fundamental premises of the Westphalian system. In this scheme of things, the Gramscian notions of legitimacy and hegemony, as applied to states, is under threat. However it is still a fact that there is no alternative sovereign power in sight.

In the field of sustainable development, the shift from local and national resources to global goods has been perceptible. We all know that the 1980s was the decade when the concept of global common goods came into prominence. The Vienna Convention on 'Ozone Layer Depletion' and the Montreal Protocol on 'Ozone Depleting Substances' heralded the advent of a world that gave priority to global common goods. The Framework Convention on 'Climate Change' and the Convention on 'Biological Diversity', popularly referred to as the Rio Conventions, completed the quest for putting in place a regime of management for global public goods, that included the ozone layer, climate, and biodiversity. Interestingly, if we situate these developments against the backdrop of globalization that was unleashed in the 1990s, one can see certain interesting trends. The advent of the World Trade Organization (WTO) in 1995 aided the process of globalization. However a fallout of the Agreement has been the rise of global environmental movements which have highlighted the possible adverse impacts global trade and investment regimes can have on the environment. Interestingly, these impacts are not just about global public goods such as ozone layer, climate, biodiversity, but also about terrestrial environmental resources such as forests, land, and water, which largely fall within the domain of nation-states. Resistance to globalization has also been coming from socialist states and local bodies that have taken up 'green–red' or 'red–green' causes. A case in point has been the instance of a small local body in Communist Party-ruled Kerala (Plachimada), that fought Coca Cola for blatant use of groundwater resources in the village.

Globalization has both its critics and votaries. Positive views on globalization have focussed on the positives of globalization. Among the votaries of globalization are economists who see globalization as promoting disparities in income and wealth in developing countries. Hirst and Thompson (1999) consider globalization as contributing to growth in trade and flows of capital investments between countries. Other scholars like Frankel (2000) advocate globalization on account of its great potential to provide a free trade environment. Frankel also states that the problems of national sovereignty and intra-civil disagreements in the globalized era, have not been on account of policies followed by multilateral institutions such as the WTO. On the other hand, he feels that states that are sensitive about national sovereignty, have, by not agreeing to the WTO regimes, caused a slowdown on efforts to free global trade tenders from protectionist tendencies. Frankel and others would consider globalization to be successful only when it liberalizes the world from the power of nation-states.

Yet another way has been to view globalization as ushering in universalization. This view logically leads to the argument that globalization promotes the rapid spread of modernization across national borders. In terms of this perspective, globalization is modernistic or is characterized by modernity.

By far, the critics of globalization focus on the evil effects of globalization in achieving economic liberalization and weakening the power of the nation-state. These critics would also bring out the potential of globalization in homogenizing cultures and identities, thereby engendering diversity deficit. There is, of course, the view propounded that globalization creates a crisis of identity or deprivation for the have nots. A related criticism of globalization is that it promotes footloose capital that does not have any commitment to any particular location. There are other shades of criticisms against globalization. For instance the internationalist school considers economic globalization as facilitating the hold of transnational corporations which do not have any commitments to any particular economy. This school believes that global institutions should be democratized and that nation-states should hold on to their identities.

There are other theories that look at the methods and strategies employed by players in a globalized world. Institutionalists who believe globalization is an inevitable trend but needs reform, would support social

learning theories which could empower institutions to achieve coopera-
tive solutions through bargaining. Similarly, scholars like Hajer (1997)
who talk about discourse coalitions, specify how particular discursive
frames help to promote and shape perceptions and align networks of
actors into coalitions. This perspective strongly emphasizes the fact that
globalization is a social construction.

Knowledge-based theories, which have propounded the idea of epistemic communities, speak about the role played by business groups
and corporates in knowledge construction in the globalization era. This
theory mentions coalition building by business groups across borders
as compared to earlier times when these groups only functioned within
national borders to achieve their ends. Indeed, experts like Haas (1992)
have attempted to situate epistemic community approaches within the
framework of regime theory and highlight the role of business as knowledge brokers. These schools of thought have also formulated theories
about how business entities that employ stratagems of bargaining and
coalition formation could 'privatize' the United Nation systems. These
theorists also point to the role of business houses in the negotiations on
WTO's Trade Related Intellectual Property Rights (TRIPS) and related
agreements.

Internationalization is also said to happen when close co-ordination
exists between business interests and the WTO dispute settlement processes. Newell says that the TRIPS agreement of the WTO has been
heavily driven by US business interests. Indeed, Paterson, Humphreys,
and Pettiford (1998) observe that business firms directly seek to influence
the United Nations system. A case in point is the Codex Alimentarius
Commission (a standard setting body) dealing with health and environmental issues connected to the WTO Agreement on 'Sanitary and
Phytosanitary Measures'. These bodies, as is well known, are supported
by UN organizations such as the World Health Organization (WHO) and
the Food and Agriculture Organization (FAO). And yet, Codex proceedings are tempered by business interests. Business associations played an
important role at the United Nations Conference on Environment and
Development (UNCED) deliberations. Indeed, as Newell (2000) states,
the term 'new constitutionalism' refers to the process by which capital
asserts its control over states and international agreements such as the
WTO-TRIPS, and the North American Free Trade Agreement (NAFTA).

Environmental movements have tried to counter this trend through frontal attacks and exposés. As Cox (1996) states, while the power of business is articulated through nation-states, transnational organizations, and domestic firms, environmentalists take to public forums and social media in order to whip up community sentiments against businesses, than rely on silent lobbying measures. However it needs to be noted that environmental NGOs such as the World Resources Institute (WRI) and the Environment Defense Fund, have a different philosophy that advocates market-based solutions and private-public partnership models to address environmental problems (Newell 2000; Helvarg 1994; Rowell 1996).

Epistemic communities have helped the world in other ways. These communities seek to provide expert solutions to problems through technical indicators and yardsticks. These communities are for democratization of the WTO and World Bank. They are against perverse or distorted subsidies. Further, they advocate moving away from the Western model of industrial development. These communities have also focused on the rationale of coalition building by civil society groups and other interest groups at the trans-national level. Their role also extends to advocating new networks that connect governments and civil societies and supporting horizontal linkages between sectors. In the field of environment, the favourite slogans of epistemic communities, include eco-efficiency, technological improvements, product sustainability, and so on. These slogans are supposed to uphold implementation of global agreements, compacts, and protocols such as the Kyoto Protocol on climate change.

Indeed, experts like Haas have tried to situate epistemic community approaches within the framework of regime theory. This approach highlights the role of business groups as knowledge brokers. The perspective also looks at issues connected to the construction of policy-relevant knowledge. Haas (1992) and Hajer (1997) argue that regimes are socially constructed. To this extent, their views are closer to the neo-Gramscian framework of stable and effective regimes that are derived from the notion of hegemony. Scholars like Hajer and Maarten explore the interaction of material and discursive practices and the roles of structures and stratagems in sustaining corporate dominance and legitimacy. The Gramscian and neo-Gramscian approaches leads one to the transnational approach developed by Risse-Kappen (1995). According to

Kappen, a state-centrist approach to regime analysis is an anachronism in the modern world of globalization. This is because in a globalized world, national-level interest groups and institutions seek to form transnational coalitions for pursuing common issues that have a global purport. Thus, as per the Risse-Kappen theory, NGOs, scientific communities, corporates, and other stakeholders build up strategic alliances and coalitions in order to articulate their positions in international policy forums.

It is stated that the theories of International Relations have never been comfortable with the role of non-state actors and global civil society in international affairs. However, Wapner (1996) and O'Brien et al. (2000) use the expression 'complex multilateralism' to explain the impact of environmental and other related movements on global institutions such as the WTO. Then, there are the transformationalists, who, while conceding that globalization is inevitable, see great scope for democratizing global institutions by empowering nation-states, to once again retain their key role in policy frameworks that uphold legitimacy and accountability based on territorial identities. This school of thought, therefore, recommends a partial if not complete revival of the Westphalian system. In a world where terrorism seems to have insidiously dissipated across national boundaries, the sanguine hopes of transformationalists may invite scepticism. Though economists like Galbraith have convincingly argued about adverse economic prospects for the 'poor in poor countries' on account of liberalization, competition, and deregulation, there have been other scholars who have argued that globalization has levelled inequalities in developing countries. This view gets support from the increase in offshore and onshore outsourcing jobs from the United States and Europe to countries such as India and the Philippines. The logic of offshoring has paradoxically created critics of globalization within developed countries such as the United States. Indeed, these critics could take considerable solace in Sassen's (2001) point that offshore production and outsourcing have only served to weaken organized workers in developed countries. Thus, the opposition to global business interests, especially in the area of offshoring and outsourcing, would now come from the developed rather than from the developing world. Most of this opposition will be directed at 'footloose capital' that is not rooted to any local environment. Peter Newell (2000) argues that firms and business groups often seek to extend their influence by forging connections between domestic and international entities and constructing international coalitions in a bid to transcend narrow domestic opposition. As Keohane and Nye (1972) state, this approach amounts to internationalization of domestic politics and the domestication of international politics. There is some truth in these observations.

It needs to be however noted that this kind of coalition and alliance building has been happening more in the developed world (comprising of the United States and European Community (EC) countries) than in developing countries. India has not witnessed trans-nationalization of policies in the wake of globalization. Rather India has insulated itself from forces of globalization. India's Central Government has always played a nodal role in mediating for national groups in the WTO as well as in the global environmental forums.

In their paper, 'Whether To Govern Globalism At All', Levy and Newell (2005) say that the best way to approach environmental governance is to view them from the broad range of political, economic, social structure, and processes that shape and constrain an actor's behaviour towards environment. Therefore, they debunk the regime theory and suggest a broader system of order and structure that is always present and not artificially created. Indeed, Levy and Newell argue that one could conceive of a market-based system running the globalized world where private firms are functioning as primary agents.

Standing on the other extreme is Scholte (2000), who states that globalization destroys pre-existent cultures and the culture of local self-determination by introducing the social structures of modernity, namely, capitalism, rationalism, industrialism, bureaucratism, and so on. Scholte argues that this kind of a process creates a reconfiguration of geography, leading to what he describes as supra-territoriality. In other words, for Scholte, globalization is modern and not postmodern and it is supra-territorial in the sense that it is characterized by trans-world simultaneity and instantaneity. However, as Appadurai (2000) states, the trend of ethnic and religious violence in recent times has altered the states of competition within contemporary globalization. At the same time, Appadurai also says that the 'newness' of what Scholte calls supra-territoriality would prove to be difficult for the globalized world to handle or to manage.

What could be the essence of supra-territoriality? Scholte (2000) has no clear answer. We get a clue about supra-territorialism from Hardt and Negri (2000). According to them, supra-territorialism transcends national boundaries, while at the same time not having any economic or political centre since the power of an empire is diffused both geographically and institutionally. A different model of supra-territoriality is brought out by the neoconservative school in the United States in the wake of 9/11. As per this thesis, the new emerging world would be run on a Washington consensus involving the US Government and US corporations, whose interests the administration represents.

Joseph Stiglitz (2002) feels that a global world government is not a great idea. He laments that no world government can ever be accountable to the people of every country. Nor will such an entity oversee the globalization process in a manner that national governments would.

To understand the fundamental transformation process achieved by globalization, one needs to look back to history, particularly the history of continental Europe, which dominated world politics from the Middle Ages onwards.

We return to the Treaty of Westphalia. This Treaty of 1648 was basically meant to promote order in a world where disorder was the norm. The peace of Westphalia was valuable. It ended the model of globalization which was based on the conquest of territories. The peace of Westphalia clearly recognized the territorial sovereignty of the member states which signed the agreement. These member states were given the freedom to enter into treaties with one another. The idea of a secular state also came from the Treaty. The classical nation-states of northern and western Europe evolved within the framework of the Westphalian agreement. The birth of the nation-state as a specific form of state or as a cultural entity also owes its origin to the Treaty. The nation-state had to be culturally distinguishable, territorially demarcable, and politically distinct. Nation-states could not be part of or subsidiaries of a grand Roman empire or a grand Greek Macedonian empire. They had to be independent sovereign units. Napoleon's wars were a challenge to Westphalianism. Westphalianism suffered a major jolt during the two world wars of the twentieth century. However, even after the Second World War, nation-states did not bounce back with vigour as Stalin had spread his tentacles over East Europe and Mao over East Asia and Indo-China. It was not until the collapse of Soviet communism in 1991, that East Europe re-drew its boundaries on the lines of nation-states.

There are no clear answers to the question whether globalization undermines nation-states though one sees clear trends of Westphalianism weakening. It is intuitive that globalization, by promoting an integrated world, has somewhat reversed the notion of the Westphalian nation-state. Indeed, the concept of global cities, which has been advocated in the wake of the globalization process by anthropologists and social analysts like Saskia Sassen (2001), completely negates the concept of the nation-state and its identity. But if one were to analyse the transformative dimension of globalization, one should go beyond the definition of globalization and probe the fundamental political philosophy that globalization has tried to overturn. Here, one sees that both globalization and religious fundamentalists are on the same platform! Both Islamic fundamentalism and globalization operate in a seamless world—both in the virtual and real senses.

Where do the global environment movements stand in relation to the Westphalian State? Since the year 1985, when the World Commission on Environment and Development submitted its epochal report entitled Our Common Future, the paradigm of 'sustainable development' has been the defining philosophy of development. Since the year 1992, a spate of Conventions of significance to the global environment have made their advent. This included the UN Framework Convention on Climate Change, the Convention on Biodiversity, the UN Convention to Combat Desertification (the UNCCD or the Desertification Convention in short), the Rotterdam Convention on Chemicals, and the Stockholm Convention on Persistent Organic Pollutants. The pre-Rio Convention, namely the Vienna Convention on Ozone Depleting Substances, and Rio's UN Framework Convention on Climate Change stand on the same pedestal. They talk about a global public goods which do not obey the territorial boundaries of a nation-state. By contrast, the Conventions relating to Biodiversity, Transboundary Movement of Hazardous Wastes (the Basel Convention) and the POPS do not talk about global public goods per se—rather they talk about environmental goods which are of common concern of humankind, but occurring within the territorial confines of nation-states. We would, therefore, go a step further and say that global environmental movements and civil society groups which have strongly focused on the climate and ozone layer, the two global goods that transcend nation-state boundaries—are distinct from those which are involved with the Conventions of POPS, Basel (Basle), Biodiversity, and Desertification.

One is tempted, therefore, to come to a very amusing conclusion about who stands where in the world of politics, economics, and environment.

The votaries of global public goods like climate and ozone layer, stand on the pedestal of transnationalism. On the other hand, environmental groups concerned with the biodiversity convention (which has given primacy to national sovereignty and the rights of social and ethnic groups), the desertification convention (that talks of land degradation), and chemical-related conventions stand on Westphalian premises. Logically, the latter seek to resist universal truths and standards.

Now, where do we place critics of globalization? As was stated earlier, critics of globalization do not form a homogenous group. Those who criticize globalization on the grounds that it promotes poverty, economic inequalities, and cultural homogenization do not necessarily stand on Westphalian premises. The idea of economic development subscribed to by these groups is based on universal ideas of welfare and well-being propounded by classical and neo-classical economics.

Whatever be the pattern of divide characterizing the governance of the global environmental and political systems, the simple fact that emerges is that even a non Westphalian system is in search of an order. Likewise, governance of global public goods also calls for an 'order'. Some thinkers would like a super-territorial order, while others would desire a 'world order'. This desire for order causes approaches that seek to resolve global environmental problems getting lost in instrumentalism. An order that gets caught in instrumentalism loses out on diversity and plurality. This needs to be avoided.

Despite the great appetite for globalization, the existence of Westphalianism in parts of the world is a healthy sign. This holds true for epistemic communities that articulate local points of view. Though all global environmental agreements uphold the spirit of global commons, each one displays its unique feature. What needs to be recognized is that global commons cannot be managed effectively without sound national and local policies. A mission for reversing climate change cannot succeed without the co-operation of nation-states and local communities. The advent of 'distributed network' digital technologies like Blockchains and crypto coins and the value that data holds in modern-day economies, have raised new possibilities for local communities by way of new economic opportunities that provide them with sustainable means of living. Meanwhile, as the world advances to Web 3.0, there will be radically new opportunities for local communities to create their own content on the Web. The coronavirus pandemic of 2020, which has caused digitization to extend to poorer communities in countries like India, raises new visions for managing the global commons.

This then are the key messages that succeeding chapters seek to convey.

We seek to explore the principal global commons issues confronting the world in the succeeding chapters with reference to global environmental agreements, the COVID-19 pandemic and the ongoing digital revolution exemplified in blockchains. More fundamentally, we seek to explore the national impacts of these global conventions against the backdrop of India.

2

Stereotypes on Development

The roots of non-Westphalian thinking in the 20th century can be traced to the emergence of the unipolar world in the wake of the collapse of the Soviet Union. The rise of the United States as the sole superpower in the 1990s gave Americanism a major push. Owen Harris (2003) in his Boyer lecture characterizes the United States as a revisionist power that aims to transform the whole society of states into what looks suspiciously like an image of itself writ large (Bell 2005). Harris is not off the mark. As Condoleezza Rice, the former US Secretary of State, once said, 'The United States is still a pretty popular place'. American culture, both good and bad, is very much sought abroad; and I still think that the values of the United States are the most universal of all values (Garfinkle 2005). This statement clearly brings out the sentiment of cosmopolitanism in a unipolar globalized world. American values are considered universal—to be practised by different parts of the world, both in its good and bad senses. However, unlike Rice, Harris talks about an 'imposition'. Yet, this does not create a deep point of difference. Ideas and norms that change from a 'rule' to a 'maxim' lose their 'imposing' nature. Discursive practices achieve this transition. The well-orchestrated discourses on America as the new and only superpower possessing military and economic might has slipped through the crevices of even the most hardened societies that have tried to insulate themselves from the rest of the world. If one reads these trends with what Condoleezza Rice considers as transformational diplomacy, it is not difficult to say that Americanism has acquired great significance around the globe, either as a credo to be embraced or as a not-so-desirable idea that needs to be opposed.

The real essence of the US-related discursive practices is that it is not a boorish repetition of 'doctrinarian jargon' as was the case with Communist propaganda. This script is re-written and re-nuanced to underscore the central point that the United States and only the United

India, Climate Change, and The Global Commons. A. Damodaran, Oxford University Press. © A. Damodaran 2024.
DOI: 10.1093/oso/9780192899828.003.0002

States can be the power centre of the unipolar world's economic and se-curity fortunes. The brand of Americanism promoted in the wake of the 9/11 attacks and in the wake of the Iraq invasion in 2002 is fundamen-tally different from the kind of universal ideas of peace propagated by Woodrow Wilson in the aftermath of the First World War. The new credo of cosmopolitanism is Americanism and is best reflected in the manner in which Donald Rumsfeld, the former US Defense Secretary, brushed off the Geneva Conventions when defending the war against Iraq. Indeed, the concept of American cosmopolitanism, its values and its desirability for the world is something which excites some American NGOs as well. This is also reflected in the manner in which Americans are self-critical about their problems and were willing to accept change, as was proved by the election of Barack Obama as the 44th President. In 2009, faced with the worst ever economic crisis since the 1930s, the United States embraced the 'radically hopeful political consensus' that Obama talked about before he became the US President (Obama 2007). Nevertheless, the sub-text remains the same. With all its problems, the United States still holds the privilege of offering the best solutions to the world's prob-lems. Although the United States withdrew into a shell (enabled by the America First doctrine) during the four years of the Donald Trump presi-dency, the onset of the Biden Presidency promises to take the country back to the forefront on critical global environmental problems like cli-mate change.

There have been similar efforts at emulating the US example in other parts of the world. Francis Fukuyama (2005) mentions how Asian multi-lateralism has cut across the boundaries of China, Japan, and South Korea and other states under the auspices of the Association of South East Asian Nations (ASEAN) plus. Fukuyama also talks about a Latin American triangle involving Cuba, Venezuela, and Bolivia forming a great alliance of Marxist and Left regimes that cuts across national boundaries—something that 'proletarian internationalism' could not achieve in the twentieth century. However, it is doubtful whether these instances have dented Westphalianism. There are many countries in Asia and Europe which do not like nation-state boundaries to be dissolved. They prefer to be on the Westphalian mode despite benefiting from the global marketplace. They like 'Americanism' for all the free-enterprise virtues it has promoted, but would not like 'Americanism' in its cultural essence to run riot within their borders. Russia, China, and India fall in this category.

When the Soviet Union disintegrated, it appeared as if Russia and its erstwhile republics were getting more and more separated from the ideal of the 'multi-nation' state welded by Communism. The formation of Ukraine, Estonia, Latvia, Georgia, Armenia, Lithuania, and the Central Asian Republics along 'national' and 'ethnic' lines, served to indicate that it was the resurgence of national identities that led to the collapse of the Soviet empire. The big residue called 'Russia' had to live with the image of being a collapsed superpower. When Boris Yeltsin gave way to Vladimir Putin as the Russian President at the turn of this century, it was felt that Putin would focus on giving Russia its identity as a cultural and military superpower. However, the manner in which Putin handled the Chechnya affair and the swift manner in which he co-opted Crimea into the Russian Federation in 2014 clearly indicated that he would not like to yield his ground on efforts to undermine Russia in its traditional sphere of influence. Russia's current Ukraine war re-affirms this doctrine. The Russian diaspora in these breakaway ex-Soviet republics (including Eastern Ukraine) adds grist to his political strategy. Complementing these moves has been Putin's efforts at mobilizing Russia's oil and natural gas power through strong state monopolies to consolidate Russia's presence in Central Europe. Russia's overwhelming presence in the OPEC + group and the effort of the group to steer independent of the Saudi Arabia-led OPEC cartel in late 2019 and early 2020 indicates Russia's resolve to prevent its sphere of influence waning in the Caspian Sea littoral. However, Russia's military intervention in Syria is motivated by the need to consolidate the country's presence in Africa and Middle East. Interestingly, after years of indifference towards the UNFCCC, Russia went on a pro-active drive in 2015 by submitting its climate action plan to the UNFCCC even before the Paris Agreement came into force. Way back in 2001, when he was elected Russia's President, I had written that Putin was the true inheritor of Joseph Stalin's mantle, projecting himself as a strong leader running a large empire, fighting efforts on the part of the constituent States to project their sub-nationalism based on alternative political ideologies that are closer to Western liberal democracy ideals (Damodaran 2001a). In many ways, Putin's response to the sanctions imposed by the EU and United States for his war on Ukraine has been retaliatory in nature. He has cut off gas supply to EU countries on the one hand, while insisting on conducting the transactions between EU countries and Russia's oil and gas companies in Roubles. This move has shored up the exchange rate of the Rouble vis-à-vis the US Dollar and the Euro. Thus Russia's Ukraine war has shaken the complacency of a world that was glued to oil and natural gas despite protestations to the contrary. Paradoxically the Ukraine effect in accelerating the drive to net zero targets could be significant, unless European countries that have hopelessly depended on Russian natural gas seek to accelerate their transition to green energy.

Where does China stand in the scheme of things? Unlike the superpowers mentioned, China is Westphalian in its approach. China, as an emerging superpower, has a different weapon to use. Today, China's strength lies in its ability to use its military and nuclear power along with its economic might to pursue national interests. China finances US trade deficits. As a net importer of oil, China cannot play the oil power game that Russia is engaged in. However, China has been using its transboundary economic power to acquire control over oilfields in Africa. 'Lesser nationalities', to use Edgar Snow's expression (1970), have been an essential (though uneasy) feature of the People's Republic. China's strategy in the post-Mao period has been to seek global presence of its economy through Chinese goods and products and more. Deng Xiao Ping, the architect of modern China, once said, 'Observe calmly; secure our position; cope with affairs calmly; hide our capacities and bide our time; be good at maintaining a low profile; and never claim leadership.' Compare this with what Confucius said, 'When prosperity comes, do not use all of it'; and you understand why China refuses to fritter away its huge foreign exchange reserves on conspicuous consumption and land itself in a Dutch disease quagmire. It also explains why China is trying out its new brew—a cocktail of Marxism (read Maoism) and Confucian thought. Many years ago, K.P.S. Menon, India's ace diplomat and civil servant, who witnessed the difficult days of civil war in China, had the following to say, 'China could be saved only by fire and sword and the holy ghost of Karl Marx, which had taken a new and congenial form in Mao Ze Dong' (Menon 1972). This summed up the Mao personality. Later, it was Deng who provided the face of modernization for the country. Deng's mantle fell on former President Hu Jintao and former Premier Wen Jiabao. The ascendence of Xi Jinping as the President of China in

2013 has ushered in a profound change in China's profile in world politics. By unleashing China's 'One Belt One Road Policy' (OBOR) in 2013, Xi Jinping has pushed China's sphere of influence to Central Asia, West Asia, and South/South East Asia through massive doses of capital investments and technology in the countries falling in the region. Currently, China is working hard to develop a central bank-driven digital yuan to take on the US dollar as a rival reserve currency of the world. This move has been aided by the International Monetary Fund recognizing yuan as an official reserve currency in October 2016. Despite reports of environmental disasters caused by the infrastructure projects undertaken under OBOR, China continues with its relentless drive to secure its foothold in the region through such projects.

Some analysts consider Xi Jinping and Barack Obama to be the main architects of the Paris Agreement on climate change. Indeed, President Xi Jinping announced in September 2020 that China will hit peak emissions before 2030 and strive to achieve carbon neutrality before 2060. China's motivations for embracing the Paris Agreement also stem from the great potential the agreement offers the country to dominate the solar panel and wind turbine markets across the world.

Looking at India, at the dawn of independence, India declared itself as a nation-state comprising multiple linguistic and ethnic groups cemented by a sense of common consciousness and common culture. Critics would point to the difficulties India had in projecting itself as an integrated multi-nation state, drawing reference to the north-eastern states of India, which have looser integration with the rest of the country. Cynicism about India's 'national identity' (by its enemies across the border) comes from a misunderstanding of what constitutes a nation-state in its spiritual sense. India believes that a nation-state can exist in a multi-ethnic and multi-linguistic context without strategically brandishing the crude weapon of enforced 'assimilation'.

India's efforts to reverse the adverse impacts of its age-old caste system are work in progress. It is only in very recent times that researcher/faculty positions in India's elite institutions have been opened to members of non-privileged castes.

India is similar to post-Mao China when it comes to ideological conquest. It cannot afford to push for an 'Americanism' kind of ideology all over the world, partly because of its status as a developing country and partly because of its relatively limited military and financial muscle. India's achievements have come from a kind of hallowed spiritual system, which sees Indianness as a way of life rather than as a religion. In the past, this spirituality of India was supreme and was considered to be a sign of happiness in a materialistic world; in recent times, India has translated its spirituality into a kind of intellectual power that handles nimble technologies (such as IT). These technologies require computing and soft skills that are refined and sophisticated when compared to crude machine-handling skills associated with the running of machine tool industries. India's emergence as a developing superpower has to be viewed in this context.

India's carbon emission intensity has reduced by 21% over the period 2005–2014. The ascendance of Narendra Modi as India's Prime Minister in 2014 and his emphasis on economic growth through infrastructure development raises issues about environmental safeguards, especially on the forestry front. However, since 2017, India has shown rapid progress on the renewable energy front with substantial increase in solar and wind energy capacities. Indeed, the Prime Minister himself announced increase in the country's renewable energy capacity to 450 GW. India's nationally determined contribution submitted to the UNFCCC envisages reduction of emission by 33% to 35% by 2030 from 2005 levels. Moreover, NDC commitment is to create an additional carbon sink of 2.5 to 3 billion tons of carbon dioxide equivalent through additional forest and tree cover by 2030.[1]

Thus, despite the play of big power politics in the world, there has been some effort to take action on global environmental problems in the preceding decade though much more needs to be done.

As mentioned, global environmental goods such as climate and the ozone layer transcend nation-states. However, 'global environmental concerns' such as biodiversity and transboundary movement of hazardous wastes are distinctively based on nation-state. Although in the field of economics, neo-liberalism spearheaded the movement against state control in economic affairs; in the field of environment, the movement against command and control systems is led by two streams—neo-traditionalists, who advocate village republics that have a say over all natural resources that lie within their territories (Gadgil and Iyer 1987; Damodaran 1992) and economists belonging to the neo-liberal persuasion, who advocate use of market-based instruments to resolve environmental problems. It is common for some sections of experts to condemn neo-traditionalism as a revivalist form of thinking. At the same time, 'market enthusiasts' are also condemned by others for their neo-liberal streak that seeks the removal of the state from environmental affairs.

I will now come to the issue of how the non-Westphalian factor has worked in the case of the WTO Agreement. The free multilateral trade doctrine that the WTO upholds is based on the inherent assumption that state-inspired protectionism is economically inefficient and distortionary in nature. Thus, the WTO regime implicitly requires facilitating economic reforms in member countries (Kiely 2005, 119). However, the most interesting part of the WTO is that its rules detail 'exceptions to free trade' rather than elaborate the rules of free trade. This will be evident from a close reading of the WTO Agreement on agriculture, sanitary and phyto-sanitary measures and TRIPS. These exceptions perhaps lie at the basis of statements made by Clare Short (as cited in Kiely 2005) that the WTO is a precious international institution, which really protects the interests of the poor and powerless in a world which is moving towards the anarchy of pre-global trade (Kiely 2005, 119). Now, when I talk about the exceptions to free trade being the most significant element of the three WTO agreements, namely TRIPS, General Agreement on Trade in Services (GATS), and the Agreement on Agriculture, my reference is to the following exclusions permitted by the WTO regime. In the GATS Agreement, there are provisions that exclude defence, central banking, and social security from the provisos of free movements of services. However, the agreement also states that if parts of the services are being delivered commercially or in competition with the private sector, then they can, in principle, be counted as part of the agreement (Kiely 2005, 120). The flexibility provisions of WTO TRIPS, centring on compulsory licensing and parallel imports, form the main exceptions to the rule of intellectual property (IP) protection. These flexibilities have provided the much-needed space for developing countries in HIV-stricken countries such as South Africa to get around tight IP rights over obtaining life-saving drugs. The Doha Declaration, which came against the backdrop of the 9/11 attacks and the subsequent outbreak of the anthrax cases in the United States, further underlined the flexibilities of the TRIPS.

The welcome exceptions to the rule of free trade in the WTO Agreement on Agriculture include exemptions on *de minimis* limits on aggregate measures of support that can be provided by countries to farming communities by way of product-specific and non-product-specific support services. However, unlike the WTO TRIPS and GATS, the agreement on agriculture is especially significant on account of two important issues. First, it tries to provide special and differentiated regimes for developing countries and within developing countries, it gives extra special treatment to the least developing countries. In effect, these concessions create a sub-world within the developing world. Countries such as India and Brazil are in the category of developing countries, while Bangladesh and Nepal are in the category of the least developing countries. Therefore, the real purport of the WTO Agreement on agriculture is that it divides the developing world. This precludes effective political mobilization of the developing world on common issues of concern arising from market access for their agricultural products.

The other issue is about the impact of the WTO on regional trade agreements. A number of regional agreements have sprouted up after the WTO agreement came into existence. However, South Asian countries (including India) have not been comfortable with regional trade agreements. The South Asian Preferential Trade Agreement (SAPTA), the trade arm of the South Asian Association for Regional Co-operation (SAARC), is for all practical purposes non-functional. Despite its numerous problems, the WTO is still preferred to regional trade agreements by many developing countries in the world.

The pre-WTO era was marked by strong nation-states that enforced control over their economies and saw global trade as an aberration rather than as a rule. Critics like Kiely, for instance, argue that most of the distrust towards the theory of global free trade has come from the critique of the comparative cost theory propounded by David Ricardo. In the Ricardian scheme of things, trade involves specializing in commodities in which a country had a comparative advantage in relation to its competitor. Indeed, Heckscher and Ohlin (hereafter HO), two Swedish economists in the Ricardian mould, advance the theory further by noting that comparative advantage is related to factor endowments. In an IT-driven world, human resources emerge as a strong factor endowment that promises comparative advantage. But is such specialization good for developing countries?

India is certainly emerging as the global hub for IT and business process outsourcing (BPO) activities in the world. In terms of the growth pole concept, India's IT and business process outsourcing sectors form its vibrant segments. In contrast, the 'non-poles' of growth are heavy industry (mostly in the public sector) and agriculture. Agriculture in India has been witnessing signs of change, particularly by way of forward integration with retail market chains. Contract farming systems are emerging as new ways of organizing agricultural operations. However, there are civil society and political movements in the country which are against such covert privatization of agriculture. Many heavy industries in the public sector have not been privatized despite their indifferent performance. In reality, the public sector, with its powerful trade unions, is not easy to handle when it comes to changes in ownership.

India's IT sector has managed to attract substantial overseas investments. Despite this, debates on foreign investment in the sector have not been as contentious as those involving agriculture. IT services are 'intangible' and its end consumers are, mainly, well-to-do companies. The IT sector is the growth pole of the Indian economy and the greatest beneficiary of globalization. Indeed, Thomas Freidman (2005) considers the burgeoning middle class of India, the products of the country's IT boom, as having the greatest stake in globalization compared with the workers of India's engineering goods industries, who must take to red flag demonstrations to prevent privatization or to ward off threats of competition to their products.

Since the late 1990s, India has had to balance liberalization of its growth poles with a policy of offering safety valves to its laggard sectors. This has created another paradox. On one hand, the state in India is seen as a champion of modernization and knowledge-intensive processes; while on the other, it is viewed as a strong advocate of the notion of sustainable livelihoods. The state has dropped the pretension of balanced growth that was the hallmark of economic planning in the 1950s. It is once again this dual character that explains why India is no longer a predictable G77 player in the WTO negotiations forum.

Jeffrey D. Sachs, in his book *The End of Poverty* (2005) makes an interesting observation, which is relevant in the context of the discussions on foreign direct investments (FDIs). He considers India as an economy which has climbed many steps on the ladder of economic growth, thanks to its great achievements in the fields of IT, electronics, textiles, pharmaceuticals, automotive components, and so on. He feels that it is this remarkable growth centring on certain sectors such as IT that makes India an attractive destination for investors around the world. As Sachs goes on to add, the problem has been that India and China are two countries whose remarkable success story is viewed in the United States as having come at its expense. However, Sachs proceeds to note that the world is not a zero sum struggle in which one country's gain is another country's loss, rather it is a positive sum opportunity in which improving technologies and skills could raise living standards all over the world. Looking at very poor countries such as Malawi and Bangladesh, Sachs proceeds to note that even though they are in dire need of life-saving solutions, the respective governments have failed to mobilise investments required to address the phenomenal problems they face in the field of public health (2005, 18–20). At the same time, as a senior advisor to the UN Secretary General on the implementation of the United Nations MDGs, Sachs is realistic enough to understand that the scale of the problem is so high that assistance through Official Development Assistance (ODA) has its limits. Hence, he comes up with the suggestion of 'modest financial help'. Like Kiely, Sachs also recognizes the fact that there are enough reasons for a developing country to feel insecure with Adam Smith's notion of specialization and division of labour. Specialization and division of labour are right, provided there is an outlet of markets available for specialized goods. Sachs has his meeting ground with Kiely about the perils of comparative advantage in promoting economic inequalities all over the world. In some ways, Sachs also promotes a rather pessimistic thinking on the comparative cost doctrine, when he points to the limitations of the division of labour.

My problem with Sachs is on a specific issue. He ignores the immense wealth of intellectual capital that lies embedded in traditional communities in developing countries. Although it may be true that new technologies have not taken roots in various parts of the rural world in developing countries, it is equally a fact that the entire emphasis on modern technologies at the cost of traditional technologies has contributed to the decline of growth in various countries. The biggest problem faced by the developing countries is the erosion of their fund of traditional knowledge. It is this crisis that no development goal seems to have addressed and which needs to be handled in the right earnest.

The reference to traditional knowledge and community modes of survival has much to do with the growth of environmentalism and environmental thinking. The Convention on Biological Diversity (CBD) and the UNCCD have placed great emphasis on the importance of traditional knowledge and its role in the upkeep of local community living standards. Legislation has been promulgated by many developing countries to protect biodiversity and traditional knowledge. This is greeted with cynicism in sections of the developed world. An important functionary of the Japan Biotechnology Industries Association once wryly told me that many developing countries suffer from the illusion that they are sitting on a 'green goldmine'. His quip was, 'If they are indeed sitting on a goldmine of knowledge, especially a green goldmine of knowledge, then why is it that they allowed this gold to erode in the first place?'

My counter was simple, 'Can you deny that plant-based bioresources and ethnic knowledge have contributed to the coffers of drug and pharmaceutical companies from your country? If bioresources and traditional knowledge have disappeared, it is due to costless access to traditional knowledge and bio-resources by drug companies in the past.'

The real paradox lies elsewhere. As I will explain later, while communities that are custodians of traditional knowledge have failed in putting a price tag on their knowledge and drugs, pharma companies that get these assets for free have been eminently successful in valuing their Intellectual Property Rights (IPRs) assets and claiming royalties on them. But for the active role of environmental movements in the world, the role of traditional knowledge in development would not have been appreciated. In economics literature, the role of traditional techniques of agriculture in contributing to the development of stationary economies has been forcefully argued. Indeed, bio-environmentalists like Herman Daly have eulogized the positive environmentally benign effects of steady state economics. If one were to look at the commercial success of global pharmaceutical, agriculture, and food companies that tap traditional wealth and create innovative products, one is left wondering why these capabilities have not blossomed in developing countries whose knowledge base acts as the springboard for these ventures.

Debates on economic development and globalization should focus on ways and means of tapping the huge ethnic community knowledge base that exists in the developing world, namely medicines, food and biotechnology industries to build sustainable bio-enterprises that are relevant to the modern world. As the examples of third generation bio-tech companies in India such as Biocon India and Avasthegen Ltd show, developing countries can make their presence felt in the globe through appropriate knowledge generation, focused investments and concerted global marketing strategy. In this manner, we should be able to give some of our laggard sectors a major push in newer directions. This would stop our reliance on a narrow set of industries for economic growth. This will also reduce our vulnerability to global economic crises like the one the world has been witnessing since 2008.

Markets, Trade, Development, and Global Environment

This brings us to the larger issue of how and in what forms could ICT be linked with markets as an institution. Ha-Joon Chang (2003) and Ocampo (2003) offer a few clues in this regard.

Ha-Joon Chang mentions how neo-liberalism was born out of an un-holy alliance of neo-classical economics and Austrian libertarian traditions. According to Chang, market failure refers to a situation where the market does not work in a way expected of it. While some would say that an unacceptable level of income inequality is a sign of failure of the market, neo-classical economists would not consider this as a failure because in the Paretian version of efficiency, inequality is not supposed to be such a bad idea. Chang is also critical of neoliberalism on various grounds. He argues that even in very advanced capitalist countries which have well-developed market systems, the state always tries to regulate or facilitate creation of new markets (Chang 2003, 50). Neo-liberals, on the other hand, consider politics as interfering with political rationality, and therefore, advocate a high degree of de-politization of policymaking processes. In the neo-liberal scheme of things, the role of the state ought to be minimized.

Environmental pollution and environmental bads are widely viewed in development and environmental economics as arising from market failure. The aspect of increasing income inequality is not seen as an externality because it is something which, according to the theorists of externalities, existed 'in spite' of the functioning markets. Indeed, market failure has produced two kinds of solutions and two kinds of analyses. While the welfare and neo-classical schools mention that market failure could happen due to under-pricing of goods and services, which in turn arises from information asymmetry or adverse selection, environmental economists who are bred in the neoclassical tradition always consider market failure to occur only when a particular resource gets to be outside the pale of markets and hence not amenable to pricing. Some economists consider the absence of prices to be an externality; however, others consider 'underpricing' of goods and services also to be an externality. Two centuries ago, Karl Marx had also talked about 'externalities' without employing the term. For Marx, discharge of municipal wastes into the Thames river was a by-product of the industrial society (Marx 1974, 101–4). Of course, he went on to notice the great potential for re-employing these wastes. Today's environmental economists would have called this 'internalization'.

Chang also states that the concept of market failure is politically constructed and has been used in different ways, with the dominant discourse linking market failure to non-pricing of natural resources and environmental bads such as pollution, solid wastes, and so on. The deeper issue is why the 'failure of markets' is confined to environmental 'goods' and 'bads' and does not extend to poverty.

The problem with viewing poverty as an externality created by the market mechanism is that it does not explain poverty in non-market economies like the erstwhile socialist countries and traditional societies, where market structures are non-existent or are poorly structured. Indeed, socialist countries have had their share of environmental pollution and, more significantly, have provided some of the worst examples of managing hazardous and nuclear wastes. In addition, environmental pollution is not just a consequence of market failure. It could result from a failure of the government. By the same token, income inequalities and poverty need not be just a sign of market failure but could also be a sign of government failure.

Jose Antonio Ocampo (2003) has an interesting perspective of dealing with the problem of government failure. He argues that improved governance structures at the international and national level could promote a global order, which is more efficient and balanced in terms of power relations. According to Ocampo, action at the regional level plays a critical role as a midway point between global and national orders for the following reasons:

1. There are complementarities between global and regional institutions in a heterogeneous international community.
2. The unequal size of the actors involved in the global process would mean that voices of countries will be better heard if expressed as a regional voice.
3. There is a greater sense of ownership of regional institutions by small countries.
4. The scope for autonomy of economic policy is higher at the regional level.

Thus, Ocampo not only talks about global and national but also of regional institutions. He feels that regionalism avoids government failures, thus insulating the world from the perils of globalization (2003, 91). However, the Ocampo thesis suffers from certain inherent problems, especially when viewed in the Asian context. First, there are areas in South Asia which are sensitive to regionalism, particularly when it comes to pursuing a common trade or political agenda. The political differences between different countries in South Asia being what they are makes it difficult to see regionalism as really offering a feasible solution to the institutional vacuum of the type described by Ocampo. Second, his argument about the asymmetry between capital and labour mobility has its limitations when it comes to regionalism. Ocampo's argument is that capital is better off when compared to labour as it is more mobile. There is merit in this argument, but it also needs to be noted that if capital flows are facilitated more by certain countries compared to other countries, this by itself can inhibit regionalization. For instance, in Asia, two countries have accounted for the bulk of outsourced jobs in the field of IT; the first being India, followed by the Philippines. China, on the other hand, has been in the forefront of attracting FDI into its industrial goods sector. It is rapidly growing as a superpower in the areas of IT hardware and various electronics industries, including micro-electronics applications. Taiwan and South Korea have forged ahead in manufacturing silicon wafers, which form the building block of the semiconductor industry. Despite differing strengths and skills, the reality is that these countries compete for FDI even in areas where their competencies have not been proven. At the same time, the emergence of G20 in the WTO has been on trans-regional lines. It is an alliance of developing countries, which seek correction of some of the imbalances that characterize the WTO. Indeed, on critical WTO issues, countries such as India and Brazil do not typically follow standard developing country positions. This is because emerging economies that have aspirations and substantial capabilities for integrating into a globalized world see opportunities to redeem themselves and join with forces that accelerate their integration into globalization rather than join with forces always opposed to it. Similarly, when it comes to agricultural issues, they join hands with other developing countries for strategic reasons. Thus, the hope that regional structures can provide governance mechanisms that can insulate the world from the negative effects of globalization is wishful thinking. It is the national and economic interests of nation-states, which would drive coalitions of parties in the fight against globalization. This may not always have a regional slant. Rather, they could have more to do with their economic development profile. Global agreements and treaties that recognize the special character of developing countries may promote activities that transcend regional sentiments.

This brings us to the difference between the Rio Agreement principle of common but differentiated responsibilities and the principle of special and differential treatment underlying the WTO. In basic terms, the common but differentiated responsibility principle deals with exceptions to the rule of sacrifices for developing countries. The special and differentiated treatment clauses in the WTO are about providing greater opportunities to developing countries by way of tariff reductions or subsidy provisioning. There is no element of sacrifice here. Thus, the main difference between the special dispensation principle of the Rio Conventions and the WTO is that the former seeks to minimize 'development deficit', while the latter is about providing a special development opportunity to the less privileged countries.

For nearly 21 years after it came into existence, UNFCCC has witnessed stiff resistance from its developing member countries when it came to accepting mitigation targets. Similarly, developing countries feel that their development pursuits are undermined by conservation goals contained in the Aichi Biodiversity Targets adopted by the CBD for the decade ending in 2020. The fact that developing countries endowed with green resources have not been able to tap their economic value in the global marketplace adds to their 'development deficit' concerns. Developing countries, therefore, argue that environmental concerns can be best addressed by rich countries because they have the wherewithal to handle global environmental concerns better.

The principle of common but differentiated responsibilities underlying the two Rio Agreements reflect the effort of these conventions to address the 'development deficit' problem, whereas the special but differentiated principle underlying the WTO provides special dispensation to developing countries to persist with their time-tested competencies in commodities. Although it is true that free trade and winding down of the tariff walls create problems for small farmers in developing countries, the WTO provides for safeguards to be adopted by developing countries to stop a surge of imports. Unlike global environmental matters where developing countries fear to take up commitments at the expense of their development aspirations, developing countries view WTO as not asking for direct 'development' sacrifices. On the contrary, they are hopeful that they would be rewarded for their competencies, provided the trading system is fair and recognizes their problems. Since the 1990s, developing countries which aspire to high economic growth see advantages in putting up a good show on the trade front. They participate in the WTO negotiations with enthusiasm, despite having reservations about the agreement on different counts. Indeed, developing countries such as India have lowered import barriers on many commodities as part of their WTO obligations despite apprehensions.

The Gender Dimension in Poverty

It would be interesting to examine how academic literature on poverty has changed in the globalization era. John Sender (2003) states that while there has been an explosion of literature on rural poverty since the 1990s, the gender dimension of the poverty has not been sufficiently addressed. Part of the reason for this is what Sender considers to be the hegemony factor in relation to the gender issue. Sender observes that many rural women in sub-Saharan Africa lack secure access to land. In large parts of Asia, where the population density is high (as in Bangladesh, India, North-East Ethiopia, and Kenya), the majority of women would be effect-ively landless due to the simple reason that land is not available. Sender proceeds to discuss policy issues that have been advocated to obviate such situations. He examines the policy initiatives that seek greater off-farm female self-employment. He adds that this kind of an approach is influenced by the literature on livelihoods, which accepts the evidence that poor rural people may not be small farmers but usually those who are constrained to combine non-agricultural assets and activities through diversified livelihood packages as a coping strategy (2003, 411). Although not excessively sanguine about this strategy, Sender also says that small farmers, who may find the scale of their tiny enterprises not good enough, can nevertheless achieve efficiency through new institutional arrange-ments that are driven by NGOs.

Sender goes on to argue that in India, periods of sharp decline in agri-cultural output have disappeared with increase in the prices of agricul-tural commodities vis-à-vis industrial goods (2003, 417). At the same time, he also says that the price formation system is asymmetrical as the price of agricultural products did not decline steeply as was expected during periods when large increases in agriculture output occurred. Therefore, those states in India that experienced fast rates of growth were not necessarily the ones that eliminated poverty at a fast rate. Sender is obviously referring to the study by Ghosh (1989) to prove his point. Ghosh's argument was that India's performance on the poverty allevi-ation front is not directly related to the growth of the agricultural sector. Rather, it is state intervention through state procurement and fair-trade shops that limited the range of fluctuations in basic food grain prices. This had its positive effects in alleviating poverty. Ghosh also argued for stepping up state investment in agriculture, particularly through ir-rigation and water-augmenting measures, as he feels that this would increase the demand for rural female labour. Sender is of the view that poor women must rely on wage incomes to survive and escape poverty.

They may not find microcredit or small enterprises to be attractive alternatives. He makes an interesting point that aid agencies promote the development of small-scale holdings and corrupt decentralized organizations and shun any organization that has a realistic prospect of increasing political and economic bargaining power of the lowest-paid wage worker (Sender 2003, 419). Obviously, this weakens the position of women who are dependent on wage labour.

John Sender's thesis is interesting because it tries to demolish the stereotypes associated with livelihood security and gender-related poverty issues. His point that women workers generally rely on wage incomes rather than self-generated incomes and, therefore, would not find the so-called livelihood ventures supported by aid agencies innovative is plausible, original, and brave. Indeed, some of these observations can be substantiated or weakened by the author's own observations about irrigation-deficient, dry land agricultural villages in Karnataka. In the semi-arid villages of southern Deccan, the author's own observation is that women are mostly employed in agricultural operations associated with dribbling and sowing of seeds, winnowing, and harvest. Despite the constitutional obligation to reward women and men equally for daily labour, discrimination exists between male and female wage workers in large parts of peninsular India. Women are depended upon in a big way to mop up livelihood resources for running their households. They collect fuel wood and related biomass, take up cooking and attend to domestic chores. Indeed, it is not a stereotype to say that women have a greater stake in common property resources and also a greater concern for depleting natural resources than men because their labour process is entirely twined to the fortunes of the global commons. Women spend long hours collecting fuel wood, biomass and water and therefore suffer on account of depletion of these resources in the village commons. Other things remaining equal, relative depletion of fuel wood and biomass prolong the time spent by women to collect them for household use. In addition, women are required to earn money as wage labour. In such circumstances, it is quite natural that their participation rates in the wage sector are limited. Their capacity to bargain for better wages also suffers due to multitasking. This then acts as a very big disincentive to reward women for their contribution to agriculture.

Sender's thesis that alternative ways of income diversification is not entirely effective is quite valid because most of the alternative sources of income and enterprises are foreign or exotic to women and call for new skills. It makes greater sense to stabilize the role of women in promotion of the commons and to involve them in conservation activities in a greater way because their stake in these resources is high and their understanding of the ecology of common lands better. Unfortunately, the entire system of livelihood security for rural households in the developing world is premised more on alternative or new enterprises than on reinforcing the capacity of women to manage their traditional means of livelihood.

Even the Joint Forest Management (JFM) programme in India does not seem to have given women a fair deal. The JFM has not really promoted democratic governance structures in the manner desired. It has also failed in its attempts to confer financial autonomy to joint forest committees. Although all efforts are made to improve JFM through greater financial empowerment and greater inclusiveness in the running of forests, there is no bold effort to impart a gender angle to these functions. Notwithstanding the fact that JFM committees provide for active inclusion of women representatives in relatively decent numbers; in practice, most JFM committees do not witness proactive participation by women. This is partly due to the existing patriarchal prejudices and partly due to the lack of proactive support on the part of the forest establishment and government agencies to go beyond statutory provisions and seek such participation of women. Instead, by diverting the energies of women to new and alternative types of ventures, the establishment has sought to divert them into new vocations, which derails their traditional association with natural resources.

Another point worth mentioning is regarding the role of women in coping with risks faced by rural households during years of drought and natural calamities. Women belonging to poor rural households bear incidence of risks associated with mortality, destruction of property and loss of lives of family members as the burden of asset or livelihood reconstruction falls on them on account of their essential role in providing means of subsistence in rural households. Unfortunately, most calamity management programmes do not focus their activities and resources on improving the capabilities of women to cope with disasters and natural calamities.

P. Sainath (1996) gives a very interesting account of the role of women in coping with the risks arising from droughts and frequent failure of rain. His reference is to tribal women in Jhabua and the women of the Bilala tribal community in Jal Sindhi in Jhawar district. Sainath mentions how, when faced with drought and deprivation in Jhabua, tribal women prepared the fields for rains, ploughed and raked the soil and carried out activities which can be considered hard labour and unfitting for women (1996, 104–8). He also talks about the great bounties, the forests that the Bilala tribals customarily accessed for their use, and explains how they lost this privilege following their resettlement. As Luwaria, a Bilala woman told Sainath, 'Our firewood comes from the forest. Our 'chara' (fodder) comes from there; our herbs and medicines and the mahua flowers which we collect for making wine comes from there; our fish comes from the river down here' (1996, 106). The loss of their forest habitat has been very painful, and women have been the worst sufferers on account of this. Their displacement is silent and subtle and hence is seldom compensated properly. Similarly, the impact of technological interventions in agriculture, especially associated with the advent of chemicals and fertilizers, on women has been under-assessed. It is not very uncommon to see how the advent of poisonous and toxic chemicals has had a deleterious impact on women workers toiling in the coffee and tea farms of Africa and Asia. This raises the degree of occupational hazards in women employed in agriculture and its related activities.

The role of women is substantial in organic farming; however, it is unrecognized. It is really doubtful whether there has been any systematic effort on the ground level to link the benefits of organic agriculture to gender empowerment, although manuals on organic farming do talk about women being important partners of the process. It is equally doubtful whether the benefits of organic agriculture really trickle down to women by way of improved wages.

These instances compel us to conclude that state intervention in common natural resources is retrograde and undesirable. Withdrawal of the state from the economic domain is what neo-liberalism desires. Given the link between neo-liberalism and free markets, it is quite likely that the idea of community empowerment as an alternative to state intervention will support the neo-liberal cause of free markets as well. A point that is emphasized when referring about silent displacement is that not all movements against the state are neo-liberal or advocate the free market dogma. It is argued that management systems whereby local communities are custodians of natural resources could achieve better social results, despite their many inefficiencies and biases. The basic reason is that under such a system, community members are not denied access to the resources they have traditionally subsisted upon. State intervention or takeover of natural resources, which leads to silent displacement, does precisely the opposite—it denies permission to access resources. The many abuses of local community governments could be overcome through restructuring measures that favour gender empowerment.

The fear that state withdrawal from the natural resources sector will lead to rapacious exploitation of natural resources is genuine. There is scope for correcting gender biases inherent in the functioning of markets. Indeed, as Barbara Harriss-White (2003, 481–97) argues, the most important point about markets is that they are socially and politically constructed. It is extremely important to understand the fact that changes in the regulation of market structure and behaviour are brought about by political and social ideologies as well as material conditions in which exchanges take place (2003, 492). This means that markets are not neutral technical institutions; they are products of ideologies. Barbara Harriss-White proceeds to discuss how gender is one of the important dimensions of markets. She mentions the role of patriarchal authority in influencing gender relations, which in turn regulates market exchanges through restrictions on tasks that can be performed by women. These restrictions are achieved through ideologies of subordination, which render rules of market participation prejudicial to women (2003, 489).

As we have mentioned earlier markets need not, be inimical to the ideals of social equity and justice. They do have their mechanisms for correcting social costs, by conferring property rights (public or private) over resources that are open access in nature. Markets can indeed work well to end gender discrimination provided there are enablers for this.

According to Harriss-White, markets achieve order by means other than purely economic. Politics of the marketplace is an extremely important factor in market transformation. Therefore, if you influence politics and change the politics of markets, you could secure changes in the marketplace to the advantage of vulnerable sections of the society. In that event, the market ceases to be part of a dominant relationship. It could be galvanized and reworked into new systems, which incorporate the weaker and the marginalized sections, including women, into its scheme of things. While this may be true of 'physical markets', the larger question is whether e-commerce and the virtual Internet markets can correct the gender biases associated with the normal, physical markets. It is not easy to answer this question. However, it is a fact that e-commerce and the Internet do insulate women from face-to-face transactions and haggling that is associated with patriarchal markets of the yore. This, by itself, should give women a greater sense of empowerment. The larger challenge is to firmly institutionalize gender balance in the MEAs.

To sum up, the birth of a unipolar world notwithstanding, nation-states are here to stay. At the same time, the impact of globalization and the WTO in promoting imbalanced growth in developing countries is apparent. The Rio Agreements entail sacrifices on the part of developing countries, which makes these agreements complex to handle. However, since 2010, developing countries are also on board regarding global environmental agreements like climate change. The Paris Agreement on Climate Change symbolizes the change. Empowerment of women is an issue that indicates the vibrance of diversity in a society as it has the ability to promote more inclusive local approaches in the management of natural resources. The importance of gender empowerment in promoting agriculture and sustainable natural resources management cannot be wished away. However, they need to be more pervasive than at present. The new rules being framed to guide the UNFCCC and CBD need to pay special attention to this aspect.

3

Challenges of Global Governance

Opinions and Formulations

World statesmen like Tony Blair spend considerable time lecturing on the challenges of globalization. Global institutions such as the United Nations (UN) and the World Bank have approached the challenges of global governance in their own ways. Apart from their perceptions, these two institutions have crafted blueprints to ensure that global governance works well. There are many messages and lessons that can be gleaned from their perspectives and actions. One strong message that comes out is that global governance is about prioritization. The other message is that they are not always about zero sum games.

Blair's Changing Vision of Challenges for the Global World

Way back in April 1999, Tony Blair, then British Prime Minister, delivered an interesting speech at the Economic Club of Chicago in the United States. His address, titled 'The Doctrine of the International Community', surveyed a world that had just recovered from a major North Atlantic Treaty Organization's involvement in the Balkans. Blair's effort was to spell out what constituted an ideal international community. He sought to situate his points from a human rights perspective. Ever since the end of the Cold War, there have been many debates within developed countries regarding the extent and the circumstances under which they should get involved in the conflicts of other countries. Blair argued that violation of universal human rights through genocide can never be considered as an internal matter. Genocide had transborder effects as it causes mass movements of refugees to neighbouring countries. This endangers the security

India, Climate Change, and The Global Commons. A. Damodaran, Oxford University Press. © A. Damodaran 2024.
DOI: 10.1093/oso/9780192899828.003.0003

of neighbouring states, which could ultimately cascade into a threat to international peace and security. Thus the transborder effects of tyrannical despotic regimes in various parts of the world, gives legitimacy to international intervention in nation-state affairs. Though one could have serious reservations about the manner in which some regimes have been categorized as 'tyrannical', there is no denying about the force behind the argument that dictatorial regimes that ride roughshod over human rights are not desirable entities both for their citizens as well as for the world.

Seven years later, in 2006, while still Britain's Prime Minister, Blair came out with another noteworthy contribution—this time on the challenges of globalization. In an article written for *Newsweek* entitled 'Europe is Falling Behind', Blair stated that globalization is something that calls for both economic competence and social justice to cope with. He also argued that there are very important reasons for countries such as the United Kingdom (UK) to focus on sustained investment in education. Drawing reference to the situation of India and the wonderful progress the country had achieved in churning out qualified graduates in large numbers to run the IT juggernaut, Blair lamented that developed countries were not able to emulate this feat. He also talked about the concept of global cities and the importance of public and private sectors. But the major thrust of his article is about the challenges emerging from the marginalization of developed countries in the new economy. Blair, who seems to treat the new economy as the most visible face of globalization, was concerned about Britain's inability to capitalize on the 'new economy' wave. He further added that the UK, in particular, and Europe in general, would need to work harder to secure increases in productivity and put in place social policies that enhance the capacity of the continent to cope with globalization.

Clearly, by 2006, Blair had changed his tack. His take was no longer about the importance of democracy and rule of law to straighten tyrannical rulers. His focus was now on economic changes wrought by globalization and the importance of bracing up. This was a sea change, given 9/11 and the subsequent involvement of his country in the fight against terrorism in Afghanistan and the war to topple Saddam in Iraq. While in 1999, Blair was trying to project an apologetic version of cosmopolitanism by trying to situate this idea within the rubric of misgoverned nation-states, seven years down the line, he realized that 'cosmopolitan ideals' were less important as compared to the more nationally pressing economic problems his country needed to address following globalization. Significantly, a year later, Blair launched the Climate Change Agenda at the Gleneagles Summit of G8, highlighting the grave risk, global warming posed to human beings. By then, the priority of correcting errant nation-states had even receded further from his horizon.

In hindsight Blair's *Newsweek* article anticipated Brexit. As Robert Fay (2019) so appropriately put it, the real reason for Brexit was stagnant incomes arising from languishing growth in productivity, the same point Blair had underscored way back in 2006. However Blair's point had little to do with the EU bureaucracy.

Blair was to take up the threads of his global perspectives when he expounded on his philosophy on universal human rights in Chicago.

The United Nations' Perspective on Global Challenges

A year after Blair's exposition of universal human rights in Chicago, the UN brought out a report of what constituted human rights in the era of globalization. The report was formulated by a Sub-commission on the Promotion and the Protection of Human Rights. Its text was prepared by two independent scholars, namely J. Oloka-Onyango and Deepika Udagama in accordance with the sub-commission resolution of 1999/8. The report provided a comprehensive survey of globalization and its impact on human rights. More specifically, the report looked at how globalization affected the basic human rights principles of equality and non-discrimination. The tremendous role of telecommunications in spreading equality was highlighted in the report. The report observed that despite its promise of seamless communication, telecommunications was restricted by geography, gender, income, and language. The authors adduced the example of Romania (an ex-Soviet Bloc country) to highlight their point in this regard. The report went on to note that the globalization divide has also manifested itself in a divide between the rural and the urban. The report noted that globalization has not contributed to improving social welfare in the African continent one bit. The report however underscored the enormous significance of the Vienna Declaration and Programme of

Action of 1993 in rendering human rights universal, indivisible, inter-dependent and interrelated. The report also proceeded to highlight how the Charter of the United Nations recognizes the importance of the link-ages between the goal of maintenance of international peace and security with the desiderata of economic and social progress and the promotion and protection of universal human rights. The report seriously ques-tioned the view that the states or state actors cannot be held responsible for the violation of social, economic, and cultural rights.

In their report, Onyango and Udagama (2000) also referred to the Limburg Principles of 1986, which deals with implementation of the International Covenant on Economic, Social, and Cultural Rights, 1986 and the Maastricht Guidelines on Violations of Economics, Social, and Cultural Rights, 1997. Both principles recognize that the right of self-determination of people is fundamental to the enjoyment of other rights. Similarly, the United Nations Declaration on the Right of Development, by focusing on the process of development, requires that a human being should be an active participant and beneficiary of the right to develop-ment. The authors suggested that the UN should provide leadership in dealing with the challenges posed by globalization. The report cites Kofi Annan (former UN Secretary-General) to highlight the strategic need to balance market forces with social needs in the world.

The UN-commissioned report is a significant contribution to advancing our understanding of a cosmopolitan approach towards the issue of human rights. The report is a serious critique of the communi-tarian principles that proclaim the primacy of the nation-state in guiding a nation's destiny. The indivisibility and multi-dimensional perspectives about human rights are the elements that make the report interesting. Significantly, the report also called upon the International Monetary Fund (IMF) and The World Bank to pay attention to the protection of the right to food, while drawing up lending policies, credit lines, and structural adjustment programmes. The report also talked about treaty-based human rights mechanisms, which are sensitive to rising economic disparities in the world. Further the report also referred to the role of Convention on the Elimination of All Forms of Discrimination against Women in preventing feminization of poverty.

While talking about indivisibility of human rights and the centrality of integrating social, cultural, and economic dimensions of human rights, the report focused a bit too much on individual statesmen and rulers rather than on the basic constituent of the UN, namely, nation-states.

In terms of the spirit and the nature of its arguments, the study is centrally rooted in non-Westphalian principles. This is not to argue that the authors have stated something which is radically different. The United Nations Declaration of Human Rights goes back to 1948. The concept of human rights law has since then systematically expanded in scope as pressures for expanding the range of individual rights intensified. But the real point is that in the initial years, while the UN emphasized international peace and security and focused on the importance of resolving disputes amongst nations in a peaceful manner, this did not prevent the organization from getting into intra-nation disputes as peacekeepers. UN organizations such as the International Criminal Court have gone a step further by issuing warrants for the arrest of rulers with proven genocide records, as had happened in the case of Omar Hassan Ahmad al-Bashir, the former President of Sudan for his role in the Darfur killings. In a world where globalization has elevated individualization as a way of civic life, it is quite natural for the UN to effect a mild shift in its emphasis towards human rights and its stipulated laws as compared to its traditional pre-occupation of maintaining international peace and security. Terrorism and drug trafficking have added to the agenda load of the UN.

The evidence of this shift in the United Nation's focus is further reflected in a paper which was prepared by UN Secretary-General (UNSG) in March 2006 for an overhaul of the UN Secretariat. The paper calls for a fundamental change in the 'rule systems' and the 'culture' of the UN Secretariat and advocated re-tooling measures to ensure that the organization catered to the growing expectations and demands of the international community. The restructuring plan seeks to modernize the UN management practices. Further, the reform proposals outline the fact that all these changes are in tune with a globalized world that has placed great demands on the UN and its Secretariat. Interestingly, the paper dealt with the role of the UN in peacekeeping activities and the enormous budgets required to keep these activities going. It is also noted that the number of humanitarian and human rights operations has dramatically increased. The point mentioned earlier, that the UN approach to world affairs has changed on account of the pressures of globalization, is significantly borne out by the paper on UN reforms.

There is a difference between Blair's position on universal human rights and the perspective outlined in the UN Secretary General's (UNSG) paper of 2006. While Blair took 'the philosophy of universal human rights' to mean adoption of an uncompromising position against torture and other violations of human rights, the UNSG's approach has been to view human rights in its universal essence, namely as a multifarious and indivisible concept.

The World Bank

Now let us look at how the other major institution of the world, namely the World Bank, has taken to the challenge of globalization. In the year 2002, an independent evaluation group of the World Bank released a report entitled 'The World Bank's Approach to Global Programmes' that provides good idea of the Bank's approach to globalization. The report is an evaluation of the different programmes of the Bank. The report underscores the following four major issues:

1. The overarching global relevance of World Bank programmes;
2. outcomes and the impacts of World Bank programmes and their sustainability;
3. organization management and financing of the programmes; and
4. the World Bank's role as a partner in the programmes.

After exploring the four segments, the World Bank report comes out with certain interesting findings. The first finding is that the Bank has managed to leverage its comparative advantage more at the global level than through country-level operations. The second point is that the programmes of the Bank that have delivered global public goods have added value to all stakeholders involved. The reference is to global public goods programmes implemented through the Consultative Group on International Agriculture Research (CGIAR) and other institutions which are supposed to have had an impact in reducing poverty. The report also mentions how the Bank has focused on institutional, infrastructural, and technological constraints faced by developing countries in achieving sustainable economic growth.

Thus the World Bank today sees its competencies heightened in its transnational operations which is a testimony to the manner in which the institution has evolved.

The report is also important for its fundamental recommendation that the Bank's programmes need independent oversight, particularly its in-house programmes. This is emphasized in the context of a globalized world.

Both the UN and the World Bank, which are major institutions in the arena of development, are adapting to the realities of a world enveloped by globalization. While the UN has tended to focus more on human rights and has shown a tendency of looking at issues of human rights universally, the World Bank has decisively and strategically tried to give country-level programmes a potential global flavour by focusing on transnational impacts that mere national impacts.

This portends well for the global commons movement unleashed in the world after UNCED 1992.

From Zero Summing to Sustainability

Tony Blair has been smart enough to understand that cosmopolitanism must be linked with serious efforts to address competency gaps at the country level. He is also clear that the world can at best prevent torture and other extreme forms of human rights violations. This, then is the reality of globalization in the twenty-first century. The world's leading international institutions such as the UN and the World Bank also realize the 'virtue of the median'. Their operational programmes seek workability (that is, the focus on extreme forms of poverty in the MDGs and SDGs), though at a more fundamental level they talk about cosmopolitan ideals such as indivisibility and integrated approaches to poverty and human rights issues.

Indeed, there could be situations where nation-states facilitate the realization of human rights in its composite essence. Countries such as Indonesia have wisely avoided the worst impacts of globalization by building social capital. Shafiq Dhanani and Islam (2002) have referred to the severe financial crisis that hit Indonesia in mid-1997. Contrary to what was widely expected, Indonesia's economic crisis of 1997 did not blow up into major social unrest. The main reason for this was the implementation of a social safety net programme by the Indonesian government. This programme had two features. The first feature was the supply of subsidized rice to poor households while the second feature aimed to prevent children from poor families from dropping out of schools by instituting scholarships for them. Another feature of the social capital-building programme in Indonesia was the focus on the severity of poverty which went beyond head-counting poverty-stricken people. This caused the focus to shift to differences in economic welfare levels within the poor categories, and differentiating those households on the verge of the poverty line from those below the poverty line and focusing on the latter more intensely. The study argues that a social protection policy which is fiscally sustainable and capable of improving the resilience of households in coping with economic crisis, was what the Indonesian Government concentrated upon in its social capital development programme. Indeed the real achievement of the Indonesian structural adjustment programme, which was introduced in the wake of the 1996 crisis, was that it provided social safety nets without impairing the fiscal situation.

Diversity and Social Capital

It seems that I was born to chart the evening sky ... they had cut me out for baking bread. But I had other dreams instead ... the baker's boy from the west country would join the Royal Society.
Mark Knopfler, 'Sailing to Philadelphia', Circa 2000

A nation's diversity of life can be traced back to the pattern of historic evolution and social capital construction. Social capital is an insular mechanism that buffers local communities from economic shocks. Social capital is also instrumental in providing the wherewithal for empowering and strengthening local democracies. However, in his paper, Inoguchi Takashi (2004) proposes a slightly different concept of social capital. Takashi endorses Robert Putnam's view that social capital is conducive to building democracy. At the same time, he also accepts Fukuyama's argument that social capital facilitates prosperity. He supplements these two principles with a third one advanced by Karl Deutsch (2004, 34–6), which states that social capital is essential for the integration of countries into regions. Takashi proceeds to group countries in Asia into five categories. In the first category comes China and Vietnam. In the second category comes Sri Lanka and Uzbekistan. Malaysia, Myanmar, and India fall in the third category. On the other hand, Japan and South Korea are placed in the fourth category with Thailand falling in the fifth category. Takashi explores three major dimensions of fairness, utility, and institutions to analyse social capital (2004, 36). He considers utility to be a concept employed by economists and rational choice theorists who were not sensitive to the role played by cultural differences in the formation of social capital. Fairness, according to Takashi, is associated with the views of those philosophers, sociologists, and political scientists who argue that political cultures matter in differentiating communities. Based on his analysis, Takashi states that in developing countries or in non-democracies where no countervailing forces are present in societies, the utility dimension of social capital assumes an upper hand.

The Takashi thesis has certain unusual features, especially when it comes to the categorization of different groups. For instance, it is not clear how India could be equated with Myanmar and Malaysia. However, what strongly comes out from his study is that social capital is necessary to promote identities and diversity, which in turn is significant in nation building and in preventing the negative effects of top-down discursive practices associated with globalization.

Talking of social capital and social protection measures, it is important to realize that there have been many initiatives on the part of local self-governments in developing countries to build social capital at the grassroots level. A case in point are the villages of Bodampally and Channarayanahalli in Kolar district in the state of Karnataka in India, where villagers have been practising a system called Damasha, which is a unique effort to redistribute scarce water resources amongst members of village communities concerned. This system has been unique, as it has served to blunt the sharp edges of social friction during times of extreme scarcity of water. In drought seasons when the two tanks of the villages recede, it was common for village communities to shift to the Damasha method of allotment, whereby farmers whose lands are available near the tank agreed to allot their land to deprived farmers at the tail end of the tank command. This was basically to ensure continuance of temporary cultivation by deprived sections, which in turn enabled them to avoid deprivation (Mishra et al. 2005). In the same villages, despite these interesting self- initiatives, there was no enthusiasm on the part of the villagers for carrying out 'capital works' such as de-silting of the tanks. These works were not carried out by village communities even though de-silting was considered extremely important to improve water storage. The reason was that villagers felt that such capital works had to be carried on by the government which owned the tanks. Elsewhere, Damodaran (1997) has noted that traditional village communities of India are not capital-asset creators. They believed in asset maintenance. Villagers are more tuned to maintaining structures such as tanks and other natural resources rather than creating new tanks by making heavy capital investments. But where social capital is built, insular structures are positioned to ensure that scarce resources are well distributed taking into account social inequalities.

This aspect was highlighted in the World Development Report 2006 (World Bank 2006). The report, entitled 'Equity and Development', focused on a topic that the World Bank had not paid adequate attention till then. The Development Report relied on cross-country information and historical narratives to substantiate its propositions. A very careful reading of the report indicates that while the World Bank report rightly emphasizes the significance of the issues of equity, unequal opportunities, and the widening gap between rich and poor, its faith in market-based solutions remains unchanged.

The WDR 2006 is different in its approach to the solution of the problem. While it is neo-liberal in its approach it aims to re-tune the cold face of neoliberal prescriptions in order to silence its critics. The Report clearly states that good economic institutions are equitable. The Report also stresses the need to set up incentives for a vast majority of the population to induce them to invest and innovate. But an equitable set of economic institutions can emerge only when the distribution of power is not highly unequal and under circumstances where there are constraints on the exercise of power by office holders. But is this a realistic situation in the public sphere? Is there something more about social capital that we need to learn from the corporate sector? Alternatively, can one take any cues about nation-state governance from changes that have happened in the enlightened segments of the corporate world? The most important observation of WDR 2006 is that unequal power leads to formation of institutions that perpetuate inequalities in power, status, and health. This is typically bad for innovations in investments and risk taking that underpins long-term growth (World Bank 2006, 8–9). The key question is how 'just' institutions can be created, given the grip of existing power structures in a state. The World Bank prescriptions include, grant of property rights, through proper titles and access to land and related resources. However, the best way to ensure that insular institutions fulfil their objective of pursuing equity, would be by putting in place transparent and accountable systems. But then, the basic reality is that these conditions cannot be ensured in a situation where governance and political power structures remain the same. This was the reason why the Communists advocated the overthrow of an iniquitous State.

However, the communist revolutions in Russia and China did not deliver the promised paradise. Rather communist states created their systems of inequality and inequity which turned out to be as unjust as the systems they overthrew. Further, the Soviet Union and the People's Republic of China (during the Mao phase) suffered from massive problems of economic stagnation and bureaucratization. Revolutions do not necessarily effect changes in political power structures.

Ronald H. Coase (1937) states that firms exist to economize on the cost of coordinating economic activity. Sumantra Ghoshal (2005, 1–27) takes Coase to the corporate world by arguing that corporates can replace markets. Ghoshal employs the theory of organizations and, more specifically, cites Herbert Simon (1991) and his concept of the ubiquity of organizations to argue the point that in an economy where an industry or a firm is considered to be organizational, companies matter not only to investors, employees, and customers but also to all members of the society. Ghoshal cites Herbert Simon's observation that when organizations are ubiquitous, markets become irrelevant. The author goes a step forward to claim that organizations can substitute markets (Ghoshal 2005, 5 and 8). He takes the reader to an interesting concept of proactivity by organization-based firms. He cites Richard Nelson (1994, 8) to the effect that 'the new formal models continue in the spirit of older ones in treating the actions taken by firms as determined by the environment they are in, and ignoring anything like Schumpeter's entrepreneurship and the Abramovitz enterprise'.

Therefore, Ghoshal not only argues that organizations can replace markets but goes on to further argue that corporates are increasingly looking at leadership that can effect changes and transformation (Ghoshal 2005, 10). Referring to the Royal Dutch Shell system of governance, he argues that where the organization predominates, no individual can exercise unwarranted power. Hence companies of continental Europe, Japan, and North America have devised complex systems of checks and balances. This holds a great lesson to policy makers in the context of the Satyam Computers Ltd scam in India, and the Madoff investor cheating scandal in the United States (that caused $50 billion to vanish from the scene). The havoc created by non-transparent, closely controlled corporate governance system can be widespread.

Apart from corporate scams, there are other major lessons to be drawn from the experience of the corporate world. This has to do with complications induced by operational complexity. Oliver Williamson (1996) mentions how simple contracts give way to complex ones, thereby raising new governance issues. The advent of complex derivatives and associated accounting processes in recent years has made it difficult to track corporate frauds. Derivatives, particularly the third-generation ones, run by quant managers (who used computer-driven statistical models to identify high return investments) had trillions of dollars invested in by hedge funds. By exaggerating expected performance, quant models caused investors to be fooled by numbers (Taleb 2005). When the bubble burst, it dragged leading investment funds and insurance groups (such as Lehman Brothers and AIG) down the drain. By early 2009, it was clear that these developments had yanked the world economy down to one of its worst economic crises since the Great Economic Depression of 1929. Grand stimulus plans floated by Barack Obama and Gordon Brown marked desperate efforts to pull the banking sector out from its worst liquidity crisis. Indeed, as Shiller (2008) states, bail-outs are not the long-term solution to the problem. The simple fact is that nobody knows where the problem lies as they do not understand the instruments that created these products. The fall-out of simple retail derivatives products that are understood by a common investor is easy to handle. Their potential damages could be checked in time. The reality is that the world of derivatives was a simpler world until the mid-1980s. The quant funds of the 1990s changed the landscape of finance capital towards increasing complexity. Greed added to the problems, while globalization gave greater breadth to the crisis of 2008 that defied even the wildest imagination. As Paul Krugman states:

> ... yet until very recently, Americans believed they were getting richer, because they received statements saying that their houses and stock portfolios were appreciating in value faster than their debts were increasing. And if the belief of many Americans that they could count on capital gains forever sounds naïve, it is worth remembering just how many influential voices—notably in right leaning publications such as The Wall Street Journal, Forbes, and National Review Online—promoted that belief, and ridiculed those who worried about low savings and high levels of debt.
>
> (Krugman 2009)

What Is the Way Out?

Douglas North (1990) gets it right when he states that the role of institutions is central in providing the rules of the game. Additionally, if institutions could tap what Arrow (1974) states to be 'trust' and 'balance of authority and responsibility', the Satyam scam in India and the Madoff affair in the United States could have been avoided.

The main point that comes out of the discussions above is that in a world which is changing and heading towards greater social consciousness and concerns about social probity, corporates themselves have to change by embracing non-profit causes. There are even more fundamental issues to be addressed. Vaclav Havel (1990), one of the leading playwrights and intellectuals and the first President of post-communist Czechoslovakia, once said: 'IBM certainly works better than Skoda plant. But that does not alter the fact that both companies have long since then lost their human dimension and hence turned man into a little cog in their machinery utterly separated from what and from whom the machinery is working and what the impact of its product is on the world.' This is more so true of workers in developing countries such as India who perform outsourced tasks without having any idea what their output means to themselves, their organization, or to their country of birth. This could push them to be cogs and prevents them from being creative and different in the workplace. That this trend should happen in a flattened world is even more surprising. Clearly, as Nandy (2007) has pointed out, a flattened world that is homogenized, reduces the possibility of diverse futures

When this is the reality for an industrial entity or an industrial organization, which had traditionally focused on profit maximization, why shouldn't the traditional ways of nation-states change? Indeed nation-states have a responsibility to investigate the social problems created not only by the forces of globalization but also by corporates.

A related point is about decentralization as a check on power excesses.

I go back to an old theory of circulation of the elites by Vilfredo Pareto to bring out what I am basically driving at. Pareto (1935) talked about circulation of elites or cyclical mobility of people in power. One of the easiest methods to ensure circulation of elites in a country is to limit the tenure of functionaries who occupy the executive, legislature, and judiciary and enforce a periodic advent of a new system of elite formation. The elevation of Manmohan Singh as Finance Minister in 1991 and later on as India's Prime Minister in 2004 from a position of techno-bureaucrat is an example of 'elite circulation' attempted by the Indian political system. Such measures tap the plural essence of democracy. This way, one can ensure that democracy in its true sense will be brought in. The other measure which can be tried out, is a system of cyclical mobility even in the bureaucracy. As per the current practice, a bureaucracy provides the steel frame in every country. It is the symbol of continuity. But hyper-specialized bureaucracies create hyper-specialized power interests that would lead to hyper-specialized decision making—all of which could badly splinter social groups and create fissures in the society. The idea is not to shift bureaucracies from one sector to the other but to induce bureaucracy to shift to corporate sectors for some time. This would ensure that a government system does not fall into the trap of governmentality.

What would all these discussions imply for the nation-state concept in a situation where equity is considered, the central policy goal at the national level?. A strong nation-state which is resilient to the negative aspects of globalization could do so by nurturing social capital and insular institutions based on a process of circulation of elites and decentralized institutions. Such systems, by ensuring cyclical mobility and creating different power equations that promote equal opportunities for citizens, could ensure that nation-states are able to the negative effects of globalization.

In practical terms, one can re-conceive the situation by changing the terms of reference of a nation-state from one of predominant pre-occupation with political security to one of economic self-sufficiency and global competitiveness. This is what Tony Blair seems to have realized in 2006. This is what India under Narendra Modi's stewardship appears to be focussed on India's independent 5G initiative, which has surprised the world and has been propelled by the country's desire to be economically self-sufficient.

At present, efforts on the part of the governments to address so-cial justice are greeted with disdain. People see government systems as obstructing the quest for equity. But when the governments change their track and announce that their chief mission is to ensure that citizens profit from globalization and not fall victim to it, a new confidence level is created.

Let me get specifically into certain issues, which would substantiate the point mentioned. In his article entitled 'To De-value or to Defend?—The Political Rate of Exchange Policy' in the *International Studies Quarterly*, David Leblang (2003) makes an interesting observation regarding the politics of exchange rate policy in developing countries. Leblang based his findings on data analysis of 90 developing countries during the period 1985–8. He stated that speculative attacks on national currencies occur when economic fundamentals are weak and people are uncertain about the capability and willingness of governments to defend their currency. Government decisions to defend the exchange rate peg have often been moved by institutional, electoral, and partisan incentives.

The interesting issue is what would have happened if there was decen-tralization of decision-making systems whereby electoral politics was subjected to the principle of cyclical mobility of the governing class. It is very clear that none of the Leblang factors of institutional, electoral, and partisan incentives would have then mattered.

I am not trying to say that cyclical mobility of the elites would lead to better decision making. What it achieves for sure is the avoidance of the perils of partisan incentives and narrow electoral politics from clouding a country's economic policies.

The other issue that needs to be considered is whether globalization has promoted a zero sum game whereby one's prosperity is diametrically proportional to the other's loss. We have earlier discussed this concept in relation to globalization literature that focuses on inequalities between the world and inequalities within a nation-state. Commentators like Allen Sinai and Phillip Merill (2005) say that the size of the US economy, its growth rate, its economic performance and so on, have made the United States an attractive place to invest, work, and live in. At the same time, Sinai goes on to argue that in today's global world, no country is an island and that interdependence with other countries is a reality. There are scholars like Merill who argue that the US economy, the largest economy in the world with a GDP of $11.7 trillion in 2004, is driving the world economy more definitively now than it did in the 1960s. This, according to Merrill (2005), is not because of its size but because of its innovative capabilities.

However, Merrill predicts that the US share in GDP will diminish because other countries in Asia and parts of Europe will grow at a much faster rate than the global average. This, in turn, will force the United States to work on collaborative partnership arrangements. Merrill does not, however, agree with the analysis of Sinai that wealth creation in the world is a zero sum game. He argues that the United States would not be better off if Germany, Japan and other major countries in Europe were as weak today as they were at the end of the Second World War. Likewise, the United States would not have been better off if China and India remained poor. While the United States has outsourced 6,00,000 to 7,00,000 US jobs in recent times, it has also sourced in at least six to seven million jobs into the country. Siemens employs more than 70,000 people in the United States. Merrill, while recognizing the fact that China and India are headed towards high-trajectory growth, also contends that these two emerging powers cannot catch up with the United States. Presumably, he considers the strength of the United States as lying in its ability to catapult from the present stage to the next stage of innovation and growth.

Putin's current war in Ukraine has changed some of these assessments. Europe is bleeding from the aftereffects of the energy crisis imposed by Russia. The United States is in the throes of high inflation with a recession looking imminent. However with all this the US economy looks like the only beacon of hope for the world.

Why is it that the zero sum game, so characteristic of international economic relations until the 1990s, has changed? In the 1950s, the 1960s, and
the 1970s, developing countries in the world including China and India
focussed heavily on production of food, fibres, and industrial raw materials. Exports from developing countries partook of natural resources or
agricultural commodities that were produced by systems that underpaid
workers and farmers. In this scheme of things, the rapacity of companies
coupled with the weaknesses of small individual farmers led to the emergence of intermediaries who held a position of strength in negotiating
with parties on either side of the fence. Their gain was the producer's loss.
It was a classic play of zero sum game. India Commodity Boards were set
up for export-intensive agricultural commodities such as coffee, tea, and
spices to obviate the problem. But the high transaction costs associated
with the commodity board's intermediation more than neutralized the
benefits of win-win deals.

On the contrary, the business outsourcing practices generated by
the Information Technology (IT) industry in developing countries
such as India at the dawn of this century had created win-win situations. Referring to the US job market, Bhagawati et al. (2004) state how
outsourcing, while proximately reducing jobs in certain firms or sectors,
can increase jobs elsewhere. This situation is in many ways responsible
for the changing of the zero sum concept. Thus, systems of global integration promised by the information society and a globalized world enabled by the IT industry, has given a much better deal to large sections of
producers.

Certainly, leaders and international organizations have brilliantly outlined the challenges of globalization. While Tony Blair has shifted his
perspective from a cosmopolitan approach of 'values' and 'order' to the
more fundamental challenges of addressing the requisites of national development, the UN and the World Bank have gone the other way round,
from international and national priorities to global concerns. The simple
reality is that nation-states and local communities have in some parts
of the world demonstrated that with good governance, it is possible to
withstand the threats of globalization and increase their attraction
of their economies to the global communities of investors and technology providers. Lessons from the corporate world on 'social responsibility' hold valuable lessons for nation-states in their effort to nurture

social capital and carve out a genuine decentralization process that helps them optimize returns from a globalized economy. The experience of the global IT industry indicates that global opportunities can be tapped without depriving the fortunes of other states. Circulation of elites, dis-intermediation, localization, and non-complexity can further enable the process to ensure that globalization works well for nation-states.

4

India

The Multi-Faceted Nation-State

In his book 'The Collapse Of Globalism: The Reinvention Of The World', that came out in the year 2005, John Ralston Saul takes an unusual look at globalism and its future. Saul offers the view that nation-states need to play a greater role in the era of globalization. He states that though globalization appears to have led to the marginalization of nation-states and to the emergence of global markets, the prophecy that 'economics and not politics would determine the course of human events' has not turned out to be true. He notes that growth in international trade has neither fostered prosperous markets in the world nor eliminated poverty, much less, changed entrenched dictatorships. Rather, Saul argues that globalism has created a chaotic vacuum. Instead of surrendering or sharing sovereignty, governments are re-asserting their national interests. The United States appears determined to ignore its international critics. Europe is plagued with problems of immigration, racism, terrorism, and renewed internal nationalism and is looking for 'European' solutions. In short, Saul says that the concept of nation-states is back and on the rise. He quotes the instance of India and China, the so-called unexpectedly booming countries that are driven by national imperatives. Saul draws on Robert Cooper's statement, 'what keeps governments in power is politics at home, not foreign relations', to substantiate his argument. As Saul states, the view that the domestic prevails over the global will tell you to what extent the world at large has left the globalist ideology behind it.[1] Saul adduces many examples of the progressive change in thinking about nation-states. One of the most unexpected developments in recent years has been the growing confusion among neo-liberal apostles when it comes to the trade-off between low taxes and public debt. Traditionally, neo-liberals saw low taxes as good and public debt as bad. Suddenly, many of them are leaning so

India, Climate Change, and The Global Commons. A. Damodaran, Oxford University Press. © A. Damodaran 2024.
DOI: 10.1093/oso/9780192899828.003.0004

heavily on the low tax side that they cannot help being acquiescent to the rise of public debt. This includes icons like the former Federal Reserve chief, Alan Greenspan.

Coming to the miracle economy of the twenty-first century, Saul states that 'China's problems are so massive that only exponential improvements in healthcare economics and governance can pull China together' (Saul 2005, 227). Of course this was 8 years before the formidable Xi Jinping assumed charge of the country.

Saul proceeds to argue although hedge funds have been powerful, the dominant business discourse in the United States has been about job creation, transparency and social responsibility and applying self-regulation where there is none. As we have noted in the preceding chapters, corporates in the United States have learnt a bitter lesson from the derivatives scandal and the economic crisis of 2008–9, while countries such as Indonesia have avoided the worst effects of economic globalization by building up on social capital.

However, Saul goes a step ahead and advocates the concept of negative nationalism. He considers insecurity, poverty, and ambition as three causes of destructive nationalism or negative nationalism. For him, the true expressions of negative nationalism are 'ethnic loyalty', 'appropriation of god to one side', a certain sense of pride in ignorance and a conviction that you are permanently wounded. Saul's theory here resembles Huntington's idea of 'clash of civilizations', except that for Huntington, civilizations clashed across national borders while for Saul, it could also have been within nation-state borders. The real issue is that the brand of negative nationalism that Saul advances has more to do with the overall logic of economic growth envisaged in a globalizing world. The negatives of negative nationalism were seen in the ruthless genocide witnessed in parts of Africa and in East Europe and the steady but systematic rise of neo-Nazi movements in Russia, Germany, and certain other parts of Europe. None of these negative nationality streaks has promoted economic growth. However, it will be premature to suggest that negative nationalism is not conducive to economic growth. The Indian economy booms even when Hindu fundamentalism is on its rise. India as a country has focused on keeping its postmodern traditions and its identity as a nation-state, despite having a great capacity to play and prosper strategically in a modernity-driven globalized world.

Indeed, Kiely advances the argument that the phenomena of globalization and global markets have not really weakened or destroyed the concept of nation-states. Kiely's counter argument is that some states, more
than others, are agents of globalization. In this context, Kiely notes that
it is not enough to reduce globalization to the actions of nation-states.
Kiely's alternative approach is not to set up a rigid dichotomy between
the national and the global or suggest that one dominates the other in different historical phases. He states that one needs to recognize the global
character of capitalist social relations from the outset, and the ways in
which these have interacted with national organizations that are purely
political (2005). Interestingly, Kiely also says that there is an institutional
separation of economics and politics within the development of capitalist
social relations (2005, 277). This separation also presupposes a territorial
dichotomy between global markets and national states, something that
holds true for capitalist social relations.

This is precisely what brings us to the core philosophy of globalization.
There are globalists who consider globalization as economic in nature and
sufficient enough to dissolve national boundaries. If this contention is
true then how can one explain the presence of nationalism in many parts
of the world? Dynamic nation-states do not resist globalization but try
to combine globalization with nationalism. They do this by re-imagining
globalization and co-opting it within the boundaries of a postmodern
national consciousness. A nation-state might embrace globalization and
permit its economy to cross national borders, while building up national
consciousness amongst its citizens and its diaspora. This is made possible
because many nation-states have undergone a strong phase of seclusion
to build up nationalism prior to opening their doors to the world.

This is evident from an interesting study on the evolution of globalization by Kawaktsu Heita (2004). According to Heita, countries proceed
from a phase of 'national seclusion' to a phase of opening up to the world.
The interesting point of Heita's thesis is that the process of national seclusion is strongly associated with a strong and vibrant agricultural economy
and cultural and religious resurgence. He notes that China in the eighteenth century pursued a policy of national seclusion by concentrating on
building wealth in its agricultural sector. Similarly, he states that Japan
also underwent a national seclusion phase during 1603–1867 which saw
Japanese agriculture outperforming China's. He also feels that the process

of national seclusion centring on agriculture lays the foundation of subsequent economic progress achieved by countries in the phase of globalization. The United States too followed a policy of isolation or national seclusion under the Monroe doctrine, whereby it consolidated its power based on a strong agricultural sector.

Heita goes on to argue that it was during the period of national seclusion in Japan that Japanese civilization was able to shrug off its influence from China and revive itself on the cultural front (2004, 43). At the same time, Heita on account of a period of economic and cultural consolidation that a country is able to work its way up the ladder of competitiveness in a globalized world.

Global civilization has also evolved, based on identities coming from the religious dimension. For instance, Henry Pirenne (2001) argues that the European identity was born out of a sense of crisis created by the capture of the Mediterranean Sea by the adherents of the Islamic religion. Similarly, Fernand Braudel (1992), the French historian, considers Europe's victory over Islam as causing the rise of Christendom and the first hegemony of Spain under the rule of Philip II between 1527 and 1598.

These arguments interestingly bring us to the fact that Huntington's theory of the clash of civilizations is not something as recent as 9/11, but has been there since the fifteenth and sixteenth centuries or even earlier during the period of the crusades. A nation's identities, in other words, could be created by religious and cultural factors and not just by economic factors. Economic factors might have either supplemented national and cultural identities or invigorated them. However, at the same time, nation states that underwent a process of seclusion have remained, relatively speaking, impervious to the notion of diversity of cultures.

India as a country could not practise the seclusion principle. Notwithstanding the geo-political presence of the Himalayas, India had to contend with invasions for a long period in its history. This resulted in the evolution of a composite culture that transcended religious and cultural boundaries. Though India had its share of rule of religions (the period of Hindu rule followed by the period of Islamic rule and by Christian presence during the British period), the fact remains that India is still considered a plural society and a deep civilizational identity that defines its own stature in the comity of nations. This causes the modernity element of the Indian state to have its own character.

Peter Bogason (2000) argues that a state survives on account of its broad and over-arching truth that it has managed to nurture over time.

Antony Giddens (1990) has a different perspective. He says that modernity is a post-traditional order. In contrast to feudal societies that pine for ascribed status, there are no fixed identities in a modernity-driven world to which one is inevitably compelled to belong. Although sensitive to the notion that the compulsion to choose is a source of anxiety, Giddens increasingly emphasizes that pluralization enhances opportunities for all concerned. He is, therefore, optimistic about the prospects of a global capitalist economic and political order that adapts to changing times. Giddens addresses the question of politics in the neo-liberal era and concludes that neo-liberalism has promoted an individualized postmodern society in which free market neo-liberal capitalism primes over collective values. In terms of politics, the current era is characterized by an unprecedented shallowness in which old ideological differences are displayed through personality disputes and celebrity culture. While at one end, Giddens considers modernity as synonymous with individuality, he also negates any fixed identity for modernity. At the same time, he also considers the postmodern state as highly individualized.

Richard Cooper has a different position on what is the 'modern' element in politics. Speaking against the context of globalization, Robert Cooper (2003) states that postmodern Europe and a premodern group of failed states have undermined the Westphalian system of nation-states. We deduce from Cooper's theory that a Westphalian state stands for modernity.

Postmodernism is difficult to define. For sure, it is a reaction to modernism. Postmodernism could also mean the adaptation of traditionalism to a new order. Postmodernism questions meta-truths.

However a Westphalian order that believes in the territorial dimensions of a nation-state, can also induce and nurture diversity and plurality. These trends may reinforce each other and promote the re-imagination of the nation-state. It is this duality that has characterized India as an emerging economy that is diversity driven. However, when postmodern conditions make their appearance, in a modern society, it can bring changes in fundamental ways. In the first place, centralization and co-ordination of state power characteristic of modern states, gives way to the power of local networks and local communities. A postmodern situation displays the trend towards individualization, fragmentation, and decentralization—this system basically works on interaction networks wherein people work as employees of other organizations even while they cooperate within their organizations. As postmodern conditions start bubbling, bottom-up approaches and community-based collective actions surface. In some societies, there is a healthy mix between modern and postmodern conditions, which create situations where the state is in control over certain sectors of the economy, while shedding or giving up control on certain other sectors to local communities. Nation-states such as India have tried to bring about a healthy blend between modern and postmodern conditions. In the wake of globalization and liberalization, India has taken to measures that loosen the grip of the state over its economy. Also, in India, the onset of economic reforms in the 1990s was accompanied by a major effort to introduce the 72nd and 73rd constitutional amendments, designed to decentralize governance, especially in matters concerning local administration and local service provisioning. Though Panchayati Raj Institutions (PRIs) in India have since then gained immense constitutional powers, they have not really experienced true empowerment, since transfer of power has not been adequately affected. There are exceptions like Kerala's People's Planning Progress, where PRIs were granted large volumes of funds to execute projects designed by them.

By the turn of the twenty-first century, it was evident that successive national governments in India were laying greater focus on decentralization. Indeed, by 2004, the Panchayati Raj or the local self-governing process in India had progressed much in terms of designing and delivering services. The key question is, how many of these services are truly modern and how many of these have been endogenously designed? In one of my earlier papers (Damodaran 1992) on local self-governments of India and in a recent paper that considered the tribal issue in the Wyanad district in Kerala, I have argued that most of the bottom-up or decentralized approaches in India have not promoted local idioms. In the case of the People's Planning Process about which much has been written, the effort has been to implement schemes which partake of modernity. Local driven approaches were not given emphasis.

In short, postmodern structures which have evolved in societies like India are not necessarily independent from modernity. Ostrom, Bish, and Ostrom (1988) consider service provisioning as involving two types of decisions, namely 'providing the service' and 'producing the service'. Service provision means a process of collective choice which involves decisions on what service to provide, how to finance the service apart from deciding on the quantity and quality of service. According to the authors, while service production requires the service provider to stick to parameters decided upon a priori, delivery of the service is not a priori determined. The choice of whether delivery needs to be franchised or assigned is not taken a priori. The key thing, according to Ostrom and Bish, is that service production is a matter of 'price' and 'trust'. One need not stretch one's imagination far to understand that the process of provisioning public services, though resting with pre-modern local self-government units in countries such as India, are basically driven by forces of modernity that are located above. The over-arching idea and the contours of service production are decided by the service seeker, who also controls delivery systems. A postmodern space comes into existence to deliver modern services. In such a situation, to pre-suppose that a postmodern space has to, ipso facto promote postmodern design and delivery of services may not necessarily be true in countries like India. On the other hand, my argument is that postmodern conditions are crafted by modernity, keep the nation state alive in a globalized world. It is this strategy of subtle diversity which has enabled countries such as India to keep up their relevance even in a world where globalization has taken strong roots.

The phenomenon of modernity and postmodernity in India go back to the pre-British and the British periods. Prior to the advent of the British rule in India, the country was dominated by the traditional socioeconomic and political order which was characterized as the 'oriental' paradigm during the British period.[2] It was on a 'non-reasoning' superstitious world of the 'orient' that the British rule attempted to impose the ideals of modernity, scientific reasoning, and rationality. Warren Hastings, the second Governor of India (and its first Governor General), respected the customs of his subjects and their traditional Indian legal Institutions and explored orientalism. He encouraged Sir Charles Wilkins, Sir William Jones, and H.T. Colebrooke to study Sanskrit and produce masterpiece translations of the Bhagavat Gita (Wilkins) and Shakuntalam (Jones) in English. He actively worked to reduce the inequality between Hindus and Muslims by setting up the Muhammadan College in Calcutta 'to get the sons of Muhammadan gentlemen for respectful and lucrative offices of the State. Hastings earned great respect among Indians. And yet, when he returned to England in 1785, Edmund Burke took the lead in impeaching him for minor felonies. After Hastings, the tide changed. Cornwallis, who followed Hastings, set up the permanent settlement system in Bengal that created the obnoxious zamindari system to extract land revenue for the English East India Company. Cornwallis fancied the Zamindars to be the 'squires of the Indian country side'. This was a disastrous hallucination. In the process, Cornwallis destroyed the finer tenets of traditional land tenancy and revenue assessment systems put in place by Raja Todar Mal during Akbar's rule.

Since Warren Hastings, the British system in India subsisted on the fable of the inferior ways of the 'orient' vis-à-vis its other, namely the superior ideals of 'reason' embodied by modernization and modernity. The British system in India cast the 'orient' against the ideas of modernization and modernity. However, it is equally noteworthy that, despite its many failures, the British period had succeeded in implanting the germs of modernity by way of English education, railways, roads, and public institutions, particularly in the fields of health and agriculture.

The real problem was that these benefits did not percolate to the masses. It was appropriated by the Indian elite from the economically and socially advanced sections. Therefore, at the dawn of independence, India inherited a large segment of the economy which was still trapped in both 'oriental' thinking and 'oriental' ways of life. However, the statesmen who took over the reins of the Indian state in the post-independent period, led by Jawaharlal Nehru, conceived a state that could stand on its own terms by embracing modernity. During the Nehruvian and post-Nehruvian periods, the major focus was to infuse modernity in different layers of society. The steel plants of Durgapur, Bhilai, and Rourkela stood as pillars of modernity and modernization. They were located in places which were considered to be agrarian/tribal belts. The Indian Institutes of Technology were set up to churn out students imbued with 'technical skills' and 'scientific temper'.

The 1990s, which saw the onslaught of globalization all over the world following the collapse of the Soviet Union, placed the Indian nation-state in a new situation. The goal of modernity and modernization to which India remained committed through a controlled planned approach, had to be given up for a more 'open' system. The result was that the nation-state in India had to transfigure itself into a new role. Initially, the pace of economic liberalization and the globalization of the Indian economy was limited to a few sectors. However, by the close of the twentieth century, when India found that the benefits of globalization were trickling in by way of demand for its qualified human resources from the developed world there was greater emphasis on opening up the Indian economy to global forces. It was at this juncture that the State continued to promote itself as a modern or modernity state with certain postmodern features. Tradition was re-invented within modern spaces that capsuled the 'new economy'. The emphasis of the National Democratic Alliance (NDA), the front that initially ruled India in the late 1990s at the dawn of the present century, on Indian identity and its civilizational context, was a case in point of a postmodern turn. As steps towards integrating the Indian State into the global order were undertaken in the economic sphere, a reverse move was made in the cultural and spiritual spheres, which sought to project India as an oriental state with a modernity impulse. This was consistent with the teachings of the ideologues of the Rashtriya Swayamsevak Sangh (RSS), the parent organization of the Bhartiya Janata Party (BJP), which was the dominant party of the NDA.[3] This movement received further rigour when the NDA came back to power in 2014 with Narendra Modi as the Prime Minister.

Thus, the state in India, with its spaces of tradition and modernity, also created its postmodern spaces in what was otherwise a modernity-based empire. Until the turn of this century, the fault lines mirrored on, what Jeffrey Sachs refers to as 'the highly progressing urban base' in the large coastal cities of Mumbai, Kolkata, and Chennai, standing in marked contrast to the huge Gangetic hinterland that suffered from poverty and 're-gional backwardness'. This was the pattern of regional diversity in British India as well. With the advent of the IT revolution, postmodern spaces evolved.

Cities such as Bengaluru, Chennai, Pune, and Hyderabad had the flavour of IT cities of the United States. However the new band of IT professionals practised postmodernity lifestyles that showed pride in 'Indian' identity (cultural and religious), while marvelling at the achievements of Jeff Bezos, Mark Zuckerberg, and Bill Gates! Today, India as a nation-state is kept alive in terms of a mix of modernity and postmodernity which not only reflect economic vibrancy but also the quintessence of India's culture and national idiom. This has its paradoxes as well. While IT cities such as Bengaluru have been experiencing 'high growth', this has not whetted the appetite of the IT industry for more infrastructure and further improvement in high-end amenities such as roads and communications. At the other end are rural areas that have been crying out about farmers' suicides, drop in prices of food grains, and the ravages perpetrated on the Indian farmers due to the glorious uncertainty of the world trade rules exemplified in the WTO. This, then, has been the defining trait of India as an emerging economy.

Interestingly, the slogan of 'India Shining', which was coined by the NDA government, which functioned in India between 1998 and 2004, in its dying days, was, for all practical purposes, the idea of the dominant party in the front, namely the BJP, a party that espouses Hindutva. The 'India Shining Campaign' portrayed the achievements of its modernity-driven sector, with a postmodern slant. Similar has been Prime Minister Narendra Modi's efforts to combine feverish nationalism and Hindutva with the quest turning India into a modern 5 Trillion Dollar Economy.

The real issue is whether there has been a transformation in India's image in the globalized world. If, in the past, India projected its image as a state striving towards modernity with postmodern features, in future it is likely that India would promote itself as a postmodern state with modernity integrated to it. This will be particularly true when the adverse pressures of globalization become apparent. In such an event, it is quite likely that the nation-state concept to which India has been traditionally wedded, will assume greater importance. Interestingly, the pressure for a postmodern-driven state will be greater, given the global economic crisis the world is pushed into after the COVID-19 pandemic.

Traditionalism would mean the tendency to have a greater focus on, traditional agriculture, and rural ways of life, while modernity refers to the modern industries that came up in the 1950s and 1960s that India took pride in, during the initial decades of independence. The IT and the Communications Infrastructure sector straddles both the modern and the traditional in terms of its potential to help these sectors adapt to globalization, while at the same time defying the logic of modern and traditional sectors when it comes to its labour process. It is, therefore, postmodern in its essence.

A mix of three, namely, modernity, traditionalism, and postmodernity, will, by promoting diverse impulses, keep the nation-state in India from withering away or losing its relevance. Every significant political party in India would, in the long run, have this mix of modernity and postmodernity built into its perspective. It is not just confined to the BJP or the NDA. A party like the Indian National Congress (INC) had an agenda for all the three worlds. Its employment guarantee schemes (influenced by the welfare principle of the modernist welfare state) stand in marked contrast to its legislation for conferring modern property rights to the 'traditional' tribal communities that are not tuned to the concept of property rights over lands. This is a postmodern adaptation. Even the Communist Party of India (Marxist), also known as CPI (M), which is the largest leftist party in India, has adopted a mix of modernity with its postmodern concerns. Under such circumstances, economics gets separated from politics and culture, each one following its own trajectory, which in many ways serves to deny the general structuralist prophecy that economics produces its logic of politics and culture.

To sum up, the nation state is on the rise. In countries like India neo-nationalism has complemented economic boom. Indeed, countries like India do not resist globalization—rather they co-opt them through a postmodern process. India's IT cities mirror a postmodern space. In the years to come, a postmodern state that embeds modernity will be the character of India and this will be based on local identities and pan-nationalism that promotes a non-standardized approach to the challenges of globalization. A co-opted approach of the traditional, modern, and the postmodern adds to the diversity and hence plurality of responses to the world of globalization. This will have implications on how India will approach global commons.

5

India's Rurality and Its Different Faces

How is national seclusion related to national identities? This is a critical question that has engaged scholars who work on nation building. Indeed, rurality plays an important role in fostering identities. Tom Nairn (1997) who analyses 'rurality' and its role in obstructing modernization, sees a nexus between seclusion and agricultural growth. Nairn provides insights on how national identities are reinforced by seclusion. He also analyses how civic nationalism is linked to civic societies. He states that urbanization is a smooth sounding impersonal term (1997, 91). This is not the case with rural communities for whom the myth of rootedness is extremely important. It is this myth that galvanizes community feelings amongst rural folk. For Nairn, the idealist nation is perceived as a vastly extended family since it exudes a general sense of psychic belonging to a community (1997, 97). In fact, Nairn goes a step forward to suggest that ethnic nationalism gets transmuted into a nation, with the peasantry being the catalyst (1997, 91). Peasantries, if reimagined, could help in creating the modern nation. The peasantry can also form the bulwark of green politics and ecology.

Nairn's observations are interesting as they talk about the influence rurality can have in the construction of nations and nationalities. In some ways, Nairn's analysis brings out the fact that if fashioned well, rurality could be handy for a developing country to fight against the debilitating forces of globalization.

Nairn does not deny that nationalism could be abused by autocrats, particularly when it is situated within the framework of a fictive kinship. However the benefits of properly channelized nationalism far outweigh the negatives.

There are a few problems in applying Nairn's ideas to countries like India. During its initial phase of planned economic growth, India did not produce a vibrant agricultural economy despite moving from a state of

India, Climate Change, and The Global Commons. A. Damodaran, Oxford University Press. © A. Damodaran 2024.
DOI: 10.1093/oso/9780192899828.003.0005

food shortages to relative agricultural surplus by the 1970s. While it is true that the Green Revolution heralded a major change in the agricultural production apparatus in India in the late 1960s, it was only after the liberalization process in the mid-1990s and late 1990s that agricultural production surpluses in the country translated into large food buffer stocks. While the growth rate of Indian agriculture was unimpressive at 3 per cent, by the turn of the twenty-first century, rural India was buzzing with activity. Huge stockpiles of food were packed up in the godowns of the Food Corporation of India (FCI). There were pockets of rural prosperity visible in India's rural scape. Incidentally, this phase of agricultural prosperity coincided with lowered tariff barriers and removal of quantitative restrictions on the import of essential agricultural commodities.

The farmers' movements against the WTO's Agriculture Agreement were mounted by the vibrant section of India's agriculture sector. Organizations such as the Karnataka Raytha Sangha vociferously protested against the adverse impacts of the WTO import regimes in rural India. While one set of farmers demanded closure of the borders to ward off imports, there was another category which was against WTO regimes that permitted developed countries in Europe and other parts of the world to provide liberal subsidies to their farmers. Farmers groups of India, notably those led by Sharad Joshi, argued that the WTO regime provided a great opportunity for Indian agriculture, as it allowed our surpluses to move across the borders to different markets in the world. Therefore, any effort on the part of developed countries to deny this opportunity needs to be opposed.

Thus, the post-WTO phase presents a complex picture of India's rurality.

Unlike Asian countries like Kampuchea, India has a huge rural landmass with substantial ethnic and linguistic diversity. India's nation formation process extended to rural areas a few years after the country gained independence. The regions which came under the core influence of the Green Revolution in the mid-1960s became the engine of agricultural growth for India, while the traditional farming areas which were unaffected by the Green Revolution were viewed as laggards. In the Green Revolution zones, farmers took to aggressive commercial approaches when it came to agricultural production and marketing. The so-called laggard sector, on the other hand, reeled under the pressures of crop failures and dropping incomes. For the laggard agri-zones of India, the priority was to insulate themselves from the vagaries of weather.

Thus the response to the WTO Agreement on Agriculture differed for two segments of rural India in fundamental ways.

Lessons in Development from the Deserts of Rajasthan

As an advisor to the UN Millennium Development Project, Jeffrey Sachs (2005) delved into the philosophy and process underlying the MDGs which came into operation in the year 2000. According to Sachs, the UN Millennium Development Goals (MDGs) unleashed a major debate amongst national policy makers and practitioners on possible strategies of implementation (Sachs 2005, 222).

There are a few features of the MDGs which are worth mentioning. In the first place, MDGs require all UN member states to work towards realistic targets. Second, the MDGs recognized the inherent limitations faced by developing countries in crafting governance systems that are critical for rapid economic development. This explains why the MDGs did not talk about total eradication of all forms of poverty. Rather, the Goals only emphasized the need to eradicate or eliminate extreme cases of poverty. This feature of dealing with 'extremes' was what made the MDGs realistic. A close look at the MDGs shows that their focus was spread amongst the concerns of poverty and hunger, universal primary education, gender equality and empowerment of women, child mortality rates, maternal health, HIV/AIDS, malaria and other diseases, and environmental sustainability.

Notwithstanding their wide-ranging nature, the MDGs afforded scope for action in each cluster. For instance, in the cluster pertaining to poverty and hunger, goals were laid down to reduce by half, the proportion of people living on less than a dollar a day. This was in addition to the target of reducing by half, the proportion of people who suffered from hunger. Within the scheme of primary education, the MDGs required all boys and girls to complete a full course of primary schooling. When it came to the issue of child mortality, the MDGs laid down that two-thirds of the mortality rate among children needed to be eliminated.

On maternal health, MDGs emphasized reducing maternal mortality rates by three-fourths. On HIV/AIDS, malaria, and other communicable diseases, the MDGs called for reduction in the speed of their spread. When it came to environmental sustainability, the MDGs talked about normative ideas such as integration of principles of sustainable development into country development policies. The MDGs also called upon countries to achieve significant improvements in the lives of at least 100 million slum dwellers by the year 2020. On global partnership for development, the MDGs advocated open trading and financial systems based on rules-based, predictable, and non-discriminatory systems. The MDGs focused on addressing the special needs of least developed countries by way of debt relief. Finally, the MDGs also lay stress involving the private sector to make available new technologies, especially information and communication technologies for the needy.

Perhaps the intriguing part of the MDGs is that they did not expect developed countries to provide Official Development Assistance (ODA) to developing countries at the desired level. It is noteworthy that the MDG goals did not even talk about the importance of developed countries fulfilling the target of 1 per cent of GDP as their ODA commitment. By talking of global partnership through private sector involvement and highlighting the special needs of vulnerable countries, the MDGs tried to hedge around fundamental issues such as transformation of the world trading system and related perils of globalization. Nevertheless, the real utility of the MDGs lies in the fact that they gained the acceptance of many developing countries. Indeed, MDG-related programmes performed well in key areas of strategic importance to vulnerable countries which included access to drinking water and sanitation, reduction of child mortality, improvement in maternal health, control over HIV/AIDS, etc. However, in many countries, the implementation of MDGs was hamstrung by financial constraints, low focus on sustainable development programmes, and absence of private sector initiatives and global collaborative frameworks.[1]

The MDGs had a timeline of 15 years. At the United Nations Conference on Sustainable Development held in Rio de Janeiro in 2012, the United Nations decided to launch the Sustainable Development Goals (SDGs). The SDs, which comprised 17 goals were designed to improve upon the MDGs in more innovative ways. A noteworthy feature of the SDG agenda is the higher degree of interconnectedness that exists amongst its goals. In this sense, the SDGs mark an improvement over the MDGs.[2]

Implementation of the SDGs commenced in January 2016. The UN High-Level Political Forum on Sustainable Development (HLPF) monitors the implementation of SDGs. This Forum functions under the auspices of the United Nations Economic and Social Council.[3]

The 17 Goals of the SDGs cover the key development and environment problems facing the developing world. Indeed the SDGs goals on climate change provided the foundation for the Paris Agreement on Climate Change.

The 17 goals of the SDGs include 'No poverty', 'Zero hunger', 'Good health' and well-being for people, Quality education, Gender equality, Clean water and sanitation, Affordable and clean energy, decent work and economic growth, industry, innovation, infrastructure, reduction of inequalities, sustainable cities and communities, responsible consumption and production, climate action, life below water, life on land, peace, justice and strong institutions, and finally securing Partnerships to achieve the goals.[4]

In its four years of existence, the SDGs have undergone a few reviews. One of the plus points about the SDGs has been the effective manner in which the goals have been communicated to stakeholders concerned.[5]

A 2018 study published in *Nature* found that while a large number of African countries demonstrated improvements in the health conditions of children under five years of age, many of them have lagged behind when it came to the target of ending malnutrition.[6]

A major criticism about the SDGs goals is that they are large and unwieldy with too many targets. There have also been critical comments about the manner in which the SDGs have been implemented in various countries. There are also concerns about the high costs of implementing SDG goals which necessitate greater mobilization of financial resources than would be necessary had implementation been efficient.

It will be interesting to see how the pursuit of the SDGs can contribute to poverty reduction. Let us examine the SDGs in the light of the development problems faced by certain regions or states in India which are considered to be laggards when it comes to the parameters of economic and social development.

India has been characterized by regional inequalities in development. We have a few States that rank high in human development indices. We have many States that rank low in human development index. States that figure high in human and general development index are located to the west, south, and north of India. Most of the underdeveloped states in India are located towards the east, north-east, north-west, and central India. One of the largest states in north-west India which has a relatively low level of human development index is Rajasthan (traditionally known as Rajaputana). Way back in the 1970s, Rajasthan was the first to announce its Antyodaya scheme—a scheme designed to raise the welfare of the poorest. Three decades later, the MDGs were to state the same idea when they proclaimed their focus on the poorest of the poor. The focus of SDGs too is on eliminating extreme cases of underdevelopment such as hunger and poverty.

It will be interesting to go through the human development profile of Rajasthan for an idea of the challenges the State has faced in its development mission. It will be even more interesting to see how, given the profile and pattern of human development noticed in the state, the SDGs could make a difference.

Rajasthan is a desert region that suffers from the problems of unpredictable weather. At the same time, Rajasthan is noted for its bountiful mineral resources. Human communities that inhabit Rajasthan include pastoral nomads, marginal agricultural communities, commercial agriculture practising farmers as well as communities that live on mineral extraction and mining. One would imagine that as a desert state, Rajasthan would be largely rural. Interestingly, the findings of the Human Development Report (HDR) prepared by the Rajasthan government in the year 2002, paints a totally different picture regarding the livelihood issues and the trajectory of growth that the state has achieved. These findings are borne out by the author's visits to Alwar and Barmer in 2005. Much of the succeeding descriptions are based on the Human Development Report of 2002 (HDR 2002).

Though 60 per cent of Rajasthan's area is covered by deserts and the population density is relatively low, the absolute growth of population has been high with decadal population growth rates reaching their highest level in the 1990s. The literacy level for girls is the lowest in Rajasthan as compared to the rest of the states in the country.

As per the Human Development Report of 2002, the growth rate of Rajasthan, in terms of Gross State Domestic Product (GSDP), compares favourably with national averages, though there have been slippages in recent years. In the 1980s, Rajasthan had the highest GSDP growth rate in the country while in the 1990s, partly due to the high decadal growth rate in population, its rank slipped down by a few notches. It is creditable that, despite rising population and a stagnant agricultural sector, the State did not witness a drastic rise in unemployment figures. It is equally note-worthy that the industrial sector in Rajasthan has a very low share as far as employment is concerned, with just 7.5 per cent of the employment avenues coming from the industry. At the same time, the share of labour in total agricultural employment increased, despite a fragile agricultural sector.

It is noteworthy that government jobs have been the major source of employment in the state. According to the HDR 2002 Report, the state's employment base has been contributed by government and public sector undertakings such as the Rajasthan State Electricity Board (RSEB) and the Rajasthan State Road Transport Corporation (RSRTC). The other interesting aspect of Rajasthan is that despite its predominantly rural profile, the problems that the state faces in its urban centres have been for-midable. The growing incidence of urban poverty has outstripped rural poverty levels and this is on account of the fact that Rajasthan experi-enced nearly 40 per cent growth in its urban population between 1980 and 1991, in contrast to the population growth rates in its rural areas, which was only 25 per cent during the same period.

Leather forms a vital segment of the state's industrial sector. This is understandable given the fact that livestock is the main asset of the people of Rajasthan. However, the leather sector does not generate suffi-cient employment opportunities for women. The HDR 2002 report con-cludes that the state suffers from feminization of poverty, malnutrition, sanitation problems, and growing incidence of communicable diseases such as HIV/AIDS. As the HDR 2002 report observes, over a period of time, the state's problems have been compounded by its major failure in utilizing its natural resources base in a sustainable manner. Loss of com-munity lands, pastoral lands and grasslands coupled with deforestation, encroachment, and privatization have created severe livelihood problems for local communities that depend on livestock and dry land agriculture.

Similarly, even though the urban situation in Rajasthan had improved, no serious improvement has occurred in the job markets. Entrepreneurial opportunities have also been insignificant in the nonfarming sector in rural areas.

These inadequacies have been in spite of the Rajasthan government's sincere efforts to achieve political de-centralization by strengthening the Panchayat Raj Institutions (PRIs) and involving Panchayati Raj representatives in rural development programmes.

There has been a major effort to promote the literacy movement in the state since the 1990s and a clear initiative to empower Panchayat Raj Institutions (PRIs) to handle subjects stated in the Eleventh Schedule of the Indian Constitution. The government had attempted to create 'islands of prosperity' by undertaking the ambitious Indira Gandhi Canal Command Area in the district of Bikaner. However, the distributive dimension of this major technological intervention is not clear. While farmers who benefited took to commercial agricultural crops, the impact of irrigation on the food economy of the state was negligible. Similarly, the HDR 2002 report observes that there has been failure on the part of the Extension Department of the state government in extending and making available sound technologies to poor farmers who have been suffering from frequent crop failures and decline in yields. There has also been no serious effort to find a solution to the problem of over-population of livestock in districts such as Jalore, Churu, Bikaner, and Jaisalmer. While it is true that the quality of milch cattle stock in the state had improved in the 1990s, the stock of draught animals and small ruminants which give subsistence to both small and marginal farmers, has deteriorated both in qualitative and quantitative terms. The sheep and goat population increased only modestly in the 1980s and 1990s. Development efforts based on technological interventions could only create islands of prosperity that focused on dairying in terms of high milk-yielding cows instead of improving sheep rearing amongst the marginalized pastoralist population.

Given that the agriculture and rural areas have been stagnant, the key question is, what has accounted for the growth of Rajasthan's Gross Domestic Product (GDP)? The answer lies with the mining, quarrying, and the forestry sectors. Thus limestone, silica, sand, zinc, and calcite, including iron ore, have formed a very important basis for the phenomenal growth of the state's GDP in the preceding decades. Following a high-tempo privatization drive, many mines in the state fell into private hands. This weakened the hold of Public Sector Undertakings (PSUs) over mineral resources. However, despite its ability to contribute to the state GDP, the mining sector in Rajasthan has been characterized by serious inter-gender disparities in wages. Interestingly, much of the leatherwork in Rajasthan has been carried out by small-scale units, particularly when it comes to operations like treatment of hides. These activities are carried out by the poorer sections of the society. Similarly, the returns to the primary workers and cottage industry entrepreneurs have been minuscule. What is more, communities that are traditionally connected to the leather industry have been subjected to social discrimination.

What lessons can one learn from Rajasthan as far as the SDGs are concerned? Let us take the case of the SDG objective of eradicating extreme poverty and hunger. The SDGs, while specifying targets for elimination of hunger and poverty, do not consider the fact that such progress can be achieved only if there is a smooth restructuring of the traditional vocations of vulnerable people. In the context of Rajasthan, agriculturists with small and marginal landholdings and the nomadic pastoralists have suffered the most by way of poverty and hunger. In both cases, the key necessity is to eradicate extreme poverty and hunger through restructuring or re-situation of traditional vocations, namely agriculture and pastoralism. For the poorer people of Rajasthan, perhaps the greatest tragedy has been their inability to access the benefits of state-driven technological interventions. The Indira Gandhi Canal Command Area, which was a technically successful, centrally administered water augmentation system, has not benefitted the poorer sections. In other words, technological interventions have not produced benefits to poorer communities. Had the tenure over natural resources such as water been rationalized and had community property rights obtained over ground and surface water resources, perhaps the poorer sections of the community would have gained benefits from improvements in the availability of natural resources. The experience of the Indira Gandhi Canal in Bikaner, however, shows that the problem with the project was not the lack of finances. It was the inability of the project to deliver its benefits to local communities that was key issue. It is quite possible that modern vocations such as mining and energy-intensive industries would have contributed to unsustainable trends in a desert state already reeling under aridity. However, people attached to traditional vocations continue to suffer from near-poverty conditions for want of effective reorganization measures.

It is also clear from the Rajasthan example, that the focus of the poverty and hunger eradication programmes ought to be on those urban centres where vocations for employment are low. The biggest challenge facing schemes for eradicating extreme poverty and hunger in urban centres is to ensure that the organized sector adheres to labour standards and laws. When it comes to universal primary education, gender equality, and empowerment of women, the key problem in Rajasthan has been that education has not spread evenly. Besides, the process of political decentralization has failed to improve existing education services. It is not clear whether standard SDG projects could improve the situation.

Long ago, in 1985, a committee chaired by L.C. Jain, which was set up to evaluate the Zilla Parishad and the Mandal Parishad Acts in Karnataka, opined that the biggest contribution of Zilla Parishad and the Panchayat Raj Institutions (PRIs) in the state, lay in their ability to improve education and welfare in rural areas. Indeed PRIs in Karnataka, by ensuring that schools and primary health centres worked to the satisfaction of the locals, created faith amongst local communities about decentralized governance. Had a similar situation obtained in Rajasthan, the performance of the state in the realm of public services would have been radically different.

As far as environmental sustainability goes, the problems in Rajasthan arise from the substantial erosion of the public goods base in the state. By not taking effective action against encroachments and the conversion of forests and common lands for non-community or non-forestry purposes, the state failed to prevent the shrinkage of the natural resource base of rural poor. The traditional livestock economy of Rajasthan, which operated by nurturing local breeds of livestock over a wide land base, stood in marked contrast to systems of stall-fed livestock that were tried out through the rural development schemes. It is not clear how the SDGs could alter the situation.

There are many environmentalists who feel that small ruminants are responsible for the problem of land degradation. While the Government of India's State of Environment Report talks about nomadic pastoralists being a problem to the society and advocate their 'sedentarization' (or the process of conversion of nomads into sedentary communities), the UN Conference on Desertification (UNCOD) held in Nairobi in 1977 had a different view altogether. It talked about nomadism and transhuman pastoralism as the best possible land use system (from an ecological point of view) for arid and semi-arid lands. It is true that the traditional sector in the livestock economy of Rajasthan suffers from poor economic productivity. Equally noteworthy is the weakened ability of the traditional livestock economy of Rajasthan to subsist on locally available biomass and cope with scarcities due to the decline in the area under forests and common lands. Therefore, going back to the original point, the key challenge for SDG projects is to resituate tradition within the matrix of modernity without destroying the former.

In the comity of international organizations, two sets of institutions can be seen—the UN and the Bretton Woods institutions (that comprise of the IMF and the World Bank). Historically, the World Bank has been in the forefront of providing development aid to needy countries. The World Bank has also played an important role in addressing the poverty issues through land-based and non-land-based approaches. However in recent times the UN organizations have been in the forefront when it comes to advocacy-based activities connected to poverty reduction. With the announcement of the SDGs, the UN has proclaimed its role as the supreme goal setter in the sphere of sustainable development. The larger challenge is to go beyond advocacy and develop a framework for implementing SDGs in a manner that balances the traditional with the modern, thus promoting diverse options for development.

What do global environmental benefits mean to the poor people of Rajasthan? It is obvious that climate change would only add to the woes of Rajasthan's farmers and pastoralists. The key issue for the agriculturists of the state is to adapt to climate change by improving rainfed agricultural practices, conserving water, and reversing land degradation. Biodiversity conservation would also be critical in conserving habitats associated with the Thar Desert. By stopping the spread of mining desertification can be arrested. A state such as Rajasthan, that is on the brink of economic stagnation, should not be expected to contribute to carbon sequestration and mitigation measures that reduce quantitative emissions of CO_2 and other greenhouse gases (GHGs). Its per capita energy consumption is extremely low, its livestock is undernourished and it is inhuman to expect such a state to sacrifice its growth for the cause of climate change. The climate action goals of the SDGs should be conscious of this reality.

The Rajasthan story, in short, offers fundamental lessons in managing global commons.

Rural Woes in the WTO Era

No discussion on rurality is complete unless it explores the impacts of the WTO agreements in rural areas. WTO agreements fall into various categories. While the agreements on Agriculture, Sanitary and Phytosanitary Measures, Pre-shipment Inspections, and Rules of Origin clearly do not support monopoly rights by any entity, the same cannot be stated about the WTO-TRIPS. Here, the emphasis is on protecting the rights of IPR holders than on upholding the interests of nation-states and consumers. The problem with TRIPS is that it does not recognize the role of traditional knowledge in fostering new inventions. There are two exceptions to the TRIPS rule of upholding proprietary IPRs. The first is the compulsory licensing provisions of the TRIPS that enables a country adversely affected by epidemics or pandemics to invoke the provisions of compulsory licensing in case the patent holders refuse to work on their patents. The second provision of the TRIPS that lends it a distributive edge involves two forms of collective IPR rights upheld by it, viz. Geographic Indications and Community Trademarks. These collective rights have the potential of empowering rural communities with IP rights over their crafts.

Unlike TRIPS, the beneficiaries of the Agriculture and Sanitary and Phytosanitary Agreements are largely nation-states or their farming communities and not multinational corporations (MNCs). Thus tariff measures introduced by food-importing countries under the provisos of the Agreement on Agriculture is primarily designed to protect the interests of farming communities in importing countries. Similarly the sanitary and phytosanitary measures undertaken by importing countries is primarily designed to protect the lives and health of domestic consumers.

Is it possible to address the inadequacies of WTO agreements? To answer this question we need to take a look at how development economics has in recent times, looked into the issues posed by neo-liberal policies and the free market dogma.

The post-Second World War period witnessed the triumph of modernity in nation-states. Ever since Harry S. Truman made his famous description of poor countries as underdeveloped countries in 1949, there has been serious effort to spread the dogma of modernity and the virtues of economic growth amongst developing countries. As John Toye (2003) states, the first votary of a development formula for under-developed countries was Arthur Lewis. Lewis produced his report en-titled 'Measures for the Economic Development of Under-developed Countries' in the year 1951. He presumed developing economies to be labour-surplus, capital-scarce, and low wage-driven, which for him opened opportunities to these countries to specialize in labour-intensive products. For Lewis, the problem of underdevelopment was associated with underemployment in the agricultural sector and the only place to transfer the surplus labour was the industrial sphere. Such transfer could be achieved at real wage cost with least damage to agricultural produc-tion. There were many problems with the Lewisian model, including mat-ters connected to human capital formation. However, the most significant criticism of the Lewis model came from Bauer (1956), who argued that the Lewis model was basically negative about agriculture and was wrong in presuming that it was rational to sponge off labour from agriculture. Another point advanced by Toye (2003), was that the Green Revolution was instrumental in overcoming agricultural stagnation in many parts of the developing world (Toye 2003, 25–6). However, Toye proceeds to note that the effective rate of protection for agriculture has turned out to be negative (Toye 2003, 28–9). This, according to him, was partly due to agricultural inputs being taxed and partly due to liberal imports of agri-cultural products. A few Organization for Economic Co-operation and Development (OECD) reports went on to argue that governments were not only neglecting the agricultural sector but also exploiting it to the hilt to promote uncompetitive industries that could be established in min-imal time.

There is a counter viewpoint, which states that the WTO Agreement on Agriculture, by recommending limits on the amount of domestic sup-port to be extended to agriculture and agricultural products through *de minimis* product-specific and non-product-specific support, led

to agriculture in developing and developed countries to be over protected. The special and differentiated treatment provisions of the WTO
Agreement on Agriculture however seeks to protect the agricultural
sector in the developing world more intensely than the farm sector in the
developed world.

If one were to reckon the fact that agriculture in countries like India,
Indonesia, or Thailand is predominated by small and marginal farmers
who practise low external input usage processes, we can very well visualize the consequence of adopting the Lewisian system of economic
change. Since agriculture in developing countries is labour intensive,
any process which shifts labour from the agricultural sector to the industrial sector could create two possible outcomes for the agriculture
sector. The first outcome could be that the agriculture sector will shift
to capital-intensive production processes. The second possibility is that
traditional agriculture holdings will be deployed for non-agricultural
activities like forestry. In India in the Green revolution zones of Punjab,
Haryana, and Western Uttar Pradesh cultivation operations experienced capital intensity. In other parts of India which experienced mi-
gration of human population from villages to cities, the abandoned
farm lands were turned into forest farms, thus endangering conventional agriculture habitats. By the 1980s, the prosperous green revolution zones started experiencing the phenomenon of high incomes
which substantially enhanced their purchasing power that absorbed
large volumes of consumer goods that were generated from urban industrial agglomerations.

In zones where the pull of cities or urban industry was limited, the
conventional agricultural sector fell into a state of stagnation. It is a well-
known fact that Indian agriculture had suffered heavily till the 1970s or,
more specifically, until the mid-1970s, on account of rural unemployment, poverty, and related issues.

In the first decade of this century, ICT and e-commerce portals made
their advent in the rural areas of India. This shift from physical markets
to electronic markets caused a major shift in the orientation of farmers.
Farmers commenced selling their produce online. Indeed, the online-
driven trading kiosks in rural India have been successful in overcoming
the problems of information asymmetry and transaction costs associated
with traditional agriculture markets channels.

Nevertheless, with all these possibilities, agricultural commodity producers in India still suffer from wild swings in prices and fluctuations in their incomes, resulting in grave distress to their lives. In developing countries, this has led to farmers' suicides. Unfortunately, none of these developments concern the WTO. For farmers cultivating price-sensitive globally traded crops like cotton, the free trade rules of the WTO did not matter since subsidies were positioned along different segments of the cotton value chain in order to protect the farmers. In the United States, cotton is a highly subsidized commodity. It was estimated during 2001–2, the United States, China, the European Union and to some extent, Turkey, Egypt, Mexico, and Brazil Cote d'Ivoire had pumped in subsidies in their cotton sector, to the tune of nearly $5.8 billion. Similarly, subsidies on cotton amounted to $1.2 billion in China and $97.9 million in the European Union (World Bank 2006, 212). The tragedy with such subsidies was that it had the effect of compressing costs of production, thereby creating conditions for the sale of cotton at low prices. Though world cotton prices plummeted due to supply gluts, this did not in any way harm the farmers in the countries mentioned.

Unfortunately, India, which requires cotton for feeding its burgeoning textile industry, finds itself saddled with cotton subsidies that have been framed or designed in a different way. Cotton farmers in India, especially in the state of Maharashtra, have been provided with minimum support or floor prices for their crops. Indeed, in states such as Maharashtra, it has been customary for the state government to give a premium price above the minimum support price announced by the Public Sector Undertakings (PSUs), namely the Cotton Corporation of India (CCI). In this scheme of things, farmers are not subsidized to help them breakeven—rather they are subsidized in order to ensure that they get a decent profit margin. Thus while world over, cotton prices remain depressed, in India the price of the crop is propped up way above its market clearing price through subsidies. This prima facie creates conditions for cheap imports of cotton by India. To ward off such imports, the government imposes duties on imported cotton that ensures parity between import price and domestic imported price. Cotton farmers in India are particularly keen to avail of the higher prices offered for the produce by the government and were disturbed when the Government of Maharashtra reduced its subsidies. Unfortunately this led to some farmers committing suicide.

Subsidies of the kind operating in India's cotton sector need to be restructured. For instance, the Cotton Corporation of India, which is supported by the federal/central government, has a policy of limited procurement at a minimum support price if certain quality parameters are fulfilled. However, the state government's scheme does not discriminate between quality cotton and non-quality cotton. The state government procures cotton of differing qualities at a premium above the MSP offered by CCI. This fundamentally distorts the market.

Had the US subsidy regime shrunk and had the Indian subsidy regime promoted procurement of high-quality agricultural produce at greater than MSP price, the situation would have improved for the cotton farmer in the long run. Indeed, in the state of Gujarat, M/s Navbharat Seeds Limited, with the active support of the Government of Gujarat, distributed Bt cotton seeds and plant materials at prices which were much lower with a view to helping needy farmers. It was found that the Navbharat 151 was a successful variety, since it enabled farmers to reduce their need for pesticides and chemicals besides recording good yields. The result has been that farmers have found it easier to cope with low price regimes in a much better way than before.

The main argument here is that subsidies create distortions in the World Commodity Market. Subsidies of the type which promote unsustainable Minimum Support Prices (MSPs), create longer chains of intermediation between producers and the final consumers thus reducing producer margins. The real solution to the problem in agriculture can come about only when end consumers are able to convey their preferences for quality produce directly to producers. In many ways, therefore, the current effort to integrate supply chains and to shorten the length of intermediation channels need to be welcomed.

The tendency to shorten supply chains and closely integrate supply chains is what 'codes of conduct' attempt to do for commodities such as coffee. For some time, there have been major efforts to promote international guidelines and performance standards on environmental and social sustainability for key agricultural commodities like coffee. The International Finance Corporation (IFC—the private sector lending arm of the World Bank Group) is one of the major institutions that have taken the lead. Others include the Deutsche Gesellschaft für Technische Zusammenarbeit (GTZ). The thrust of these measures has been to regulate the commodity supply chain, through guidelines on sustain-ability which are required to be adhered to by players in the chain. The Code of Conduct for Coffee Community Project, which was launched by the GTZ and the Swiss Development Agency in 2003, aims to provide a set of social, economic, and environmental guidelines to render main-stream coffee production sustainable. Another performance standard worthy of mention is that of the IFC. The IFC standards lays down guide-lines and goals to be adhered to by corporate entities which have taken up development projects with IFC assistance (Sethi 2006, 24–5).

In the year 2003, ten large commercial banks in the world agreed to set up the so-called 'Equator Principles', which formed a set of policies for financial institutions to determine, assess, and manage environmental and social risks in project finance. By the end of 2005, 37 of the world's largest private financial institutions had signed up the Equator Principles. The principle categorizes projects into A, B, and C, where A is high risk, B is medium risk, and C is low environmental risk. For category A and B projects, Environmental Impact Assessment (EIA) is mandatory and it should be clearly demonstrated through the environmental impact ex-ercises that national laws have been complied with by banks which have adhered to the Equator Principles treaty, namely ABN Amro, Barclays, Citigroup, Credit Lyonnais, Credit Suisse group, Dresdner, and the Royal Bank of Canada.

Interestingly, the Codes of Conduct projects mentioned earlier and the Equator Principles basically aim to strengthen the hands of nation-states to act as regulators. It is quite possible for nation-states to see how far IFC guidelines and the Equator Principles are really followed by entities and firms operating within their borders, in spite of their global routes. Thus, thanks to this process, nation-states are getting re-empowered to keep a watch on international entities operating within their borders. In the case of agricultural enterprises, the additional benefits that flow from these guidelines or performance standards is that they enable the pri-mary stakeholders, namely the producers and processors in developing countries, to be closer to consumer groups without in any manner under-mining the strength of the nation-state. Many other interesting trends complement these developments. The emergence of fair and ethical trade movements for commodities such as bananas, cocoa, coffee, brown sugar, tea, and a few other products have seen the emergence of an inclusive movement involving consumer groups, trade unions, civil society groups, and other independent technical bodies that seek to overcome the defects of limited inter party interactions across agricultural supply chains.

In the context of the agricultural negotiations in the WTO, measures adopted by importing countries to tighten supply chains have been viewed by developing countries like India as a kind of a non-tariff effort to control production systems in developing countries. National governments, which have played a role in facilitating commodity development and trade in developing countries, feel that transboundary integration of supply chain entities threatens the policy latitude of nation-states in developing countries. Many of them have voiced their concerns about commodity chains (especially about tight commodity chains) as possibly violating the basic WTO philosophy of liberalized world trade. More specifically, developing countries feel that labour and environmental standards function as non-tariff barriers (NTBs) to trade and have the potential to disturb the final delicate production that characterizes most of the commodities in the market systems.

My personal view is that labour standards can be problematic for agriculture and traditional industries in developing countries. This may not be the case with environmental standards. At a broader level, nation-states do not have to take up the responsibility of intermediating on behalf of farmers to insulate them from the ravages of international markets. On the contrary, by permitting producers within the country to have direct linkages with consumers or their direct representatives, it is quite possible to ensure that fair returns accrue to producers. The role of the nation-state would not be to create intermediate structures but to create insular mechanisms which ensure that contracts between producers and consumers are direct and help producers to earn a fair remuneration. States need to intervene only in situations when producers feel cheated.

A careful look at the slant of India's negotiation position in the WTO agricultural negotiations indicates that the country's representatives at the WTO have effectively ventilated the aspirations of agriculturists. This was the case at the Doha and the post-Doha rounds. India has very fervently argued for paring subsidy regimes in developed countries as it feels that these subsidies help developed markets to ward off agricultural imports from India. By comparison, India has been relatively uncomfortable with the idea of characterizing its agricultural system as an 'ecosystem', though there have been very persuasive arguments to this effect. India's position has been that in case it characterizes agriculture in ecological terms or in terms of its ecological diversity or attributes, it would give strength to similar arguments by European Community countries, which will in an overall sense weaken the case for agricultural trade liberalization.

On the other hand, the concept of multi-functionality which was advanced by the European Union in the run up to the Doha round has been an ecological argument for protecting European agriculture against the ravages of free trade. India has kept a clear distance from the concept of multi-functionality, despite the efforts of the European community to rope in India's support for the concept. There have been sections of academia in India which have argued for a multi-functional type of argument to buttress India's position in the agricultural negotiations. One such argument was the notion of ecosystem multi-functionality, which was advanced as a method by which India could protect its agriculture from the ravages of low and cheap imports (Damodaran 2002). However, these suggestions were dismissed in official trade negotiations policies as it was feared that we would be unwittingly creating situations where such a concept would be used by developed countries to block potential exports from India. While agricultural trade liberalization would help farmers in India with export surpluses to have access to global markets, such market access has no meaning for the majority of the peasantry with small holdings and miniscule agricultural surpluses. Rather, small farmers producing food crops could be threatened by massive imports that may result from India having to work towards granting reciprocal access to overseas agricultural producers.

By arguing about market access possibilities, we have unwittingly succeeded only in supporting islands of prosperity in agriculture rather than protecting the segment of mainstream, subsistence farmers who practise cropping systems that are resilient to droughts and respect ecological diversity.

Indeed, sections of India's agricultural systems associated with export-oriented plantation crops like tea and coffee, have been showered with substantial policy support when faced with import threats. Successful lobbying by the United Planters Association of Southern India and the Indian Tea Association compelled the Government of India to raise bound and applied import tariffs levels on imported tea and coffee products, from a low level of less than 30 per cent to 85–90 per cent. However, it is also significant that support for the modernized agricultural plantation system has been made within the framework of the flexibilities afforded by the WTO in the matter of tariff regimes. The ostensible reason for supporting the plantation industry in its quest for import controls is the role played by the industry in providing employment to a large number of labour households. The main reason for the Government of India providing enhanced protection to plantation crops against the forces of competition has been the persuasive powers exercised by parastatal bodies, namely the Commodity Boards set up by the government through Acts of Parliament, to protect the interests of plantation crops. Commodity Boards have acted as insular institutions. They are empowered to legitimately lobby on behalf of the coffee and tea producers in order to secure favourable concessions from the Government of India. Similar systems of insular institutions do not exist for cereal crops. Farmers who produce cereal crops rely on street protests to vent their grievances. A case in point is the movement led by the Raitha Sangha associated with the State of Karnataka. The States of Uttar Pradesh and Haryana too have farmers movements.

Arguments for incorporating environmental concerns into agriculture and trade negotiations can look towards environmental movements that are supportive of these causes. The tragedy with most of these developing countries including India is that there are no insular structures or civil society groups within the country to espouse the cause of integrating environment concerns in agricultural trade. There seems to be a strange sense of withdrawal when it comes to arguing for incorporating environmental considerations in trade involving agricultural commodities. This has been because of the fear that environmental dimensions are highlighted by developed countries to create non-tariff barriers that will serve to weaken India's agricultural share in world trade.

Darjeeling Tea as a Postmodern Response

The phenomenal progress achieved by organic foods in world markets has given respectability to many agricultural enterprises in India which would normally have been situated at the lowest tier in terms of competitiveness. India, Bangladesh, Nepal, and Sri Lanka are well positioned to turn out large volumes of organic products. African nations also enjoy a great advantage in the organic foods market. Many small and marginal farmers of the developing world, including India, practise organic food production as they cannot afford use of inorganic fertilizers and chemicals. Either way on account of the small size of their land holdings, these sections of farmers do not enjoy the advantage of economies of scale that is necessary to carry out input-intensive agricultural practices in a viable manner.

For quite some time, small-scale farmers of India have been pressurized by 'free inflow of competing commodities' from across the borders. The growing demand for organic foods has opened up new possibilities for tea farms of Darjeeling. Darjeeling tea has always enjoyed an iconic status as the 'Champagne Tea' of the world, by virtue of its unique flavour. What adds to the aura of Darjeeling Tea is that it is produced in limited qualities, which in turn can be attributed to conventional tea cultivation and manufacturing practices that eschew the use of chemicals and fossil fuel energy. It is axiomatic that the higher capital intensity of an agricultural enterprise should motivate producers to intensify production and achieve high yields per unit land area. This enables them to bring down costs of production and capture larger profit margins. In a situation where large agricultural enterprises continuously encounter declining yields and low volumes of production, they cannot survive for long. They have to either close down or switch over to alternative crops.

The traditional tea plant in Darjeeling is the 'China Jat' variety, which is rich in aroma and taste and low in productivity, if reckoned in terms of the quantum of tea leaves plucked from a bush. At the same time, Darjeeling tea plants have never been subjected to technically-intensive systems of cultivation in the nineteenth century, partly because modern fertilizers and chemicals had not made their advent then and partly due to the peculiar nature of the production environment in Darjeeling. Even in the twentieth century, after the advent of chemicals and fertilizers, some Darjeeling tea plantations were not quick to transition to intensive cultivation systems for various historical and economic reasons. There was no effort to introduce new high-yielding plant varieties which could have paved the way for high-input cultivation operations. The archetypal Darjeeling tea enterprise, represented a case of traditionalism. However, the tea enterprises of Darjeeling relied on modern marketing skills to realize higher revenue per unit of production and thus survive through higher revenue realization per unit of output. Many units fell into the loop of low-productivity-low-input use and had to make up for this deficiency through higher revenue realization. However, sections of the tea plantation industry in Darjeeling, which fell into a vicious circle of low productivity and low market realization, due to insufficient success in marketing, became sick units.

In the 1990s, the advent of the organic foods movement came as a big relief to these units. Their sick farms were suddenly found in demand 'because they were sick'. The factor that kept these units sick, namely low input use, turned out to be a boon. Their virtual organic Darjeeling tea got a premium over regular Darjeeling tea (which by itself was superior compared to other teas of the world). Old vices became new virtues. Many other 'sick' or 'to be sick' plantations in Darjeeling enthusiastically got their units certified as 'organic' farms and managed to reach the gourmet tea markets in Europe and the United States, something they were not able to achieve earlier. Today, the organic tea plantations of Darjeeling not only talk about organic products but also of biodynamic agriculture. Some of them have even introduced management plans that talk about conservation of both biodiversity and natural areas within plantations. This is a sea change for a number of agricultural enterprises in the world which have grown up to believe that competitiveness and competitive advantage arise only when enterprises are productivity-driven.

Admittedly Darjeeling tea is an outlier. Its brand image has been cultivated over centuries. Those virtually organic Darjeeling tea estates that never enjoyed high productivity levels, did not have to suffer yield drops following their switch to organic cultivation. By contrast, tea farming systems in Assam in north-east India or the Nilgiris in the South or other large horticulture enterprises in north and central India, are not in a position to emulate Darjeeling, as they find their transition from capital-intensive systems to low external input agency systems highly costly and uncertain. Further, they have to put up with serious loss of output during the transition. On the other hand, small enterprises growing tea, spices, coffee, and other products on the fringes of the Western Ghats find the organic movement as a wonderful opportunity to make their holdings and enterprises look attractive, viable, and sustainable, but do not have the resources to market their produce.

The Darjeeling story leads to an interesting insight. Globalization is a constellation of forces that has a hybrid characteristic in terms of two contrasting triggers. While one strand of globalization attempts to re-inforce the virtues of the Industrial Revolution that centre on production and movement of highly standardized, mass-produced goods of uniform quality, there is another strand of globalization which triggers the post-modern sectors to adapt itself to the global markets. The postmodern trend in globalization reifies the virtues of the pre-industrial revolution phase, while selectively taking to modern adaptations. Unfortunately, this segment only has a small presence. This could be because the global trade regime sought to be implemented through the WTO does not pay much attention to the world of niche commodities.

The author's study of the organic agriculture movement in India, espe-cially in the plantation sector, clearly shows that where organic farming is practised by small enterprises, they fail for the want of complementary economic resources. Thus, the small coffee and spice producing farmers of southern India located in the biogeographically sensitive Western Ghats, found organic farming to be a self-defeating exercise, since the products that they produced through organic methods were only ac-cepted as normal commodities. As a result, most organic farmers who thought that their systems of farming could find favour in a globalized world were in despair. Indeed, the more serious limitation of the organic food movement is that farmers of developing countries find certification services connected to organic farming, fair trade, and biodynamic agri-culture to be expensive. They would prefer to have their own standards and set up their own certification mechanisms. This is not acceptable to countries in the North that have promoted international certification sys-tems. In the early decades of the current century there was a fair amount of effort to indigenize organic certification systems by locating resource persons from within developing countries to undertake advisory and cer-tification services. The obvious attraction of this move was that these lo-cally recruited inspectors were paid less for their services. Leaders and thinkers of the organic movement in India like Sanjay Bansal (the owner of the globally reputed Ambootia Tea Garden in Darjeeling), have been toiling hard to improve the lot of the ordinary organic farmers in India through indigenization of certification systems.

The message of the globalization process in the world is thus very loud and clear that 'large is beautiful when inefficient'.

The positive impact of organic production processes on global commons is certainly tremendous. However, the organic movement does not go well with norms of competitiveness that underlie the WTO Agreement on Agriculture.

The NAMA Phenomenon and Non-Tariff Barriers to Great Craftsmanship

One of the major issues taken up in the WTO negotiating forum after the Doha Summit of 2001 was about trade related to non-agricultural goods. The Non-agriculture Market Access (NAMA) negotiations sought to cover products not covered by the WTO Agreement on Agriculture, namely, natural resources such as fisheries, gems, and minerals amongst others. The idea behind the NAMA negotiations was to ensure that there were few obstructions to trade in these goods by way of border measures like tariffs. The NAMA was fashioned to address the following issues: (a) measures employed by developing and least developed countries to control the surge of imports of non-agriculture goods, (b) providing opportunities for developing countries to export employment-intensive, non-agricultural commodities on favourable terms to developed countries. In other words, the two planks of the NAMA negotiations centred on protection of developing countries from import competition for sensitive non-agricultural sectors on the one hand, while negotiating to provide export opportunities to developing countries in respect of non-agricultural goods, on the other. Many studies have indicated that the NAMA negotiations had opened up new opportunities for the export-intensive sectors in developing countries (Ranjan 2005). The NAMA negotiations (hereafter NAMA for short) was designed to facilitate export-intensive sectors like textiles to bloom in developing countries. The NAMA was central in removing the non-development image of the WTO.

Let us take a very specific case of India's silk industry to examine how the NAMA negotiations could have made a difference to developing countries. The silk sector of India's textile industry has the trappings of a traditional vocation that has immense economic, social, and cultural significance. The silk sector draws its raw materials from a variety of sources. South India produces mulberry silk (or silk produced by worms raised on mulberry leaves) in the main. Mulberry worms are reared by mulberry-cultivating farmers in their households. Mulberry is an annual non-food crop which yields leaves that silk worms feed on to produce silk. The state of Karnataka in India has been home to mulberry silk for centuries. Indeed mulberry silk is considered a traditional cottage industry in the state of Karnataka.

The more interesting part of the mulberry silk industry is the segmentation of its value chain. The first stage of the value chain is creation of cocoons at the farm. These cocoons have to be reeled for raw silk production to take place. Even after raw silk yarn is produced, the yarn has to be twisted and turned before it becomes a product worthy of getting into the weaving system (Damodaran 2004). Raw silk production system displays fine differences in its sub production systems in terms of the nature of technology and yarn processing techniques employed. The more interesting aspect of the mulberry silk value chain is the striking social differences amongst people involved with different operations. Thus the mulberry cocoon producers are drawn from the agricultural communities of the Mysore region of Karnataka most of whom are Hindus. However, when it comes to the cocoon reeling, it is seen that this is done mostly by members of the Muslim community. The social cohesiveness ensured by the mulberry silk value chain is in many ways interesting. Indeed, it is said that communal harmony between Hindus and Muslims is on clear display in the mulberry silk zones of Karnataka due to the social bonding ensured by the silk 'value chain'.

For some time, the Government of India and the state of Karnataka have been trying to upgrade and modernize mulberry silk production system by introducing high yielding mulberry plant varieties. However, high-yielding varieties require more irrigation and the adoption of advanced farming practices. Similarly improvement in the productivity of mulberry leaves would be meaningless unless it was matched by advancements in the cocoon and yarn production segments. Over a period of time, mulberry silkworm has also undergone genetic change. The traditional Mysore races of silkworm were sought to be replaced by bivoltine races of worms that are endemic to Japan and China. Bivoltine silk is supposed to yield yarn with higher tensile strength which goes well with weaving practices that create high-quality wefts (which forms the vertical thread of the traditional Indian saree). The introduction of bivoltine worms and the cross-breeding between the traditional multivoltine and bivoltine worms in the 1990s, created two significant technological interventions in the silkworm rearing sector. On the reeling side too similar technological improvements were brought in. The changed process seeks to remove the old 'Charkha' system that relies on manual operations with 'multi-end reeling systems' which are supposed to be mechanized and driven by electrical power. Multi-end reeling machines are costlier. The advantage with these machines is that they have the ability to produce high-quality reeled silk. Notwithstanding these attempts at technological interventions, the fact remains that the Indian mulberry silk industry is characterized by a dualistic structure. There are sizeable sections of farmers who still believe and practise traditional systems of mulberry plant cultivation in the fields and rely on traditional or the endogenous races of silkworms. These sections of farmers are so attached to traditional systems of cultivation that they consider changes in cultivation and worm-rearing practices as severely undermining traditional lifestyles. Unsurprisingly, these adherents to traditions are mostly small farmers who cannot scale up their production levels to cater to the large volumes of cocoons demanded by multi-end reeling machines.

While mulberry silk in its raw or twisted form is produced in Karnataka, the weavers of the silk worm are from the adjoining State of Tamil Nadu which is noted for the world-famous Kancheepuram sarees. The traditional artisans of Kancheepuram sarees employ manually-operated handloom machines rather than going in for automated systems which deny products the stamp of creative craftmanship. Countries that import Indian textiles and fabrics will not have any of this. The labour standards that these importing countries lay down on imported goods go against the age-old systems of labour process associated with traditional industries. The trouble with these labour standards is that they do not look at the immense sustainability advantage that traditional systems of craftmanship enjoy in terms of energy efficiencies.

The issue of labour standards has been hotly debated, contested, and flatly repudiated by countries such as India in various forums. The reasons are not far to seek. In the name of improved production systems, it has almost become a habit for developed countries to bring in issues of labour standards. Countries such as India are understandably apprehensive of this trend, which they feel is a non-tariff barrier (NTB) that affects their freedom to trade in valuable products. Indeed, Rajesh Mehta (2005) brings out how NTBs faced by India's export goods have been steadily rising. According to Mehta, in 1999, 23.3 per cent of exports from India were subjected to NTBs, while the figures were 44 per cent for the United States and 45.9 per cent for Japan. Similarly, Parashar Kulkarni (2005) states that India has extensively notified its objections and reservations on a wide variety of NTBs affecting marine products, hessian bags, tyres, textiles, pharmaceuticals, and leather products. In most cases, Indian export products have been subjected to detentions at the ports of entry on account of chemical residues, microbial contamination, and non-compliance with packaging standards. India is also opposed to imposition of voluntary standards such as ISO 14,000 and SA 8000 on suppliers by importers. India has also complained against customs clearance delays and the introduction of comprehensive product liability insurance policies which add to the financial burden of exporters. Thus NTBs are highly sensitive to the trade fortunes of developing countries. There are no NTBs which are favourable to goods produced by the traditional sectors in developing countries such as handloom clothes, handcrafted products, or articles. Therefore the NAMA negotiations hold little attraction for developing countries that enjoy the presence of a prominent traditional sector in NAMA goods.

From a global commons perspective, the traditional sector of the mulberry silk industry with its emphasis on indigenous silk worms and local landraces of mulberry plant are closer to the ideal of biodiversity conservation. Had the NAMA negotiations been sensitive enough to distinguish these products from the rest in terms of product differentiation, the fate of the NAMA negotiations would have been different.

Are Externally Aided Rural Projects Sustainable?

The role played by externally aided development projects in developing countries offers major lessons for globalization and global conservation movements. The literature on social capital refers to the role of this unique form of created asset in empowering and enabling communities to meet translocal challenges. However, very few assessments have been made about the impacts of externally aided projects in promoting social capital.

It is well known that most of the UN, World Bank, and bilaterally aided projects in developing and least developing countries route their resources through governmental mechanisms. Currently, many externally aided development projects in rural areas are conceived sectorally and are implemented through specialized government departments rather than as holistic integrated projects through local government bodies. There are various reasons for this. One reason is the absence of capacity on the part of local governments to implement such projects.

The key question is whether local execution of development projects is desirable or not. To put it in a different way, if World Bank development projects were implemented through local self-governments, would it have contributed to the social and economic betterment of vulnerable communities?

To answer the above question, we have to take a closer look at some of the deficiencies of the sectorally implemented external aided projects. There are a few instances from India which are worth mentioning. The first case in point is the World Bank-assisted Rubber Board Project, which was implemented with a lot of fanfare during the Eighth and the Ninth Five Year Plan periods that coincided with the economic liberalization phase of the 1990s. The Rubber Board is a statutory Commodity Board set up by an Act of Parliament. For all practical purposes, the Rubber Board functions as an arm of the Government of India. The Rubber Board is mandated to look at production and processing issues concerning natural rubber. Over a period of time, the Rubber Board has contributed financial resources and technical assistance to its target groups, namely rubber producers and processors. This has resulted in the robust development of the rubber sector in India in terms of area, productivity, and trading channels. This support has also enabled small rubber farmers to reach their product to end users at low costs. The World Bank project sought to supplement the efforts of the Rubber Board by providing financial resources for further enhancing production and processing of natural rubber. The aim was to improve the lot of small farmers and processors of rubber by providing them with the means for ensuring stable livelihoods. One of the outstanding results of the World Bank Rubber Board Project was the stupendous growth that it ensured to improve the productivity and processing systems associated with natural rubber. At the same time, the World Bank project also unconsciously promoted a large establishment within the Rubber Board for carrying out what it considered to be technology-extension activities. The increase in 'rubber bureaucracy' created a paradoxical problem when the project came to a closure. The Rubber Board found itself with the liability of maintaining the 'project staff' that was left over on the closure of the project. In order to prevent retrenchment of the project staff the budgetary allotment to the Rubber Board was raised by the Central Government. The irony of the whole story was that the project stood for all that the World Bank did not stand for. While the World Bank has always harped on downsizing the government apparatus, facilitation of markets, and reduction in government expenditure, its Rubber Project in India was expansionist in nature.

The Indian Rubber project has failed on three counts. It aimed to increase the production of a commodity whose prices fluctuated according to the laws of supply and demand. The project did not provide any novel approach for solving the problem of volatile prices for Rubber. Nor did the project seek to correct the fiscally profligate manner in which natural rubber was procured from farmers. Rather, the project only served to negate the World Bank's philosophy that the State should keep its hands off production and market intervention operations.

The problem could have been avoided if the implementation agency was localized. In case the World Bank had concentrated its resources for developing local systems of technology, extension, and management rather than focus its resources on a centralized commodity board system for project implementation, the situation would perhaps have been different. Perhaps then, the natural rubber project would have met with greater success because it would have ensured that the technologies disseminated through local governments were more relevant to local economies. A decentralized approach would also have not created the kind of imbalances which the Rubber Board experienced.

The Indian Rubber Project created a supply-side explosion of sorts in terms of natural rubber output. The result was that between 1998–2004, natural rubber prices fell drastically and much below the expectations of the rubber producers.

As a tree crop, rubber plantations contribute to irreversible land use. This makes it difficult for a farmer to switch away from rubber in times of price downturn. The fact that natural rubber is a monoculture product reduces its potential as a biodiversity enhancer.

Another interesting project of the World Bank, which was implemented with a lot of enthusiasm, was the tank irrigation project in Karnataka. The project was put on a mission mode as it aimed to rejuvenate traditional water bodies referred to as 'tanks' that served the purpose of irrigation. The tank irrigation project of Karnataka was largely implemented through the irrigation bureaucracy attached to the state government. The project aimed to rejuvenate large tanks which have been in a state of neglect for a long period of time. If one considers the fact that tanks in Karnataka were historically managed by local institutions (Tank Panchayats), one would understand the serious limitations of the World Bank Tank Irrigation Project. The technocratic or sectoral approach to tanks attempted under the project focused on enhancing the irrigation capacities of tanks. Traditionally, tanks in Karnataka or Tamil Nadu had community functions as well. Thus tanks provided drinking water for cattle and livestock. The second community function of tanks was by way of providing fishery resources. The third community function of tanks was that they provided grazing grounds for small ruminants and livestock during summer months when the water receded. Unlike irrigation facilities that accrue only to well-to-do farmers who own lands in the command areas of tanks, the grazing and drinking water facilities provided by tanks are availed by poorer sections of the village community for whom livestock is the key means of survival. The problem with the World Bank Tank Irrigation Project is that these small community benefits were ignored. This was contributed by the thinking of the State Irrigation Departments that it was only the irrigation function of tanks that needed to be focused upon. On the other hand if local institutions were entrusted with the project, they could have produced much better results by optimizing the community benefits of tanks.

A third project that is worth referring to is the World Bank's 'India Eco-Development Project', funded under the aegis of the Global Environmental Facility (GEF). This project, which was targeted at the national parks and Project Tiger Reserves of India, aimed to promote biodiversity conservation through an 'ecodevelopment approach' that aimed to provide alternative livelihoods to village/tribal communities living inside these reserves. The problems with the project were threefold. In the first place, the project was designed on the premise that conservation efforts in protected areas like Project Tiger reserves are weakened by human communities inhabiting the reserve. This thinking was wrong and outdated. The second 'not so desirable' feature of the project was that it was implemented sectorally—that is, through the Project Tiger and wildlife establishments of the central and the state governments respectively. If one were to consider national parks and Project Tiger reserves only to be habitats of tigers and other carnivorous animals, then one would be correct in pursuing projects that seek to multiply the tiger population in the reserve to achieve conservation goals. The problem with such narrow conservation goals is that they eschew participatory approaches. The India Eco-development Project ignored the participatory management structures promoted by the Government of India since 1990 to jointly managing forests.

There were healthy precedents that could have provided a cue to the manner in which the India Eco-development Project needed to be structured. The ODA UK-funded forestry project in the Western Ghat zones of Karnataka, which was taken up in the early 1990s, attempted to couple conservation and regeneration programmes with participatory forest management structures. The positive element of this project does not seem to have been captured by the World Bank Eco-development project that subsequently followed. Indeed, the theatre of the India Eco-development Project as well as the ODA UK-supported forestry was Karnataka. However, the lessons of one were lost on the other. This could have been because the wildlife wing of the State Forest Department which was in charge of the Eco-development Project had a strong adherence to the virtues of singular stakeholdership unlike the Territorial and Development wings of the Forest Department which were in charge of the ODA Project.

The basic lesson that one draws from the three cases is that externally aided projects need to improve their delivery of outcomes through the choice of decentralized systems of implementation. The other lesson is that the departmental and sectoral approaches that these projects adopted did not serve to promote the ideals of welfare, equity, and sustainability. In this manner they did not promote the cause of biodiversity conservation as defined by the CBD.

The Modern Face of Rurality? ICT and Rural Areas

Information and Communication Technologies are perceived to be liberating influences on account of their ability to transcend space. ICT has the wonderful ability to situate social power in altered contexts. There have been many observations regarding the growing disjuncture between political space and technology space. It is said that the IT industry in India is dominated by the upper and middle castes with the less privileged sections receiving marginalized status (Vasavi and Upadhya 2005, 37–41). At the same time, there are views that ICT has induced reimagining of the state, which has enabled the sector to project itself as the arbiter of a state's destiny. In Karnataka, IT company honchos have been playing a major role in guiding the fortunes of the city of Bengaluru.

Discussions on the ICT phenomenon do not deal with the issue of how such technologies can help lower castes and the depressed economic sections of the society such as small and marginal farmers to secure a fair deal for themselves. Damodaran (2001b and 2007) notes about the power of ICT to empower small and marginal farmers to take on market forces. The role played by unscrupulous intermediaries in denying small producers their due is well documented. ICT can change this limited world. Online trading systems help farmers located in remote areas to be connected to a wide range of customers outside local areas and thereby trade their products in a wider market than at present. Though this norm is great in theory and to some extent can be demonstrated as a realistic possibility, the bare fact is that this concept has not been implemented on a large scale, due to organizational and logistical problems. However, it is conceivable that in the handicrafts and textiles sectors, small artisans can be connected to a wider network of areas for marketing their unique products. Thus, it is possible for the tribal crafts persons of the State of Chhattisgarh to be linked to world markets through a network of online hubs that not only advertise their unique products but also seek out new customers who would be willing to pay the kind of remuneration that such products deserve to get. It is also possible that local communities including tribal communities can advertise their livelihood systems and cultural traditions through online networks which would help the world to carefully look at instances where such traditions or livelihood systems have been violated. The key issue is whether ICT has been able to do all this. The simple answer is 'No'.

On the contrary, India's ICT prowess has been utilized for meeting the needs of the developed world. We have already seen the antagonism that India's Business Process Outsourcing (BPO) systems and IT industry have generated in the United States on account of its supposed adverse impacts on the job markets there. The extent of antipathy towards off-shoring was a major election issue during the US Presidential election of 2016. A few intellectuals have also come in favour of US nationals who feel 'cheated' of their jobs. Indeed, ICT and BPO have benefitted the United States and Europe more than India. The ICT service boom has not gravitated towards India's agricultural sector or to its niche segment, namely the natural farming sector. Rather India's ICT prowess has enabled the growth or competitive efficiency of modern sectors such as telecommunications, insurance, banking, and heavy industries in the United States and other developed countries. This erosion of technology skills from India has been enabled by premium enjoyed by the US dollar and euro vis-à-vis Indian rupee.

On the other hand, the pattern of flow of services from the North to the South has been in the high-tech industrial segments. These flows involve large capital investments with very little labour content. The reasons for this trend are not far to seek. Many countries in the world, especially those in the early stages of development, are showing undue haste in embracing modular systems of construction, fabrication, and installation. Similarly, developing countries in the world are constantly upgrading their infrastructure construction skills to meet international standards. As standards in developing countries improve and the gap between developed and developing countries narrow down, it opens immense potential for personnel from developing countries to transfer their services or make themselves available as consultants and technical advisors for projects in developing countries. Paradoxically, the adage that technologies, plans, and programmes ought to be tailored to the need of developing countries has been abandoned. It seems that developing countries are tuning themselves to technologies coming in from the developed world.

E-Commerce, E-Governance, and Agri-Trade

In the WTO forum, one of the issues that have proved to be intractable pertains to e-commerce transactions across borders. While it is true that e-commerce transcends nation-states or national boundaries and assumes the characteristics of international transactions in goods and services through cyber space, the actual process is extremely complicated on account of taxation issues. The prospects thrown up by e-commerce within national boundaries can be equally formidable given the impressive strides made by Amazon, Ali Baba, Otto, and Walmart in developing countries across the world. While it is important to regulate electronic trade across nation-state borders, it is equally important to recognize that e-commerce in agricultural goods within nation-state boundaries, can have positive impacts for the poorer sections of the community such as marginal and small farmers. Unfortunately, the relevance of e-governance and electronic trade for primary agricultural commodities in developing countries has not been discussed much.

However, in the previous decade there has been a serious effort to transact agricultural commodities through Internet-based systems. This has taken the shape of certain notable ventures set up by multinational corporations such as the Indian Tobacco Company Ltd (ITC) in India to tap businesses in the rural farm produce. The ITC chowpal or kiosks, which were set up in various parts of rural India in the last decade, aimed to transact trade on a wide variety of agricultural commodities using online systems.

The interesting feature of e-commerce initiatives in India is that these have been initiated by private companies. These initiatives effectively compete with the conventional regulated markets of the government. The e-chowpals are not liked by commercial tax authorities of governments, since they cause tax leakages. There could be many other problems with e-commerce systems that operate within national borders. E-commerce hubs which trade across provinces are bound to attract state intervention for fear of tax leakages. It is likely that inter-provincial transactions will be adversely affected by state governments clamping restrictions on physical movement of goods resulting from electronic transactions. This is likely to happen for commodities such as silk, coffee, and tea where production and processing of raw materials occur in different provinces or states. The solution lies in uniform indirect taxes that are levied, collected, and made over to sources concerned. Notwithstanding these irritants in the physical movement of electronically traded or transacted goods, it remains a fact that e-commerce has drastically expanded in India during the COVID-19 pandemic. Unless electronic commerce transactions stabilize within national boundaries and integrate different regions, it is inconceivable that a global regime of e-commerce will emerge to link primary product producers, especially agricultural producers, to the globalized world. In other words, empowerment through electronic commerce should start 'at home' before we discuss its broad contours at the international level. The most significant aspect of e-commerce within national boundaries would be its liberating effect and wider reach. It is quite likely that a mulberry farmer or a reeler in Karnataka is directly linked to a consumer of silk or a fabric producer in Mumbai instead of confining his small world of production in trade within the boundaries of his village. In this manner, he not only understands the requirements of the end consumer and the changes in the global marketplace but would also appreciate the huge advantages that he gains by getting directly connected to end clients rather than work through intermediaries. The producer will know his end consumer rather than knowing only the person who comes to the farm gate to buy products.

Despite criticisms, e-chowpals have succeeded in pooling resources from far-flung areas and in providing opportunities to traders and farmers to transact with a wider network of clients or customers, not only drawn within the region but also across regions. In a situation of networked or extended markets, benefits of trade would, other things remaining equal, devolve on the producer or the seller of the products. A farmer can liberate himself from the yoke of middlemen who customarily come forward to the farm to collect the harvested produce at a very nominal price. These middlemen make large margins by selling it at much higher prices to intermediaries and consumers who are at the apex of the supply chain. Though ITC e-chowpals are also motivated by the strong corporate interest of procuring agricultural commodities at cheap prices, the fact that they have the potential of reducing the layers of inter-mediaries in the value chain makes them attractive for direct producers. Farmers feel empowered by being able to negotiate and bargain for a fair price. Fair trade movements at the global level also try to work towards this goal. However, since the latter is concerned with international trans-actions, disputes can be rife and the sensitivity of charges about possible unfair treatment meted out to farmers is greater.

Having said this, it should also be noted that supply chains, especially those which attempt to provide direct links of connection between the producer and the end consumer (like the code of conduct of the coffee community) tend to be customer-driven and in most cases, customers tend to be large multinational corporations who use the link to snuff out alternative methods of marketing. Electronic commerce or virtual com-merce which is offered through trading kiosks should be encouraged, but if required, be regulated by the government to ensure that the farmers are not at the mercy of a senior supply chain partner at the consumer end. In this manner, electronic commerce is a matter of concern for governments, private companies, and multinational corporations that have direct transaction interests. To reduce chances of buyers asserting their monopoly position (monopsonies) and putting pressure on pro-ducer prices, it would be necessary for the state to step in with regula-tions. It is conceivable that as the process of electronic commerce gets underway within national borders, it cannot be kept long under wraps within nation-states. It has to spill over borders. Conceivably, in the days to come, with contract farming a reality in India and China, the chances of global companies entering the farming sector are higher, with ICT facilitating the process further. A chowpal will not confine itself to buying or selling finished output but could be transacting on inputs. They could also act as hubs to enable farmers to make informed choices about con-tracts that they enter into. The significant point is that the lessons of na-tional integration perhaps hold lessons for global trade. These lessons should be tapped in the WTO negotiations on e-commerce. It will also serve them with a model tool to analyse what would be the impacts for non-supply chain-based electronic commerce initiatives which involve direct buying and selling without any contract or obligation.

A related issue is the potential offered by ICT in facilitating transac-tions in futures contracts. Traditionally, the Indian agricultural sector has been under a closed control regime, with the state placing heavy controls through price controls. Futures trading in agricultural commodities used to be a common phenomenon until they gave way to controlled conditions by the 1960s and 1970s. Indeed, many sensitive commodities such as edible oils and cereals were taken off futures trading, fearing that transactions in futures contracts in these commodities would abet speculation and encourage rampant fluctuations in prices. With price control regimes brought in through the Essential Commodities Act 1965, futures trading business held no prospect in India until the 1990s. In the wake of the economic liberalization programme initiated in the 1990s, there was a major effort to revive futures trading in agricultural commodities and the government appointed expert committees to look into this issue. The Kabra Committee set up by the Government of India in the early 1990s to review the futures trading issue was in favour of futures trading in commodities. In the period following the mid-1990s, there was gradual relaxation in futures trading in all agricultural commodities and by the year 2000, virtually every commodity was listed in the commodity basket for futures trading.

Now, even metals and crude oil contracts are traded in India's commodity exchanges. The real problem in India in the 1990s was the proliferation of 'single commodity' futures exchanges. Thus a spate of bucketed exchanges sprung up to trade in futures contracts involving singular commodities like Coffee, Soyabean, and Pepper. These exchanges proved to be unviable on account of their narrow focus. By 2004, multi-commodity exchanges came into existence, which was supposed to trade in futures contracts in multiple commodities. Indeed, by 2001, the Forward Markets Commission, which was the regulatory body in India in charge of futures trading in commodities, adopted the policy of only permitting the establishment of multi-commodity exchanges in India. Barring exceptions such as soyabean and wheat, the general experience with futures trading in agricultural commodities in India has been disappointing. The main reason for this was lack of volumes in futures trading on account of limited participation by primary producers. Indeed the futures exchange for agricultural commodities in India is largely driven by traders. This creates a credibility problem for these exchanges. Had farmers and primary traders embraced futures exchanges, the volume of trade in futures contracts would have picked up and the credibility factor could also have been high. Part of the reason for futures trading not taking off amongst farmers is that futures trading facilities are not available in far-flung rural areas. The other reason is the fact that farmers do not understand the intricacies of futures trading though three generations ago their forefathers were adept at it. The situation calls for establishment of facilities in far-flung rural areas for futures trading. This will enable futures trading to pick up in rural India. However, the well-capitalized brokerage houses that are required to facilitate trade are based in urban areas and are not keen to spread to agricultural zones.

ICT trading platforms like ITC kiosks have filled up this gap to some extent. Kiosks should not only be in a position to transact in spot markets but also, more significantly, be in a position to trade in futures contracts, by actively enlisting participation of farmers and traders. In the absence of such structures, futures trading would be confined to a few urban, semi-urban, or highly developed rural areas. There are many critics who still question futures trading. The occasional scams and economic crisis add vigour to these criticisms.

Way back in 1945, Hayek stated that a state-driven Price Board was a bad idea as it snuffed out the 'assiduously dynamic and organic nature of market price fluctuations and the benefits of this phenomenon' (Hayek 1945). Subsequent revelations about the distortions brought in by the visible hand of planning in the Soviet Union, proved Hayek right. But then, after 2008, the pendulum seems to have swung the other way. The third-generation derivative instruments have grandly distorted price discovery instead of facilitating it. In the wake of the 2008 economic crisis, the European edition of *Time* magazine that came out on 2 February 2009 carries the visage of Karl Marx to point to the mess capitalist institutions got into. It is natural that India's Left Parties have been making demands for banning derivatives in India.

There is another notion that futures trading is antithetical to government's price intervention schemes. This is a myth as far as India is concerned. As we mentioned in the case of physical markets, governments in developing countries such as India have a major role to play in facilitating futures trading through creative market literacy programmes so that farmers and small processors could hedge themselves against volatile prices. Many wonder why in the United States agriculturists are active in futures trading. The simple answer is that in North America and

Europe, farmers who trade in futures have larger farm holdings. They are reasonably well capitalized to participate in futures trading. On the other hand, in India, the size of the farm holdings of an average farmer household being small, it precludes the majority of the farmers from taking the plunge into futures trading. Indeed, if small and marginal farmers, and small traders of India can hedge prices for their crops through commodity futures, it can have a salutary effect on the trading environment. However, there is the constraint that small farmers or traders are not in a position to buy trading membership from existing commodity exchanges due to the hefty membership fee and partly due to the fact that they do not have the technical capacity to execute trade transactions. By forming themselves into groups, farmers can have agencies that transact for them in futures exchange. Governments, by facilitating the process of capitalization of such groups, could provide a stimulus for the empowerment of small producers and traders.

A proper hedge by a farmer in India produces a different effect as compared to a hedge practised by an American farmer. While a hedge practised by an Indian farmer who is small or medium or marginal, may reinforce systems of farming based on sustainable principles, in the United States every hedging position taken by a typical farmer serves to promote commercial agriculture with its attendant consequences of high input usages by way of chemical fertilizers and other inputs which are inorganic in nature. This, in turn, creates conditions for the success of highly polluting fertilizer and chemical industries that provide inputs to commercial farmers. Thus, futures markets in countries such as India can be beneficial in more than a sense. They save on wasteful crop procurement programmes that add to the public expenditure of the state, besides enabling farmers practising sustainable agriculture to stick to their practices. Such farmers would be encouraged to 'cultivate by conserving nature' than to 'cultivate by destroying nature'.

The advent of the new generation of digital technologies like Blockchains (or distributed ledgers) can substantially add to the efficiencies of futures markets by improving price discovery through data-driven approaches and in ensuring that the glitches associated with conventional online trading and payment systems are overcome.

To sum up, the prosperous fringe of rural India seeks greater liberalization of world trade in agricultural goods, while the not-so-prosperous fringe seeks greater protectionism from imports. But diversification that is induced from the above does not capture the essence of diversity. The richness of diversity comes in its rich socio-economic and cultural essence. In the case of Rajasthan, despite the best efforts of the administration at diversifying the income base of the rural population, the issue of redistribution of benefits of growth is not addressed. Further, environmental degradation has added to the depletion of public goods in the state. Externally aided projects also suffer from the absence of bottom-up, de-bureaucratized approaches that harp on the centrality of sustainable development. Similarly, the WTO agreements have provided opportunities to large sections of Indian agriculture. However, there is no effort to utilize environment and sustainability as assets to improved market access. The exception is the unique case of Darjeeling Tea, which has ensured that the virtues of organic agriculture, geographic indications, and brand equity come together. A postmodern approach has succeeded in prominently positioning Darjeeling Tea in the global market. However, when it comes to crops like silk, it is seen that traditionalism has not been reinvented as a market access tool. This may have been due to the absence of local initiatives to change marketing systems. India's ICT sector offers to its agriculture sector immense potential of linking farmers to a larger network of global buyers, thereby preventing exploitation by local middlemen. ICT can also promote futures trading for agricultural commodities and help them cope with price volatility, thereby helping an Indian farmer to shed his inhibitions about participating in larger markets. More fundamentally, these technology platforms enable a small farmer or a member of a tribal community to effectively sustain their livelihoods. Such measures would immensely contribute to India's quest for conserving the global commons.

6

Adapting to Globalization or Fighting It?

Tradition, diversity, and local adaptations to metanarratives are issues that have engaged thinkers like Mahatma Gandhi (Rehnema and Bawtree 1997). Interestingly, these issues are helpful in providing us with an understanding of the deeper political implications of information and communication technologies (ICT) in today's world. Today the ICT networks have permeated almost every nook and cranny in the world. Some of these sites have turned into local 'sites of resistance' against the forces of globalization. All the same, it is equally noteworthy that there are many local spaces that have adapted themselves to the forces of globalization.

Arturo Escobar (1997, 85–93) traces the pattern of discourses on development that arose after the Second World War. In the post-Second World War period the narrative of development sought to relate the problems of poverty to insufficiency of technology and capital, rapid population growth, inadequacy of public services, and archaic agricultural practices in poorer countries. However, these discourses were relatively cagey or cautious when it came to dealing with cultural attitudes and the racial, religious, geographic, or ethnic factors associated with backwardness. According to Escobar, most of these discourses emanated from international organizations, government offices, or from distant capitals.

Ivan Illich (1997, 94–102) goes a step further and says that the notions that seek to relate development to progress in infrastructure, emanate from the affluent class. Illich highlights the importance of undertaking counter-research to arrive at an alternative definition of development. According to him, most of the alternatives projected by existing development theories call for, long-term planning with a view to strengthening existing institutions and artefacts. However as Illich says, 'the only way to reverse the disastrous trend of increasing underdevelopment, hard as

India, Climate Change, and The Global Commons. A. Damodaran, Oxford University Press. © A. Damodaran 2024.
DOI: 10.1093/oso/9780192899828.003.0006

it may be, is to learn to laugh at accepted solutions (1997, 101). Illich is obviously referring to Vietnam, a country with bicycles and sharpened bamboo sticks, that successfully challenged the pre-eminent superpower of the world, namely, the United States (1997, 101).

David Clark (1977) describes the rebellious activities of local communities in his own inimitable way.[1] Clark says that there are communities of interest in the world which live or try to live differently. These are alternative communities which try to look at issues from the viewpoints of group lives and communitarian ethos and in the process, endeavour to rework and discover alternatives to the present order. Clark mentions the case of alternative communities which try to reshape family ties, work for conservation causes, or seek to find small, but manageable ways of handling modernity or the modern discoveries of science. These communities enjoy the advantage of being springboards of resistance against 'arrogance', 'prejudice', and 'grief'. Quite a lot of these alternative communities have sought linkages across the borders of nation-states through the Internet and other communication facilities. For those who advocate the cause of postmodern ideas, ideals, and techniques such as organic or sustainable agriculture, ICT can be handy as it can be fashioned into a tool to create empowerment structures for small and marginal groups.

Very often, alternative communities are unable to articulate their 'alternative' without resisting the hegemony of existing ideas. James Scott's concept of infra-politics is about resistance to accepted ideas. For Scott (1997, 311–28), 'infra-politics' is real politics. According to Scott, informal assemblages of markets, neighbours, family, and community provide structures and forums for resistance (1997, 325). Resistance is fermented in small groups with folk culture, playing a key role. There are no leaders to round up, or any membership to investigate. The entire structure would appear to be unruly and incoherent. According to Scott, it is this kind of infra politics that counters hegemonic discourses (1997, 325).

A slightly different thesis on resistance and adaptation in the Internet era, is suggested by Esteva and Prakash (1997). The authors note that the Internet affords equally interesting ways of coping with globalization. Grassroot-level populations engaged in movements such as Community Supported Agriculture do not deny the reality that the world is globalized or that economies are internationalized. However, they seek to oppose globalism with radical pluralism. And in terms of the Zapatista movement in Chiapas, it meant that people's choice to live, think, and act on a human scale is supreme, though this does not prevent them from conveying or circulating their views through email networks. This alternative system forms the ultimate symbol of a globalized world. Grassroot level human communities, while accepting that globalization is here to stay, seek to make use of the wonderful technological facility offered by globalization to promote its opposite, namely radical pluralism. This then sums up the resistance movements induced by the Internet and e-commerce facilities.

This perspective about utilizing the forces of globalization and its artefacts to work against it, challenges some of the assumptions developed by Thomas Kuhn, that a corpus of knowledge which becomes mainstream normal science seeks to brush aside as illegitimate other questions and evidence which does not fit into its scheme of things (Shanin 1997, 69). The Kuhnian notion holds that hardened politicians who establish normal politics and rub aside alternative views or visions, which do not fit into their scheme of things, perpetrate hegemony. Going by the Chiapas rebellion and the technique of plurality of resistance adopted by the local communities there against globalization, one could say that the Kuhnian notion could be subjected to a great challenge in the Internet and the social media era, where both the channels and systems of communication cannot be blocked unless there is a serious system of blockages and surveillance in place. After the global advent of terrorism since 2001, there have been serious efforts to exorcise information which is considered subversive and to the ideals of globalization and global nation-states. A similar kind of situation obtains today when it comes to 'fake news'.

Mahatma Gandhi (1997, 306–7) considered a village to be a complete republic, which is independent of its neighbours for its vital wants and yet interdependent on many others. Life in such a situation is not a pyramid with the apex sustained by the bottom. On the other hand, it is an oceanic cycle whose centre will be the individual. Gandhi advocated this concept against the backdrop of what he considered to be a mad desire of present-day human civilizations to destroy distance and time. For Gandhi, an ideal society or a village community will eschew machinery and particularly the machining trends of culture.

Clark's concept of alternative communities resonates with that of Gandhi's except that for the Mahatma, village communities carried an implicit geographic notion. Clark's alternative communities are not circumscribed by territorial space.

The point then is that the information age and the Internet era not only promises space for the politics of the local but also for the politics of alternative communities. Thus the Internet provides space for revival of the Gandhian concept of Swaraj. It also provides space for those who do not share the Gandhian vision. In the event that all empowerment movements are able to ventilate their ideals, the world will turn into a plural community. Globalization would by itself become more humanized.

To go back to our original thesis, peasants and artisans in the developing world who find the influx of highly standardized mass-produced goods to be an oppressive feature on their modes of living, would be tempted to see the alternative of the information explosion and 'global pace' afforded by the Internet, to be a great opportunity for liberation and empowerment. Indeed the Internet would also bring out the limitations of modernity. Similarly, the Internet would be a valuable platform for articulating different forms of resistance to the ideological, economic, and cultural domination of the globalized world. In a world where the WTO discourse on free trade seems to have taken root in officialdom, it is quite possible that the plurality of alternative discourses and identities, and the alternative of the second commons would, if aided by the Internet, succeed in resisting and overturning the ugly features of free trade unless such movements are suppressed by Governments. The more fundamental question is how these forms of resistance translate to constructive missions like the revival of traditional agriculture.

It is abundantly clear that all attempts to promote organic farming and traditional agriculture within the framework of the global multilateral trade rules of the WTO, have failed to achieve results. This is due to the fact that alternative agriculture stands against the modernity implicit in the global trade rules, which is based on the ideal of mass production of goods of standard quality. What is also clear is that in case WTO rules are to be redefined, this should be achieved through orchestrated movements of resistance across the Internet. Support for traditional forms of agriculture can be secured through networks of the largest civil communities and groups which operate on the Internet. Discourses in the cyberspace about local identities could pressurize the WTO to see the world differently. Similarly, one should also be aware of the fact that movements involving 'alternative communities' from the North, attempt to build connections with the traditional agriculturists of the South to advance their common agenda of offering alternatives to modern agriculture. Thus the Internet could not only be a platform for propagating the ideas of modernity, fair trade, and fair labour standards but also help promote traditional agriculture and other craftsmanship practiced in developing countries. Thus, it could serve as a welcome tool for all the three forces, namely traditionalists, modernists, and postmodernists.

Kant once remarked that 'the ultimate test of a maxim is whether, when universalized, is something that logically cannot be done'. This observation is of significance to understanding the debate between sustainable development and free market dogma. To appreciate the meaning of Kant's statement, we need to go Thomas Kuhn and his idea of belief systems. Thomas Kuhn's proposition was that belief systems of individuals affect the way they perceive things. His point was that individuals do not just see the world as it is but see it as affected by the belief systems (Hayward et al. 2001, 6–24). Hayward closely examines the Kuhnian notion of disciplinary matrix, where a shared commitment of a particular scientific community to particular models and values, provides the basis for professional communication. He goes on to cite David Bohm, a physicist who states that science is communicative action within an unbroken wholeness that is infinite in its qualitative and quantitative depth and complexity (2001, 24). Bohm's argument is that the communication process or actions of a group of scientists bring into consciousness an abstract picture of a limited domain. Any laws or theories formulated within the matrix of this domain are necessarily relative—valid only within the domain and false beyond it (2001). It is quite clear that this kind of a notion is true of the free market dogma of the 1990s. The same also holds for sustainable development.

If the free market principle can be traced to Adam Smith, the discursive practices associated with sustainable development can be considered to have originated with the World Commission on Environment and Development (WCED).[2] However, it is quite likely that the discourses on free markets or of sustainable development have not reached every nook and corner of the world. There could be sections of the world community (say, tribal and indigenous groups), which might not have heard about or understood either the underlying philosophy of free markets or of sustainable development, in spite of practising these ideals based on their own thinking.

One also needs to distinguish between the concept of discursive formation and its applicability in the operational sense. It is one thing to talk about the basic definition of sustainable development as propounded by the Brundtland Commission and quite a different thing to propose an operational model of sustainable development (2000). As a universal idea or truth, sustainable development has not only failed to permeate all layers of society but may not carry any operational significance to those sections of the communities for whom it is basically meant.

There could, of course, be a question as to whether the concepts of sustainable development and the free market are essentially phenomenological or structural. The answer to this question is that structuralism does not posit any change. One could also visualize sustainable development as having been brought about by the merger of the concepts of the free markets and economic development.

Whatever the reality, the fact remains that sustainable development in the true sense of the term, as developed by the Brundtland Commission, was dictated by a certain kind of political reality that called for cooperation between the North and the South to integrate the notions of economic progress and development with environmental sustainability. The Commission Report never specified its position regarding the role of markets in an economy. All that the Commission's definition of sustainable development said was that it is a form of development that meets the needs of the generation without compromising the requirements of the future generation. In this manner, the WCED attempted to provide a universalized definition of the concept.

Further, the idea of sustainable development is closer to the notion of 'paradigm shifts' developed by Thomas Kuhn, which states that scientific regions develop in more or less linear progression, with each paradigm discovering things which its predecessor was not able to. Kuhn posited a linear progression from one paradigm to another. However, for Foucault linear progress in paradigm evolution was unthinkable. Foucault did not see a linear development from 'Renaissance' to the 'Modern Age'. He always felt that epistemes work and speak for themselves through production of discursive formations that 'rupture' the existing order. The WCED definition of sustainable development did not rupture the existing wisdom on development. It merely built over it. It is obvious that sustainable development is not the same thing as an epistemic break. It can be at best taken as a shift in the existing paradigm.

In terms of the preceding discussions, let us now look at where the modern and the postmodern concepts of globalization are positioned. We have earlier noted that global agricultural trade is sufficiently premised on the principle of modernity that believes in mass production of quality standardized goods across the globe. At the same time, global agriculture has also created space for traditions of organic and sustainable farming. In terms of the Kuhnian paradigm, if modernity had triumphed over the traditional, then it should not have created such postmodern trends. In terms of the phenomenological doctrine, it is the perceptions of different sections of communities or individuals that influence approaches adopted towards the modern and the postmodern trends. Indeed, belief systems do play a major role in providing the basis for postmodern trends such as organic agriculture and biodynamic agriculture. But in the Kuhnian sense of the term, it is obvious that modernity has not been able to achieve what it should have achieved, that is, complete universalization. There are pockets of resistance to modernity, despite the grand efforts to take the 'idea' to every speck of the globe, through the Internet).

This brings us to the larger question we discussed a little while ago about the relevance of the Internet in promoting discursive formations. With the advent of the Internet, discursive formations have not followed a unilinear trajectory. The Internet provides space to multiple discursive formations. But very often, as Kuhn, Foucault, and the phenomenologists argue, it is the belief systems and our fundamental values which make us look at certain paradigms more closely than others. To this extent, one can surmise that in a world of pervasive globalization, it is impossible to universalize or to pre-eminentize postmodernity. At the same time, for a world which is exposed to the discursive formations of postmodernity or is rooted in the postmodern, the Internet provides enough substance for alternatives to flourish. Indeed the World Commission on Environment and Development (WCED) (in the case of sustainable development) or the World Trade Organization (WTO) (in the case of free trade) are seized with the issue of postmodernity. Therefore we can state that in some ways, postmodernity can survive if the nation-state makes an effort to help them survive.

It is well known that India and the Philippines have been major hubs of Business Process Outsourcing (BPO) in the IT sector. However, one notices discourses that state that these countries have only projected their old strengths—of cheap labour—to conquer the new economy.

The cheap labour discourse which one comes across in the context of BPO, Information Technology Enabled Services (ITES), and the IT industry is something which is modernistic in approach. The cheap labour discourse seeks to reinforce the concept of international division of labour propounded in the 1950s, which in turn goes back to the classical theory of comparative advantage propounded by Ricardo and Adam Smith. By relating ICT revolution to low-paid labour jobs and by linking the BPO model to lost employment opportunities in developed countries, discursive formations create mistrust between the labour force in developed countries and their counterparts in developing countries. During the Industrial Revolution, the conflict dynamics between labour of the developed and developing worlds was focused on the textile industry. Indian textiles that were handwoven, unique, heterogeneous, and products of consummate craftsmanship, were set in opposition to large volumes of mass-produced higher-than-average quality products from mechanically or machine-driven production processes. The point here was that the uniqueness of the 'craftsmanship' could not take on the onslaught of the mass-produced, standard products that machines yielded. Human labour and craftsmanship were shown in a derogatory light because the opposition was set between craftsmanship and 'machine-ship', where the craftsman's inability to cater to large sections of the population across the globe, was touted as the reason for its demise. The question of a clash between workers of the mechanized factories of Manchester or the craftsman in countries such as India was never there. It was a zero sum game where the former very clearly gained at the expense of the latter. However, in the information technology age, labour forces of the two worlds seem to be lugging it out, with the developing countries winning partially. In more than one way, the euphoria over 'India Shining' campaign initiated by the first NDA Government in India could be taken to convey the victory of Indian labour or its craftsmanship-driven abilities over the labour of the developed world, which has lost on its ability to acquire craftsmanship-like qualities in production of high-technology goods. There is no reason to suppose that this was not true or lacked validity.

In other words, the discursive formation of a structurally different industry like the IT industry (in the Kuhnian sense of the term) is situated within the matrix of modernity and not the postmodernity concept, as one gets to see in the case of agriculture.

The key question then is why is it that there has been no postmodern interpretation of the ICT-related industries. To answer this question, we need to know as to how postmodernity would have viewed the ICT and the global job outsourcing movements.

What is the essential quality of craftsmen that enables them to stand up against modernity in the twenty-first century? The answer is qualities of aesthetics, brilliance, and craftsmanship that renders products of crafts different from those turned by machines. Therefore, in a postmodernistic sense of the term, the concepts of uniqueness and non-standardization stand in opposition to the concept of mass-produced, high-quality mass-produced universalized homogenous goods. In terms of this way of thinking, if the BPO sector were to be reinterpreted in a postmodernist sense of the term, India and other developing countries would be springboards of creativity and intellectual craftsmanship that is required of a digitized age. Unfortunately, this has not happened. But at the height of the ICT revolution in the 1990s, the concept which came close to a postmodernistic interpretation of workmanship was the expression 'knowledge worker'. This expression was closer to postmodernity. The concept of knowledge here was not unfortunately related to craftsmanship but to workmanship, which in some ways was an unusual attempt to combine a modernity virtue within a postmodern scaffold. It was quite natural that this description went out of circulation once the software industry was hit in a big way by the dotcom meltdown during 1999–2000.

Is there a similar evidence of craftsmanship embedded in India's traditions in the field of sustainable development? Certainly, India has a great tradition of having practised conservation agriculture. Other developing countries in Asia and Africa also have great traditions of being purveyors of knowledge about natural resources and natural products, which is of great fundamental relevance to the global community in terms of medicinal plants and medicinal resources. And yet, when it comes to the glorification of India's achievements in the environment sector, very little is heard about this feat as compared to the achievements it has made in the field of IT. Why is it so? The simple answer is that while IT is treated as a definite product of modernity, the achievements in the conservation sector have been associated with traditional and endogenous systems of management that are considered to be anti-modern and, therefore, deserving to be treated as secondary.

Indeed, the basic question is how one defines 'tradition' or 'traditional'. Modern science is an ever-evolving discipline, that commenced from very primeval or formative processes before consummating into what it is today. In this scheme of things, there is a tradition associated with science. The problem with the traditional knowledge of endogenous communities in India is that they are viewed as static and non-evolving. Therefore, one of the reasons why traditional knowledge has lost its deserved place in the pantheon of modern-day knowledge is the presupposition that their evolution has ceased. This explains why the modern jurisprudence on intellectual property rights harps on the concepts of novelty and non-obviousness when it comes to the patentability of an invention. In this scheme of things, novelty can only be ensured if a body of knowledge is evolving and continuously improving. Since traditional knowledge is not supposed to have this feature, it is considered as a moribund body of knowledge which cannot enjoy intellectual property rights (IPRs).

The spate of bio-prospecting activities carried out by modern drug and pharmaceutical companies in bio-diversity-rich developing countries portrays a different message. Traditional knowledge and its stagnant nature can be galvanized by modern science, which could, on the basis of the leads offered by the former, churn out modern medicines that are more effective than their traditional counterparts.

Intellectual Property Rights (IPRs) and the Second Enclosure Movement

Technology flows that take place between developed countries to developing countries are protected by IPRs. Thanks to the World Trade Organization Trade Related Intellectual Property Rights (WTO-TRIPS) and the pressures put on developing countries by the developed world to tighten their IP regulations, countries such as India were compelled to amend their IP laws. India amended its Patent Act, not by virtue of the fact that it was obliged to do so as a WTO member, but more due to the fear of retaliatory action by the United States and Europe, which had dragged the country to the WTO dispute settlement system for failing to secure changes in its patent laws in accordance with TRIPS regimes, within a reasonable period of time. Many technology-related services that flow from North to South are also subject to patents, designs, and copyright protection. However, when it comes to the software products exported by countries such as India, there is very little talk about protecting intellectual creations contained in them.

The BPO sector in India has also been under pressure to comply with security norms related to data protection and data security. These one-sided approaches to IPRs mirror the asymmetric nature of trade relationships between developed and developing countries.

The play of IPR issues in the agricultural sector merits attention. The most prominent IPRs that are mentioned in the context of agricultural relate to plant breeder rights and geographical indications. Plant breeder rights do protect innovators of new plant varieties from their products getting multiplied. Countries such as India, which were not inclined to provide IPR protection over agriculture-related products, had to bow to the dictates of the WTO-TRIPS and put in place a regime of plant breeder rights. On account of its many exemptions on IPR right granted to innovators, India's plant breeder rights legislation does not assure plant breeders with monopoly control over their products. Third-generation plant breeding technologies based on recombinant DNA techniques ma the supreme triumph of 'modern science' over forces of nature. Extraordinary inventions call for extraordinary rewards. In developed countries such as the United States, new plant types are protected by stronger IPRs such as plant patents and plant utility patents. This, then, represents a great incentive for products of modernity. By contrast, plant breeders rights have very little to offer to third-generation inventors.

By comparison, a Geographical Indication (GI) is a non-glamorous IPR. This IPR has nothing to do with new inventions. It harps on the hallowed virtue of a product, namely its distinct geographical origins, which gives it its uniqueness compared to similar products. Unique traditional products like Darjeeling tea qualify for GI protection. Developed countries in the world, especially those with aggressive agricultural export interests, consider GIs to be a form of NTB which prevents them from exporting agricultural products, either in primary or processed forms, based on the imported materials.

Primary biological materials that are wild-crafted from forests or traditional cultivars that are collected from farmers' fields, do not enjoy a market clearing price or a standard reward system for their unique properties. They do not enjoy any IP protection as they are products of nature. Though the CBD seeks to reward these products for their true values, through benefit sharing and compensation regimes, there are complexities in estimating the benefits accruing from these products. The mode of realizing value from bio-resources through an IPR regime has also not made progress. Developed countries in the world view patents as inappropriate for holders of traditional knowledge. This, as we have pointed to a little earlier, comes from the notion that traditional knowledge is stagnant and non-evolving. At the same time, modern industries have no problems in appropriating or accessing these resources and bringing out new products, which fulfil the criteria of novelty, non-obviousness, and application. In this manner, the efforts of developing countries to secure IPR protection, has not succeeded. Though it is a fact that institutions such as the World Intellectual Property Rights Organization (WIPO) have been making efforts to craft *sue generis* legislation that protects traditional bio-resources and associated traditional knowledge; such legislations do not provide robust protection' for the custodians of traditional knowledge. Developing countries such as India, the Philippines, and others have been trying to grapple with this issue. For quite some time, some developing countries have been exploring the possibility of applying GIs to biological resources, to be only told that a GI legislation that is based on WTO-TRIPS only applies to goods in the course of trade.

However, as mentioned earlier, there is scope for a network of small craftsmen or agricultural communities with unique technical skills and artistic products, to protect their creations by making use of Internet platforms. Though it is very widely accepted that IPRs are individualized and proprietary in nature, it is seldom noticed that a few of them respect traditions of community ownership and community proprietary rights. Trademarks and GIs are two forms of IPRs that promote and protect community IPR. Community Trademarks (CTM) and GIs afford collective rights over products emanating from a geographical area. The benefits of these IPRs accrue to farmers and primary processors. It is quite likely that small and marginal producers belonging to a region or a local community could practise their unique craftsmanship to commercial advantage in the digital age.

Let us imagine a small community of artisans in India, who have a high reputation of being weavers of a unique fabric. The advent of the Internet makes it possible for these artisans to be connected to buyers, or consumers in other countries who desire to buy their products for their unique value. The watchdog and product promotion functions exercised by the stakeholders of unique craftworks could be far more efficacious than the efforts of governments to protect such items from possible infringement. The new generation digital technologies, viz, Blockchains, are able to exercise watchdog functions much more efficiently, since they involve a very large network of stakeholders to record and verify transactions in protected commodities and craftswork.

Clippinger and Bollier (2005).[3] Clippinger and Bollier discuss how the revival of the ideology of collective wisdom and networks can be an antidote to the free market doctrine that goes back to Adam Smith's 'invisible hand'. The authors state that the renaissance of the commons enabled by the Internet raises fundamental questions regarding the viability and efficiency of the free market doctrine, which is accepted as the gospel truth by classical and neo-classical economists. The authors cite Karl Polayni (1957) to the effect that no free market can survive long without the presence of extensive social institutions and shared ethical norms (Clippinger and Bolier 2005, 265). For the authors, the advent of the Internet brings in its wake the emergence of a collective networked system of 'imagining' and 'doing'. This helps to revive the tradition of common resources. The authors discuss the part played by the General Public License (GPL) in contributing to the free software movement. By differentiating works coming under the GPL category from standard market products and by legally identifying them as commons, it is ensured that the source codes underlying GPL category products are not treated as open access resources that can be privately appropriated by free riders (2005, 279).

The authors proceed to state that though a handful of economists such as John Kenneth Galbraith and Kenneth Arrow have dwelt on the serious contradictions and problems of the free market doctrine, it is only the behavioural economists such as Vernon Smith and Daniel Kahneman who have contributed to the demolition of the doctrine. Behavioural economists achieve this by bringing out the chinks in the free market doctrine, which rested on the assumptions of 'unbounded rationality', 'unbounded selfishness', and 'unbounded will-power' (2005, 272). The authors argue that the contribution of behavioural economics has been to explain non-linear behaviour and underline the social context of markets (2005, 274). The authors state that the behavioural economics school has attempted to suggest new principles for coping with issues of externalities, market failure, irrational behaviour, agency costs, and public goods. Citing Coase (1937), the authors argue that corporations can be formed outside of formal boundaries with greater efficiency and creativity, thanks to the Internet. Apart from creating highly efficient commerce, the Internet has provided grist to the mill of political, environmental, and human rights movements including those which seek to ban landmines and clean up chemical spillages (1937, 278).

David Bollier (2003) similarly mentions how the Internet has managed to unify diasporic ethnic communities in different parts of the world at the least cost. Interestingly, Bollier also argues that the appearance of network societies in the digitized age marks the advent of the second enclosure movement, which creates regimes and proposals, that attempt to lay down the rules of the game for a decentralized order. He adds that IPRs on digitized products lead to the desire on the part of the IPR holders to price each consumer according to his willingness to pay. Here, IPR holders seek to explore 'Consumers Price Points' (Boyle 2002, 248) through enforceable shrink wrap or click wrap contracts so that consumers can be locked up in licence-based contracts. Boyle proceeds to argue that in such situations, there could be demand for change in anti-trust rules to allow for a variety of practices that are illegal (2002).

Boyle also argues that while a second enclosure movement is very desirable in terms of productivity and efficiency, it could lead to suffocation of individual rights. As he also proceeds to argue, the broader the scope of IPRs, the greater is the attraction of the Internet to civil libertarians. But there is a likelihood that the second enclosure movement would fall into the trap of property rights, thus finding themselves in the company of neo-liberal orthodoxy.

The main point that emerges from these discussions is that the advent of the Internet and digitized economies in the twenty-first century has created a fundamentally different paradigm. It has ensured the functioning of a world which accords the 'invisible hand' a supreme position as the guarantor of market efficiency and equilibrium.

As mentioned earlier, the advent of blockchains and distributed network technologies since 2008 has given a body blow to the idea of centralized control over economic operations. Blockchains enhance the capabilities of local communities to ensure that trade transactions are fair and transparent. This is done by entering details of transactions in the ledger and encrypting the entries in order to render them tamper free. Since the ledger is operated by a large community of users, it is impossible for any single person or group of people to change entries as is the case with ledgers operated by closed groups. In the process blockchains open the transaction details for numerous people to see while at the same time protecting the anonymity of the parties that carry out the transactions.

All this brings us back to the original point that for agriculture and primary goods, the second enclosure movement augurs well as it achieves protection by cleverly utilizing non-modernity IP rights like GIs in a better way. The second enclosure movement, that involves a network of sustainable communities promoted by the Internet, can be harnessed in a better manner to bring benefits to custodians of wild-crafted products and traditional knowledge. Sustainable Internet communities can bring out stories of huge revenue flows appropriated by the commercial users of these products and goad local communities in developing countries to bargain for their rightful share in benefits. It is quite likely that a producer who practises sustainable agriculture, fair labour, and good production standards is rewarded appropriately for her efforts. If the liberating effects of e-commerce and the Internet are put to use, an entirely new system of production, marketing, and consumption can replace conventional systems. In such a situation, new networks which emerge to promote radically different systems of economic operations, could encourage new forms of identities

The whole process by which IPRs have been formulated has much to do with movements which promote the neo-liberal agenda of market reforms. Indeed, the free market concept, if tailored well to IPR regimes, can stand as the bulwark of modernity against the forces of tradition.

Having argued this way, it is also pertinent to note that when Adam Smith wrote *The Wealth of Nations* and the classical economists delved into the issue of industrial production and economic structures of production, they never had the vision of grandeur that the multinational corporations (MNCs) of today are said to possess. The classical economists certainly did not imagine that the humble joint stock companies of their times would evolve into mammoth corporate structures that would prosper at the cost of economic efficiency and social justice. True, during the neo-classical economic revolution associated with Pigou, there was an effort to delve into the impacts of social costs on welfare. Indeed, Keynesian and left Keynesian schools had gone even further to talk about the adverse effects of oligopolies and monopolies on developed economies of the world. Despite all these aberrations, the fact remains that the ideal of free markets has much to offer for the brave who brazen it out by taking risks in the marketplace.

This is not to deny that there have been counter-currents against the efforts of the WTO proponents to embrace the model of globalization that centres on transnational and multinational corporations. While liberalization of capital and services flows may offer relief to developing countries plagued by capital shortages, the negative consequences of the stranglehold of foreign capital on the national economic structure, may outweigh the positive ones. This is precisely why developing countries oppose the inclusion of the agenda of investment liberalization in WTO agreements. The WTO agenda is yet to integrate the concepts of investment and competition into its fold, despite the best efforts on the part of lobbyists to have investments on the WTO agenda. Strangely it could be one of the major concessions of the WTO agreement that it soft peddles the issue of foreign direct investment (FDI) flows across borders. Global regimes on cross-border investments are a sensitive issue for nation-states, as they do not provide nations with enough elbow room to take their own decisions. In any case, as we shall explain in the subsequent chapter, FDIs do not address the basic development problems faced by developing countries.

To recapitulate, the ICT Revolution has enabled the development of new institutions that inform small craftsmen and agricultural producers on the profitable avenues where they can dispose their products. The Internet also carries stories of deprivation across the world, which informs international policy makers of the spots in the world where they are required to pay attention. Another feature of the Internet is that it provides a platform for dissenting voices against the ugly face of globalization. The success of the Bhoomi Project in Karnataka in improving land records and in providing ordinary farmers with easy access to their land titles is another story about the social success of the Internet (Chawla 2005). Similarly, Internet sites that deal with trade in commodities facilitate efficient and informed transactions which induce producers to seek changes in traditional market systems. As has been discussed already, most of the ICT systems which have been employed in rural areas have been driven by corporate or quasi-marketing entities that seek to channelize products from rural areas to urban centres. Some of these systems are transparent as they have protocols that inform consumers and producers about the value realized from various transactions.

Likewise, the relevance of the second enclosure movement catalyzed by ICT is that it offers immense potential to capture plurality of thinking on key development issues. Similarly, local resistance against globalization enables diversity to thrive in a globalized world. Viewed in this manner the second enclosure movement taps local impulses better, thereby ensuring that the forces of globalization are successfully modulated by local communities with a view to improving their collective wellbeing.

7

Environmentalism in the World

The phase of globalization that the world entered into in the 1990s co-incided with an upsurge in environmentalism. Globalization, while integrating different parts of the world through extensive trade and investment networks, also created its share of frustrations in large parts of the developing world on account of poor trickle-down effects. Indeed, the resultant opening of trade brought in its wake serious agrarian distress. Many microenterprises that subsisted on local and regional markets faced closure as transnational corporations made their entry in developing countries.

Environmentalism also assumed a global character in the 1990s. In the 1970s, while environmental movements were guided by the ideals of conservation, by the 1980s environmental movements had pitched their agenda within the matrix of development. This led to the rapid spread of environmentalism in developing countries like India. However, the 1990s witnessed a major change. Environmentalism across the world shifted its focus towards global public goods such as climate, biodiversity, and land degradation.

The roots of globalization and the global environmental movements can be traced back to the 1970s when significant changes were taking place in the realms of economics and environmental science. The Stockholm Summit on Human Environment in 1972 triggered environmental awareness amongst policy circles in both the developed and developing world. This resulted in the advent of a spate of global conventions and agreements during the 1970s and 1980s.

As far as India was concerned the period between the Stockholm Summit of 1972 and the Rio Conference of 1992 was marked by a series of national legislations that advanced the cause of conservation and environmental protection. One could argue that the Stockholm Declaration on Human Environment was a clarion call for resolving

India, Climate Change, and The Global Commons. A. Damodaran, Oxford University Press. © A. Damodaran 2024.
DOI: 10.1093/oso/9780192899828.003.0007

pressing environmental problems occurring within countries. Most of the Stockholm concerns, though universal in appeal, related to matters that lay within the jurisdiction of nation-states. The post-Stockholm phase marked the onset of a few global conventions like the Convention on International Trade in Endangered Species of Wild Fauna and Flora (CITES) which entered in force in 1975. It was in the 1980s that focus on 'global environmental' issues became the major credo. This was due to the awareness that the more fundamental environmental problems that the world as a whole was facing arose from the destruction of global commons. Global commons included two broad categories of resources, namely those that transcended or spilled over national boundaries (climate, ozone layer, and desertification) and those which occurred nationally but were of critical importance for the survival of the planet (biodiversity). In other words, the conventions and agreements which were signed during 1972–80 were not really associated with global public goods—they had more to do with national environmental problems of international concern.

Before we explore the two conventions, which were signed at Rio, let us look at the origins of the Rio Summit. By 1980, the UN was required to take stock of the results achieved after the Stockholm Summit. It was noticed that there were far too many environmental problems confronting developing countries that needed to be addressed. Most of these environmental problems were a concomitant of under development. Accordingly, the UN General Assembly desired that the linkage between environmental concerns and development aspirations be carefully examined. The World Commission on Environment and Development (WCED) was constituted in 1984 to formulate a new paradigm of development. The WCED was established as an independent Commission by the United Nations.

The WCED was constituted as a think-tank of 21 members, with Gro Harlem Brundtland as the Chair.

The Commission, after taking stock of events and surveying critical developments that took place after the Stockholm Summit, came out with a report which was titled 'Our Common Future' (1987). The report called for major rethinking on the issue of environmental protection and strongly emphasized the significance of viewing environmental protection in an integrated manner, by incorporating development concerns.

It was felt that without such a paradigm change, it would be difficult for the world to accept environmentalism or environmental protection as a maxim of growth. The central principle advocated by the WCED was 'sustainable development'. The Brundtland Commission defined sustainable development as 'development that meets the needs of the present generation without compromising on the needs of future generations'. The concept of sustainable development differed from the manner in which the idea of development was viewed until then. Prior to the inception of the term 'sustainable development', economic development was neutral to environmental issues or to the maxims of environmental protection. While it is true that conventional economic theory did focus on the concept of inter-generational equity in relation to income and wealth, the idea of viewing development in terms of nature and natural resources came into vogue on account of the WCED report.

By incorporating the principles of inter-generational equity and by insisting on the coupling of environmental protection with concerns of economic growth, the WCED Report called upon the world to deliberate on these issues and requested the UN to take up these issues in right earnest. The WCED report was placed before the UN General Assembly. Based on inputs received from the WCED and taking into account the gravity of the problems caused by climate change and biodiversity loss (as reported by scientific studies), the UN General Assembly passed Resolution 44/228 of December 1989. The resolution announced that a United Nations Conference on Environment and Development would be convened in Rio de Janeiro in the year 1992.[1]

Apart from the Convention on Biodiversity (CBD) and the UN Framework Convention on Climate Change (UNFCCC), the output of the Rio Summit included the Rio Declaration on Environment and Development, the non-legally binding statement of forestry principles, and Agenda 21. While the UNFCCC dealt with low carbon and cleaner pathways of economic growth to avert climate change, the CBD dealt with conservation of biodiversity and its sustainable use with due regard to the efforts, needs, and aspirations of countries and local communities. By comparison, the Rio Declaration on Environment and Development was a strong affirmation of the principle of sustainable development. The programme document of the Rio Declaration, namely Agenda 21, outlined all major areas where the principle of sustainable development could be integrated as the underlying paradigm. Thus, by the end of 1992, the world had placed the issue of global commons as a part of its development agenda. Two years after the Rio summit came the United Nations Convention to Combat Desertification (UNCCD), a convention that was chiefly driven by the need to bring in a sustainable development agenda of central concern to African states. The UNCCD was primarily formulated to alleviate the distress faced by agriculturists and pastoral communities of Africa on account of land degradation and desertification. The UNCCD addressed land degradation as a global commons issue and recommended national, regional, and global action to combat the problem.

We begin with a survey of principal developments that led to the shift in focus from national environmental issues of international concern to global environmental concerns.

The Propellers of the Global Goods Cause

Let us take a look at the origin and evolution of global environmental concerns. In the 1970s, there was a flurry of research on four issues of global concern. The first one is related to the transboundary movement of hazardous wastes. It was observed that hazardous substances which were generated from mining, shipping, industrial electronics, construction, and a host of other activities in the developed world, were deleterious and undesirable to human and ecosystem health. As environmental legislations tightened in developed countries, industrial units that generated hazardous wastes in these countries, attempted to transfer their deadly wastes to the developing countries of Asia and Africa. Grave concerns on this score led to the formulation of 'The Basel Convention on Transboundary Movement of Hazardous Wastes'.

The second major global environmental issue of the 1980s related to the phase out of chlorofluorocarbons (CFCs), methyl bromide and related ozone depleting substances. The CFCs were considered a wonder chemical of great industrial significance for a long time, ever since the 1930s when they were discovered. They were not only odourless, but were also very effective as coolants and as de-greasing agents. However subsequent scientific research by Sherwood Rowland and Mario J. Molina established that CFCs and other Ozone Depleting

Substances (ODS) created deleterious impacts on the earth's ozone shield that shields UV-B radiations from reaching the planet. As discussed earlier, one of the consequences of UV-B radiation is that it increases the incidence of skin cancer. Progress regarding work on handling ozone depletion issues proceeded at a very fast pace in the 1980s. Events reached their peak by the mid 1980s and by 1985 one could see that there was sufficient commitment on the part of different countries to set up a Convention and a follow-up Protocol to address the issue. The result was the Vienna Convention on Ozone Depleting Substances in 1985 and the Montreal Protocol on Ozone Depleting Substances of 1987.

Studies were also carried out to explore the possible negative impacts of anthropogenic factors on global climate. For some time, there were concerns that the fast pace of economic growth in the post-Industrial Revolution period was causing Green House Gas (GHG) emissions to increase, which had the potential to cause global warming and climate change. The source of GHG emissions were the fossil fuels, notably coal and oil, both of which had formed the energy base of economic activity since the eighteenth century.

By the 1980s, these theories assumed greater credibility amongst the scientific community and were spilling over to the policy sphere. As a result of improving awareness, by the mid 1980s one could see certain structures evolving that sought to provide a sharper action-based agenda to handle the issue. The UN Environment Programme (UNEP), which was set up in the post-Stockholm Summit period, initiated the first moves. The First Climate Conference held in Geneva in 1979 underscored the importance of climate change. However, more had to be done to push the climate change agenda to the forefront. There was a strong necessity to establish an organization that would provide evidence of climate change. The result was the creation of the IPCC (Inter-governmental Panel on Climate Change), as a joint venture of the World Meteorological Organization (WMO) and the UNEP. The IPCC went into the issue of climate change assessments in detail and came out with scientific evidence regarding the relationship between fossil-fuel use and GHG emissions as well as between global warming and sea level rise. As a result of all these efforts and the 'scientific treatment' that climate change received at the hands of the IPCC, the first assessment report of the IPCC was formulated. This report formed the basis of the work towards an international legal framework for addressing the scourge of climate change.

At the Second World Climate Conference of 1989 in Geneva, Heads of States accepted the possibility that climate change was real and called for action on the part of the world community. The outcome of the Conference accelerated the pace of a global convention on climate change. The spadework for crafting the Convention was carried out by the UN General Assembly, which set up an Inter-governmental Negotiations Committee (INC) to work on the text of the Convention. By June 1992, the INC had drafted a convention. The draft Convention was placed before the Heads of States for their signatures at the UNCED Summit held in Rio de Janeiro in June 1992. The Draft convention, as approved and signed at UNCED by the heads of state, was named the United Nations Framework Convention on Climate Change (UNFCCC).

A parallel issue of great importance was the goal of conservation of biodiversity. The International Union for Conservation of Nature (IUCN) was the progenitor of the CITES Convention having initiated the process of crafting the basic document relating to the trade in endangered species in the 1960s. Over time, the document was transformed to the text of the CITES. The CITES finally came into force in 1975. It was deemed as a Convention of critical importance to wildlife conservation since it sought to control and regulate illegal transboundary movement of endangered and threatened plant and animal species. Inspired by the CITES, many developing countries undertook measures not only to conserve wildlife but also to prevent trafficking in wildlife products (especially products and by-products) derived from the endangered species listed in the Red Book of the CITES. The CITES was effective in creating awareness about the danger to threatened and endangered species in the world. However it failed in preventing trafficking of threatened and endangered animal species such as pangolins. The Convention has also not entirely succeeded in preventing the illegal movement of rare plant/tree species like mahogany and rosewood. The principal limitation of the CITES was that its agenda was not situated within the matrix of development and livelihoods in member countries. Indeed the zoonotic roots of the COVID-19 pandemic of 2020 brought into sharp relief the inadequacy of the Convention. Despite listing all species of pangolins as endangered since 2016, the CITES was not able to prevent illegal trafficking of the species to the wet markets in Asia. Indeed, COVID-19, which was traced to the wet market at Wuhan in China, was widely considered to have jumped from pangolins to human beings. In spite of this, the CITES pleaded that the convention had no provisos to deal with zoonotic diseases even where such diseases could be traced to endangered species in the course of trade.

In hindsight one can argue that the relative narrow nature of CITES was anticipated by the IUCN. The IUCN's World Conservation Strategy (WCS) of 1972 attempted to craft a wider conservation agenda. The WCS, for the first time, outlined the significance of protecting and conserving different forms of biodiversity such as wildlife, rare animals, and so on through effective policies and programmes. However, the important point, which proved to be contentious as far as the WCS was concerned, was regarding ownership over biodiversity. The WCS emphasized and underlined the significance of viewing biodiversity and conservation as a common heritage of humankind. This concept was not acceptable to developing countries of the world, which had for a very long time espoused the principle of permanent sovereignty over natural resources (PSNR) as the central concept guiding natural resources management. The IUCN strategy document also did not have other elements which would have got developing countries interested in the problem of biodiversity conservation. Further, the 1970s was a decade surcharged by acrimonious debates between developing and developed countries on development issues in the UNCTAD forum. The Group of 77 (G-77) and non-aligned countries had strongly taken up the issue of skewed international division of labour and high disparities in per capita incomes between developed and developing countries, in order to highlight the need to provide for financial transfers on fair and concessional terms from the developed world. Against the backdrop of such a surcharged environment, it was difficult for a global conservation strategy to gain acceptance amongst developing countries, particularly when such a conservation strategy did not enshrine the PSNR principle. As a result of this, the WCS did not transform into a global concern for some time.

By the 1980s the UNEP took up the cause of conservation in right earnest. The process for drafting the Convention on Biological Diversity was initiated in 1990. A draft Convention was prepared after many rounds of negotiations. The CBD, which was signed by the Heads of the

States at the UNCED in 1992, came into force in 1994 after it was ratified by the minimum number of signatories. (More on CBD to follow in
Chapter 11).

The Tragedy of the UNCCD

The UNCCD or the Desertification Convention is different from the other
two Rio Conventions. Though widely considered to be a Rio Convention,
the UNCCD was signed only two years after the Rio Summit. The United
States had played a major role in the formation of the Convention. The
UNCCD was conceived against the backdrop of the severe problem of
land degradation in Africa. The Convention's origins go back to 1977
when the United Nations Conference On Desertification (UNCOD)
adopted a plan of action to combat desertification. However, it was much
later, in the 1990s, that the UNEP took cognizance of the plan of action
prescribed by the UNCOD. The Rio conference called upon the UN
General Assembly to establish an intergovernmental negotiating committee to prepare, by the year 1994, the text of a Convention to combat
desertification. In December 1992, the General Assembly passed its
resolution 47/188 to set off the process for drawing up the Convention.
The Convention opened for signatures on 14–15 October 1994. It came
into force on 26 December 1996, 90 days after the 50th ratification was
received. Today, the Conference of Parties (COP) of the UNCCD com-
prises of 180 members. The first session of the UNCCD COP was held
in October 1997 in Rome and the second one in Dakar, Senegal a year
later. Subsequent COP meetings of the UNCCD took place in Recife,
Brazil, and in Bonn, Germany where the conference secretariat is located.
Each of these sessions dealt with the important task of implementing the
Convention at the regional and national levels. Generally, COP sessions
of the UNCCD are held on a bi-annual basis. The UNCCD website lists a
set of reasons for different countries to be members of the Convention.[2]
It is stated that by acceding to the Convention, a state could show sol-
idarity with affected countries facing the urgent and growing problem
of the global dimensions of desertification. Members could also benefit
from cooperation with other affected countries, improve access to relevant technologies and data, benefit by participation in the work of the

Committee on Science and Technology and take part in networks to support the implementation of the Convention as mandated by Article 25. In addition, it is also stated that parties are entitled to facilitate the networking of relevant institutions, agencies, and bodies. Articles 3, 4, 12, 14, 16, 17, 18, and 20 of the UNCCD are important as they lay out obligations for parties which are unaffected by desertification, but would nevertheless like to contribute to the Convention's mandate of combating desertification. More specifically, these Articles relate to international cooperation for implementing the CCD through exchange of information, facilitation of technology transfer, capacity and awareness building, promotion of integrated approaches for developing national strategies to combat desertification, and providing assistance to ensure that adequate financial resources are available for implementing the programmes identified by the Convention. The obligations also call upon countries affected by desertification in Africa, Asia, Latin America, the Caribbean, and north Mediterranean to undertake National Action Programmes. Articles 6 and 20 of the UNCCD lay down specific obligations on the part of developed countries to support affected countries through transfer of appropriate technologies.

Unlike other Rio and pre-Rio conventions which we covered, UNCCD has a regional approach to programme implementation. The annexures to the Convention are programmatic in content and thus virtually serve the functions of a Protocol. Each annexe is for a specific continent (say Africa, Central Asia, etc.) and seeks to provide a set of programmatic items for each region to realize specific outcomes. Under Article 4, all parties can implement their obligations jointly through bilateral or multilateral agreements. As per Article 26, any group of affected countries may make joint communications on measures taken up in pursuance of approved action programmes.

Chapter 12 of the Agenda 21, which deals with the management of fragile ecosystems, specifies action for combating desertification and drought as important priorities and identifies a number of programme areas to discharge the mandate of the Convention such as strengthening knowledge base information systems, conservation, afforestation and reforestation, developing and strengthening integrated programmes for poverty eradication, promoting alternative livelihood systems, developing comprehensive anti-desertification programmes, undertaking comprehensive drought preparedness/relief schemes, and promoting popular participation.

If one were to carefully read the text of the UNCCD, one would notice the presence of a section that deals with tenurial issues connected with land. The Convention also refers to climate change factors which have induced desertification while also according a significant role to traditional communities and their knowledge systems in combating land degradation and desertification. More importantly, the UNCCD also talks about sustainable livelihoods as the basic issue to be addressed in any national action programme to combat desertification. At the same time, the Convention also has its element of modernity by way of provisions for transfer of technology and flow of financial resources from the developed world. All this goes well with the objectives of the Sustainable Development Goals (SDGs).

Though the Global Environmental Facility (GEF) was mandated to focus also on the UNCCD, the facility's limited resources have constrained it to capsule desertification objectives in climate change and the biodiversity projects. Thus the GEF has been encouraging cross-cutting projects, which optimize biodiversity conservation or climate change goals, with desertification objectives taking a residuary position.

Apart from its linkages with other Rio Agreements, the UNCCD has a potential link to the World Trade Organization (WTO). Under the WTO Agreement on Agriculture, developing countries and least developing countries are given special and differentiated dispensation which permits them to avoid the regimes of subsidy reduction on agriculture and non-agricultural goods. Indeed, Annexure 2 of the WTO Agreement on Agriculture, which talks about livelihoods, environment, and food security issues, is of central importance to desertification-prone regions of the world, listed in the UNCCD. However, the UNCCD's linkage with the WTO has not been explored to the desired extent. The result is that most of the developing countries that participate in the WTO negotiations and enjoy the phenomenal advantages of concessional flow of funds and technology are not able to marshal these assets for meeting the goals of the UNCCD. This is partly for the reason that the WTO has been sensitive to multilateral environmental issues entering trade talks. While it is true that the least developing countries which account for a substantial portion of the African continent, do get a number of special concessions under the WTO by way of an enhanced latitude in the matter of domestic support and promotion of export crops, this advantage has not been reflected in country-level Action Programmes for combating desertification. In other words, programmes for combating desertification have not been twined with the development provisions contained in the WTO Agreement on Agriculture.

There are more fundamental reasons for UNCCD's weak position vis-a-vis other MEAs. It is well known that the primary reason for hunger and poverty persisting in the African continent and parts of Asia is not only connected to the weak agriculture systems and droughts that limit food production but also to the breakdown of entitlements at the household level (Sen 1983). Under such circumstances, the desertification process cannot be reduced to limitations in biophysical factors. Small peasants and farmers of Africa and Asia, as has already been noted, suffer not only from inadequate crop yields but also from a periodic fall in prices of commodities in the global marketplace. Unfortunately, the major problem with multilateral environmental agreements such as the UNCCD is that it never pays cognizance to the role of such factors in land degradation. Although there have been many studies which have gone into details regarding the economic loss posed by soil erosion and natural resources degradation in the fragile zones of Asia and Africa, none of the multilateral environmental agreements carries any firm provisos for handling such issues.

Added to this is the fact that the UNCCD suffers from serious financial problems. Despite focusing on disadvantaged regions of the world prone to desertification problems, the UNCCD has to fight hard for its own identity. The UNCCD's identity crisis explains the acute financial problems faced by the Convention. Despite protestations to the contrary, all developed countries which are obligated under the provisions of the UNCCD to financially contribute to the process of combating desertification in affected countries, have not fulfilled their obligations. The GEF, as has been noted, provides only a residual status to land degradation programmes. Thus, the UNCCD has suffered in spite of US support to the Convention in its initial stages and despite its natural compatibility with the goals of the MDG and the SDGs.

One of the most critical issues that needs closer attention in policy circles is the basic reason for the UNCCD's tight financial situation. A more fundamental question is why the climate and biodiversity conventions get more attention from the developed world in the international arena.

The tragedy of the UNCCD is that it deals with land, a resource that defies the status of a global public good. Furthermore the Convention looks for regional-level solutions, which is neither attractive to nation-states nor to global institutions. Since financial resources tend to be committed either to global or nation-state programmes, the UNCCD suffers for want of sufficient financial resources.

In the Thirteenth Session of the Conference of Parties to the UNCCD held in 2017 in China, the Convention strove to overcome its weaknesses by adopting a future strategic framework for 'more focused, targeted, effective and efficient implementation of the Convention based on systematic monitoring and assessment of progress in the implementation of the Convention's provisions'. One of the interesting features of the strategic framework was the adoption of 'Land Degradation Neutrality Target Setting Programmes' with associated indicators. This was to provide greater teeth to the implementation of the Convention's goals.[3] The Fourteenth Session of the Conference of Parties to the Convention held in India sought to keep up the tempo by firmly seeking to align the outcomes of the UNCCD with the activities of the UNFCCC and CBD with sharpened focus on land degradation.[4]

Why Some Nation-States Welcome Imported Hazardous Wastes

The 175 member-strong Basel Convention on Transboundary Movement of Hazardous Wastes is sensitive for different reasons. This has to do with the decision-making space of nation-states that accept hazardous wastes from across borders. The Basel Ban of 1994 agreed to bar the movement of hazardous wastes intended for final disposal in non-OECD countries. In 1997 it was decided to ban export of wastes intended for recovery and recycling. This ban was applied to exports from Annex V11 countries of the Convention (that is, developed countries) to non-Annex V11 countries (mainly developing). The Basel Protocol on Liability and Compensation was adopted in 1999 to provide for a comprehensive regime of liability and compensation for damages resulting from transboundary movement of hazardous and other wastes by 'locating financial responsibility' for damages inflicted upon developing countries.

In the year 2005, India was rocked by two events arising from the Basel Convention. These incidents raised issues regarding India's ability as a nation-state to take decisions on matters relating to international movement of hazardous wastes. On 15 April 2005, Connie Hedegaard, then Denmark's Environment Minister (who later became the President of the UN Climate Change Conference at Copenhagen in December 2009) alerted her counterpart in India about the illegal movement of a 51-year-old asbestos-laden ship by the name of King Fredrick IX. The ship was on its way to Alang shipbreaking yard in Gujarat for scrapping when the alert came. The ship's new owners, namely Jupiter Ship Management, a Mumbai-based company, had renamed the vessel as M.V. Riky.[5] The article goes on to state that 'King Fredrick IX' had left Denmark on 16 March 2005 on the grounds that it had to be put into service in the Middle East as a cargo ship. The report was that the ship was transiting the Suez Canal on its way to the Red Sea. However, the Danish minister alerted the Union Minister for Environment and Forests in India about the possibility of the ship docking at a Western Indian coast for dismantling. Obviously, the alert had come when the ship was on the high seas. The Danish minister wanted to alert her Indian counterpart with a view to preventing the ship from being dismantled in India. She also referred to the provisions of the Basel Convention. According to the Basel Convention, a ship must be characterized as waste if the owners intended to dispose of it. Further, the Convention lays down that transboundary movement of hazardous wastes without prior notification should be deemed as illegal traffic in waste. India's Minister in charge of the issue replied to his Danish counterpart saying that India was a party to the Basel Convention since 1992 and had its own national legislation on hazardous waste management since 1989, to ensure compliance with the obligations of the convention. However India was of the view that the ship could not be classified as waste within the scope of Article 2.1 of the Basel Convention. India's argument was that a ship sailing under its own power cannot be considered 'waste' and that the authorities of the Gujarat Pollution Control Board (GPCB) and the Central Pollution Control Board (CPCB) who had inspected the ship, did not find anything objectionable or hazardous about it. Despite the many controversies surrounding the issue (including a litigation filed by Madhumita Dutta in 2005 challenging the decision of the India's Ministry of Environment and Forests (MoEF) to admit the ship) the Monitoring Committee on hazardous wastes set up by the Supreme Court of India permitted the dismantling of Riky in the presence of the officers from CPCB and the GPCB. A Monitoring Committee was set up by the Supreme Court of India during October 2003 to monitor the progress and implementation of hazardous wastes rules.

The Riky case involved two problems. First, the ship left Denmark without proper notification, which was illegal. Second, Riky also arrived without Denmark's authorization and hence could not have carried Form 7, which is used to maintain records of hazardous wastes imported. The Basel Convention, as has already been mentioned, seeks to define hazardous wastes, minimize its generation, dispose of them as close as possible to the source of generation and reduce the transboundary movement of hazardous wastes. Further, the Convention defines wastes as substances or objects which are disposed of or intended to be disposed of, under the provisions of national laws. It is this proviso which had led the Denmark government to presuppose that Riky was a 'waste'.

A year later, another controversy erupted involving 'Clemenceau', a French ship which was sent to India for dismantling. However, this ship had to face considerable opposition even from the Government of India.

The key point that emerges from the cases discussed is that the Basel Conventions' provisos, which state that nation-states and governments can decide what is good or bad for them through a process of prior informed consent (PIC) is its weakest point. The stand of the Government of India on the Riky affair clearly indicates that they did not want any dilution in their decision-making system relating to PIC. In the case of Riky, the Government of India clearly conveyed to the international parties concerned that it retained the freedom to interpret a multilateral environment agreement and would not like its judgment to be coloured by external perceptions. Thus, though the Basel Convention deals with a concern related to modernity, namely toxic wastes that are products of the Industrial Revolution, its implementation record suggests that national interests play a greater role in decision making involving transboundary movement of hazardous wastes, than scientific assessments.

The Basel Convention has witnessed major confrontations between developing country governments and international and national civil society groups. Indeed activists have been demanding strict control in the movement of toxic exports to Asian countries. They are for developing countries not taking up environmental liabilities connected to the acceptance and processing of hazardous wastes. These groups also tried to argue very strongly and forcefully for 'extended producer responsibility' (EPR) on hazardous wastes that are shipped to developing countries. These groups seek to alert developing countries about regulatory developments in the European Union, that require source companies to phase out hazardous substances and electronic products and in the interim, take back discarded products for recycling. The underlying message is that developed countries in the world have no business to set up stringent national environmental laws within their borders at the expense of poor countries of the world and create a default situation where developing countries would act as receptacles for hazardous wastes generated by them.

As in the case of the Biodiversity Convention and the Kyoto Protocol, the United States has kept away from signing and ratifying the Basel Convention. India is yet to ratify the Basel Ban amendments calling for stricter controls in the movement of hazardous wastes.

It is worth exploring the difference how the PIC principle underlying the CBD compares with that of the Basel Convention. In the case of the CBD, PIC is a right that accrues to countries of origin of bio-resources. In the case of the Basel Convention, PIC is to be exercised by countries that seek to import hazardous wastes. While in the context of the Biodiversity Convention, India as a provider of biological and traditional knowledge, seeks to utilize PIC to assert its share in benefits, the opposite is true for the PIC employed under the provisos of the Basel Convention. In the case of the latter, India has been forthright in asserting its right to exercise PIC even in the face of pressures from civil societies and other governments since most of the arguments made by international civil societies and NGOs that the developing countries in Asia, including India, are incompetent to protect themselves from hazardous wastes. By exercising the PIC provisos of the Basel Convention, India tries to convey to the world that it has adequate technological capabilities to handle hazardous wastes.

POPS: The Twenty-first Century Convention

An interesting scenario emerges when we talk of the Stockholm Convention on Persistent Organic Pollutants (POPS or Stockholm Convention in short). Together with the Basel and the Rotterdam Conventions, the POPS has attempted to steer the management of toxic chemicals and related substances across the world by laying down comprehensive guidelines. The POPS basically tries to rein in and ultimately halt the proliferation of toxic chemicals. It targets some of the world's most dangerous substances such as polychlorinated biphenyls (PCBs), dioxins, and pesticides such as chlordane for action. The objective is to completely eliminate or severely restrict the production and use of these substances, by ensuring that they are managed appropriately or handled scientifically. The Convention also deals with the chemical transformation of POPS wastes and seeks to ensure that new chemicals are not developed with POPS-like characteristics. The Stockholm Convention was finalized in May 2001 and has been ratified by nearly 50 countries for whose governments the Convention has come into effect from 17 May 2004.

Persistent Organic Pollutants are hazardous, toxic, and persistent and do not break down easily. They can get into the food chains of marine mammals and other animals. There are 12 major POPs listed by the Convention that are slated to be banned. However, a longer phase out schedule is planned for certain PCB uses. This includes dichlorodiphenyltrichloroethane (DDT), where the agreement sets the goal of ultimate elimination within a timeline, which will be determined by the availability of cost-effective alternatives for malaria eradication. Of course, the agreement limits the use of DDT in the interim and places strict control on its use in agriculture. Similar control regimes are put in for dioxins, furans, and hexachlorobenzene, where parties are called upon to reduce their release with the ultimate goal of elimination. As in the case of the Bio-safety Protocol, the two important features of the POPS are its incorporation of the precautionary principle and its emphasis on public participation. The Treaty also emphasizes the significance of adopting environmentally sound management and scientific disposal of POP wastes. Besides this, the Convention seeks to control trade in these wastes, by requiring the importing country to certify the receipt of wastes. Perhaps the most important feature of the Convention is that the importing country is not only required to give PIC but also to notify and certify that it meets with the compliance norms laid down by the Convention.

This is mortifying for developing countries such as India which feel that they have capabilities to control and regulate POPS on their own. In the year 2001, the United States came up with its support for the POPS, much to the happiness of NGOs and civil society groups. However, in order to become a party, the United States was required to carry out its obligations towards the Treaty by ensuring passage of enabling legislations at the national level. Meanwhile, a host of other technicalities sprung up. One of them was the constraints in getting agencies such as the Environment Protection Agency (EPA) to implement the Convention standards. The net outcome was that the United States did not ratify the Convention.[6]

It is a fact that NGOs and civil society organizations play an active role in the implementation of the Stockholm Convention on POPS and have formed extensive networks for their elimination. The NGO network for POPS elimination, carries out elaborate communications with different stakeholders across the world, regarding the action points arising from the Convention. There is indeed a POPS elimination platform set up by NGOs which calls for effective implementation of the Convention.[7] This group clearly states that the goal of all concerned parties should not be confined to risk management and that the parties concerned have to take proactive steps to eliminate problematic substances that could cause significant injury to the humans, wildlife and other living organisms inhabiting the biosphere. The network calls upon the world governments and the UNEP to establish a legally binding programme of action to eliminate POPS as well as its anthropogenic sources, based on the following facts:

1. That many countries lack the capacity to eliminate POPS as well as their anthropogenic sources without significant external assistance;
2. no country or region must be required to act in matters that is substantively harmful to health or to the well-being of its people. Special consideration should also be given to the control of infectious diseases;
3. achieve elimination of POPS through both qualitative and a quantitative undertakings. Once a substance has been listed as a POPS

substance, it needs to be absolutely phased out and eliminated. The decision to list a substance as a POP should reflect the fact that the substance poses an unmanageable risk for society. There should be a commitment to work towards the elimination of the substance as well as its production sources;

4. Apart from the 12 identified POPS, steps may be undertaken to identify toxic substances at a later date. The legally binding instrument should mandate rapid, but orderly and responsible global programmes of action;

5. a reasonable criteria should be established for identifying new POPS beyond the original 12;

6. POPS elimination should proceed through a transition regime that is rapid, orderly, and that unnecessarily delays should be avoided;

7. in order to assist governments, effective POPS-related action should be undertaken by the private sector, NGOs and other interested parties in all countries. For this it is essential that a special clearing house mechanism be established;

8. as part of the global efforts to identify and eliminate POPS, Governments concerned should undertake aggressive programmes for toxicity testing which are directed to chemicals whose toxic effects remain unknown, and take up evaluation of these chemicals form the angle of health outcomes; and

9. the instruments associated with the legally binding POPS instruments need to be transparent as far as possible ensure effective public/NGO participation in decision making.

The POPS Convention has been a great learning process. It is clear that NGOs and civil society groups, which were frustrated with national governments in developing countries for their act of stonewalling the Basel Ban, got their act together when the POPS came up for negotiation in the mid 1990s. Civil society groups and NGOs played an active role in ensuring that policy making was responsibly carried out. However the absence of a provision of graduated phase out of POPs reduced the options available to developing countries. Further, although the POPS Convention recognized the fact that developing countries did not have the capacity to solve any problems created by toxic substances such as POPs, the Convention did little to resolve the issue by seeking technology and financial transfer as was the case with the UNFCCC, the Montreal Protocol on Ozone Depleting Substances, and the Basel Convention. Rather, the POPS Convention went one step further and said that no developing country should ever be given an option to try out these chemicals in a manner that dilutes the core concern of the Convention, namely elimination of POPS.

As the Convention of the twenty-first century, POPS promises to be a non-nation-state-based Convention. This is evident if one goes through the structure of the Convention and its departure from some of the established provisos of the Montreal Protocol, the CBD, and the UNFCCC. Indeed this deviation for the three mentioned MEAs was on account of the fact that the POPS received considerable support from a variety of international organizations. Thus the International POPS Elimination Network (IPEN), which is a network of over 350 NGOs worldwide, played an important role in the evolution of the POPS Convention. Indeed, the UN Industrial Development Organization (UNIDO) came up with programmes to assist NGOs present in the International Pollution Elimination Network (IPEN) in order to help them implement national programmes in countries where the network is actively involved.

The GEF has also supported POPS-related projects that foster active and effective civil society participation.

The multi-sectoral ramifications of the POPS Convention has been tremendous. The POPs has widespread ramifications in the areas of public health, agriculture, animal husbandry and urban ecosystems, not to mention, the Convention's possible impacts on wildlife conservation and forests. Perhaps the real relevance of POPS comes from the number of windows through which it can push its agenda. Some of the measures that indirectly promote implementation of the POPS Convention in the agriculture sector include codes of conduct involving sensitive agricultural commodities that seek to eschew harmful chemicals and take up practices that involve biological control methods and integrated pest management.

Similarly, in the industrial sector, the POPS Convention has come up with major suggestions for replacement of PCBs used as insulators in electric transformers and capacitators, with biodegradable substitutes such as mineral oils. Further, the dioxins and furan issues addressed by the Convention has fundamental implications on activities routinely carried out to dispose plastic wastes in local areas. Efforts to replace incineration of municipal wastes by recycling and reuse, and endeavours to achieve source reduction of dioxin generating substances aid the quest of the Convention to eliminate release of dioxins. Yet another POPS convention aiding measure is the replacement of PVC plastics with chlorine-free plastics. The fourth meeting of the COP held in May 2009 in Geneva amended the Convention to expand the list of dangerous chemicals. This move was welcomed by the UNEP for its potential to 'create a salutary impact on human health and the environment' (Steiner 2009).

The Rio Triumvirate and Uneasy Locals

> But one fact seems to stand out: that a divorce from the soil, from
> the good earth, is bad for the individual and the race.
> Jawaharlal Nehru, *The Discovery of India*

The tsunami disaster, which struck India, Indonesia, and Sri Lanka in December 2004, had little to do with climate change. Though seen as an absolutely unforeseen natural calamity, the tsunami tragedy exposed inadequacy of rehabilitation measures and the deficiencies associated with poverty alleviation schemes carried out in coastal areas. The narratives around the tsunami calamity of 2004, focused on how the disaster was exacerbated by faulty land-use changes on shorelands, inadequate protection for the poor people staying on the shores, unimaginative coastal zone regulations and inadequate disaster management preparedness.

The tsunami tragedy also brought in its wake a flurry of theories regarding the seismic causes of the tsunami wave. The tsunami was seen as a one-time disaster that struck hapless coastal communities who were dependent on marine and shoreland resources for their survival. While the diagnosis of the tsunami crisis focused on the seismic roots of the problem, the solutions that emerged were of a different nature.

In the wake of the tsunami disaster and its glaring aftermath, response strategies advanced by different stakeholders varied from short-term effective measures of protection to more realistic and long-term ecological steps that could improve the resilience of affected coastal ecosystems. Some sections of stakeholders (including prominent political leaders in the affected states), argued for the construction of seawalls to prevent tsunami-like disasters. However, other stakeholders including civil society groups and scientists opposed the concept of seawalls and argued that it would only create more problems. By the time the after-effects of the tsunami disaster had sunk in, improved solutions, which advocated ecological measures, gained currency. This included the famous idea of installing or putting in place a set of green walls in the shape of forestry plantations, involving mangroves and related tree species. Indeed, the discourse then changed to the wonderful effects green walls could have in mitigating calamities like the one that resulted from the tsunami. Since then, there has been a fair amount of emphasis, on the part of the state governments affected, to not only initiate rehabilitation measures but also to ensure that there was greater provisioning of financial resources for constructing green seawalls.

It took a natural disaster like the tsunami to convince governments of the utility of environmental and ecological services in protecting human communities from natural disasters. A natural calamity of the proportion of the tsunami had put to rest all canons of financial propriety and prudence that one normally encounters in India. Initiatives by the tsunami-affected states to carry out afforestation or reforestation programmes proved to be successful.

In reality, almost all successful environmental projects in India have focused on improving the resilience and capacity of common property resources (such as tanks, forests, common lands and related water-land regimes) with a view to catering to the livelihood needs of the rural poor. The new trend of geo mapping resources that one comes across in India's rural areas has aided the implementation of such projects.

While there has been a systematic effort at employing Geographical Information Systems (GIS) to map natural resources in different watersheds, the more interesting activity that has been undertaken by organizations such as the Foundation for Ecological Security in Gujarat involved disseminating the findings of GIS studies amongst village communities to make the latter aware of the threats to their natural resources base. The people's planning process in Kerala is also modelled on similar lines as it seeks to involve local communities and their governments to undertake self-diagnosis of the problems faced by them in order to arrive at solutions which are meaningful and add value to their welfare.

As mentioned earlier, the trouble with global multilateral environmental agreements is that they do not have a scheme for disseminating their message in rural areas, particularly on the pressing priorities identified by these conventions. By relying on national governments and the state machinery, the conventions are at the mercy of the conventional channels when it comes to execution of projects. The underlying problem with the global environmental projects that are implemented at the local level is that they do not enter the 'mental-scape' of local communities.

The main point here is that MEAs do not have rooted structures to ensure that their programmes are internalized by local communities. The MEAs need to enter the local mental-scape in a manner that results in their proper implementation without hitches. Wedded as they are to the primacy of nation-states, MEAs carry out their interventions through national-level programmes so the global message would percolate to local areas. Indeed, the UNDP in the previous decade has initiated a National Capacity Building for Self Assessment (NCSA) project for global environmental management at the national level, where the idea was to provide countries with opportunities to assess capacity needs and priorities through a consultative process with the idea of designing and implementing synergized projects that sought to meld MEA goals with national priorities.

There are many intractable issues in seeking to implement a global commons programme in local areas. The role of NGOs and civil society groups as well as the local communities could be extremely significant, though not always acceptable to governments. Similarly, the role of national technical institutions and technical personnel is critical for the successful implementation of programmes for rehabilitation of global commons in local contexts. One area where multi-stakeholder involvement can work is the energy sector. The astronomical rise of crude oil prices in 2007–8 spurred a flurry of active programmes for promoting the use of alternative fuels in developing countries. In India, commencing from the Ninth Five Year Plan, there has been a serious effort on the part of the Planning Commission and the Government of India to consider alternatives to fossil fuels such as coal and oil. One of the ambitious programmes devised during the Tenth Five Year Plan is the bio-fuel programme focused on bioenergy plants, crops, and animal feedstock. Of the various bio-fuels, pride of place has been taken by two fuels, namely those sourced from Jatropha and Pongamia plantations. While Jatropha has been advocated and strongly supported by the Government as a national programme for bio-fuel generation, the role of the tree species Pongamia Pinnata has been highlighted by states such as Karnataka, where the tree is part and parcel of village ecosystems. Pongamia Pinnata yields oil, which, after processing, acquires the traits of bio-diesel. The oil is extracted and put through a process called trans-esterification to convert it into fatty acids esters (the chemical description of biodiesel) by incubation with alcohol and alkali. The resultant oil can be blended with petroleum.

Similarly, Jatropha oil or liquid gold, as it is called, is based on the seed of a plant called Jatropha Curcas. Jatropha is a hardy plant that can grow in a variety of environments including dry and arid zones. Jatropha oil-based energy substantially reduces GHG emissions.

Apart from the two tree species, the other source of bio-energy which has been developed in India is ethanol, which is made by fermenting molasses, which is an important product of sugarcane. Ethanol represents a group of compounds whose molecules contain hydroxyl OH group bonded to a carbon atom. Its local freezing point makes it useful as a fuel in thermometers. Successive governments in India have been promoting ethanol-blended petrol since 2003.

The main problem with the bio-fuel programme in India is that though it is aimed at solving the country's energy problem and also has the incidental advantage of addressing climate change, it has to contend with operational issues at the local level. Tree plantations of Jatropha and Pongamia, in particular, meet with a host of institutional barriers. In the first place, plantations of the two tree species induce irreversible land use change. Given the fact that most of these plantations have to be taken up either on private farms or in common lands, it is bound to affect the flow of food, fodder, fuel wood, and other sources of biomass from common lands. This will affect the livelihoods of landless labour, small and marginal farmers in particular. There is great effort to counter this argument by stating that common and marginal agricultural lands are wasted, degraded lands where nothing grows. This argument tempts policy makers to introduce schemes for implementing plantations of energy-promising monocultures such as Jatropha and Pongamia. There is no effort to try local varieties in such lands. In reality, community lands have to be taken over and converted into forest lands and kept impervious to community rights before an ambitious programme for addressing a global common issue such as climate change is addressed. This could constrain local communities to view global commons as nothing but an extension of the old colonial forest policy. Even if this approach is not taken up for addressing the issue of global commons, there is the larger issue of seeking community concurrence to ensure that strategic local community support is obtained for projects involving Jatropha and Pongamia plantations.

For quite some time, there have been serious dialogues regarding the issue of synergies amongst MEAs. The exercise on synergies has involved three players, namely the UNEP, the United Nations Development Programme (UNDP), and the United Nations University. Many rounds of country-level consultations were initiated in Africa to bring about synergies amongst the Rio and post-Rio conventions. Countries such as Namibia and Uganda have gone a step further and tried to work out concrete programmes of twining different MEAs at the local level in order to achieve success. The agreements that figure in these exercises are Climate Change, Biodiversity, and the Desertification Conventions.

A UNEP-commissioned Expert Group regarding inter-convention synergies came out with their recommendations. The report highlighted the need for the identification and implementation of synergy regimes that could be executed in accordance with identified needs, work programmes, and priorities (Damodaran and Suneetha 2007). The Expert Group was also in favour of convening meetings of Joint Liaison Groups, comprising representatives of the three major Conventions, for giving greater credence and priority to the synergization process. The Expert Group also recommended a system whereby Secretariats of various conventions met on a regular basis to look at the manner in which they could affect synergies in different areas. A concrete strategy that was advanced by the UNEP-commissioned Expert Group was to link up the management information systems of various MEAs in order to support national implementation of the Conventions in different countries. Other areas where synergies have been thought of include cross-sectoral harmonization initiatives, national reporting, joint standard data forms, and systems.

At the national level, developing countries such as India have deliberated on the issue of inter-convention synergies. However, India and a few other developing countries have reservations about synergies at the global level. The fear is that inter-convention synergies could reduce the flow of financial resources and technologies, besides diluting the responsibilities of countries supposed to play a major role in these activities. Still deeper is the fear that inter-convention synergies at a global level would throttle national decision-making and programme implementation. At present, developing countries enjoy considerable freedom in these realms.

There is also the feeling that uniform and standard guidelines would act as a barrier against developing countries funding and supporting environmental projects that have global outcomes. It is politically unpalatable to promote projects that seek to achieve global economies of scale without regard for national or local level concerns. There is also the apprehension that the talk of inter-convention synergies may be extended to the issue of trade and environment, whereby the issue of synergies between MEAs and the WTO would come to the fore. For many developing countries, this terrain is dangerous as it will lead to environmental standards acting as NTBs in the global movement of goods. The incorporation of Products Related Process Methods (PPMs) in trade rules, particularly those linked to MEA objectives, could be fatal for developing country exports. This, in turn, will cause ripples in rural areas in developing countries, from where the bulk of exports emanate. We will come to this issue later.

Thus when one talks about inter-convention synergies and the operational aspects of implementing an inter-convention synergy-based programme in a local area in developing countries, we have to consider the complexities that may arise. In case such synergy-based projects do not involve local stakeholder consultations, it will engender serious misgivings amongst local communities.

Coming to the local impact of the trilogy of desertification, climate change, and biodiversity conventions, a few factors need to be noted. While it is true that the GEF has tried to situate desertification or land degradation programmes within the framework of climate change and biodiversity conservation conventions, it is seldom recognized by these international organizations that such bundling needs to be appreciated by local communities. As has already been stated, the real thrust of the Desertification Convention is on measures to combat the adverse impacts in land degradation in local areas. It is well known that communities inhabiting arid areas in different parts of Latin America, Africa, Asia, and northern Mediterranean do not understand the discourses on climate change and biodiversity emanating from Bonn and Montreal. Indeed, their awareness of climate change issues is more remote than their awareness of biodiversity, since the latter is more directly related to livelihoods and food security concerns. In such an event, even the best traditions systems of endogenous resources management cannot gel with projects that seek climate change outcomes.

Under such circumstances the idea of implementing the global conventions in a top-down manner is flawed. To avoid such a backlash, the Rio Conventions have been requesting member countries to develop National Action Programmes which have an impact of incorporating global environmental concerns of the Convention by situating their objectives within the socio-economic matrix of local areas. This is what we meant when we stated that MEAs rely on the political muscle of the state to implement their projects.

Either way, UN organizations such as the UNDP and the Bretton Woods Institutions such as the World Bank and the IMF are basically mandated to interact with governments of the countries and leave the implementation of projects to the national or sub-national governments. An afforestation project in a desert-prone area that is funded by multilateral financial institutions like the International Bank for Reconstruction and Development (IBRD) or the Asian Development Bank (ADB), has very little chance of success even if it sought to achieve climate and biodiversity goals, unless local communities or bodies welcome the mix.

This is not to state that such trilogies are not likely to succeed. Where no tensions exist amongst the objectives of different conventions, it is quite likely that the projects may meet with a high likelihood of success. Where there is an attempt to combine the objectives of climate change convention with those of the desertification convention, there could be tensions. For instance, a monoculture plantation of a fast-growing tree species, say eucalyptus, taken up in a desert-prone area in Africa, could make eminent sense from the climate change point of view because of its accelerated carbon sequestration potential. However, in terms of its impact on desertification, its success will depend on what desertification is taken to mean. If desertification is interpreted by local communities to mean arrest of soil degradation, it is a win-win situation as the project will meet climate change concerns as well as the support of local people. However, in case 'livelihood' becomes the predominant concern of the local people, it may not be possible for a monoculture tree plantation with zero food or fodder benefits to be successfully implemented with the co-operation of the local communities. At the same time, it is conceivable that if the local communities were given the funds to implement a project of their choice, they would have looked towards agro-forestry solutions to the problem. One option could be that for the project proponents to go for leguminous trees, which, while optimizing nitrogen fixation in soil, can also contribute to lessening soil erosion. On the other hand, a plan of afforestation that is designed to arrest land degradation and provide support to an agricultural community may not meet with the approval of project proponents whose central concern is carbon sequestration. Indeed, there have been protest movements against monoculture plantations in different parts of the world. India has also witnessed local protests against the planting of eucalyptus and poplars. In case global environmental projects go for CO_2 sequestering plantations, local communities may find global environmental causes as going against their essential interests. Thus, it is equally conceivable that global environmental projects that are not designed for the benefit of the local people may reverse the trend of empowerment and inclusiveness and promote top-down approaches instead of weakening them. In the process, they could meet with failure.

As Hildyard et al. (1997)[13] mention, even the Tropical Forestry Action Plan (TFAP), which was launched in the 1980s for protecting forests over 80 countries in the world, suffered from top-down approaches despite not having a global commons slant. Decisions regarding the contours of projects were drafted by experts appointed by Governments. These experts prescribed the 'ideal forest zones', despite the fact that its hundreds of millions of denizens could have a say in the matter. When it came to implementation the focus was on how to get everyone else to carry out the vision provided by the experts. But Hildyard et al. (1997) concede that the TFAP did start with real efforts to revamp existing systems of management and sought to associate NGOs in the implementation operations. However, as the authors note, the reform process promised by the TFAP came to a grinding halt due to opposition within the Food and Agriculture Organization (FAO) Council (1997, 6). Little wonder that

Agarwal and Narain (1989) advocated decentralized decision making for sustainable development projects.

Nicki Kindersley (2005: 13–14), in his article, 'Nature's Fury in Europe', states how the agenda of climate change was pushed to explain natural disasters that were at best random events. During the year 2005, while East Europe was hit by torrential rains and swollen rivers, Southern Europe was hit by a massive heat wave. In Portugal and Spain in south Europe, forest fires, which broke out due to high ambient temperatures, were put down with difficulty. Though jet streams and high-speed winds found below the troposphere were found to be the proximate causes for the natural disasters, there were strong efforts to link them to the possibility of climate change although many scientists disagreed with the analysis.

Thus global environmental problems basically struggle to get into the local matrix of local thought. They use a variety of measures to get themselves going. The basic accent of the global environmental agreements such as climate change, desertification, and the biodiversity conservation conventions has been to situate their programmes within the national matrix and hope that things happen to the satisfaction of everyone. But this faith is belied as global environmental projects fail to get local support.

The role of civil society groups and NGOs is crucial here since they can ensure that the design and content of the project fulfils the needs of villagers. They can take up local causes by working out convergent strategies to arrive at informed decisions on climate change redressal projects. However, NGOs or the civil society groups that work on the Climate Change Convention may or may not have an equal interest in the Convention on Desertification. Moreover, unless international NGO groups are broad-based and inclusive in their perspectives, they will not be in a position to carry local communities with them. Ideally, an NGO based in a water-short developing country, will have a positive orientation to the UNCCD. Such NGOs will take up projects that address climate change concerns. Such organizations will seek to take up projects that emphasize the objectives of food and water security, livelihood issues, endemic biodiversity, and agricultural sustainability based on healthy man–livestock interactions. Given the fact these outputs meet with the livelihood concerns of local communities, it is quite possible that such a project will gain local support as well. On the other hand, bio-fuel plantations that have positive climate outcomes, will have no place in a local community's scheme of things in countries which are prone to desertification.

Communicating the Conventions:
The Perils of Hierarchy

The key factor which decides the success of an MEA amongst local communities is communication. One of the greatest paradoxes of the Rio Conventions has been that their communication systems are hierarchical. In the case of climate change, one could see that the flow of communication is from the national governments to the Convention Secretariat and vice versa. There is nothing like a bottom-up flow from the local level to the national governments and then to the Convention. The hierarchical system of communication prevents the key goals of the Convention from taking roots amongst local-level communities and their Governments. National Action Programmes or National Determined Contribution Statements drawn by national governments also follow a top-down approach.

A research study, which was published in 2006 in the journal *Global Biogeochemical Cycles*, states that mangroves contribute to oceanic carbon (Dittmar et al. 2006). The article, written by Thorsten Dittmar of the Florida State University, comes out with the important revelation that 10 per cent of the essential dissolved organic carbon that is supplied to the oceans from land is contributed by mangroves. For scientists in developing countries who are used to considering mangroves as valuable biomass in shorelands, the article is a great revelation. Their views on mangroves could change drastically in the wake of the findings of the study. Thus scientists from India who have always appreciated the unique role of mangroves in the protection of shorelands, will be induced to take up research on the role of the species in addressing climate change concerns and come up with comprehensive projects that seek to utilize mangroves for climate outcomes blended with petroleum. The main point here, is that such scientific findings are never reported systematically to the Convention Secretariats or to their scientific arms, much less to local communities which live in coastal areas and are witness to the large-scale degradation and depletion of mangroves in their region. This diminishes the chance of the CBD and FCCC taking roots in local areas.

There is another problem with hierarchical communication systems associated with the Biodiversity Convention. Most of the national reporting systems on biodiversity or National Biodiversity Strategy and Action Plans (NBSAPs) are confined to status surveys of the principal ecosystems. There is no effort in any of these documents to make an honest audit of where things have gone wrong. Indeed, apart from national reporting and communication systems, countries have opportunities to ventilate their position on specific issues in COP meetings and in other forums related to these Conventions. However, such opportunities are either not availed or are wasted. Nitin Sethi (2006) mentions how India's presentation on protected area networks at CBD's Eighth Conference of Parties (COP 8) did not go beyond tall claims. According to the author, India made grand statements claiming that it has always tried to ensure that its protected areas represented a range of biological values spread across 10 bio-geographic zones and 26 bio-geographic provinces. India also went on to claim that its National Environment Policy had envisaged an expansion of networks to represent all bio-geographical zones and proceeded to talk about the grand objectives of the National Wildlife Action Plan (2002–6). There were only a couple of statements about limitations—one which mentioned financial constraints and the other which hinted at the social, economic, and political factors that worked against rehabilitation of communities inhabiting protected areas.

In some cases, corporates also play a similar game. A case in point was the Clean Development Mechanism undertaken by the corporate giant ITC (Gupta 2006). The project, which was put up in the UNFCCC website for comments from interested parties, was flawed on various counts. For one thing, though the project commenced in 2001, it took a while for it to get into a consultation mode. It was only in 2005 that the ITC held consultations with local stakeholders, namely the tribals of Andhra Pradesh's Khammam District, whose lands were being taken up for reforestation with the eucalyptus species. Experts also doubt whether the company followed the Clean Development Mechanism (CDM) guidelines that laid down that trees were to be planted only on lands that had no pre-existing activity like agriculture.

The issue that emerges from these examples is that officially mandated communications end up with tall claims that conceal the true weaknesses. What is worse, top-down communication systems fail to tap local perspectives on environment. Had these tendencies been avoided, it would have led to a more imaginative local planning of projects that carry global environmental objectives.

Reflections on the Negotiations Trajectory of Global Environmental Agreements

Let us start with the history of negotiations connected to the Montreal Protocol on Ozone-Depleting Substances (ODS). The process of setting up an international regime on ODS was initiated in the 1980s. The first international regime on ODS came in the shape of the Vienna Convention on ODS in 1985. The Montreal Protocol on ODS followed in 1987. The Montreal Protocol provided a clear charter for governments to phase out ODS. Part of the reason for the success of the Montreal Protocol was that it was narrowly focused on eliminating a group of ODS which had only a narrow consumption base in developing countries. The architects of the Montreal Protocol were however keen to ensure that the legal instrument was accepted by the major developing countries. However, there were a few features in the original framework of the Vienna Convention and the Montreal Protocol that were not acceptable to India and China. The Montreal Protocol was also not that well known to NGOs and civil society groups. Consequently, they did not play a serious part in the negotiations. It was left to the governments of India and China to spearhead the movement against the negative features of the Montreal Protocol. Both countries stood as a united team and demanded significant changes to certain important sections of the Protocol, as a precondition for joining the Protocol. The Conference of Parties to the Montreal Protocol that met in London in 1990 adopted the amended Protocol, which carried with it certain major changes to accommodate the concerns of developing countries such as India and China. Incorporation of these concerns was an important gesture. It was the first of its kind, and served as a model of other global environmental agreements that were to follow. The principles of common and differentiated responsibilities that underlay the amended

Montreal Protocol to accommodate developing country concerns, was later carried over to the UNFCCC. This proviso enshrined in the amended Montreal Protocol enabled developing countries to honour the Protocol commitments through a graduated transition period as compared to developed country members. Also enshrined in the Montreal Protocol were certain new principles that have now become leading tenets of international environmental jurisprudence. These were commitments to honour the special rights of developing countries to financial resources and transfer of technology on fair and efficient terms. The rights were later enshrined in the later MEAs that followed the Montreal Protocol, namely the UNFCCC and the CBD.

The most noteworthy aspect of the Protocol-related negotiations related to the interface between the government and the industry. It was well known that India was acquiring production capacities in CFCs since the 1980s. By the mid 1980s, India had emerged as an exporter of CFCs to many countries of the world including those in the Middle East. When the Montreal Protocol came up for renegotiations, India questioned the provisos of a uniform phase-out schedule for ODS, on grounds of equity. The nascent capacities in India were too 'new' and 'recent' to be suddenly phased out. It was felt that provisos of the Montreal Protocol would affect the capacities of these industries to produce the so-called ODS and would restrict their trade or exports. To a large extent, the common but differentiated advantage which India got out of the Montreal Protocol was driven by the needs of its 'then nascent CFC industry'. India's CFC industry took the plea that refrigerators and air conditioners were absolutely new entries in the basket of consumer durables in India and that the objective of reaching them to common households would be frustrated by the Protocol's tight regimes for CFC phase-out. The costs of substitute technologies would only serve to increase the prices of refrigerators and air conditioners in India and keep these goods out of the reach of the average middle-income households. The argument was compounded and rather legitimated by the fact that the multinational corporations which had taken up ODS substitution technologies were not willing to make them available to developing countries such as India, except on commercial terms. This was an added reason for India insisting on an amendment to the Protocol to facilitate transfer of technologies and financial resources on fair and favourable terms. In reality, the Montreal Protocol represents a supreme success story in the realm of technology transfer regimes and is touted as a model for other conventions.

When it comes to the UNFCCC, the basic issues of concern have been about 'lifestyles' and 'modernity'. The structure of the Convention clearly distinguished between developed and developing countries. The issue at stake was not just about stabilizing GHG emissions but also about achieving substantial reductions in these emissions through quantitative restrictions. In the initial stages of the negotiations, there were differences of opinion about remedial measures. Countries such as India argued that the common but differentiated responsibilities principles underlying the UNFCCC were insufficient to guarantee effective participation by developing countries. Another interesting point about UNFCCC-related negotiations was that it brought to the forefront differences of opinion between the European Union countries and the United States. While the European Union countries suggested major reductions in quantitative emissions, even going beyond what was envisaged in the Framework Convention, the United States resisted this on the ground that it would hurt their economic growth. Thus, the United States supported the introduction of flexible mechanisms such as joint implementation, emission trading, and clean development mechanisms that provided latitude to developed countries to postpone their mitigation commitments. The slang match between the European Union and the United States also saw civil society and non-governmental groups chip in. The Kyoto Protocol, which was negotiated and opened up for signatures in 1997, tried to carry both factions along. The Kyoto Protocol clearly laid down the role of flexible instruments, but also committed countries in Annexure 1 (developed countries) to quantitative reductions in their emissions. Similarly the emission trading regime was not applied to developing countries, thanks to stubborn resistance on the part of developing countries like India, China, and others, backed by NGOs. The only flexible instrument that applied to the Non-annexure 1 developing countries in the Kyoto Protocol, was the Clean Development Mechanism (CDM), which was required to be run on democratic and transparent principles under the aegis of the UNFCCC.

The India-based Centre for Science and Environment (CSE) played a remarkable role in opinion building in favour of developing countries at Rio and later on in Kyoto in 1997 and Bali in 2007. The CSE's seminal paper, 'Global Warming in an Unequal World', written by Agarwal and Narain, succeeded in enshrining the 'per capita emission principle' in the UNFCCC. This paper made a strong and forceful plea to developing countries to take up obligations for undoing the damages wrought by 'historic' emissions. By showing that the important criterion was not absolute emissions but relative or per capita emissions, the study went on to point to the grave inequality in treating development-starved countries on par with their developed counterparts, when it came to taking up the obligations to redress climate change. Similar has been the effort of international thinkers, associated with the journal *Ecologist*. It is equally worthy of note that while NGOs and civil society groups have been in the forefront to ensure that equity as a concept was enshrined prominently in the UNFCCC and the Kyoto Protocol, there has been substantive effort on the part of aid institutions and financial institutions such as the World Bank, ADB and the European Investment Bank (EIB) to give a major push to the Convention and its Protocol by setting up dedicated funds to finance activities relevant to climate mitigation. Thus, in the 1990s, the World Bank set up the Carbon Prototype and other Carbon/Climate Funds to enable purchase of Certified Emission Reductions (CERs) arising from CDM projects at optimal prices. Since then the World Bank has set up many more carbon funds for servicing climate change activities. Same has been the story with the ADB and the EIB. The GEF continues to provide catalytic funds to finance incremental costs incurred by developing countries on climate change redressal projects that apply energy efficiency and clean energy options.

The issue of 'inter-generational' equity was important to the climate change debate in the initial phases. As Klaus M. Meyer Abich (2004) stated, there is a grave inequality in the climate change debate where countries that contribute three quarters of the climate change problem are least affected by its implications while those who suffer from it mostly share the responsibility of redressal. Agarwal and Narain too had made the same point. Abich goes on to argue that given the political rationality that one sees in the present-day world, there is an in-built propensity on the part of governments to shift the costs of climate change to future generations. He also goes on to say that sometimes lack of political rationality causes preference policies on climate change to pay attention to short-term goals.

Governments in developing countries (barring small island developing countries like Maldives) do not consider climate change to be a top priority issue. Faced with pressures for taking up carbon mitigation measures, and conscious of the fact that they themselves would face the brunt of global warming, emerging economies such as India and China have changed the policy of complete indifference towards climate change measures and formulated National Action Plans that focus on adaptation and voluntary mitigation efforts. India's National Action Plan on Climate Change, adopted in 2008, emphasized the importance of cleaner economic development based on low carbon emissions. The accent is on developing, sourcing, and internalizing cleaner technologies that are not only energy efficient but also backstopping in nature as far as the problem of GHG emissions is concerned. India and China however refused to take up any mandatory emission reduction measures under the Kyoto Protocol and its successor regime. It needs to be stated that India has always been cautious about the Kyoto Protocol and had agreed to sign the same only in 2002, nearly five years after the Protocol was accepted by a majority of the developed countries. Even this late act had to do with India's 'gesture of goodwill' as the host of the UNFCCC's COP of 2002.

After signing the Kyoto Protocol in 2002, there were subtle changes in India's policy on climate change issues. In a departure from its earlier stand, India warmed up to the Kyoto Protocol's CDM. India started welcoming funds for launching CDM projects. Since then, there has been a flurry of competing proposals from the industry sector for CDM projects. Indeed, India announced in 2002 that it would take up CDM projects in the areas of land management, land degradation, and other related areas. However, despite this pronouncement, the CDM portfolio of India is yet to have any agricultural-based sequestration project worthy of note. The reasons for this are not far to seek.

Barring some protests about the efficacy or the relative utility of CDMs, the issues relating to the climate change convention have not been tackled by civil society groups or NGOs to the extent required. It is a simple axiom that climate change objectives may not go well with the objectives of the CBD. This is because sequestration of carbon is efficient only when new plantations of trees are raised. Mature plantations or natural forests that have limited potential for carbon sequestration have limited GHG sequestration potential. The best 'carbon mitigation' outcome arises only when the plantations comprise of growing stock. In practical terms, this calls for cutting down natural forests and replacing them with new plantations which have high carbon sequestration potential.

Thus, here one sees a trade-off between the UNFCCC and the CBD. This issue does not seem to have acquired the kind of attention that it should have. It is quite conceivable that if greater priority is given to CDMs and GHG mitigation measures, it is bound to be at the cost of natural forests unless there is a clear effort to ensure that the CDMs do not extend to the forestry sector and even if they do take place, this will not be at the cost of biodiversity assets.

These days, negotiations on climate change are 'games of strategy'. As we have noted, the United States had kept out of the Kyoto Protocol as this would have entailed economic sacrifices. Therefore, feverish efforts are on to have a successor protocol. In terms of the game theory, a successor agreement has all the virtues of a 'repeated game', which would, as Axelrod (1984) stated, 'strongly discourage countries reneging from their commitments on climate change amelioration'. This can lead to interesting and ingenious solutions that give the semblance of 'least position change' on the part of the high-stakes players.

In the run up to the Copenhagen Summit of 2009, there were strong pressures on India and China to take on CO2 mitigation commitments in the post-Kyoto Protocol regimes. It was the underlying feeling that this will be cost effective for developed countries as it would lessen the burden on the developed world to go for a 'closer shave'. Until about September 2009, both India and China (joined by G-77 countries) had strongly urged the developed world to 'right' their historical wrongs by taking up mitigation commitments and helping developing countries adapt to climate change through an appropriate global environmental financial system (Damodaran 2009). In reality, the concept of historical debt was the central equity issue that underlay UNFCCC until the Paris Agreement on Climate Change in 2015/16. Indeed, Schelling (2006) argues that the principle of historical obligations needs to be built into a regime of allocation of CO2/GHG emission rights. As Schelling states, 'the complexity of allocation of emission rights is that they have to be allocated over decades, not just a decade at a time but cumulatively' (2006).

However India and China, by unilaterally announcing reductions in carbon intensity by 2020, on the eve of the Summit, indirectly conceded the fact that they cannot be treated as part of the G77. The Copenhagen accord that came out in the early hours on 19 December 2009 was a deal between the United States, the BASIC (China, India, South Africa, and Brazil), and European Union countries. The remaining 164 nation-states were onlookers. Though not a legally binding instrument with concrete targets on emission reduction commitments, the Copenhagen Accord produced three major results: (a) it indirectly drew the emerging BASIC countries to the Annexure 1 fold; (b) it set up oversight measures to verify emissions by China and India; and (c) it announced the establishment of the Green Climate Fund as an exclusive operating financial mechanism of the UNFCCC.

Nevertheless the Copenhagen Summit was acrimonious and fractious. The manner in which the negotiating texts were prepared and the unexpected talk about both developed and developing countries shouldering mitigation responsibilities, shocked the developing countries belonging to the non–BASIC bloc.

The GCF has been an improvement over GEF for two reasons, namely, its efforts to leverage private sector investments for climate change activities and its efforts to de-risk investments in projects that seek both mitigation and adaptation outcomes.

The most important lesson that the Copenhagen Summit provided was that any enduring arrangement hinges on a global environmental financial architecture that facilitates transfer of low-carbon clean technologies to developing and emerging countries on fair and favourable terms.

Indeed four years before the Copenhagen Summit, there was a major effort to address the climate financing issue. Nicholas Stern was commissioned by the then British Prime Minister, Tony Blair, and his Chancellor of the Exchequer, Gordon Brown, to come up with an economic assessment of climate change. Stern, who did a brilliant study on the Palanpur village in India early in his career and served a stint in the top echelons of the World Bank, came out with the 'Stern Panel Review on Global Warming' in 2006.

Stern's report stated that if a 'Business-as-Usual Scenario' obtained, average annual temperatures could rise by 5°C from pre-industrial levels. The Stern Panel stated that if action were taken immediately, the cost of measures to avoid the worst impacts of climate change would amount to 1 per cent of GDP each year. The solutions proposed by the Panel included finding a 'common price of carbon' and internalizing the price/value into decision making. He advocated the use of carbon markets to discover and internalize carbon prices. The Stern Panel laid the onus of responsibility for climate change amelioration on the United States and other developed countries, while exhorting emerging economies such as India and China to also take up mitigation responsibilities. Stern's report has been attacked on different grounds. The issue on which he got it into problems with the US economists, namely Nordhaus, was on his proposal of low discount rate that he employed to deflate future costs. William Nordhaus (2007) stated that the alarming scenario painted by Stern was due to the near-zero discount rate combined with a specific utility function. This, according to Nordhaus, will not survive 'substitution of assumptions that are consistent with today's market-place real interest rates and savings rates' (2007). Dasgupta (2008) swerves onto a different path when he states that the 'earth system's deep non-linearities' render estimates of climatic parameters based on observations from the recent past unreliable for making forecasts about the state of the world at concentration levels of 560 ppm or more. Since global sequestration technologies may not 'bite in' as easily as one would imagine, humanity should invest a lot more in reducing climate change even more than the 2 per cent of the GDP of rich countries proposed by Stern (2006). Thus, Dasgupta implicitly supports the point that the most perfect model based on perfect or deductive rationality could break down under complications (Arthur 1994). Spash (2007) has a more philosophical point of critique. He sees the dominant discourses on climate change (the Stern Report included) as seeking to collapse values within a scheme of preference utilitarianism. As Spash says, by encapsulating ethical issues within a preference utilitarian matrix, the larger issues of inter-regional inequity are ignored. The debate goes on.

It is true that there were strong pressures on China (the world's largest CO2 emitter) and India to take on CO2 mitigation commitments at the Copenhagen Summit of 2009 as it was felt that mitigation action on the part of the two countries would be cost effective and reduce the marginal abatement costs for the developed world. Since economy-wide mitigation targets will not gain acceptance, more ingenious proposals emerged. Proposals on sectoral approaches to carbon/GHG mitigation had various shades. Some proposals envisaged extensions of CDMs with tighter baselines, certain others envisaged nationally appropriate mitigation actions that were non-credited, and still others talked about sector-wise emission commitments that could provide for trade and sectoral intensity targets—a combination of elements of sectoral crediting, non-binding targets and indexed targets. Yet another variant of the proposal called for actions where some but not all emission benefits are credited.

Whatever be their emphasis, proposals on sectoral approaches were problematic for developing countries. In the first place, sectoral crediting based on prices discovered by an imbalanced and volatile carbon market had the potential to be tricky. More fundamentally, sectoral credits that were not situated within the matrix of discussions on financial and technology transfer issues were philosophically flawed.

Indeed, progress of action on climate change depends on righting the historical wrongs through an appropriate global environmental financial system (Damodaran 2009).

Interestingly, in a subsequent report, Stern (2008) does talk of credible and demonstrable action on the part of developed countries to induce emerging countries to take up mitigation commitments.

As the global climate decision makers moved from Copenhagen to Paris (*en route* Durban, Dubai, Warsaw, and Lima), their thinking about responsibilities and obligations changed. Indeed, as will be explained in Chapter 11, the Paris Agreement of 2016 ensured that both developed and developing countries contributed to mitigation of carbon emissions through Nationally Determined Contributions (NDC). The race for proclaiming net zero targets gathered momentum in the post–Paris Agreement phase. At the Glasgow Summit in November 2021, India's Prime Minister proclaimed his country's commitment to net zero carbon emission targets by 2070. A year earlier, President Xi Jin Ping had announced China's goal of attaining net zero carbon emissions by 2060. With the United States also pledging to achieve net zero emission targets by 2050, the stage is set for a more determined action on the climate change front. The Glasgow Summit did not result in the major emitters agreeing to strong measures to achieve drastic emission reduction from 2030 onwards. Rather as Rob Stavins mentions even with updated NDCs at Glasgow, the world will cross the threshold of 2 degrees centigrade.[8] The Glasgow Conference also could not persuade major coal-using countries to phase out the problematic fossil fuel. Instead at India's bidding at the closing phases of the Summit, the final communique mentioned toned down the phrase to 'phase down'. On finance, despite major efforts to get developed countries to commit to the annual financing targets of $100 billion agreed to at the Copenhagen Summit, the target is not likely to be achieved before 2024. The ambition of having a much larger climate financing target was also not realized at Glasgow. This was despite India and other developing countries calling for $1 trillion package of climate financing from 2030 onwards to developing countries to achieve emission reductions by 2030.

On the vexatious issue of carbon markets, the Glasgow Summit did manage to secure an agreement regarding the rules of accounting under Article 6.2 of the Paris Agreement, with a view to avoiding double counting of credits arising from international carbon reduction projects involving developed countries (as buyers of credits) and developing countries (as sellers of these credits) (more on this in Chapter 11). However as Schneider (2021) observes, the carbon markets agreement at Glasgow has loopholes which allow countries with single-year targets to average emissions. Similarly as Schneider (2021) observes, issues pertaining to Article 6(4) could lead to large inflow of non-authorized credits of low or zero quality (Schneider 2021).

One of the other interesting developments at Glasgow has been the phenomenon of non legally binding side deals/agreements between a few member countries of the CoP. The methane deal initiated by the United States was a side agreement of considerable importance at Glasgow, since it required countries that had signed up to achieve 30 per cent reduction in methane emissions by 2030.

The larger challenge before the Paris Agreement Contracting Parties is to address ticklish issues regarding neutralizing the carbon emissions created by raw materials extracting projects in source countries. Poor countries which supply climate-friendly commodities to developed countries do not, by themselves enjoy the benefits of carbon emission reductions, despite producing materials that bring about emission reduction in sourcing countries. The Paris Agreement does not squarely address this matter and this requires 'Paris Agreement plus' initiatives in the near future (Damodaran 2021[9]). In the preceding few years both developed economies and emerging economies like India have realized the importance of tapping international green and climate bond markets for raising the capital stock of national financial and refinancing institutions, thereby enhancing their credit flows towards green energy projects that backstop carbon emissions and help these countries to attain their net zero carbon emission targets. Climate bonds issued by developing country agencies are based on the Climate Bonds Standard and Certification Scheme instituted by the Climate Bonds Initiative (CBI), an international, not-for-profit organization that has taken upon itself the mission of mobilizing the $100 trillion bond market for climate change solutions.[10]

Let us now look at the CBD, which, as has already been noted, evolved from the WCS of the IUCN. As mentioned earlier, the CBD incorporated many welcome features which were not there in the WCS and thereby provided a firm foundation for addressing the biodiversity conservation issue within the foundations of the PSNR framework. However, it is also to be noted that despite a focus on a country-driven programme focus, the CBD has not really taken off. The main reason for this is that its provisions on benefit sharing has been non-functional. The United States, which is yet to ratify the Convention, has had reservations about many aspects of the Convention including its benefit-sharing provisions. Developed countries which are members of the Convention have been uncomfortable with the idea of protecting traditional knowledge through the IPR route. Their opposition has persisted, despite support for traditional knowledge protection from the civil society movements in the North. The simple point is that IPRs and the entire corpus of jurisprudence associated with these rights are modernity-based in approach. Traditional knowledge therefore does not fit into the paradigm. Much has been written about the larger task of devising a sui generis legislation for the protection of traditional knowledge. However, there is precious little movement at the ground level.

The other issue of contention relating to the CBD has been about access regimes, which is a prerequisite for benefit sharing to work. The Convention outlines the significance of ensuring an ordered access regime based on the principle of prior informed consent (PIC). These provisos serve to condition benefit sharing. The United States has serious reservations about the whole idea of linking access to benefit sharing. For one, it is opposed to the idea that access of biological resources, which are products of nature, calls for benefit sharing. The argument by the countries of the 'North' is that if the natural resources accessed from developing countries are strategically subjected to some degree of value addition and processes on the part of the prospecting agent, then the entire credit for deriving a novel compound should go to the prospector.

There are many problems with this argument. In the first place, very few bio-prospecting ventures focus only on germ-plasm collection activities. Tapping traditional knowledge is also the objective of many bio-prospecting programmes. The advantage of traditional knowledge is that it plays a major role as a 'lead' that enables the accessing agent to focus his creation efforts on desired lines instead of wasting his time and resources on random screening efforts that may or may not yield promising compounds or molecules. A committee set up by the Parties to the Convention on Biodiversity (CBD COP) for drawing up regimes for access and benefit sharing, looked into the matter in detail and submitted their recommendations in the year 2001. The recommendations included a comprehensive set of guidelines on access and benefit sharing. The recommendations were placed before the COP for their consideration and endorsement. These guidelines, which were called the Bonn Guidelines (named after the place where the committee met to finalize the guidelines), advocated linkages between access and benefit sharing. It also called for a definitive system of royalty payment or profit sharing between the bio-prospectors and prospected communities/country, besides proposing guidelines for tapping and rewarding traditional knowledge. The Bonn Guidelines are categorical in that countries providing genetic resources need to be adequately rewarded for their contributions. However, being mere guidelines, they do not assume the status of a legal regime. Indeed, while the clauses of access and benefit sharing has been central to the CBD, it did not receive attention for a very long time. COP 8 of the CBD attempted to revive the Bonn Guidelines, which too had remained on paper. Delegates from different countries tried to approach the issue of access and benefit sharing in different ways. While developing countries such as India, Mexico, and other G-77 countries were for the establishment of an international access and benefit sharing regime developed countries including Canada and Australia (basically protagonists of liberal trade in agriculture) tried to block the proposal. Finally, after tough negotiations, COP 8 decided that an ad hoc open-ended working group on ABS would be set up which would submit its recommendations on

ABS before COP 10 so that there would be some kind of a framework in place by that time.

One of the contentious issues that was put up by developing countries was the addition of a requirement in the ABS guidelines that there should be a certificate of origin for nature-based products. Australia and developed countries did not want to pursue this, while countries such as Mexico wanted this element to be firmly put into the agreement. Finally, after considerable discussions it was decided that there should be an internationally recognized certificate of origin. The proposal at COP 8 to include representatives of private sector organizations in the meetings of the Subsidiary Body for Scientific and Technological Advice and the COP ran into rough weather as civil society groups stoutly resisted the idea. Despite this, the proposal was pushed through (Kumar 2006).

There were talks in the WTO forum regarding traditional knowledge and benefit sharing. The opponents of benefit sharing persisted with their argument that traditional knowledge cannot be rewarded with IP rights, since they are not novel and have been in the public domain for a long time. Also, opponents of benefit sharing arrangement state that the Bonn guidelines can only be location-specific and cannot be replicated on a universal scale. Civil society groups such as Rural Advancement Foundation International (RAFI), the Third World Network (TWN) marshalled evidence from various benefit-sharing arrangements in the world (such as the Kani tribal case in India) to suggest that benefit sharing is both desirable and workable. NGOs and civil society groups, which encourage benefit sharing with traditional knowledge repositories, also have a variant in thinking. Their argument is that where traditional knowledge is not rewarded or does not look like getting rewarded through the ABS mechanism, there should be a strong effort to have tighter regimes of access to biological resources in developing countries, particularly since the CBD has tried to link access with benefit sharing rather than dealing with the two issues independently (Damodaran 2003).

Notwithstanding tardy progress globally, the ABS mechanisms proceeded reasonably well in a few developing countries. Some developing countries went ahead and crafted national legislations in accordance with the principles of the Bonn guidelines. India's National Biodiversity Act 2002 anticipated the Bonn guidelines as it came into effect around the same time these guidelines were released.

The culmination of all these trends was the passage of the Nagoya Protocol on Access and Benefits Sharing that came into force in 2014 (more on this later).

The other controversial issue associated with the CBD has been the Bio-safety Protocol, which was signed in Cartagena in the year 2000. The Protocol's features have already been discussed. Here, focus is on the negotiation trajectory of the Bio-safety Protocol.

When the Bio-safety Protocol talks commenced in the mid 1990s, the thinking was to put in place a regime of strong controls over the flow of living modified organisms (LMOs) between nations. This kind of thinking had the support of international NGOs such as Greenpeace, the TWN, and RAFI amongst others. It also had the backing of a few articulate developing countries. What looked like a protocol with tight controls on transboundary movement of LMOs, turned out to be disappointing to groups which wanted strict controls to be put in place. The Miami group of countries, which was opposed to controls on transboundary movement of genetically modified materials such as food, feed, plant materials, and other related materials, threatened to block the negotiations on the Bio-safety Protocol. Towards the final stages of the protocol negotiations, it was clear that the Miami group would not join the protocol unless it was given significant concessions. These significant concessions had the effect of diluting the control regimes originally envisaged. Thus, the Miami group succeeded in exempting food and feedstuff containing LMOs, from the purview of the advanced informed agreement (AIA) clause of the Cartagena Protocol.

The advanced agreement clause of the Cartagena Protocol was very significant and in many ways tighter than the prior informed concerned concept enshrined in the Basel Convention on Transboundary Movement of Hazardous Wastes and the CBD. The AIA clause, by stipulating that an exporter has to notify the authority concerned in the importing country about the possibility of his consignments containing genetically modified material, gave an importing country a decisive say over the consignment. This was because, without the AIA, LMOs cannot be shipped to the importing country. This informed process, which was based on the principles of transparency and accountability was diluted by the Miami group in the Cartagena Protocol.

Another contentious issue that came up in relation to the Cartagena Protocol was about identification of LMOs inadvertently present in shipments. While African countries were keen to shift the burden of testing for accidental presence to exporting countries, developing countries like Brazil did not want this arrangement at all as they felt that it would adversely affect liberalization of trade. Either way, the complex documentation connected with testing procedures would not have helped importing countries to expeditiously take informed decisions.

However it needs to be noted that despite its biosafety angle, the Cartagena Protocol's fundamental goal is to ensure conservation of biological diversity. Though it is well documented that novel biotechnology products have the effect of eliminating traditional land races and traditional genetic resources that have been nurtured by farmers in developing countries and have a strong displacement effect, the same does not seem to be factored in Cartagena Protocol discussions. The manner in which the LMO issue was discussed in the Protocol betrayed a truncated view.

The Bio-safety Protocol is also caught between the twin stools of the conservation concerns reflected in the CBD and the trade concerns exemplified in the WTO Agreement. The Miami group countries understandably view the WTO as a good antidote against any tightened measures that may come from the Bio-safety Protocol. They preferred to pursue their agenda through the WTO. For instance, the WTO clearly states that 'like products' should be treated in a 'like manner'. Armed with this principle, proponents of free movement of genetically engineered or genetically modified materials argued that products containing LMOs or genetically modified organisms (GMOs) cannot be treated differently because they are 'like products' and are to be treated accordingly without discrimination. They thus invoke the provisions of the WTO to give strength to their arguments. This weakens the implementation of a sustainable development norm, implicit in the Cartagena Protocol.

Nevertheless, the Bio-safety Protocol bears the imprint of civil society groups. Strangely, there is considerable concern in developing countries about the impact of the protocol in strengthening national decision-making process. However, when it comes to those who subsist on imports of LMO products or those who have a reason to support the larger costs of biotechnology research all over the world, the thinking is that the AIA of the Cartagena Protocol would seriously affect the growth of biotechnology products.

Thus, while the biotech industry in India has, in the preceding few years, been lobbying for bringing down regulations on LMOs and GMOs by seeking to reduce the number of decision-making layers in the decision-making system, NGOs like the Green Foundation clearly argue that the multiple layers of the Bio-safety regulations in India are not only to be maintained but also strengthened with the association of civil societies and local communities in the decision-making process. Indeed, farmers who are the end users of the products associated with plant biotechnology such as Bt cotton, are a divided lot. Some are in favour of restrictions, and others are against them.

Issues relating to IPRs, traditional knowledge, and traditional communities, which appeared to be integrated and fused together as a negotiation cluster in CBD forums, do not seem to be playing the same role as far as the Biosafety Protocol is concerned. There are civil society groups and farmers which fight against the IPR implications of the Bio-safety Protocol. These sections are indifferent to sustainability issues. Others fight against the threat of LMOs and GMOs to biodiversity.

The case of Navbharat Ltd in Gujarat shows that there is a section of indigenous industry which is nationalistic in approach. The latter seeks the right to break the monopoly of foreign multinational corporations like Monsanto by refusing to honour the company's IPRs over Bt cotton. This school of thought looks at the issues of IPRs related to GMOs from an anti-IPR perspective. The unauthorized distribution of IP-protected seeds of Bt Cotton in Gujarat by Navbharat Ltd was projected as a challenge to patenting and IPR monopolies created by MNCs. Ostensibly, the seeds of Bt cotton were distributed to farmers in Gujarat not by Monsanto, the patent holder of Bt cotton. Monsanto's seeds was itself not cleared by the National Regulatory Authorities in India for commercial release. Navbharat Ltd fashioned itself as a Robin Hood which prided in its image as a crusader against IPR monopolies.

While conventional opponents of biotechnology products and genetically modified technology products in agriculture are opposed to these products on grounds of bio-safety and the displacement effects, their cause gets undermined by companies that focus their crusade against IPRs. On the other hand, the focus of the Parties to the Cartagena Protocol seems to be primarily on bio-safety.

There exist lobbies that strongly support the biotechnology revolution and IPRs associated with biotech products. These sections strongly argue for a more inclusive process of bio-safety regulations that involves the industry in the decision-making process. The Association of Biotechnology Enterprises of India (ABLE) has always argued and lobbied for advanced biotechnology research. It is quite natural for ABLE to support the cause of IPRs over novel biotech products.

ABLE has also been demanding a more inclusive and a less constricted regulatory process on bio-safety in the larger interests of sustainability in the country. The MoEF (now MoEF&CC), which has been the nodal point for implementing the bio-safety regulations, came up with a proposal to reduce its responsibility for regulating the commercial release of the genetically modified plant biotech products, by transferring the function to the Ministry of Agriculture and the Indian Council of Agriculture Research. There have been apprehensions that this would lead to a more relaxed regime of control over commercial releases of plant biotech products, given the major stake that Indian Agriculture Research Institute (the research arm for the ICAR), has in plant biotechnology research.

After much dithering in the 1990s, India agreed to the introduction of transgenic plants in its agricultural sector. In October 2009, approval was given by the Genetic Engineering Approval Committee for the commercial release of Bt Brinjal. This created a huge controversy on the ground that the potential contaminant effects of Bt Brinjal on natural germ-plasm and wild relatives of brinjal, were not assessed or made public. Despite all this resistance, India's march towards transgenic crops looks unstoppable. India is not the only country to undergo a change of heart from being a supporter of tight bio-safety control regime to one of tolerant indulgence. Brazil is also in the same boat. After a phase of strident opposition to genetically modified soyabean, Brazil did a volteface and decided to go for genetically modified crops. Brazil's flagship research arm, the 'Embrapa', has gone full stream into research on genetically modified crops. Thus, the pro-biotech stand of the Miami group is gaining more followers with time.

To sum up, biotechnology and its related products are there to stay. The CBD seems to be on a weaker wicket here, so is its Protocol. In spite the

Nagoya Protocol coming into existence, Access and Benefit Sharing will face roadblocks.

A paper entitled 'Competing Notions of Biodiversity' by Weizsacker (2004) mentions the amazing variety of stakeholders connected to bio-diversity issues. Weizsacker states that biodiversity issues have drawn the attention of a wide range of stakeholders with sharply differing view-points. This includes farmers and environmentalists who have the heart for whales and butterflies. There are many environmentalists who want to utilize biotech products for environmental rehabilitation of degraded lands. There are others who desire to have new (biotech), which prove to be handy as climate change sets in. Weizsacker's list also includes young people with sympathy for wild things. He lists biologists, genetic engin-eers, and companies who have a stake in projecting a greener image, and older people who want their grandchildren to feel happy with nature.

Weizsacker states that it is ironic that human beings who have con-tributed to the destruction of wild habitats, are centre stage as custo-dians of biodiversity. In Weizacker's words, it is a paradox that the 'foxes' (human beings) are asked to guard the chickens of biodiversity conser-vation and climate change. Weizsacker goes on to discuss how modern plant breeders, in their never ceasing quest for food security and undying enthusiasm for locating rare germ-plasm in the wild, have contributed to the disappearance of wild relatives and the wild germ-plasm from centres of conservation. He goes on to add that the concept of biodiversity has lost its moorings in terms of space, time, and context (2004, 124). Species have become numbers or are reduced to numbers instead of being valued for their unique role in preserving the functioning and well-being of a habitat. This, in turn, has led to the unfortunate trend of viewing substitu-tion of species as desirable and feasible (2004).

Weizsacker's more interesting point (2004, 125) is where he considers the biotechnology industry for creating conditions for the further loss of species. His obvious reference is to the use of biodiversity by the modern biotechnology industry to churn out products that act to deny space for the traditional raw materials from which they have been derived.

The fact that farmers in the developing world who provide the genetic resources are themselves forced to take the products of the biotechnology industry is supremely ironical. Weizsacker's notion can be further ex-tended to describe what is seen as a race for selling genetic resources. This is exactly what has happened in most of the developing countries which are caught by a bio-prospecting fever.

Weizsacker's paper is an extremely important contribution to understanding the tragedy that has befallen the cause of biodiversity conservation. The paper offers a major critique of the influence of modernity in the debates surrounding biodiversity conservation. However, there is a larger need for someone to explain why such situations and paradoxes occur. It needs to be noted that modernism combined with intense neoliberalism has caused many advocates of biodiversity to seek market-based solutions to environmental problems. This is precisely the reason why we have tried here to integrate the concepts of globalization with the global quest for sustainable development. The logic of globalization and neoliberalism require developing countries and their governments to take a hard look at the 'economic worth' of resources in terms of the laws of demand and supply.

Developing countries have been trading in agricultural commodities for a very long time. Right from the 1960s, primary commodity prices have been subject to bouts of cyclical price swings that have only served to impoverish peasants and traditional farmers. It is also a fact that the terms of trade for most of the primary commodities in the world had decisively swung against developing countries, which are now finding ways and means of getting around the problem through diversification of exports and the export market. The real issue in bio-prospecting is the desire to ensure that the green resources of developing countries get the prices that they deserve, and are not subjected to the tragedy of globally traded agricultural commodities such as coffee, tea, spices, and so on, which are faced with the whimsical ways of the global marketplace.

The Brundtland Commission Report was clearly beckoning present generations to uphold the interests of future generations. The key issue, which has not been addressed by the CBD and FCCC, is the value system that the world would like the future generations to be imbued with. Going by the predominant tendency of the globalized world, it is clear that the custodians of inter-generational equity or sustainable development are driven by the ideal of modernity. Hence, the kind of heritage or legacy they would bequeath to future generations would also be modernity-based products. On the other hand, if the postmodern forces of the globalized world are to have their stamp on future generations, they would imbue the former with postmodern ideas of sustainable development.

The Biodiversity Convention is interestingly poised here. It has traditional, modernity, and postmodern elements built into it. While the modernity element centres on the Bio-safety Protocol, the postmodern element is contained in the main Convention, particularly in the provisions associated with 'indigenous' and 'local' communities and ABS. The manner in which the modern biotechnology industry has emerged triumphant in recent times, indicates that the slanging match will end in favour of the world of modernity. It is quite likely that even developing countries, which talk the language of conservation, will shift their perspective and start viewing biological resources and their biodiversity-rich habitats as potential sources of commodification and revenues.

Thus, in the years to come, the Seed and Plant Varieties Protection legislations in different parts of the developing world, will, in all probability, be tilted in favour of new biological resources that are created by biotech labs, thereby relegating the 'traditional' and 'natural' resources to the background. Indeed the CBD itself may undergo change in this direction. Developed countries that are not comfortable with the CBD, would then see greater virtues in the Convention and would perhaps play a much greater role in the Convention affairs.

As matters rest today, the gulf between modernity and tradition as well as between modernity and postmodernity is deep, so much so that all efforts to reconcile the 'traditional' and the 'post-modern' with the 'modern' has proved to be futile. Thus efforts to incorporate traditional knowledge within the scheme of IPRs, and the demand for conceiving benefit sharing principles within the matrix of standard economic instruments of resource sharing, such as royalties and profits, have also failed. Rather, these efforts have been stoutly resisted by the forces of modernity which would not like the traditional or the postmodern sector to acquire any characteristic that has to do with modernity such as profits, sharing, and patents. If the traditional and postmodern elements adapt themselves to the laws of modernity and to the logic of neo-liberalism, the value systems that will be bequeathed to the next generation will be a more composite one, comprising of both modernity and traditionalism.

This brings us to the more basic point that globalization and the neo-liberal movements which weaken the role of the nation-state in the economy have the potential to obliterate the traditional and the post-modern sectors. While in the global commodity market-place today, large markets are swallowing local ones and rendering the role of state regulation superfluous, in the case of biological resources which is primary and nature-based, the effort to get the State to play a greater role in the emerging markets in genetic resources has made the industrial end users of these resources uneasy. The criticism about the Philippines regulations (as being over-restrictive) and the derisive remarks about 'green gold', which we mentioned earlier, are evidence of the uneasiness that industries have about developing countries seeking to monetize biological resources.

Trade, Environment, and Climate Change

Following the demise of the Cold War, liberalization of trade and free flow of capital services across borders became the realities of the new world. The WTO evolved under these circumstances. However, the 'environmental' face of globalization, as expressed through the Rio agreements sought to have a few checks and balances that went against the grain of free trade. This explains the logic of the trade and environment debate.

Even in the early part of the 1990s, there were a few environmental matters that global trade had to grapple with. These were not connected to the Rio agreements. Rather these issues date back to the pre-WTO days. The Shrimp-Turtle and the Tuna-Dolphin cases are prime examples.

However, the advent of MEAs does raise new challenges. To be able to understand these challenges, one has to explore how the process of international political and economic relations converge or diverge from the process of internationalization of environmental accords and agreements. A related issue for exploration, is the compatibility of the unipolar world with an international economic order which is based on free multilateral trade of goods, services, and investments. There is another important point concerning how the unipolar world and the logic of neo-liberalism, which has come in the wake of the economic globalization in the world, relate to international environmental agreements. Are these forces mutually supporting or are they pulling in different directions? In one shot, the answer could be that there is a fundamental tension between the rules of economic liberalism and the concerns reflected in MEAs. As we have noted elsewhere, though the WTO did not originally take well to environmental issues as reflected in a few adverse WTO dispute settlement body rulings, the tide has changed slightly in favour of the environment in recent times. However, none of the trade and environment matters that have reached the WTO dispute settlement body owe their origins to MEAs. Thus, though tensions are simmering between the WTO and the MEAs, it is unlikely that it will assume a flashpoint in the near future, unless the EU's Carbon Border Adjustment Mechanism (CBAM) scheduled for 2023 is challenged before the WTO dispute settlement body (more on the CBAM later).

The Doha Declaration [para. 31(iii)] mandated the WTO to negotiate 'reduction/elimination of tariff and non-tariff barriers to environmental goods and services'. Currently, the list of environmental goods submitted by WTO members includes hazardous wastes (relevant to the Basel Convention). Following the call of the Basel Convention Parties to strengthen co-operation between the Convention and the WTO, trade and environmental issues connected to hazardous substances have figured in the WTO forum in a major way. The discussions are not just about bringing down tariff barriers and NTBs in the movement of environmental goods but also in defining environmental goods in terms of their process and production methods. Following the emphasis of the Stern Panel Review on the potential contribution of trade liberalization on flows of clean technologies, there have been voices that argue about the need to smoothen the diffusion of climate mitigation technologies and goods across borders by removing tariff barriers and NTBs (ICTSD 2008). The introduction of technical standards (like Process and Production Methods or PPM standards) for tracking and lowering the carbon footprint in commodities could be one of the fallouts of the CBAM, once these initial proposals on reducing tariff and non-tariff barriers go through. As Martin Wolf rightly argues, the right to act against PPMs used elsewhere is not only an infringement of sovereignty but also a protectionist barrier.[11]

For a long time, the WTO has eschewed talk about the environment except in so far as it relates to Article 20(1) of the GATT. As far as the

MEAs are concerned, there are many developing countries which play an active role in the negotiations and seek to implement the Convention at the national level, but would not support ideas that will take them to the WTO machinery. But this situation could change if the health and life provisos of Article XX are linked to climate change impacts.

Another classic case relates to the Cartagena Protocol on Biosafety in relation to WTO-SPS (Sanitary and Phytosanitary) measures. Countries such as India, which have substantial export interest in agricultural commodities, would not like the former to dominate the latter. Interestingly, the idea of payment for ecosystem services (PES), which has gained currency with the World Bank and other multilateral institutions (discussed by us later), will not have much momentum unless it leads to capital and finance flows to developing countries. Although the WTO is keen to bring environmental services within its ambit, the Organization is ambivalent when it comes to ecosystem services.

Upscaling Local Environment Success

Let us move back to the operational issue of implementing a programme of global commons. There have been countless instances where natural resources have been successfully managed in different pockets of the world. Some of these success stories have been very well documented, highlighted, and disseminated as valuable use cases. There have also been discussions regarding the replicability of some of these use cases. There is one school of thought which says that success stories are location specific. It is argued that local instances of success are not replicable on a meso scale. When we talk of implementing a global commons project, the real point is to ensure that it succeeds in multiple socio-cultural contexts. This explains why global commons discourses do not percolate to the ground level.

Indeed international organizations such as the GEF have been trying to assess performance of some of the fund-supported pilot projects in different focal areas. The main criterion of performance assessment is the success of the project in optimizing global environmental benefits. This, unfortunately, is a narrow criterion of success measurement. In many cases, it will not explain why a given project clocks higher global environmental benefits. A GEF-supported project that merely looks to optimize global environmental benefits like CO_2 sequestration, will not be successful if there are no co-benefits accruing to local communities. However, if a global commons management project is effectively twined to existing local environment projects at the local and regional levels, the outcome could be different. Let us take the situation of Sukhomajri (Haryana) and Ralegan Siddhi (Ahmednagar). These are two outstanding cases of successfully implemented local natural resources initiatives. There has been some effort to document these cases but no effort to see whether a global commons project could be successfully implemented in these spots. Indeed, the key issue is whether the communities associated with the Ralegan Siddhi or Sukhomajri experiments can ever take up global environment projects and successfully integrate them into existing activities? It is important to speculate on this issue for two reasons. First, it enables the policy team at the GEF to assess the compatibility of global goods projects in a typical rural setting where strong local institutions have displayed stellar performance in resource management. Second, it yields insights on the institutional reasons why a GEF project gains acceptance (or non-acceptance) in vibrant local communities.

Thus the performance criteria laid down by global institutions such as the GEF do not have any meaning if they are not related to the socio-economic milieu in which GEF projects are rooted. Drawing an example of the Machakos experiment in Kenya, one sees that sound management of the environment can succeed even in a situation where human demographic pressures are high (Tiffen et al. 1994). Prior to the development intervention, it was predicted that the phenomenal increase in population in Machakos would starve people of their energy sources and seriously threaten their livelihoods. This was not the case, as subsequent events showed. Macahkos was successful because the Akamba farmers experienced enhancement of market opportunities, which in turn led to growth in export markets, creating thereby a greater ability to face droughts and food shortages and handle the horrors of civil war. But then, all this was made possible due to the ability of the administration to prevent breakdown of law and order. Strong local institutions and local systems of governance explained the success of Machakos (1994: 276).

The Machakos peasants systematically inched towards agricultural intensification not only through improved water and soil conservation measures but also by successfully undertaking a programme of reaching out land (especially the crown land) to the needy sections of farmers. This led to private investment crowding in, to profit from the growth in markets for the principal agricultural commodities. But the interesting feature of the Machakos case was that the Akamba farmers themselves took a lead role in the search for new technologies and new opportunities. The peasants of Akhamba adopted the plough without any official encouragement, quickly perceived the benefits of bench terraces in relation to horticulture crops, and also succeeded in drawing the support of local NGOs and knowledge groups for taking agriculture on modern lines (1994: 278–9). Provision of credit and community investments, direct interventions in agriculture by the government especially in the field of agricultural technologies, provisions for schools, and water—all these enablers helped the Machakos peasants to take off in a big way on to the trajectory of sustainable growth.

The Machakos experience was basically centred on the application of modern knowledge to a traditional economy with a huge population growth through adaptation and modulation and changes in the local institutions, which welcomed this kind of a change. By contrast, the instances of Sukhomajri and Ralegan Siddhi clearly indicate that the pattern of growth relied mainly on local resources of the village with very little interventions from outside. While it is not entirely logical to say that Ralegan Siddhi and Sukhomajri exclusively relied on traditional tools to solve their sustainability problems, it is a well-known fact that the reliance of the two communities on external inputs by way of both capital and technology was limited as compared to the Machakos model.

In economics, it is common to look at development from the point of view of technology and institutions. There have been various schools of thought that have looked at the role of institutions and technologies in development. Ester Boserup differs from Malthus when he argues that adoption of new technology is impelled by population growth and growth of labour. In a similar fashion, Hayami and Ruttan (1985) state that technological change which brings about disequilibrium is induced by changes in land, labour or fertilizer price ratios. However, this attracts scientists, administrators and inventors to the economy, who in turn contribute by way of inputs necessary for the growth of the local economy. The Hayami-Ruttan model is based on exogenous change agents. Julian Simon and Herman Kahn (1986) also see invention as a function of population growth and argue that the more the population growth, the greater is the scope for new inventions and improvements to contribute to new thought processes amongst people. The Simon and Boserup arguments are sanguine about population growth and its ability to spur new inventions and new technological adaptations and, therefore, put the population on a high growth trajectory. The Machakos story debunks neo-Malthusian theories. Nevertheless, it is a fact that the Akamba or the Machakos model has not been replicated in large parts of Africa, let alone in other parts of Kenya. The same is true of the Sukhomajri and Ralegan Siddhi examples from India. Analysts attribute the problem of non-replicability to the inability of the state to clone social institutions. They are, therefore, tempted to conclude that social institutions, social capital, and the ability to adapt and adjust form the reasons for certain local communities doing well in the management of natural resources. To a large extent, this argument has its merits.

Would global commons projects have succeeded in Sukhomajri or Ralegan Siddhi? In other words do these places welcome projects that seek to optimize global environmental benefits. The answer to these questions will depend whether such projects can elicit interest and commitment amongst local communities for the global conventions of climate change and biodiversity. As we have noted, the restoration story at Sukhomajri centred on re-vegetation of degraded lands, which in turn contributed to the improvement of the village's biomass economy by preventing soil and water erosion. Similar has been the case of Ralegan Siddhi, where depleted natural resources were revived through community initiatives. In the event of a global environmental benefit project being introduced in these areas, the GEF parameters of operational performance will operate. There is nothing intrinsically wrong with this approach. After all, the GEF is an international organization which has India and Kenya as members. But at the same time, it needs to be realized that the bulk of GEF projects are financed by resources that are provided by multilateral financial institutions such as the World Bank, UNDP, and bilateral donors of the developed world. These sources contribute funds to be deployed on projects that optimize global environmental benefits. This criteria will certainly be not welcomed by local communities.

The second problem arises from the fact that a GEF project under-values local efforts. Let us take the hypothetical situation of a climate change mitigation project being taken up in Sukhomajri village. The fact that this village has done considerable amount of work to ensure that soil and water conservation measures have been improved is known to all. This has led to an improvement in crop productivity and income opportunities. However, from the viewpoint of the GEF mechanism, this work would not be considered as contributing to global environmental benefit.

So where does this leave us?

A global commons programme that solely measures global environmental benefits can only serve to increase the divide between the global and local worlds. There are countless local communities in the world which contribute to desertification control, climate change mitigation, and the conservation of biological diversity without realizing that they contribute to global environmental benefits as well. The custodians of global commons projects would however tend to negate these self-driven efforts in their effort to look for 'additionality'. There is further effort on the part of the proponents of global projects to show that global environmental benefits can only come about in a local area through infusion of modern technology. Local interventions of relevance to climate change redressal, biodiversity conservation and land amelioration based on traditional techniques, are not given any value.

There are two important priorities as far as developing countries are concerned. When it comes to the phenomenon of economic and social globalization, developing countries should be insulated from the shocking effects of rapid movement of capital and goods across borders that can derail their economies and disturb their ability to look after their citizens. On the other hand, when it comes to the global commons, the most important issue is the reform of global institutions which have tried to address the problem of global commons. The reforms should facilitate involvement of local communities by seeking to involve them in the conservation of global commons in a manner which befits their capabilities, traditions, and ideas. In other words, the system of delineating and separating global environmental benefits from national environment and community benefits needs to be strongly avoided in order to induce local communities contribute to the process in a better manner.

To sum up, this chapter surveys and analyses the genesis of global environmental process in the world commencing with the Stockholm Summit of 1972. The negotiations connected with global environmental conventions, though contentious, have not attempted to address the fundamental limitation of these Conventions, viz, of not being able to produce tangible ground-level impacts that improve the lot of local communities. It is argued that the main problem with the global environment conventions (with their implicit instrumentalism) is that their goals do not synergize with the development aspirations of local communities. By contrast, the Geographical Indications regimes prescribed by WTO TRIPS has succeeded at the local level as evidenced by the case of Darjeeling Tea. The story of Darjeeling tea holds vital lessons to the world of environmental agreements.

8

Policies for the Environment

The Story of India

India's entry into environment protection policies and laws can be traced to the 1970s against the backdrop of growing awareness in the world about environmental problems. India's policy and legal frameworks to address environmental problems paid close attention to national development priorities. By the late 1980s, India participated in international debates and discussions on global commons including climate, biodiversity, and desertification. India's policy framework on environment management has been in existence for nearly 50 years.

India's quest for environmental protection gained greater currency in the days following the UN Conference on Human Environment of 1972. India's forest legislation has been older, by comparison, as it can be traced to the nineteenth and twentieth centuries when the country was under colonial rule. India's wildlife-related legislations also date back to the colonial period.

In the year 1972, India's Parliament enacted the Wildlife Protection Act. Two years later, Parliament enacted 'The Water (Prevention and Control of Pollution) Act, 1974' with a view to preventing different forms of water pollution from industrial and municipal sources. In the ensuing years, a string of pollution control-related organizations was established in India to implement the 1974 Act. These assumed the shape of the Central and the State Pollution Control Boards. These boards were given powers under the 1974 Act to enforce water pollution control laws. Standards were laid down under the Act to set standards/limits on effluent generation. Efforts were made to get units generating 'trade effluents' to comply with these standards. While water pollution from large industrial units were regulated in this manner during the 1970s, the

India, Climate Change, and The Global Commons. A. Damodaran, Oxford University Press. © A. Damodaran 2024.
DOI: 10.1093/oso/9780192899828.003.0008

large corpus of small-scale industries, municipalities, and Panchayat Raj Institutions (PRIs) which were in charge of public water sources, were let off the hook.

In 1981, the Government of India came out with another legislation—this time to control air pollution. The Act was entitled Air (Prevention and Control of Pollution) Act 1981. The objective of the Act was to prevent and manage air pollution in different airsheds in terms of established standards.

During the same period, an important legislation, entitled the Forest Conservation Act of 1980 was passed by the Parliament. The objective of the legislation was to prevent diversion of forest lands in India for non-forestry purposes such as construction of dams, thermal power plants, industrial units, and other commercial ventures. The passage of the Forest Conservation Act was also prompted by grassroots environmental movements which sprouted in different parts of the country (including the sensitive Uttar Pradesh Hills, now part of the Uttarakhand state) to protest against indiscriminate felling of trees in the name of development projects and mining operations. By comparison, the Air Act was not provoked by any grassroots environmental movement. It was a legislation meant to combat industry-created air pollution problems, which were assuming increasing proportions in India in the late 1970s.

The underlying structure of governance envisaged by the Forest Conservation Act, the Air Act, and the Water Pollution Act was different. While the Forest Conservation Act basically tried to bring the federal or central government to assume control over decisions regarding diversion of forests for industrial and infrastructure projects, the purpose of the Air Act was to control and abate pollution for improved environmental welfare. The same was true for the Water Act. While the Air and the Water Acts empowered the Pollution Control Board (PCB) to implement their provisions, the Forest Conservation Act significantly shifted the onus of forest conservation from the state government to the union government. This move was enabled by the 42nd amendment to the Constitution of India which placed the subjects of forests and environment protection in concurrent lists of powers, thus enabling the Central/Federal Government to pass legislation concerning forests and environment. The Central Government has the powers to override State legislations that are not in tune with the Central legislation.

Though structures were put in place and organizations established to handle the responsibilities laid down under the Water Act, the Air Act, and the Forest Conservation Act, their effectiveness left much to be desired. Authorities and organizations in charge of air and water pollution and forest conservation could not really implement the legislation to the desired extent, mainly due to political, social, and economic pressures. Such pressures in the case of Air and Water Acts were of local nature. The problem with the Forest Conservation Act was that the pressure to soften the implementation of the Act came from State Governments, which were anxious to locate development projects in forest areas. When Indira Gandhi was India's Prime Minister it was relatively easy for the central/federal government to enforce its decisions as her party held power at the Centre and the States. During those days many non-forestry projects were disallowed and where permitted, compensatory safeguards by way of afforestation and environmental safety guidelines were laid down to be observed by the project authorities. However, in the late 1990s, the situation altered. It became easier to divert forest lands for non-forestry purposes.

The problem with the two legislations in the realm of environment protection, namely the Water and the Air Acts, was that they were 'media-specific' (confined to 'air' or 'water') and did not therefore provide for comprehensive protection of the environment as a whole. Effluents which carried toxic wastes were converted from the liquid to solid state and discharged on land, thereby beating both the air and water acts. This could not be prevented as the media-specific legislations did not provide for any scope for multimedia management.

The Bhopal gas tragedy in 1985 drastically changed the situation. Two important factors were thrown up by the Bhopal gas tragedy—first was the need to regulate hazardous substances arising from different origins and second was the need to adopt multimedia measures of protection. Thus, the Environment Protection Act of 1986, which came out from the shadow of the Bhopal gas tragedy, corrected the infirmities of the Water and the Air Acts and brought under its rubric, all elements of the environment (air, water, and land) for comprehensive protection. However, one of the most interesting features of the omnibus Environment Protection Act was its governance system that provided for the dominance of the Central (Union) Government and its designated authorities with powers to implement the Act in different parts of the country. The Environment Protection Act of 1986 brought in comprehensive rules on hazardous wastes and bio-engineered organisms including regulations of GMOs and also shifted the focus of environmental management decisively in newer directions, particularly towards multimedia environmental and toxic wastes management, which was in tune with the development context of India in the 1980s.

The provisos of the Environment Protection Act, shifted the locus of control on environmental protection from Pollution Control Boards to District Administration Authorities. However, powers to close industrial units and grant consent for functioning of industrial units or other establishments continued to be vested with the State Pollution Control Board (SPCB).

In the year 1988, the next landmark initiative was taken up in India in the shape of the National Forest Policy, which superseded the National Forest Policy of 1954. Whatever its specific features, the fundamental philosophical shift effected by the National Forest Policy 1988, was its increased focus on conservation, its respect for village community rights, tribal mores and customs, and its focus on reducing exploitation of forests even where it was necessary for meeting development needs. As discussed elsewhere, the National Forest Policy in 1988 inspired the famous JFM initiative of the central government for inclusive governance of forests by associating tribal communities and other local village communities in the management of degraded forests. In June 1990, the Federal Ministry of Environment and Forests introduced a set of guidelines for inclusion of village communities in the administration of forests. States were requested to pass similar resolutions and orders to ensure that village communities were actively involved in managing forests and were provided incentives for their role by way of access to non-timber forest produce.

The implementation record of Joint Forest Management (JFM) in its first fifteen years offers interesting lessons. As Damodaran and Engel (2003) state, JFM signified a subtle shift in the property rights regime over forests. While existing old forestry legislation of the British period enacted in 1865, 1878, and 1927 postulate strict state control over forests and curtail local rights, the JFM process in some ways re-opened community rights which were foreclosed or settled under different forest settlement systems for reserved forests. However, unlike the Forest Conservation Act, where the central government took the key decisions, in the case of JFM, the central government chose to exercise its moral suasion powers over state governments through guidelines, advisory inputs, and financial provisions. This was due to the fact that the JFM process did not have the force of a legislation. It was merely a set of guidelines that relied on the spirit of voluntariness on the part of the implementing agencies.

The difference between JFM and the Forest Conservation Act is that while the latter seeks to disallow land-use change in forest areas, the former seeks to alter the structure of property rights (not ownership rights) and governance systems of forests by including local communities in management. In the absence of any serious effort to overturn the existing Indian Forest Act and the corresponding State Forest Acts, the JFM had to entirely rely on voluntary action on the part of state governments. This accounts for the relatively poor implementation of JFM as compared to the Forest Conservation Acts. In the case of the Forest Conservation Act, one logical reason for its success was that though existing Forest Acts (namely, Indian Forest Act and the State Forest Acts) sought protection of forests, they did not deal with impact of land-use changes on forests. This was the legislative gap that the Forest Conservation Act sought to bridge.

States such as Andhra Pradesh and West Bengal have done reasonably well in not only increasing the area of forests coming under JFM practices, but also in setting up village forest committees consisting of local communities that shared the produce arising from conservation activities with these communities. Many states, in east, south, and north, have not achieved satisfactory results in implementing the spirit of the JFM concept. Another limitation of the JFM concept has been that it has not taken off in protected areas such as wildlife sanctuaries and national parks coming under the purview of the Wildlife Protection Act of 1972. Despite grave incidents involving poaching of tigers, the philosophy of protected areas management, continues to be basically guided by the concept of singular stakeholdership that relies solely on the state apparatus for its implementation (Damodaran 1998).

Taking advantage of the strong provisos of the Wildlife (Protection) Act 1972, many states effectively stonewall the implementation of the Joint Forest Management initiative in wildlife national parks and sanctuaries.

The most noteworthy legislation enacted by India was the National Biodiversity Act 2002 (NBA 2002), which brought in provisos for access and benefit sharing in respect of biological resources occurring in the country. The NBA 2002 created National Biodiversity Authority (NBA) at the Federal level, the State Biodiversity Authorities at the state level, and the Biodiversity Management Committees (BMCs) at the local levels which undertook measures for conservation of biodiversity and traditional knowledge in their jurisdiction (Damodaran 2003). The NBA regulates access and benefit sharing at the national level, by providing previous approval to overseas agencies that desire to access and collect biomaterials and traditional knowledge in India, while the State Biodiversity Authorities provide previous approvals for national entities desiring to access biomaterials and traditional knowledge from forests and other public habitats (Damodaran 2003). The NBA and the BMCs levy fees on entities that desire to access biomaterials and traditional knowledge. These assume the form of access and benefit sharing fees (by the NBA) and collection fees (by the BMCs). In addition, the NBA also charges a levy by way of royalties on entities that manage to develop and patent new products on the basis of biomaterials and traditional knowledge accessed/collected from India (Damodaran 2003).

India's NBA 2002 has significantly influenced the formulation of the 'Nagoya Protocol on Access to Genetic Resources and Equitable Sharing of Benefits' (hereafter the Nagoya Protocol), which was signed by the Parties to the Convention on Biological Diversity in 2010. The protocol came into force in the year 2014.

The NBA 2002 is unique as it seeks to collapse the CBD and the Nagoya Protocol into one single legal instrument. It unifies the access and benefit sharing functions with conservation functions, thereby avoiding truncation of bio-conservation functions at the national level.

In the field of environment protection, much of the legislative and policy work relating to multimedia management and hazardous waste management were over in India in the early 1990s. However, the issues of GMOs and transboundary movement of hazardous wastes continued to fester. The onset of the biotechnology revolution in the world since the 1980s and the serious efforts made at introducing GM products into India by national entities and overseas companies such as Monsanto, pushed the biosafety issues to the fore in the country, at the turn of the century.

The other matter which has become significant in recent times relates to hazardous wastes emanating from transboundary sources. Though the government has been adopting a pro-industry stance, the activism directed against dismantling of the French ship Clemenceu, served to raise awareness about the deleterious consequences of ship breaking on workers involved.

In general, the most interesting point is that while truncation of environmental regulations is the hard reality at the international level, the same does not seem to be the case in India as far as laws and regulations are concerned. In India, treatment of hazardous substances and regulation of GMOs are both handled within the framework of the Environment Protection Act of 1986, while at the international level, these are handled by two distinct Conventions. At the international level, while transboundary movement of LMOs and biologically hazardous substances (including invasive alien species and GMOs) are handled by the Cartagena Protocol and under the provisions of the WTO Agreement on Sanitary and Phytosanitary Measures, the entire gamut of the environmental issues related to GMOs and hazardous substances is handled under the provisions of the Environment Protection Act of 1986 in India. In short, truncation of environmental regulations is more at the global level than at the national and the local levels. This reflects the hyper-specialized instrumentality associated with global conventions.

India does not have a national legislation on climate change. The reason for this may be that India has not taken up mandatory obligations for the mitigation of GHG emissions under the UNFCCC. Even the Paris Agreement does not have any time bound targets for mitigation. The NDCs embody voluntarily chosen targets. Indeed, there are many developed countries which also that do not have legislations on climate change.

The story of the evolution of India's environmental policy and legislation serves to bring out the fact that implementation of decentralization measures has been patchy. Nevertheless, India's policy framework on environmental protection provides enough scope for promoting diverse and localized approaches to implementing global environmental issues. The larger task is to secure effective implementation of policies and programmes by effectively communicating the objectives of the MEAs to local communities and eliciting their interest in implementing global commons projects. For the latter to happen, it is important that global commons projects in local areas are in tune with local aspirations.

9

Leaders, Markets, and Values

A widely held perception is that Malthus and his disciples have been prophets of doom. Ecologists have for a long time been airing neo-Malthusian fears of a resource-scarce world which will spell the end of human civilization. The neo-Malthusian despair has been the staple story of many ecologists for a long time. However, a few neo-Malthusian ecologists do see light at the end of the tunnel. Lester Brown falls in this category. Though Brown talks about depleting natural resources in the world, he also sees interesting possibilities of the world attaining the goal of sustainable development. Brown has alternatives and blueprints for what he considers to be the challenge of ecological sustainability. Brown has been the President for the Earth Policy Institute, a non-profit body that he founded. He has been the founder President of the World Watch Institute for nearly a quarter century. He has been an influential thinker on environmental matters for years. Brown's notions about environmental sustainable development have been significantly influential. His 'State of Environment Reports' flags the most critical environmental problems of the world in a succinct manner.

Lester Brown's book, *Plan B: Rescuing a Planet under Stress and a Civilization under Trouble* (2003), actually commences with a lucid description of 'Plan A', which is 'business as usual'. Here, Brown talks about resource scarcities. He feels that without improving productivity of land and water and cutting down on carbon emissions by half, the world has no hope of surviving. He follows this up with his 'Plan B', which is a blueprint for sustainable development in the light of the problem that he sees. Brown sees world population increase as a devastating proposition and suggests its stabilization through suitable policy measures and other related initiatives. As he says, it is extremely important to break down or deflate the bubble of world population growth, which, at 7.5 billion,

India, Climate Change, and The Global Commons. A. Damodaran, Oxford University Press. © A. Damodaran 2024.
DOI: 10.1093/oso/9780192899828.003.0009

can induce economic breakdown of countries with larger population increase rates.

Brown's theory is straightforward—large populations consume natural capital assets at an accelerated pace and one needs to have alternatives to handle the problems (Brown 2003, 200). His solution is the creation of what he terms 'an honest market'. Brown cites the case of the flooding of the Yangtze River basin in China, which prompted the Chinese government in 1998 to ban tree cutting in the catchments. He commends the Chinese government for their quick and sharp understanding that the flood control service provided by forests is more important than the timber value of its trees. Another interesting example which Brown cites is that of the Amazon rainforests and its role in protecting water cycles in Brazil. Here, he cites Philip Fearnside, an Amazon specialist and researcher, to drive home the point that the agriculturally-prominent, south-central part of Brazil, depends on water that is recycled inland through Amazon rainforests (2003, 210). If the Amazon is, therefore, converted into cattle pasture, there will be very little rainfall to support agriculture (2003, 210).

Indeed Brown laments the woeful situation in the world where polluting activities and the brutal exploitation of energy resources take place without costs. Brown proceeds to give examples from different parts of the world to argue that ecological services rendered by forests and other ecosystems ought to be rewarded.

Brown's Plan B also conveys his liking for markets. He assumes that markets have to exist, but with greater transparency and honesty in declaring ecological truths. His eloquent plea for an honest market is nothing new for economists. An economist would define honest markets as those that internalize ecological costs. However, certain complementary steps are required for markets to function honestly. It is equally necessary that national income statements of the country concerned, should provide accurate information regarding depreciation of natural resources brought about by industrialization and economic growth.

Perhaps the most interesting aspect of Brown's description of the 'honest market' is based on the following remark of Oystein Dahle, the former vice-president of Exxon of Norway and the North Sea: 'Socialism collapsed because it did not allow the market to tell the economic truth.

Capitalism may collapse because it does not allow it to tell the ecological truth' (2003, 210).

Though well said, the problem with Dahle's statement is that socialism never allowed markets to function in the first place, let alone allow it to tell the economic truth. Second, his assumption that capitalism may also collapse if it does not allow the market to tell the ecological truth may not hold water. It is well known that the concept of efficient markets is not defined in terms of environmental parameters. This is because markets do not internalize resources that defy a price tag. At the same time, there are many resources in the world that do not enter markets by choice. These are consumed by local communities. Such subsistence-economies, which are 'honest', exist along with the not-so-honest capitalist markets. So, despite siding with Lester Brown and his interesting thesis on honest markets, I must state that markets are not meant to be 'honest' or 'dishonest'. They are basically meant to 'convey', 'transmit', or function as an institution in order to enable people to discover prices.

In practical terms, markets form a price relaying machinery. In case natural resources do not enter the pricing mechanism offered by markets, environmental economists say advocate the solution of non-market valuation, which relies on the tools of 'stated' and 'revealed' preference to estimate the values of such resources. Apart from the limitations pointed out in the previous chapter, the tragedy of stated preference and revealed preference methods is not that they do not give numbers but that they may not give numbers that are really amenable to the pricing philosophy in the marketplace. The reason is that market prices must be standardized to be pervasive. This perforce calls for the commoditization of goods and services. The benefits of a wildlife reserve or a natural park as worked out by non-market valuation tools, cannot be market the price of the reserve. Prices differ from the value of a resource as they keep varying from consumer to consumer, depending on her/his utility preferences. This means that a resource like forests is not amenable to standardization and pricing. There is also a related issue about the ethics of subjecting traditional knowledge or biological resources to a commodified system of price determination.

Nevertheless, markets can be more useful in handling the environmental 'bads' of water and air pollution. Though command and control systems have been set up in various countries to ensure that environmental 'bads' are subjected to rigid controls, the fact is that on account of various inefficiencies associated with such systems (such as transaction costs, rent seeking, and inefficiencies in supervision) these authoritarian systems have been discredited. The greater casualty of this is the negative image that this has given to nation-states in their efforts to handle environmental problems. This strengthens the call for reducing the policy space of nation-states. As mentioned earlier, had nation-states succeeded in implementing command and control systems with the active participation of civil societies and NGOs, the story would have been different. The struggles that a local self government in Kerala had to wage to get a notoriously polluting industrial unit such as the Gwalior Rayons Factory closed down shows that determined local communities can utilize the support of command-and-control systems to win the war against environmental damage. Authorities of the State are empowered to shut down factories, which carry huge social costs by way of pollution that damages the lives of local communities. Of course, such action could be interpreted by conventional development protagonists as the anti-development characteristic of environmental regulations.

Lester Brown is also very enthusiastic about the role of taxes in carrying out environmental correction and this is in partly due to his belief in honest markets. He feels that taxes could correct some of the distorted flow of resources towards environmentally disturbing activities. He also advocates shifting subsidies away from activities that are harmful to the environment, while at the same time stating that such bold steps require countries to be run by enlightened leaders. He admires Tony Blair for his bold statement that developed countries have to achieve a 60 per cent reduction in carbon emissions by 2050, which stood in marked contrast to the shrill anti-Kyoto Protocol campaign unleashed by the Bush Administration in the United States. Lester Brown also compliments Gordon Brown, who, as UK's Chancellor of the Exchequer, introducing a new Marshall Plan for redressing climate change. Brown gets effusive about Jacques Chirac, the former French President. He considers Chirac to be a progressive when it comes to environmental issues, despite his political conservatism. Brown's list of greats also includes the CEO of Daimler Chrysler, Jurgen Schrempp, who supported Gordon Brown's Marshall Plan.

Another exemplary leader for Lester Brown is Gro Harlem Brundtland, who headed the WCED and later on led the World Health Organization (WHO) to great heights. Brown states that basic universal health care in developing countries will require substantial donor grants. According to Brown, in case funding were substantial, it would be possible to cure the world of AIDS, tuberculosis, and malaria. Interestingly, Brown also dwells on great leaders who have been evangelists of sustainable development and poverty eradication in the United States. Brown's examples include Senator George McGovern and Robert Dole, who helped to bring school lunches for the poor. The McGovern-Dole 'International Food for Education and Child Nutrition Act' of 2002 is rated by Brown as one of the greatest gestures which enabled poor children in the United States to have access to good nutrition. Brown says that, if such initiatives were carried to different parts of the world, one could succeed in draining the swamplands of hunger and despair and solve some of the greatest problems that the world faces (Brown, 2003). Lester Brown has great faith in the ability of institutions like the World Bank to guide the fortunes of the world in areas such as education and health (Brown, 2003).

The problem with Lester Brown's approach is that he imagines that great leaders in executive positions could make a big impact on environmental management programmes across the world. It is Brown's 'realpolitik' sense that gets him to see the role of statesmen and political executives as central to the agenda of sustainable development. His approach is based on the doctrine of realism, as it centres on strong states, strong leaders, and strong will. In other words, Lester Brown tries to situate the quest for sustainable development firmly through the centres of power that run states in the world. Brown may be perversely right. He perhaps realizes that the power equation in the world being what it is—the North dominating the South—solutions proposed by politicians from the North can gain traction. Look at the Paris Agreement on Climate Change of 2015/16, an accord which compelled countries from the South to accept mitigation action, something they had tooth and nail opposed for over twenty-one years in the UNFCCC forums.

In some ways, enlightened leaders of the North are creations of the radical posturing of the statesmen of the South. The G-77 countries have for years blamed the unsustainable lifestyles of the North for climate change. This has generated a benign response from some of the enlightened statesmen of the North, who seem to be telling their people, 'please control your lifestyles and give a little bit more than what you are giving now to address the problems of hunger, AIDS, and epidemics that you see in the South'. This approach is patronizing. It debunks the capabilities of developing countries to find a solution to their own problems by creating sound market systems and good governance structures within their boundaries. Developing countries such as India and Brazil can benefit from policies that seek to develop indigenous technologies and value natural resources, but many other developing countries may or may not succeed in this direction. Given the long and brutal colonial history of African states, it is natural for the big powers of today to be concerned about their well-being. But they do not realize that Africa, if left alone, has the potential to charter its own course, which may not be in the larger interests of power equations that prevail in the world. There are obvious signs of African renaissance as shown in some of the outstanding example of Machakos in Kenya. Another noteworthy success achieved by African countries is in the realm of biodiversity regulations.

Indeed, Lester Brown has ignored successful cases from Tamil Nadu (India) related to free mid-day meals provided to students from needy families. M.G. Ramachandran, the former Chief Minister of Tamil Nadu, who introduced the scheme for the poor in the State of Tamil Nadu in India in the 1980s, was way ahead of McGovern and Dole!

Standing in contrast to Brown's optimism about the North are Ophuls and Boyan's notion that 'all is well with the American system' (Ophuls and Boyan 2005, 191–206). The authors are neo-Malthusian in their approach and consider that scarcity of natural resources, particularly energy resources, is basically posing a big problem to the United States. However, they argue that there is very little scope for environmentally sustainable decisions to be made in the US political system since the US society has been completely predicated on growth and abundance and, therefore, is not able to cope with the era of ecological scarcity (2005, 202). The authors say that though the American political system worked very well for 200 years, many of its past virtues have become irrelevant because the system has not been planned to handle scarcity (2005). In the final analysis, the authors question the premises of the existing politics, which is based on growth and abundance, and state that there is a need for a new politics where the brilliant notion of equality and freedom so eloquently bought out by Alexis de Tocqueville is placed at centre stage.

Lester Brown's thesis is thus made to stand on its head by Ophuls and Boyan. It is obvious that a neo-Malthusian perspective does not mean standard approaches towards political systems or solutions. While Brown is full of hope that enlightened leaders and senators of the North can make a big difference to the sustainable development story of the world in the twenty-first century, Ophuls and Boyan argue that enlightened leadership is not the issue. The issue for them is that of a new paradigm of political values which recognizes or tries to situate the notion of democracy and its equality and freedom within the premise of growing ecological scarcity and insecurity. One sees a similar trend elsewhere in the world when it comes to approaches related to sustainable development and industrial societies (Torgerson 2005, 509–24).

Despite their differences, Lester Brown and Ophuls and Boyan share a few things in common. Both believe that the problems in the world can be solved if there are changes in the manner the United States thinks about the world and to this extent they are again close to the old notion that the solution to environmental problems of the world lies with the United States or the countries of the North. To this extent, the neo-Malthusian school suffers from the common limitation of relying too much on the asymmetrical power relationships and its faith in the ability of the power to solve the world's pressing environmental problems.

It is one of the most interesting twists of irony that although Tony Blair and George Bush saw eye to eye on issues such as the invasion of Iraq and also took positions which were identical in terms of ideological and economic policies, they sharply differed on climate change. In the Gleneagles G-8 Summit held in 2005, Tony Blair proudly declared that climate change is probably, in the long term, the single most important issue we face as a global community. At Gleneagles, the G-8 leaders signed a communique, which included a political statement and an action plan covering climate change, clean energy, and sustainable development. Though essentially a G-8 Summit which made a major effort to give a big push to the climate change agenda, the Summit also saw the heads of governments of Brazil, Mexico, South Africa, China, and India being invited for a separate session on outreach issues like the new paradigm for international cooperation. George W. Bush, who participated in the

Gleneagles Summit, had to alter his traditional opposition to the Kyoto Protocol and also agree to the formulation that a new FCCC would become the framework for stricter implementation of emission reductions through cleaner technologies and energy-efficient measures for GHG emissions, which, according to the Gleneagles Summit, had to slow, peak, and reverse. Perhaps one reason why Tony Blair highlighted the Climate Change Convention in the G-8 Summit was the accession of Russia to the Convention, which had accelerated the pitch for both UK and the United States to act on climate change. For some time, Vladimir Putin has been demonstrating that the huge Russian oil and gas reserves can be a great political tool. By joining the Kyoto Protocol, Russia, it was reckoned, would enjoy the early bird benefits in the climate change regime as well. This was not great news for Blair and Bush.

A decade later, Barack Obama as the 44th President of the United States took up the cause of climate change in earnest and pushed the world to sign the Paris Agreement only to be stymied by his fellow countryman and successor in office—Donald Trump!

The real point is not even this. While the POPS Convention was primarily driven by civil society groups, the climate change initiatives have essentially come from the heads of the States of the G-8. In other words, the pattern and methods of addressing, discussing, and overcoming the roadblocks to the implementation of different MEAs have been different for various reasons. However, what is noteworthy is the fact that the twenty-first-century conventions like POPS are driven today by NGOs and civil society groups, something that could not be dreamt of in the 1990s.

To sum up, an optimistic view places faith in leaders and honest markets. A pessimistic view would state that leaders preserve their turf, while markets tend to distort. The truth lies in between. Values, we know, are subjective and hence contentious. The solution is for each of the elements to function well by transcending sectarian and distortionary tendencies. We need the presence of international and national institutions that uphold the virtue of broad consensus, thereby ensuring a bright future for the Global Commons.

10

Compensating for Lost Resources

Does It Work?

Noted anthologies on 'Environmental Thought' carry influential writings that question existing narratives on development. Textbooks on environmental science, economics, and politics also give considerable space to alternative discourses that question entrenched viewpoints on development. A standard anthology or textbook on the environment starts on a pessimistic note about the environmental problems in the world. The neo-Malthusian streak in environmental discourses conveys the dangers of resource scarcities and unsustainable resource consumption. Some anthologies and textbooks go a step forward to explore measures that can be taken by world organizations and nation-states to address the twin crises of resource depletion and degradation.

A case in point is the anthology of John S. Dryzek and David Schlosberg (2005). The anthology starts on a neo-Malthusian note but goes on to counterpoise neo-Malthusianism with the anti-Malthusian arguments of Julian Simon and others, which view the earth as offering infinite possibilities for growth and consumption. The anthology covers green movements and ecological democracy. On the whole, the volume concludes on a positive note.

Even books on environmental economics commence with chapters dealing with the issues of scarcity and exhaustible resources before proceeding to consider methods by which economic instruments can be used to address scarcity issues. Books such as *Environmental Economics: A Reader* (1993) by Anil Markandya and *Introduction to Environmental Economics* (2001) by Nick Hanley, J.F. Shogren, and Ben White also take a closer look at policies and regulations that govern environmental resources.

India, Climate Change, and The Global Commons. A. Damodaran, Oxford University Press. © A. Damodaran 2024.
DOI: 10.1093/oso/9780192899828.003.0010

However, there are very few books which talk about the contribution of civil society in influencing allocation of environmental resources and services by public authorities. My obvious reference is to the failure of environmental economics textbooks to look into the role played by environmental movements such as the Narmada Bachao Andolan in influencing the conventional cost benefit estimates of development and commercial projects.

Political, institutional, and environmental movements have played a major role in reversing the trend of under-assessed costs in conventional environmental impact assessment reports. They have contributed to the discovery of unmeasured social costs and succeeded in integrating them in project analysis and appraisal documents. This has in some ways led to just compensatory measures. The initial assessments of the development protagonists indicated that the Narmada Dam would displace forests. However, by supposing that this loss, could be made up by greening an equivalent area of wastelands, the initial assessment exercise reduced the problem posed by the project to one of forest loss. The larger livelihood implications of the project did not figure in the initial assessment exercises. Had it not been for environmental and social movements like the Narmada Bachao Andolan, such assessments would have dominated decision making.

The issues raised by the Narmada Bachao Andolan compelled the State Governments concerned (namely Madhya Pradesh and Gujarat) to provide for rehabilitation costs in project budgets. The volume of funds provided for rehabilitation was, however, nowhere close to the actual requirements. Perhaps a better articulation of needs by the affected communities would have helped in improving their rehabilitation.

Environmental economics has developed tools and techniques to value non-market resources. The most pervasive tools used include contingent valuation and willingness to pay approaches. The corollary of willingness to pay is 'willingness to accept compensation. The latter is relevant to people who lose (or are likely to lose) their property or habitats, either on account of development/infrastructure projects or on account of environmental calamities.

Application of these tools calls for literacy on the part of those who are required to reveal or state their preferences regarding an environmental resource. Apart from this limitation, there are other problems with these tools. In the first place, the focus of these valuation tools is on individual utility functions rather than on collective/community utility functions. Secondly, not all probable victims of development projects may settle for compensation, even if the package is attractive.

Interestingly, while environmental economics concentrates on valuation of natural resources in a big way, the discipline does not factor in the roles of civil society and environmental movements in influencing the fate of development projects.

One of the concomitants of such an approach is that environmental issues are viewed in a top-down manner. A case in point is the fashionable trend of conflating the environment–economy debate with the larger debate between the votaries of market liberalism and supporters of state-driven economies. The Narmada Bachao Andolan by placing emphasis on community livelihoods, provided an alternative way of viewing the economy–environment debate.

It is conventional to suppose that Governments in developing countries resort to command-and-control systems to accelerate economic development. Neo-liberal protagonists criticize such systems on the ground that it breeds excessive state power, corruption, and rent-seeking. Nevertheless, there are instances where Governments in developing countries have taken up the cause of local communities in their struggle against resource-grabbing corporate entities. A case in point is the support extended by the local government body to the tribals of Plachimada in their fight against Coca-Cola's bottling plant which was badly polluting the water streams in the village.

Payment for Ecosystem Services

The issue of compensating or incentivizing stakeholders of natural ecosystems for their role in providing fundamental ecological services has been complicated. In recent years, ecological services, provided by the common property resources, have engaged the attention of both multilateral financial institutions (such as the World Bank) and bilateral donor agencies, though nothing much appears to have been accomplished. A closer look at the initiative of the World Bank's work in the area of environmental economics and indicators clearly highlights the importance that the Bank accords to environmental valuations and payments for environmental services.[1] The Bank argues that natural resources which provide multiple utilities to human communities are not conserved. Similarly, landowners do not receive any compensation for the environmental services provided by them, which includes their role in preventing catastrophic floods or landslides in low-lying areas. As a result, they take sub-optimal decisions on the use of their land resources which undermines the community value of their holdings. Therefore, it is argued that measures need to be taken up to ensure that landowners are compensated for the invisible environmental services that they generate. The World Bank believes that by integrating or incorporating the scheme of payment for environmental services in its projects, it will become possible for local communities to be adequately compensated for their efforts in conserving natural resources.

The World Bank's programme accordingly focused on:

1. Identification and quantification of environmental services;
2. charging service users through appropriate payment systems;
3. paying service providers and specifying the methodologies of paying them; and
4. creating an appropriate institutional framework for making payments.

The Bank has initiated projects in different parts of the world in order to compensate stakeholders for the environmental or ecological services nurtured by them. A notable project has been the eco-markets project undertaken by the Bank in Costa Rica.[2] The eco-market project in Costa Rica, which started in June 2000, aimed to develop markets and compensate private sector providers for the environmental services generated by them. The focus of the project was mainly in the forestry sector. The project aimed to reverse the trend of deforestation in Costa Rica, by valuing potential benefits lost by local communities on account of deforestation. The project also sought to explore how privately provided environmental services could be compensated. The strategy of the project was to support the Costa Rican government's environmental services programme, with the long-term objective of building a financing mechanism that could render the programme effective and efficient. The Bank also proposed to explore different financing options to ensure that stakeholders providing environmental services were adequately compensated. In order to mobilize money for providing compensation to the affected stakeholders, the project recommended fiscal instruments such as fuel tax and watershed services taxes. The other major component of the project was capacity building of local communities and stakeholders.

Another World Bank-assisted project worthy of mention is the 'El Salvador Environmental Services Project'. The project had two components. The first one dealt with the establishment of a functioning environmental services fund from which payments were disbursed in lieu of ecological services lost on account of development/infrastructure projects. The second component of the project aimed to improve institutional capabilities and strengthen the capacity of all market participants to develop an environmental services market. The project focussed on reversing land degradation, deforestation, and arresting the conversion of forestlands into agricultural lands. Thus the thrust of the project was on restorative measures in areas where land degradation occurred. Several pilot mechanisms were initiated to implement the scheme in priority watersheds. Funding was provided for a variety of activities which included agro-forestry, reforestation, afforestation, and sustainable agricultural production.

The strategic dimension of the concept of 'Payment for Ecosystem Services' needs to be appreciated in a different context. The World Bank's 'environmental economics and indicators programme aimed to effect major improvements in policy perceptions about environmental services. However, if we delve deeper into the content of the programme (including the projects that the Bank launched in El Salvador and Costa Rica), it is seen that the basic focus of both projects was on the generation of global environmental services expected from local ecosystems. Thus the focus of the Costa Rica project was on improving the flow of private services for conserving biological diversity, and achieving GHG mitigation. Similarly, the El Salvador project focussed on carbon sequestration, climate change, and biodiversity conservation—activities which are conducive to conserving global commons. In terms of its strategic loci, the World Bank's Environmental Services and Indicators Project had an interesting multi-spectral approach. The structure of the project was unique since it attempted to combine the elements of the economics, global commons, and local institutions. Thus, the Bank sought to integrate three major international programmes in this project, namely the MDGs about which we have referred to earlier, the Corporate Advocacy Priorities (CAP), and Global Public Goods (GPGs). By integrating the three important programmes of the twenty-first century in its environmental services and indicators project, the World Bank sought to ensure that environmental services were situated firmly within the matrix of the MDGs and sustainable corporate governance parameters, while at the same time giving due regard to the goals embodied in the biodiversity and climate change conventions.

Thus the 'compensation for environmental services' project transcended the traditional development assistance approach of the World Bank. By suggesting measures by which environmental services could be paid for by the private and public sectors, the World Bank attempted to twine the process of economic reforms around the goal of sustainable development. This approach was appreciated by the host countries.

In case the concept of the scheme of payment for environmental services is implemented in its true spirit in developing countries, it could lead to far-reaching changes in the economic policies of these countries. The initiative could also have far-reaching implications for developing countries by way of (a) improving taxation regimes, (b) streamlining existing systems of resource flows through public finance systems, (c) altering the pattern of financial flows between the central and provincial governments, (d) instituting fiscal incentives to assist private environmental service providers, and (e) mobilizing foreign direct investment (FDI) for sectors that provide environmental services.

At the national level, the impact of an internationally supported 'payment for ecological services' project, would be phenomenal. National environmental policies would be reframed and reformulated. Major changes would be brought in, by way of improvements in EIA procedures and conservation legislations. Thus Environmental Impact Assessments (EIA) procedures and conservation legislations would not only deal with the prospects and consequences or diversion of ecosystems or habitats for development projects, but also work out appropriate compensation packages for environmental service providers.

Indeed compensatory measures are part of the decision-making system in India when it comes to natural resources like forests.

Let us take a hypothetical example of a tribal community in India inhabiting a forest area. One way by which we can assess the role of this community in the conservation of the forest ecosystem, is to explore how well the community has contributed to the protection of traditional land-use systems and natural biota in their habitat.

Similarly, in case a mining project or irrigation reservoir is proposed to be taken up in a tribal inhabited forest area in India, the present regulatory mechanism requires the forest bureaucracy to assess the implications of the project on the Forest Conservation Act of 1980. The most important exercise is to make a clear assessment of the loss of forests entailed by the project. The forest bureaucracy submits its assessment to the Federal Government for a decision. The Federal Government has the option to consult the affected tribal communities in order to obtain their inputs through public hearings. Based on different inputs received, the government would either disallow the project or convey its approval. If the decision is to go ahead with the project, a compensatory reforestation plan is required to be undertaken by the project authorities along with other measures such as a robust rehabilitation plan for the affected local communities.

Does the scheme of compensating for lost ecological services fit into the scheme of things described above?

The concept of PES is based on the idea that a community which can estimate the environmental services provided by their habitats or ecosystems, is in a better position to influence decisions regarding their habitats. However, tribals or local communities seldom calculate environmental or ecological benefits in terms of the toolkits prescribed by environmental economists. There are a few other complications which arise when it comes to estimating compensation for habitat loss. Many tribals consider 'displacement' from their habitats as unthinkable. They view their habitats not as forests but as living spaces that are inseparable from their cultural values and lifestyles. For a typical tribal community in India, the cost of displacement is immeasurable and literally speaking, priceless. Normal rehabilitation measures that involve payments or payouts would not compensate for the loss of their cultural identity. A tribal community, if given an option to decide on the issue, would surely seek abandonment of the project rather than seek compensation. This possibility is not addressed by PES schemes.

The discipline of environmental economics, which harps on the tool of Willingness to Accept Compensation (WTAC) for lost environmental services, suffers from limitations. An individual's willingness to accept compensation may differ from that of his fellow community member. One of the reasons for this is that each individual's initial wealth endowment plays a critical role in determining her/his desired compensation. Since tribals have low levels of wealth endowment, a member of a tribal community may not quote a high compensation figure, even if she is pushed to indicate her WTAC.

What compounds the problem is that tribal communities of India are not fully integrated into the cash economy. Indeed, many food-gathering tribes of India live outside the pale of organized markets. They do not seek to exchange their goods and services in the marketplace. Consequently, compensation packages for marginalized communities are worked out by Government functionaries.

In short, monetized compensation packages for environmental support services, will not bring justice to tribal communities.

There are compensation awarding juries, which consider environmental goods to be of 'zero market value' or to be of no consequence. An important case in point is an article by Cymie R. Payne (2005), a lawyer by profession regarding the issue of compensation arising from Iraq's invasion of Kuwait in 1990–1, which came up before the United Nations Compensation Commission (UNCC). The Commission in its fifth and final report of June 2005, awarded compensation for the environmental and public health damages caused by Iraq's invasion and occupation of Kuwait in 1990–1. The Commission held that Iraq's invasion of Kuwait had created both direct damages (to Kuwait) as well as collateral damage in neighbouring countries. Thus Jordan, which had to accept many refugees from Kuwait, faced a massive destruction of its rangelands. The other state which had to bear the collateral damage of Iraq's invasion was Saudi Arabia, which also had to suffer on account of refugee movements from Kuwait. Kuwait was, of course, the primary victim of the war. The main issue before the panel was that Kuwait, Jordan, and Saudi Arabia had suffered ecological and human life damages which had to be compensated by Iraq. Indeed, an extreme case of collateral damage was presented by Iran when it stated that the oil well fires that were set by the retreating Iraqi troops had caused major damage to its cultural properties. Thus, when the UNCC started looking into the issue, it received a number of written submissions regarding environmental and human health-related damages that needed to be compensated. There were many other contentious issues that came up before the Commission. One such issue was whether a natural resource with zero commercial value needed to be compensated. The Commission decided that compensation should be awarded even if it was not a commercially-used natural resource. The second important issue that came up before the Panel was whether pure environmental damages need to be compensated, particularly in the light of certain international conventions on civil liability excluding pure environmental damages from the ambit of compensation. The UNCC went into the matter and clearly ruled that pure environmental damages too need to be compensated. However, the Commission laid down that such damages had to be estimated in an objective manner.

The interesting result that came out of the Panel deliberation was that one must adopt evidence-based approaches when it came to assessing the costs of damage. Iran's contention that the fumes of oil wells, which were put on fire by the retreating Iraqi troops had affected its heritage sites, was not accepted by the Commission on the ground that Iran was not able to provide sufficient evidence to link the fumes with the damage inflicted on the country's cultural heritage sites. The Commission also examined, what Cymie Payne refers to as 'compensatory alternatives'. The Commission stated that valuation measures were too big a problem to be confined to simple compensatory payment awards. The UNCC, therefore, relied on the cost of compensatory alternatives as a surrogate for deciding upon compensation payments. Another important result of the UNCC deliberations was the finding that the cost of monitoring and medical screening also needs to be reimbursed by the perpetrator of the damages.

The above example clearly brings out the fact that both compensation assessment and compensation awards are extremely tricky matters that have to be carefully handled. Where local communities are primary victims and need to be provided compensation for being displaced by projects, care should be taken to ensure that assessment of possible damage is properly done. Similarly, where local communities are required to be rewarded for the ecosystem services they have helped to preserve, nuanced approaches are called to determine what is due to them. This reinforces our earlier point that preference eliciting methods like contingent valuation do not hold much relevance for local communities suffering from low income and wealth levels. In such countries, where local communities are on bare subsistence regimes, a better approach would be to adopt damage assessment exercises based on physical and cultural parameters. By contrast, where relatively affluent private corporate entities are involved, willingness to accept compensation can be a promising tool, since these stakeholders have a fairly clear estimate of the compensation package they require or are willing to accept.

Way back, Gordon (1954) noted that an asset that is everyone's property is, in fact, no one's property and, therefore, it is in the common interest to restrict its use. The issue was how to restrict the use of such resources. In the earlier stages of its evolution, the discipline of environmental economics placed major emphasis on privatizing common property resources in the larger interests of unifying the costs and benefits of using a common property resource on a single agent who would be the sole owner and sole consumer of the resource. This, in effect, meant that the tragedy of the commons could be avoided by creating private property rights. However, over time, as countless instances of collective action came to the attention of scholars, the perspective changed. Today, large sections of environmental economists have discarded the theory of privatization of common property resources as a way out of the free-rider problem affecting the commons. The focus is on how and under what circumstances, collective action can be brought in to resolve the tragedy of commons. As Ostrom (2000) states: 'Instead of pure pessimism or pure optimism ... the picture requires further work to explain why some contextual variables enhance cooperation while others discourage it'. There is a compelling reason to suppose that incentives like payment for ecosystem services can be a major incentive for communities to cooperate in managing common property resources. The issue is how to work out appropriate incentive packages.

As we discussed earlier, despite multiple success stories of sustainable common property regimes by local communities, we still struggle to estimate the monetary value of ecosystem services. We need to move from the office rooms of decision makers and set up improved systems for mapping preferences of 'money-illiterate' or 'cash-deficient' primary stakeholders, to arrive at robust systems of valuation of environmental resources and services. Such an approach would encourage the over-whelming presence of local community preferences in exercises that seek to estimate monetary values for ecological services.

11

The Local Impacts of Multilateral Environmental Agreements

The UNFCCC, CBD, and The Basel Convention

Hannah Arendt's idea of instrumentalism can be charmingly seductive to those who are baffled by the Kafkaesque ways of governments and transnational public institutions. Instrumentalism defeats the intrinsic purpose of an activity through processes, procedures, and monitoring systems that have been set up to achieve the purpose. Arendt (1958) analyses why labour and work get into an instrumental mode. Work is a matter of constructing artefacts that last or endure over time; however, more importantly, labour is an economic activity that enables human beings to interact with nature. For Arendt, speech is recognizable and action is conduct that is meaningful and inventive. The revelatory quality of speech and action comes to the fore when people are neither 'for' nor 'against' others. As instrumentalism removes the intrinsic nature of a phenomenon, Arendt highlights the importance of advancing non-instrumentalist approaches (1958, 510). Torgerson (2005), who has analysed the concept of instrumentalism in the context of green political processes, mentions how Arendt is criticized for maintaining non-instrumental positions about politics and why the distinctive dimension about her position is not appreciated by her critics. Rather, Arendt's triad—namely 'labour', 'work', and 'action'—suggests the way of retaining the uniqueness of a concept.

Using Arendt's formulation, Torgerson goes on to discuss the three dimensions of green politics, viz., 'functional', 'constitutive', and 'performative' green politics. Functional green politics shows a face of reform and inclination to work within established systems to make them more economically rational. Here, the focus is on public policy changes aimed at

India, Climate Change, and The Global Commons. A. Damodaran, Oxford University Press. © A. Damodaran 2024.
DOI: 10.1093/oso/9780192899828.003.0011

making an advanced industrial society ecologically rational. Functional green politics also displays a constitutive inclination and appeals to notions such as sustainable development and economic mobilization, but in a way that is sharply rejected by radical greens (2005). In Torgerson's second category comes 'constitutive green politics' where the accent is on social transformation. Constitutive politics usually presents a radical face, which is concerned with qualitative change which ultimately induces transformation of socio-economic systems, cultures, and human identities (2005, 504). The problem with constitutive green politics is that it does not have a coherent programme for radical change.

The third school of thought, called 'performative green politics,' argues that green politics needs to make sense outside of itself. As Torgerson explains, at times, performative green politics aims to project comic gestures (such as Green Peace marches), which provide a humorous dimension. According to him, the important point about these marches is not their antics, but their message that the seriousness of the officialdom is a mask that hides its irrationality. Performative green politics involves evocative measures and practical symbolisms, which harp on the performative element (2005, 528–9). Based on these three concepts, Torgenson goes on to define the green public sphere as a clearly defined institution, which has emerged from the changing patterns of interconnection among the places where green discourse is practised (2005, 520). However, Torgenson says that the boundaries of the green public sphere are inclined to be contested as they are permeable and indeterminate. Indeed, for Torgenson, 'green performative politics' is the only phenomenon that is interested in the 'intrinsic value' of politics.

The basic problem with Multilateral Environmental Agreements (MEAs) such as the UN Framework Convention on Climate Change (UNFCCC), the Convention on Biological Diversity (CBD), the Basel Convention, and the Rotterdam Convention is that they have not focused on the fundamental philosophy for which the conventions exist, namely ensuring equity and fairness when it comes to their operations. These ideals get displaced by 'instrumentalism'. To understand why instrumentality is not desirable for global environmental resources, one has to take a deeper look at the essence of the concepts of equity and fairness in relation to MEAs.

The Convention on Biological Diversity 1992

The two cardinal principles that guide the CBD are fairness and equity. The CBD was signed at the UNCED by 150 heads of states. The convention, which came into force in 1994, has 196 states as its members. The United States is not a member of the convention.

The CBD defines biodiversity as 'the variability among living organisms from all sources, including inter alia, terrestrial, marine, and other aquatic ecosystems and the ecological complexes of which they are a part; this includes diversity within species and between species.'[1] The three key elements of the CBD are (a) conservation of biological diversity, (b) the sustainable use of the components of biological diversity, and (c) fair and equitable sharing of the benefits arising out of the utilization of genetic resources. The biosafety dimensions of biodiversity conservation are associated with the first two elements.

The Nagoya Protocol on Access to Genetic Resources and the Fair and Equitable Sharing of Benefits' is associated with the third element of the CBD, viz., 'fair and equitable sharing of the benefits'. The Nagoya Protocol came into force in 2014 and has 92 members. The CBD principles of fairness and equity are best exemplified in the operational principles of access and benefit sharing enshrined in the Nagoya Protocol.

The CBD and the Nagoya Protocol seek to empower bio-resource-providing countries with the mechanism of Prior Informed Consent (PIC) in order to enable these countries to realize a fair share in the benefits accruing to resource-accessing agents from the commercial development of the resources they have collected from these countries. In many countries, PIC or equivalent access-regulating measures are exercised by national governments through access and benefit-sharing contracts that comprise of material transfer agreements. These contracts are entered with bio-resource seeking overseas entities on mutually agreed terms. Certain countries have empowered lower government formations to exercise these rights. Thus, countries such as the Philippines provide for a local PIC regime for access and benefit sharing. In contrast, India has gone in for a 'previous approval principle' whereby the federal or central government plays a decisive role in regulating access to germ-plasm by overseas entities. This is to ensure that benefit-sharing arrangements are properly worked out.[2] The CBD does provide prospectors of biodiversity with the opportunity to develop improved, value-added products that have commercial significance. However, the condition is that the benefits flowing from the developed commercial products would be shared with people or entities that provide these resources. Nevertheless, it needs to be appreciated that the CBD also implicitly recognizes the right of the rest of humankind to access bio-resources and develop commercial products. Thus the equity and fairness principles underlying the Biodiversity Convention do not negate the right of transnational bio-prospectors in accessing and developing bio-resources and traditional knowledge located in custodian countries. As a matter of fact, the primary function of the Nagoya Protocol is as much to ensure that there is legal certainty, clarity, and transparency in access measures laid down by bio-resource-providing countries.

The mission of the CBD has been to correct historical wrongs associated with colonial transfer of genetic resources from developing to developed countries. When Vasco da Gama landed in Calicut, India, in 1492, his mission was to seek spices from India. Subsequent sea voyages undertaken by other explorers to other countries or continents resulted in the free transfer of valuable and rare agricultural crops and plant materials from these countries or continents to voyage-sponsoring countries. This 'historical wrong' had to be corrected. However, some economists from developed countries consider the benefit-sharing provisions of the CBD to be problematic and inherently not acceptable. In their scheme of things, traditional knowledge and bio-resources which have been obtained from developing countries, do not deserve to be paid any more than what it costs to access them. These experts are swayed by the principles underlying the nature of IPR (intellectual property right) regimes that had evolved in the wake of the Paris Convention on Protection of Industrial Property of 1883. In terms of the Paris Convention and the subsequent corpus of intellectual property law that evolved in the developed world, any product which does not fulfil the criteria of novelty, non-obviousness or industrial application cannot be protected by patents. All the same, IPR laws enable IPR holders to have monopoly control over commercialization, marketing, and sale of the invented products or processes. One logical corollary of the arguments against benefit sharing is that any knowledge, which is traditional and old, or any biological resource that is considered to be a bounty of nature, cannot be treated as a product that can qualify for any IPR. However, any new product which is developed from these traditional or dated products is novel, has an application, and is thus eligible for the grant of a patent.

In terms of the IPR paradigm, bio-resources are like any other ordinary raw materials that enter a regular production system. The focus is on conferring monopoly rights by rewarding novelty and value addition attempted by an inventor through exclusive production, marketing, or licensing rights.

The World Trade Organisation-Trade Related Intellectual Property Rights (WTO-TRIPS) of 1994, which came into force two years after the Biodiversity Convention was signed, has sought to strengthen IPR regimes all over the world (barring minor exceptions and flexibilities by way of the provisions of compulsory licensing and parallel imports). In the wake of the opposition to the WTO-TRIPS Agreement voiced by developing countries, NGOs, and civil society groups, there was an effort to review the impacts of IPRs. The WTO set up a Committee on Trade and Environment in 1996, with the mandate to look at the entire gamut of trade and environment issues, which included IPRs. The committee could not come out with an approach that harmoniously reconciled trade, environment, and IPRs.

What is clear is that the CBD's benefit-sharing principle goes against the monopoly rights sought to be conferred by IPR laws.

While traditional economic organizations struggle to hold on against the onslaught of IP regimes, the IT industry has witnessed a successful struggle against the monopolistic grip of IPRs. Civil society and NGO groups, led by the Free Software Foundation, have come out with strong movements that have focused on open-source software systems. Today, IT companies such as Microsoft, IBM, and Oracle which have advocated proprietary technologies and strong patent regimes for protecting strong software and ICT technologies, face tough competition from the open-source movement that promises to make software available free for development applications in return for a license agreement to comply with the common pool characteristics of the open-source software. In essence, this meant that those who access open-source software could improve upon products and processes and contribute the improved product back to the common pool. Though in the initial stages, the open-source movement was seen as a revolt on the fringes led by mavericks like Richard Stallman, the kind of problems Microsoft faced in China with its IPR-based proprietary products, prompted the open-source movement to go a step further and promote their products in the government sector. As a result, the open-source movement has now reached a stage where companies which believed in proprietary IPR technologies are themselves trying to contribute a great portion of their developed software into a common pool after a phase of exclusive use. Today, the situation is that while the open-source movement has taken off in the cutting-edge IT sector, the same world is not willing to put new products developed from bio-resources and traditional knowledge in the public domain. Rather, the demand of the industry is to treat traditional knowledge and germ-plasm as 'open-source' resources.

Though the right of innovating and coming up with improved products has been successfully applied in the case of software and other ICT products, the same has not taken off in the drugs and pharmaceuticals sectors. As life-saving materials, 'drugs' are still under the proprietary control of the so-called innovators. Indeed, even with COVID-19, AIDS and related diseases reaching epidemic and pandemic proportions, companies that have discovered vaccines and essential medicines have been reluctant to unconditionally supply these medicines to poorer countries. This is true of the COVID-19 vaccines developed by Pfizer Inc. and Moderna Therapeutics. This also explains why developing countries like India and South Africa had submitted a proposal in October 2020 to the TRIPS Council for the waiver of IPRs on vaccines, COVID-19 test kits, and PPE kits for a period of three years.

The dimensions of equity and fairness that one discerns in the case of the ICT sector is different from the dimensions of equity and fairness laid down by the CBD and the Nagoya Protocol. A few analysts advocate the notion of open-source mode to be applied to bio-resources. The idea is to highlight the fact that being part of commons, they should not be appropriated for private use without prior permission of its custodians, namely local or tribal communities. These analysts argued that even if improvements are effected on these resources, the end-products should be fed back into the domain of the commons. However, the logic as far as the drugs and pharmaceuticals sector is concerned is that the basic raw materials, which are traditional and/or occur naturally, need to be made available freely, although the final products developed by the industry need to be protected by patents.

There is a flaw in trying to mechanically apply the open-source concept in the software segment to the bio-resources sector. For one thing, the ICT industry is based on continual and incremental innovations, unlike in the case of the drug and pharmaceutical industry where the proclaimed focus of innovation is on radical improvements to existing drugs. The second point is that the beneficiaries of open-source movement in the ICT industry do not stand on the same pedestal as beneficiaries of traditional resources. While companies in the ICT sector that benefit from open-source mode are largely those that produce application software, in the case of biological diversity, the beneficiaries of open-source movement are plant-breeding companies that look for unique germplasm for producing new plant products. Farmers or tribal communities who provide bio-resources to these companies do not benefit from open-source approaches. Similarly, the beneficiaries of a possible open-source movement in the drug and the pharmaceutical industry would be drug manufacturers who produce drugs using improved processes, which are better than traditional medicines available in the market. Even where the provisions of compulsory licensing are invoked by countries, the beneficiaries are generic drug manufacturers. As the cases from Burkina Faso, Malawi, and South Africa demonstrate, it is mostly private generic drug manufacturers of other countries that have been the primary beneficiaries of compulsory licensing regimes invoked under the provisos of the WTO-TRIPS.

CBD: Post-2010 Developments

In the tenth Session of the COP held in Aichi in Japan in October 2010, the member countries of the CBD adopted a list of 20 biodiversity targets popularly referred to as the 'Aichi Biodiversity Targets' (ABTs). The idea behind adopting the targets was to sharpen the focus of the convention on key focal themes. The Aichi targets included prevention of biodiversity loss, prevention of pollution that causes biodiversity destruction, mainstreaming biodiversity in development plans and programmes and awareness about biodiversity, ensuring sustainable production and consumption, creating conditions for fair and equitable access to benefits, safeguarding ecosystems (including agriculture, aquaculture, forestry, and coral reefs ecosystems) and protection of species (including fishes and invertebrates) and genetic diversity.[3] The Aichi Biodiversity Targets targeted the protection of 17 per cent of terrestrial and inland waters and 10 per cent of coastal and marine areas for protection. It also harped on action against invasive alien species.

The ABT succeeded in terms of targets connected to the protection of protected areas and threatened species. The most important element of the ABT was the emphasis on resource mobilization to ensure attainment of other targets spelt out in the ABTs. Thanks to research inputs provided by 'The Economics of Ecosystems and Biodiversity' (TEEB) and the 'Wealth Accounting and Valuation of Ecosystem Services' (WAVES) projects, a sharper system of valuing biodiversity was employed by the CBD to assess the challenges of resource mobilization. Two high-level panel reports established by the CBD undertook global assessment of costs required to meet the ABT based on the valuation estimates arising from the TEEB and WAVES projects. Simultaneously, efforts were afoot to reorient and calculate public investments made by countries on core and ancillary activities of relevance to biodiversity conservation. These were based on methodologies developed by Damodaran (2012).[4]

The birth of the United Nations Development Programme (UNDP)-sponsored Biofin Project in 2012 was successful in introducing new accounting practices and methodological frameworks to delineate flow of budgetary and non-budgetary resources towards biodiversity conservation in CBD member countries.[5]

Though many countries have robust systems in place to assess the flow of resources to biodiversity conservation, there are significant gaps between mobilized funds and those required for implementing the ABT.

The first high-level panel on Global Assessment of Resources for Implementing the Strategic Plan for Biodiversity 2011–2020 (HLP 1) in their report presented an estimate of the global costs of meeting the Aichi Biodiversity Targets by 2020. The panel estimated funds required to implement the ABT could range between US$130 billion and US$440 billion per year.[6] The panel, however, noted that the actual flow of financial resources was not more than US$52 billion.

The Post-2020 Global Biodiversity Framework

With the time horizon of the ABT concluding in 2020, the CBD initiated steps to formulate a post-2020 Global Biodiversity Framework (GBF) with a longer time horizon that extends to 2050, with certain intermediate targets slated for attainment in 2030.[7] In terms of priorities, the framework does not differ from ABT. Indeed, goals such as conservation of freshwater, marine and terrestrial ecosystems, avoidance of increase in the threatened species list, enhancement of genetic diversity and access and benefit sharing specified in the draft framework, are not new. However, by mentioning the link between development programmes associated with nutrition, safe drinking water, and climate change goals set in the Paris Agreement, the post-2020 framework seeks to cement the links of biodiversity conservation with the Sustainable Development Goals (SDGs). What is more, by proposing an intermediate time horizon of attaining the goals, the post-2020 framework seeks to be more realistic in its approach as compared to ABT. In the run up to COP 15 at Kunming, there were intense discussions on the need for the CBD to craft a comprehensive agreement that defined the milestones to be achieved in clear terms as has been the case with the Paris Agreement on Climate Change. Indeed, the President of Costa Rica even exhorted the Biodiversity community to embrace the goal of protecting 30 per cent of the planet by 2030. This line was further pushed by the High Ambition Coalition led by Costa Rica, UAE, Mozambique, Gabon, the Seychelles, and Monaco amongst others. The effort was not welcomed by other parties on the ground that the proposal would undermine the post-2020 GBF. Indeed, the GBF seeks to overcome the deficiencies of ABT by mainstreaming biodiversity conservation goals against the social matrices of gender equality, women's empowerment, youth, gender-responsive approaches, and effective participation of indigenous peoples and local communities in conservation programmes. In this manner, the GBF aims to situate the performance of countries in terms of quality-of-life parameters rather than getting lost in instrumentalism like the ABT.

On 13 October 2021, more than 100 member countries of the CBD adopted the Kunming Declaration, which underlined the importance of ensuring the development, adoption, and implementation of an effective post-2020 GBF which includes provisions for having in place a solid implementation strategy.[8] In the first virtual segment of COP 15 that followed two days later, the UK announced an additional contribution of £200,000 to the Special Voluntary Trust Fund to facilitate participation in the convention's processes, while China underlined its commitment to establish the Kunming Biodiversity Fund with a contribution of 1.5 billion yuan/renminbi (approximately US$230 million) in accordance with the spirit of the Kunming Declaration.[9] The declaration also highlights the role of sustainable and environmentally friendly supply chains in conserving biodiversity.[10] These initiatives are expected to provide a boost to the adoption and implementation of the 2030 framework.

Climate Change Convention during 1992–2016: The Cooper Thesis, CDM, and Carbon Funds

Let us take a closer look at the issue of equity, fairness, and instrumentality in the context of the Climate Change Convention. There has been a substantial amount of writing on the Climate Change Convention. These have assumed the form of scientific and technical reports, policy statements, economic assessments, and social and institutional analysis. However, from the point of view of understanding the essential structure of the discourses that existed in the initial twenty-two years of the Convention. The Climate Change Convention seeks to address the problem of global warming posed by the steady accumulation of greenhouse gases (GHGs) in the atmosphere since the industrial revolution. The change in climate induced by the rise in temperature in turn has led to droughts, floods, sea-level rise, and changes in the bio-physical environment. The United Nations Framework Convention on Climate Change, which came into force in 1994, advocates the twin response strategies of mitigation of GHG emissions and adaptation to climate stress to cope with the problem of climate change. The Kyoto Protocol, signed in 1997, vested the responsibility for emission mitigation in developed countries. This was the state of affairs until the Paris Agreement on climate change came into force in 2016. The Paris Agreement requires all countries to contribute to mitigation in a nationally determined manner.

The Kyoto Protocol is a sterling example of how instrumentalism plays out in the governance of global common. The three flexibilities of joint implementation, emission trading and Clean Development Mechanism (CDM) enshrined in the protocol, served as important mechanisms for ensuring that the climate change process is arrested through an active programme of co-operation amongst different contracting parties. The protocol had put in place these flexible instruments to incentivize developing countries to voluntarily contribute to carbon mitigation, with reference to the 1990 levels of emissions. The flexibility mechanism of the Protocol which has been of great interest to developing countries, was the CDM. Under the CDM scheme, developing countries took up low-carbon projects, either with own resources or with the financial assistance of developed countries. CDM projects taken up in developing countries earned carbon credits which, in turn, were sold to developed country companies to offset their mitigation obligations. The real problem with CDM was that while it promoted clean energy projects in developing countries, the local impact of these projects was limited. This was because the sole criteria of success attributed to a CDM project hinged on the instrumental parameter of 'avoided CO_2 emissions' that a project achieved.

The other aspect of instrumentalism has been the technicalities associated with IPCC reports. Climate assessment reports prepared by the Intergovernmental Panel on Climate Change (IPCC) discuss the climate change problem in terms of a plethora of scientific facts, theories, data, and information. The focus of the response strategies proposed by these reports is also technology driven. Thus, as with the CBD, instrumentalism is a major characteristic of the climate change convention.

In the case of CBD, the focus is on arresting the deterioration of biodiversity wealth through a system of technical fixes that includes *ex situ* conservation, *in vitro* collection of genetic materials, and so on. In the case of the climate change convention, the technical fixes are more pervasive and come in the form of robustly implemented, technically efficient projects that mitigate carbon emissions or sequester carbon emissions. It is here that Cooper (2000) makes a major contribution. In his paper, Cooper survey the issues that caused climate change. He considers a wide range of issues to argue the case for a robust international compact to reduce GHG/carbon emissions. Cooper's point is that while the rewards from restraints on GHG emissions will come only in the distant future, costs have to be incurred at present (2000, 151). Developed countries, and especially those which are located in intensely cold areas like Russia, expect that climate change and global warming would help them to clear ice-clad lands. Under such circumstances, such countries have very little stake in arresting climate change. At the same time, Cooper also points to the fact that the issue of controlling GHG emissions from fossil fuel use, rice cultivation, and cattle production are sensitive matters for developing countries since it would entail fundamental shifts in their traditional or conventional systems of natural resources use. Therefore, Cooper's argument is that no major binding regulating treaty can afford to confront all these issues in one go. He also feels that because of this fundamental limitation, it is difficult for collective decisions to be implemented on issues connected with global climate change (2000, 151). Since costs have to be incurred immediately while benefits would accrue only in the uncertain future, the issue of discount rates on future incomes becomes extremely important. If a country does not undertake investments to mitigate climate change today, it would only serve to imperil future generations (2000, 153). Cooper thus argues that the debate on the choice of a discount rate is also about eliminating imperfections in collective decision making (2000, 154).

Here, Cooper cites Nordhaus (1994) and his theory of optimal mitigation policy. The Nordhaus model of optimal mitigation policy is based on existing information. It is difficult for the optimal policy to remain in the same shape if new knowledge comes in to show that the damages or benefits of climate change mitigation are more significant than one thinks (1994, 157). Cooper states that most of the transfers of financial resources meant for climate action in developing countries, do not reach local citizens or communities as most of it gets undisbursed on account of Governments not passing them to intended beneficiaries. Therefore, a moral issue arises when money intended for citizens is held up in Government coffers (1994, 159).

The notion of instrumentality in climate change is perhaps best illustrated by Cooper in his discussion regarding the US government's stand on the Kyoto targets for emission reduction. Cooper estimates that in the normal course, the US government would have to incur an expenditure of US$200 per ton of carbon in order to achieve the Kyoto target of reaching 1990 emissions by 2012 (1994, 165). However, in case the flexibilities of the protocol work to the complete satisfaction of the United States, that is, if emission permits were allocated and traded not only with developed countries belonging to Annexure 1 but also with developing countries in Annexure 2, the United States would have found its cost of reducing emissions declining substantially from $200 per ton of carbon to as low as $56 per ton. The interesting point made by Cooper in his paper is that Russia promises a great market for the United States when it comes to emission trading regimes, mainly because of the de-industrialization induced by the collapse of the Soviet Union in the early 1990s. Cooper argues that if China and India also opened themselves to emission trading, it would be even more advantageous for the USA, as it would have to spend only $23 for every ton of carbon emission.

Cooper's arguments, however, go against the spirit of the Kyoto Protocol. The Council of Economic Advisors Report of 1998 tried to drive home the point that the technicalities of mitigation strategies have to be entirely seen in terms of economic parameters and therefore need to be completely divorced from the ethical issues that crop up in debates that seek to address trade-offs between economic development and the environment. To consider that the collapse of the Soviet heavy industry would afford a great chance for the United States to bring down its mitigation cost is a perverse argument. Cooper takes us on a different trajectory when he points to a possible emission trading scenario involving India and the United States. He argues that India's per capita income would have grown substantially; but even after 20 years (say by 2020), India's per capita income would be only 14% of the per capita income of the United States, while the per capita consumption of energy would be many times higher in the United States than in India (1994, 159). Had the Paris Agreement not come into force in 2016, countries like India would have emerged as hubs for offset projects on behalf of developed countries which would result in an enormous amount of financial transfers from the United States and Europe to India. Cooper goes on to conclude that countries such as China and Korea, which aim at high economic growth rates, are definitely likely to insist on high-energy growth consumption patterns. He feels that low emission targets, without assurances about flows of technology, would not be an acceptable proposition to China and other developing countries (1994, 160).

The essential point of Cooper's old paper is that within the framework of the Climate Change Convention, it is difficult to achieve results so long as the kind of problems that he envisages between the developed world and the developing world exists. Rather, Cooper speculates that faced with the scientific truth of a severe change in the global climate, many countries may need to adopt contingency planning to supplement research and to develop 'cheap low emitting sources of energy to satisfy human wants' (1994, 169). The intense heat wave that the world at large experienced in 2022, attests to the immense significance of Cooper's prognosis.

Cooper's paper also has the significance of underlining how the technicality of the problems outlined by the Climate Change Convention could have its own intrinsic contradictions and problems. The same year that Cooper wrote his paper, the World Bank established the Prototype Carbon Fund (PCF) for climate change. In the words of the then World Bank President James Wolfensohn, the fund seeks 'to address the issue of vulnerability of poor people in poor countries, which were subject to the threat of climate change'. The PCF was also supposed to serve as a market creator in emissions reductions by investing in a wide range of cleaner technologies.

In the post-2005 phase, the world experienced an explosion of Clean Development Mechanism (CDM) projects. As of 2006, India had a total of 85 million Certified Emission Rights (CER) rights registered or pending for registration with the CDM executive Board of the Framework Convention on Climate Change (FCCC). It is stated that in 2006, nearly 82 million CERs were registered or were under registration with the CDM executive board in the large-scale project category (Gopichandran and Prakash 2006). During the same period around 50 per cent of the CERs earned by Indian projects came from hydrofluorocarbon 23(HFC 23) incineration projects, with the remaining projects drawn from biomass fuel, co-generation, wind energy projects, waste heat recovery projects, and methane to energy conversion projects.

The difficulty with the CDM projects was that the bulk of them centred on cleaner business practices that had negligible community impacts. CDM projects in India never looked beyond the instrumentality of optimizing CER generation from the projects. Though CDM project documents did talk about community participation, it was tokenistic. They were not incorporated as an institutional process. Thus CDM projects offered very few benefits for local communities. For example, the methane recovery projects and methane-emission capping projects taken up under the CDM, did not focus on the interests of pastoral communities whose livestock subsisted on grazing in common lands.

Indeed, one of the essentially interesting features of the CDM projects was that they were proposed to be implemented in countries such as India on a project mode instead of on a programme mode. The other feature was the neutrality of CDM projects as regards the issue of ownership of process. The CDM schema went a step further and sought to draw in private corporates to execute CDM projects on behalf of the investors, in the larger interests of technical efficiency and optimality.

Thus, in the case of India's forestry sector, where the process of Joint Forest Management (JFM) and participation by local communities in the management of degraded forests have been moderately successful, the guiding principle of equitable access to common/public natural resources is well established. The fact that the responsibilities and obligations of executing CDM projects were done on a project mode, serves to show that the aspects of institutionalization, fairness, and justice are not important. Instrumentality, which has been the hallmark of CDM projects, is heavily rooted in the end product these projects seek, namely CERs. This is unlike the social objective of equitable access to forest-based products, that underlies the JFM programme.

The fever of CDM projects in developing countries had led to a blind alley, where the focus was entirely on attracting financing for narrow earnings from low-carbon projects. In reality, the CDM projects could have also focussed on employment generation, income growth, and rise in the standard of living in countries that host them. This would have resulted in greater linkage of climate change issues with fairness and equity.

Another case of instrumentalism in the Kyoto Protocol is in the area of emissions trading. Economists like Robert Stavins see virtues in cap and trade schemes as they provide greater certainty about emission levels and thus offer easy means of compensating for the unequal burdens imposed by the climate policy. The caveat is, of course, that the scheme needs to be designed well (Stavins 2008). The problems of an ill-designed cap and trade system can be daunting going by the European experience. In 2005, the European Union Emission Trading System (EU–ETS) went on stream. Allowances worth more than 2 billion tons of CO_2 were allocated to nearly 11,500 factories drawn from five industrial sectors. However, these allowances were so liberally and munificently allotted that despite levels of CO_2 emissions from these sectors being high, it was found that the allowances provided did not bear any correlation to the actual emission levels. The actual result was that though the emission trading markets started off with high price levels of say €31 per permit, it came down to €11 since many companies realized that they really did not need to buy large volumes of permits to keep themselves going. Despite high-level debates on the mechanics of allocating allowances, there were too many loopholes in the manner in which the allowances were allocated. The problem had clearly much to do with data on historic emissions and future projections submitted by the individual countries. What was more amusing was that investors and watchers of the emission trade market prices were not focused on the defects of allowance allocations. They were more concerned about the manner in which prices of the permit allowances fluctuated.

The EU–ETS in its initial phase was a world unto itself. It had little to do with emission reduction performance and more to do with the 'profit margins' of CO_2-guzzling enterprises. The focus was on tempering price fluctuations of allowances rather than looking at ways and measures by which the GHG emissions could be proactively reduced by the industry. Such instances create misgivings amongst developing countries about carbon markets in general. Indeed the EU–ETS itself put an end to its shoddy ways by tightening the allowance market in the post-Paris Agreement phase (more on this later).

Let us now consider the philosophical problems raised by the UNFCCC. The key issue with the UNFCCC is that global warming is contributed to by a handful of developed countries in the world. Given that the levels of per capita income of developing countries are considerably lower, it is clearly unjust to expect developing countries to bear the burden of mitigating CO_2 emissions. This then is the equity and fairness dimension of the UNFCCC; however, the instrumentality mode of the convention has a different face. It focuses on (a) inventorization of GHG build-up in the atmosphere, (b) assessment of GHG emissions for different trajectories of growth, and (c) devising frameworks for monitoring, reporting, and verification (MRV). The Kyoto Protocol also spawned an extensive system of emission trading by way of allowances, derivatives contracts, trading exchanges, and platforms.

None of these instrumentalist measures has a bearing on the need of developing countries to achieve energy self-sufficiency. They are also not conducive to the idea of developing countries following a pattern of economic growth that is based on sustainable livelihoods and industrial development. What one gets from reading the large volumes of documents produced on climate change is that they deal with the consequences of global warming on sea levels, water balance, and food security. Very few studies talk about how the climate change convention will facilitate the rights of developing countries to achieve higher growth rates in their agricultural, industrial, and tertiary sectors in a sustainable manner.

One of the most interesting paradoxes of climate change in relation to the WTO is that while under the climate change convention regimes, developing countries can receive investment resources for CDM projects, the focus of the WTO is on the rules regarding imposition of tariff barriers on products exported by developing countries to developed countries. Despite this focus, there are safeguards provisions in the WTO agreements for preventing rural livelihood means and resource husbandry practices from collapsing. In contrast, the CDM projects which were taken up to fulfil the requirements of the Kyoto Protocol did not integrate livelihood concerns. This might have been due to excessive focus on instrumental issues such as carbon emission reductions, 'additionality' determination norms and the technical soundness of projects undertaken under the CDM scheme. The other issue is that while the Kyoto Protocol emphasized the transfer of state-of-the-art low-carbon clean technologies that meet the needs of developing countries, not much progress has been made on this front. Even if we assume progress in future, it is not clear whether such transfers can give a good deal for local communities.

The greater the instrumentality of a particular regime, the less is the possibility of valuable public and local goods emerging from activities connected to the regime. Thus, solar power, fuel cells, wind energy, and hydro-projects, which are recommended as the right technologies for arresting climate change or back-stopping climate change, cannot be considered as really emancipatory unless they are in tune with the essence of equity and fairness as perceived by underprivileged communities.

Way back in 1985, there was a curious incident associated with a solar street lighting scheme in a village called Shanbhoganahalli on the outskirts of Bengaluru. Though the solar lights worked well in the village, a few people went on an arson spree to destroy the solar lamps. To a large extent, this was on account of the new technology creating resentment amongst some people who felt that the new technology would eliminate the old street lights to which local communities were adapted.

Another case in point was the introduction of hand pumps in the villages of India. Though the hand pump was a boon for the water-starved people of villages, a large number of wells faced breakdown, and the communities reverted to the old open wells since many villages did not internalize the technique of maintaining them. In reality, decentralized technologies like rain-water storage (based on gravity flows) would have achieved greater success in improving adaptation to climate change at the local level. This is due to the fact that they have greater possibilities of internalization and social acceptance if backed by capacity building, but the policy thrust seems to be moving in other directions.

The real success lies not only in getting a technology to be internalized but also in ensuring that the technology is in sync with the fundamental values for which a local community stands. Both the cases mentioned convey the challenge of communicating and applying climate change redressal technologies in rural areas. Climate change is too distant and far away for local rural communities to really appreciate and understand. Even in the case of more relevant technologies which are directly related to natural and biological assets of rural communities, like biogas based on livestock wastes, households in rural areas of India which are used to burning cow dung and other animal wastes to meet their energy needs find it difficult to internalize a technology which generates a new form of energy. The technicalities associated with the running and maintenance of biogas plants is another reason for small and marginal farmers keeping away from the technology. Similarly, mega solar power projects that require mammoth investments clearly lie beyond the reach of local communities.

In many ways, the instrumentality of climate change causes the scale of projects to be large. Scale effects preclude small and marginal groups from participating in climate change mitigation. Collective action can be useful in addressing climate change in rural areas provided they are catalysed through awareness programmes. However, this calls for a new approach to communications. It is true that the Paris Agreement has replaced the CDM with a Sustainable Development Mechanism, which seeks to achieve 'overall mitigation in global emissions' thereby get rid of the curse the CDM suffered from—of being an 'offset tool'. However, it is too early to say whether the sustainable development mechanism (SDM) will have a greater impact in developing countries or will get lost in instrumentalist parameters as was the case with the CDM.

The Paris Agreement has induced developed and emerging economies to come up with harder, national mitigation targets (or Net Zero Goals). One positive result of this goal has been the strengthening of carbon markets. Thus the EU–ETS market underwent major streamlining in recent years. Thus the era of free allocation of allowances has ended for EU–ETS participants. Today, participant companies in the ETS need to bid for allowances at auctions. The results are there for everyone to see. EU permit/allowance prices have steadily climbed and even reached the height of Euro 95 in mid-2022. Indeed the EU's proposed Carbon Border Adjustment Mechanism (CBAM) (that seeks to impose carbon levies on imports of carbon-intensive goods to the EU) is indexed to the EU–ETS prices.

The Historic Paris Agreement of 2015 and After

The failure of UNFCCC's COP 15 at Copenhagen marked the beginning of a new era in global climate change regulations. By the time COP 17 took place in Durban in 2011, impressive strides were made by the convention to develop convergent views on the desirability of containing the increase in global temperatures above pre-industrial levels. Apart from providing a second commitment period for the Kyoto Protocol beyond 2012, the Durban COP adopted the idea of preparing a blueprint for a fresh, universal, and legal agreement to deal with climate change beyond 2020 (where all the countries will play their part in reversing climate change) and launched a new platform of negotiations to work toward a new universal 'greenhouse gas reduction protocol' by 2020. This move set the stage for the Paris Agreement in 2015.[11] The Paris Agreement on Climate Change was signed on 22 April 2015, at the 21st Conference of Parties held in Paris. The agreement came into force on 4 November 2016, 30 days after the date on which 55 parties to the Convention, accounting al for an estimated 55 per cent of the total global greenhouse gas emissions, had deposited their instruments of ratification/acceptance/approval with the designated depositary. As of November 2020, the agreement has been signed by 195 members. The main objective of the Paris Agreement is to strengthen global response to the threat of climate change by keeping the global temperature rise in this century well below 2°C above pre-industrial levels while pursuing efforts to limit the temperature increase to 1.5°C.[12]

The key elements of the Paris Agreement include formulation of nationally determined contributions (NDCs) by member countries, whereby each country declares its contribution to the attainment of the agreement's central objective of the Agreement, viz. limiting the increase in global temperature below 1.5°C as compared to pre-industrial levels. The limitation of the agreement is that NDCs provide flexibility to individual countries to set their mitigation targets. To ensure that countries do not go for soft mitigation targets, Article 13 of the Paris Agreement provides for transparency frameworks that assess the functioning of their NDCs through harmonized monitoring, reporting, and verification mechanisms. The Paris Agreement also has other elements such as 'global stocktaking' (Article 14) (that evaluates information submitted by member countries on the steps taken by them to provide climate finance), the 'sustainable development mechanism' (Article 6.4), 'adaptation provisions', technology development and transfer (Article 10), and financing commitments. The agreement provides balanced emphasis on mitigation and adaptation. The 'loss and damage' dimension of the agreement (Article 8) seeks to address the impact of abrupt damages in vulnerable countries (including small island developing countries) that cannot be managed through standard adaptation measures. The flexibility mechanisms of the agreement provide for the capacity-building needs of developing countries.

Article 6 of the agreement is particularly relevant (and contentious) as it deals with both market and non-market factors that guide policies to achieve the targets of the convention. Market mechanisms include emission trading markets, while non-market approaches include application of taxes and related fiscal instruments. The thrust of Article 6.2

is to develop a system of interlinked carbon markets to trade in NDC-related carbon credits. The idea is to ensure that carbon markets are larger entities than narrow, regional-level bucket shops that trade limited volumes of carbon credits. Article 6.4 of the Paris Agreement establishes SDM as a replacement for clean development mechanism (CDM) and facilitates trading in carbon permits/allowances by countries as well as corporates. The caveat is that such trading shall be additional to mandatory reductions or without compromise on 'overall mitigation in global emissions' (often referenced as OMGE). As Kelly and Rambharos (2019) state, the Paris Agreement was explicit about continuing support for adaptation and administrative purposes under Article 6.4 (trading credits from emissions reductions resulting from specific projects), but did not mention it in Article 6.2 (when two or more countries transfer emission reductions, for example, through linked emission-trading schemes). The COP 25 in Madrid was supposed to determine how countries will share proceeds under Article 6.4 and also whether there will be a share of proceeds from Article 6.2 through transfers to generate revenue for the adaptation fund.[13] Article 6.8 of the Paris Agreement establishes a work program for non-market approaches, which includes taxes to discourage carbon emissions.

The real significance of carbon markets is that they help developed countries to minimize the costs of implementing their committed NDC-related targets. As Kelly and Rambharos (2019) elaborate, half of the countries' initial NDCs (constituting 31 per cent of global emissions) include the use of international cooperation through carbon markets. According to IETA, the potential benefits to cooperation under Article 6 include cost savings of $250 billion per year in 2030.[14] The second benefit of carbon markets is that they can leverage financing and give a push to emission reducing activities in countries that have accepted the mitigation targets.

However, much depends on how the rules of functioning of the carbon markets will be set. These include rules on mutual transfer of permits generated from activities mentioned in Articles 6.2 and 6.4. Though these rules were supposed to be laid down in COP 25 held in Spain in 2019, it did not work out. The COP 26 at Glasgow held in November 2021 succeeded in resolving the issue by setting rules to avoid 'double counting' of carbon credits accruing from inter-country projects through scientific book keeping practices.[15]

There are a few deeper issues regarding carbon markets that need to be addressed in future CoP meetings. This concerns a global-level carbon pricing mechanism

that would help the global community to arrive the tempo of action being taken to achieve net zero goals (Damodaran, 2022a). Similarly, a unified global carbon price of carbon is neither desirable nor feasible. Instead, a global price index that provides for a sliding scale of prices will make for a more efficient price discovery process that reflects the differentials in marginal abatement costs between developing and developed countries (Damodaran 2022a).

At Glasgow, the issue about carrying forward unutilized CDM credits was resolved.[16] Yet another unresolved issue at Glasgow was the financing of loss and damage activities as envisaged under the Warsaw International Mechanism (WIM) set up in 2013. The issue of whether these needed to be funded under a separate mechanism or through an extended window of the GCF was left unresolved at COP 25. The Glasgow Conference partly managed to resolve this issue as well.

Despite the ambitious targets laid down under the Paris Agreement, progress on the mitigation front has been tardy. The top four emitters (China, the United States, EU27, and India) contributed to over 55 per cent of the total emissions over the last decade. According to the United Nations Environment Programme (UNEP), to limit global temperature rise to 1.5°C, it has to be ensured that global annual emissions are pegged below 25 gigatons (Gt) by 2030. To limit the global temperature rise to 1.5 °C, the global annual emission reduction needed is 7.6 per cent every year between 2020 and 2030. Indeed, the international watchdog Climate Tracker describes how the United States has slipped on its commitment of reducing carbon emissions by 20–25 per cent over 2005 levels on account of Trump administration withdrawing from the Paris Agreement in 2017.

The NDCs are in reality, 'best endeavour statements' as they do not provide for accountability for shortfalls in stated commitments. Many developed countries have taken up net zero commitments by 2050. India's 'Paris Pledge' envisaged reduction of the intensity of carbon emissions by 33–35 per cent over 2005 levels by 2030. At the Climate Ambition Summit 2020 held in December 2020, to commemorate the fifth anniversary of the Paris Agreement, Prime Minister Narendra Modi announced that India had already reduced its carbon emissions intensity by 21 per cent compared to the 2005 levels and that it would even exceed its Paris Agreement goals. At COP 26, Prime Minister Modi announced that India will achieve net zero target by 2070. However, despite strong arguments at the Glasgow Summit that a 'phase out' of coal by 2040 would be essential for the world to stave off a 1.5°C rise in temperature above the pre-industrial levels, India and China refused to toe the line and instead opted for a milder regime of 'phase down' of this fossil fuel. The 'phase down' formulation got carried into the final agreement adopted at Glasgow. At the Sharm el-Sheikh Climate Summit (CoP27), a year after Glasgow, though there were active efforts on the part of India and a few developed countries to have phasing out extended to all fossil fuels (including oil and gas), the proposal did not go through. Sharm el-Sheikh also saw no further follow-up on the phasing down of coal that was adopted at Glasgow.

As mentioned in Chapter 7, the most intractable issue with the Paris Agreement is on the climate financing front. Article 9.1 states that developed country parties shall provide financial resources to assist developing country parties to carry out mitigation and adaptation in continuation of their existing obligations under the convention. Article 9 (3) mentions that developed country parties should continue to take the lead in mobilizing climate finance from a wide variety of sources, instruments, and channels, noting the significant role of public funds, through a variety of actions, including supporting country-driven strategies and taking into account the needs and priorities of developing country parties. Article 9(4) mentions the provision of scaled-up financial resources to achieve a balance between adaptation and mitigation after taking into account the thrust of country-driven strategies. Despite these clear directions and the commitments of developed countries, the target of mobilizing $100 billion a year for climate financing has not been achieved. The spate of climate bonds issued under the auspices of the Climate Bonds Initiative (CBI) have not met with the required success on account of the economic slowdown that the world has been witnessing since 2020 on account of the COVID-19 pandemic. However, despite not being able to meet their commitments by 2020, developed countries, agreed at Glasgow, to take up transparent commitments for providing $100 billion per annum to developing countries. At Glasgow, the parties to the Paris Agreement also agreed on the need to provide financial resources for countries suffering from grave climate calamities. However, in the wake of the Ukraine war, it is doubtful whether even the minimal commitment of $100 billion/year will be met anytime soon (Damodaran, 2022b).

However, at CoP 27 held at Sharm el-Sheikh in November 2022, vulnerable developing countries secured a victory by getting the idea of a dedicated fund to address 'loss and damage' problems, incorporated in the final agreement.

A noteworthy feature of the Glasgow Summit Agreement was its emphasis on the role of biodiversity and forestry conservation in achieving mitigation. Another interesting feature of the Glasgow Summit Talks was the emergence of *in situ* plurilateral pacts amongst a select group of countries present at the summit. This included the pact amongst 25 country parties to the COP to cut off new international finance for fossil fuel projects by the end of 2022 and the pact by more than 100 countries to bring down emissions of methane.

More fundamentally, despite progress on Article 6(2) and related issues mentioned above, the Glasgow Conference could not succeed in getting major emitting countries to come up with ambitious mitigation targets by 2030 by phasing out coal and other fossil fuels. This has reduced the scope for achieving desired quantitative cuts in CO2 emissions that could help the world community to achieve the goal of limiting the rise in global temperature to 1.5°C. At Sharm el-Sheikh, despite efforts on the part of developed countries to advance the emission peaking schedule to 2025, the proposal did not go through.

The onset of CBAM from 2023 on carbon-intensive imports to the EU (referred to earlier), and the 'Just Energy Transition Partnerships' (JETPs) proposed by the Group of Seven Countries (G7) in August 2022, mark efforts on the part of developed countries to nudge and push developing countries to rapidly transition to low carbon technologies through trade measures and targeted financing.

To sum up, the Paris Agreement is broad-based and balanced. However, the Agreement's focus on measurable mitigation tools smacks instrumentalism. The Agreement places more emphasis on emission reduction targets than on the outcomes of climate action in terms of livelihoods protected and losses and damages avoided. To be an equity-based compact, it is essential for the Paris Agreement to focus more on the vulnerability story of poor countries affected by the rise in global temperature. The agreement at CoP 27 to institute a 'loss and damage fund', perhaps marks the first step in this direction.

The Basel Convention

We now take a look at the implications of instrumentalism in relation to the Basel Convention on 'transboundary movement of hazardous wastes'. The Basel Convention which was signed in 1989 came into force in 1992 and has 53 members as of 2019. As has been already pointed out, the Basel Convention has been essentially instrumentalist in its approach to problems and is relatively neutral for social and community matters. This is because the Basel Convention has been seen to a large extent as a pure inter-state convention that deals with national policies in relation to global issues. Right from its inception, the Basel Convention was designed to control transboundary movement of hazardous wastes. While the industry wanted fewer restrictions on inter-country movements of hazardous wastes, environmentalists wanted a total ban on such movements. The middle road solution was to have a formula for controlling or regulating movement of hazardous wastes rather than impose an outright ban. The Basel Convention was, essentially speaking, an 'extreme focus' convention that focussed only on trade in wastes. Indeed, as the Earth Report (2001) on its website, entitled 'Up the Ladder' states, the Basel Convention had carried with it provisos for recycling hazardous wastes. Industries in developed countries, which generated and transported hazardous wastes, took advantage of the recycling provision of the convention to their advantage. Their argument was that recycling of hazardous wastes needs to be seen as a legitimate and productive activity as it added to the supply of valuable raw materials in the importing country.

The annexes of the convention had other instrumental features. These annexes provide detailed information on various forms of hazardous wastes, their regulation, the degree of toxicity of various types of wastes, and a plethora of related technical aspects. The solution of recycling, advocated by the convention, was also based on the credo of instrumentalism. The simple idea revolved around the technical point that as long as toxic wastes were recyclable and reused, they would not spill over or contaminate natural ecosystems. Until the Basel ban thousands of barrels of hazardous wastes were shipped to developing countries creating havoc in these countries. A prominent case was the dumping of large quantities of Italian carcinogenic chemicals, poisonous solvents, and decomposing pesticides in Lebanon, a country wrecked by civil war, with minimal capacity to handle these wastes (Earth Report 2001). The toxic chemical substances seeped underground and contaminated soil and water supply sources in the dumping area.

There have been a few other cases involving exports of toxic wastes. In the year 1988, another Italian entity was reported to have dumped hazardous wastes in Nigeria's Koko Beach. The chemicals were so poisonous that they caused burns, vomiting of blood, and paralysis among sections of the local population that came in contact with the dumped materials. The collateral problem was that the substance affected people who happened to be closer to the site of dumping but also had far-reaching adverse impacts on other natural resources.

The Basel Convention's emphasis on environmental management of hazardous wastes is its strong instrumental feature. The issue of instrumentality, as embedded in the concept of 'environmental, management of hazardous wastes,' has prevented an absolute ban on toxic waste movements. The votaries of the 'environmental management plan' provisos in the Convention argued that countries which import hazardous wastes could deal with the issue in an efficient and sustainable manner. By breaking down hazardous wastes into simpler chemicals, toxicity could be reduced in the importing country. However, very little effort has been made by the convention to advocate source-reduction technologies that could have totally avoided the generation of hazardous substances from production systems. Such a line of action could have been a far better proposition than emphasis on reuse and recycle that runs the risk of accidental leakages and spill-overs in developing countries.

The basic issue of 'justice' in the Basel Convention centres on the argument that developing countries in the world, which have little economic means to back up their delicate fragile livelihood systems, have an intrinsic and inherent right to conserve water, air and land resources for supporting their livelihood. Unfortunately, the Basel Convention, with its almost exclusive focus on environmental management plans and programmes for hazardous waste treatment, has tried to overlook the basic right of common citizens in developing countries to access clean and high-quality natural resources. The Basel Protocol on Liability and Compensation adopted by the fifth COP on 10 December 1999, marked a major effort to reiterate an instrumental view on the issue of hazardous waste movement rather than take a look into the equity and justice dimensions of the move. The protocol seeks to provide for a very comprehensive liability regime and a system of compensation payment for damages.

A related issue is that of technical guidelines adopted by the Secretariat of the Basel Convention regarding environmentally sound management norms guiding the complete or partial dismantling of abandoned ships. The 'Technical Guidelines for Environmentally Sound Management of the Full and Partial Dismantling of Ships', adopted in 2006 contain a variety of parameters, guidelines, and recommendations on how to ensure that the ship-dismantling yards maintain environmentally sustainable management systems to prevent hazardous emissions or spillage of hazardous substances that exceed waste reception facilities.[17] Major ship-dismantling nations such as Bangladesh, China, India, and Pakistan import obsolete vessels for dismantling. It is alleged that developing countries take up the task of dismantling obsolete vessels without regard to environmental health and safety standards for their citizens. It was to address this deficiency that the guidelines were prepared. The technical guidelines aim to render ship-dismantling activities in developing countries, safe for local communities. Thus the guidelines fight shy of banning the practice of sending ships to developing countries for dismantling and breaking. The core issue of inequity arises from the base fact that developed countries that manufacture ships do not want to accept any form of social or environmental costs associated with its dismantling once the vessel's commercial life is over. In some ways, the Basel Convention and its technical guidelines legitimatize the hazardous practice of ship breaking in developing countries. It is doubtful whether industries in the developed countries of the world, which send ships for dismantling to the developing countries, would ever consider adopting the Basel guidelines for safe dismantling of ships in their dockyards themselves even if compliance with the guidelines assures safety!

The skewness and the absence of fairness and justice in the Basel Convention comes from the fact that developing countries in the world are viewed in sections of the developed world as not being able to carry out menial tasks associated with processing of hazardous wastes. To a large extent, this kind of thinking is reinforced by industrial groups and lobbies in developing countries, which support processing of hazardous wastes. In India, zinc ash importers have lobbied with the government to relax imports of zinc wastes. For some time, the Government of India was also in favour of hazardous wastes recyclers importing zinc wastes. It was felt that recyclers formed a very important base of the Indian economy as they catered to the small-scale sector, which had good employment potential. Besides, it was also felt that it was important to protect the raw material base of these industries in the larger interests of economic development. From this perspective, India's environmental system facilitates adoption of cleaner technologies that are 'recycling-oriented' when it comes to hazardous wastes. However, recycling technologies only serve to prolong the phase-out of hazardous substances. If the Basel ban was respected in its true spirit and the countries of the West decided to implement the ban in its true sense, this would have constrained the world to take to source reduction technologies that substitute hazardous substances for more benign ones.

As a result of all these factors, citizens of developing countries would still be denied their genuine entitlement to an environmental crucible, which is free of pollution and hazardous substances. India could seriously consider eliminating its recycling industries in a phased and less painful manner and seek to redeploy the employees and the employers of the recycling industries to alternative vocations that are green and clean.

There is a deeper reason for arguing along these lines. In the 1970s, the Indian trade delegations which went for the UNCTAD meetings had vociferously argued, and for valid reasons, the need to correct the crude inequities associated with an imbalanced international division of labour that constrained developing countries like India to stick to low-value yielding agricultural commodities while enabling developed countries of the world to concentrate on high-value industrial goods. India's argument in the Climate Change Convention was also precisely on the same lines. Developed countries, by insisting on reduction of GHG emissions by emerging economies such as India, are forcing them into a state of de-industrialization. However, when it comes to the Basel Convention, India's stand seems to be in favour of perpetuating an iniquitous division of labour, which survives on scavenging and recycling of materials that are hazardous.

Post-2010 Developments

In recent times, the Basel Convention, the Stockholm Conventions on POPS and the Rotterdam Convention (along with the Secretariat of the Minamata Convention) have come together to co-operate on common programmes such as the plastic waste partnership. A case in point was the joint meeting convened in April–May 2019 under the auspices of the joint secretariat of the three conventions to address interconnected issues, such as establishing clearing house mechanisms for information exchange relevant to preventing and combating illegal traffic and trade in hazardous chemicals and wastes.

The Biosafety Protocol

The most interesting part of the Cartagena Protocol on Biosafety is that it carries within it the proviso of Advanced Informed Agreement (AIA) whereupon an exporter of a product that is potentially not bio-safe has to secure an AIA from the government of the importing country for the import of the product. The Cartagena Protocol is, therefore, like the Basel Convention when it comes to its scope. Like the Basel Convention, the Cartagena Protocol talks about transboundary movements of materials and seeks to put a check on free transfer of Genetically Modified Organisms (GMOs) through the system of AIA. Indeed, the CBD also talks about PIC. However, at the same time, countries have the discretion of using different expressions when regulating access to genetic resources. Both the principles of PIC and the AIA facilitate entitlements and equity. The entitlements of importing countries and communities are not only to a 'clean' and hazard-free environment but also to the right to be informed about the threats or hazards to their environment.

The Cartagena Protocol stipulates that it is the right of a farmer to be well informed about the seeds that he purchases for sowing. A farmer who cultivates a plant that is genetically modified has every right to be informed about its biosafety aspects. This calls for labelling of such products in the interests of fairness and equity. However, the biotechnology industry resists labelling of genetically modified products. As a result, the 'right to be informed principle' enshrined in the Cartagena Protocol (through the AIA) is virtually nullified.

Unfortunately, the progressive elements in the Cartagena Protocol have been badly affected by instrumentalism. Similar to the Basel Convention, the Cartagena Protocol is instrumentalist as it talks about inventories, information on scientific and technical characteristics, risk assessment, and a whole lot of scientific protocols that are not normally present in other conventions. What is more, the instrumentalism of the Cartagena Protocol gets further reinforcement from WTO-SPS measures, which covers interstate movement of LMOs and GMOs 'in the course of trade' that pose a threat to plants, animals, human health, and life. Indeed, the WTO-SPS also talks about risk assessment. The agreement also stresses on precautionary approaches. The Codex Alimentarius Commission proceedings are characterized by discussions of a highly complex technical nature.

The instrumentality element in the Cartagena Protocol serves the same purpose as the Basel Convention in obfuscating the basic concept of fairness and equity for which it stands.

In reality, the negative impact of instrumentalism on equity and fairness is much more harmful in the case of the Basel Convention and the Cartagena Protocol compared with UNFCCC and CBD. Indeed, Damodaran (2006) argues that the level of scientific understanding of communities and civil societies in developing countries needs to be upgraded if they have to play an effective role in regulating biotech products.

In India, national systems exist to give greater meaning to the principles of equity and justice implicit in global conventions. India's EIA procedures provide for a process of public hearing in the case of certain projects of fundamental importance. The concept of public hearing in some ways is a kind of an information dissemination process, whereupon local communities are informed about the project, its scope and potential consequences. To this extent, environmental laws and legislations in India have progressive features, although there are serious concerns about the manner in which the public hearing processes have been sidetracked in some cases.

The Global Environmental Facility, National Action Plans, and Civil Societies

The GEF, which is considered to be the main financing arm for climate change, biodiversity and desertification control projects, has focused on supporting projects that promote development of scientific and technical data on key environmental issues connected to the three conventions. Thus, major GEF-sponsored studies on climate change have emphasized the significance of conducting country studies based on scientific information. For instance, the GEF working paper (1994) titled, 'Review of Country Case Studies on Climate Change' highlights a set of country studies from different parts of the world (Fuglestvedt et al. 1994). These country case studies have worked out GHG inventories of sources and sinks, carried out impact and vulnerability assessments and assessed the feasibility of cost-effective interventions. The GEF considers such country studies as enabling decision-makers to take cost-effective national response strategies. Indeed, India's Policy Statement on Climate Change (Anonymous 1998) and the later National Action Plan on Climate Change focus on assessment of sustainable development issues confronting the country in the light of climate change priorities. The Action Plan of 2008 scans various sectors, including agriculture and rural development, the health sector, waste minimization, and pollution prevention matters before getting into the core issue of energy utilization in the power sector. The reports highlight issues and policy frameworks that could make a difference to climate change mitigation measures and propose measures to achieve energy efficiencies through energy audits and renewable energy production.

However, the problem with the previously mentioned GEF reports is that they suffer from the burden of having to provide periodic assessments, despite recognizing the importance of the principles of entitlements, fairness, and justice.

Anil Agarwal and Sunita Narain (1991) explain how a negotiating position that highlights the role of equity is important for global conventions such as climate change to gain acceptability in the developing world. The authors demolish a World Resources Institute (WRI) report of 1990 that focused on CO_2 releases by developing countries on account of deforestation and methane emissions originating from rice fields and livestock, instead of looking deeper into CO_2 emissions contributed by the developed world on account of their fossil fuel-intensive industrial path. Agarwal and Narain advanced a set of eloquent and logical points to highlight their central thesis that no global commons issue could afford to ignore the central fact of an unequal world. The authors stated that to carry out the strategy of improving land productivity and meeting survival needs, development strategies will have to be 'ecosystem-specific' and 'holistic'. According to them, 'it would be necessary to plan for each component of the village ecosystem and not just trees'. To do this, India would need real peoples' participation in wasteland development, which in turn requires local democracies to be set up without the nagging interference of bureaucrats. Finally, the report argues that those who talk about global warming should concentrate on what ought to be done to solve the problem (1991, 25). As the report goes on to state, it is important for third world countries to participate in debates on global environment issues and counter the Western perception about global environmental problems (1991).

A few years later, Agarwal wrote about the GEF in the context of the facility's assembly meeting in New Delhi in 1998. He forcefully stated that all multilateral financing mechanisms like the GEF will have to accept the principle of local empowerment. He went on to argue that the GEF should promote a genuine learning culture, and civil society groups ought to be involved in its work in a more effective and sustainable manner (1991). Agarwal went on to state that the GEF should not allow global environment to be an isolated issue, but rather should play a clearer role in the integration of the Rio agenda with the struggle against world poverty. He was also emphatic that the identities of developing nations and their local communities had to be preserved in their cultural, social, and economic senses. Technological solutions or solutions to global environmental problems that did not respect the social, economic, and cultural dimensions of livelihoods of the local communities in developing countries would not take the world anywhere. Despite Agarwal's eloquent intervention, the final resolution of the first GEF Assembly in Delhi did not reflect any of his concerns.

Closely relevant to the issue of global commons discussed above are articles written by two eminent ecologists regarding the limitations with academic studies on sustainability. These articles consider the discipline of economics to have changed the rules of nature's problems. Donald Worster (2004) makes an interesting observation about the problem with the so-called expert analysis of environmental issues. He says that ecologists who are supposed to inform and make the layman understand about how ecosystems work or undergo modifications or get stressed by human demands have, in practice, adopted techniques of research that relate ecological ideas to economic principles of production and sales. Worster argues that by measuring productivity and treating soil, forest and fisheries as commodities, ecologists are applying economic tools to analyse ecological issues (Worster 2004, 137). Worster draws attention to the statement of Daniel Botkin (1990) that 'nature when undisturbed by human influence is like a symphony whose harmonies arise from variation and change over every interval of time' (1990, 139). Botkin goes on to argue that 'nature in the 21st century will be a nature that we make'. Worster's criticism is that despite starting on a promising note of providing a comprehensive enquiry into the nature of nature, Botkin proceeded to reject nature as a norm for human civilization. On the other hand, by presupposing that humans could control, shape and order nature, Botkin fails to understand that nature has a value by itself and has a system of retaining its own attributes (1990, 140).

In some ways, Worster reinforces the point made by Agarwal et al. about the need to see nature in an integrated and comprehensive manner, rather than just analyse it from a narrow scientific or economic perspective. However, in his quest to ensure that interventionistic models of ecosystems do not distort ecology for its own sake, Worster tends to argue against all forms of interventions including interventions made by human societies to correct natural imbalance.

Vandana Shiva (1995, 149–56) is another prominent ecologist who talks about 'green imperialism' imposed by the movements that take up global environmental causes. For Shiva, the emergence of global environment problems seems to have marginalized local issues such as deforestation, water crisis, nuclear, and toxic hazards and dumping of hazardous wastes (1995, 151). Similarly, Shiva argues that erosion of biodiversity in developing countries has caused the biodiversity agenda to be shifted from the South to the North, with the latter appropriating the agenda from the former. As Shiva argues, by shifting and deflecting socially critical problems such as loss of local community rights over natural resources and suggesting the need to empower them with property rights, the current trend in global discussions veers towards negotiations that shift decision-making systems and empowerment structures to far and distant agencies.

At a more fundamental level, the trouble with most of the technical and scientific assessments prepared by international institutions is that they indulge in hyperboles. For instance, the working group 1 of the IPCC of 2000 stated that there has been a noticeable increase in global warming on account of emissions of GHGs and aerosols contributed by human activities. This finding was not received wholeheartedly by a number of scientists. The report was welcomed by the then UNEP Executive Director, Klaus Topfer, who even exhorted the world to consider accelerated introduction of cleaner technologies to meet the contingencies. However, when the IPCC report was discussed in public, a couple of scientists are reported to have questioned the findings, stating that generalizations and predictions that the world was going to get warm faster were overstated.

Another case in point is the manner in which deforestation rates are frequently revised, both at the global and national levels in India. For instance, the FAO had, in an assessment in 2000, indicated that the rate of deforestation world-wide had slowed down to 9 million hectares per year. As per this assessment, the global figure reported in 1995 was on the higher side. In India, the Forest Survey of India, which has brought out state forest reports since 1986, had to revise its findings on a few occasions to provide the correct picture of the state of forest cover in India. There were great efforts to work around discrepancies between satellite imagery and the ground-level surveys conducted by the Forest Survey of India from time to time. Although assessment reports that are based on satellite imagery have improved in scientific veracity, they are still cross-checked with field survey figures before the final tally is released.

The point stressed here is that even the most rigorous and credible scientific assessment reports are questioned for their veracity. The alteration of a technical assessment report calls for changing operational strategies for implementing projects. Unfortunately, the latter does not happen with the same frequency as the former.

If presented in terms of their impacts on human entitlements and endowments, environmental programmes would have a much better chance of getting grassroots acceptance. There is also great advantage in viewing socio-cultural and economic variables while assessing the state of environmental resources. For long, 'deserts' were defined in terms of biophysical features. There was also a theory which stated that deserts have developed as a result of invasion of xerophytic species, which, in turn, was attributed to over-grazing by sheep, goats and other small ruminants. For quite some time, prescriptions for sustainable development proposed that households in desertification-prone areas remove small ruminants from their livestock holdings. However, it took some time for the scientific community to realize that deserts have their identity as distinct ecosystems, with their bio-physical and institutional specificities. Goats, sheep, and small ruminants, for long considered destroyers of land are, these days, viewed as the most adaptable creatures that help secure human life in deserts. Nomadic communities in deserts are not marauders of natural ecosystems. They tune themselves to these ecosystems and practice unique systems of sustainable livelihood and consumption patterns with the small ruminants helping them achieve this.

The message here is that if we undertake assessments of environment in terms of social, cultural, and economic priorities and within the framework of these parameters look at biophysical factors, we may end up with totally different strategies of development than what is being attempted at present. When we put technical parameters on the top and see socio-cultural and economic parameters within the ambit of these technical parameters, our perspectives change. The Thar Desert of the Indian subcontinent would, from a technical assessment point of view, be considered a depleted/degraded ecosystem, which needs a sustainable solution in terms of water augmentation to improve land productivity. However, a non-technical socio-cultural approach would say that the Thar Desert needs to be guarded against the spread of urbanization, mining, and tertiary activities to ensure that local communities, which subsist on the desert, continue to survive. If one considers the fact that some of the great reservoirs of genetic diversity or gene pools in the world are located in the desert zones of Iraq, Iran, and Syria; it will be evident that an approach that focuses on resource-consumption patterns and explores ways of improving existing resource-utilizing systems would be more constructive and sustainable.

Environmental movements in the world need to be strongly anchored on the foundations of equity if they have to succeed at the grassroot level.

Global public goods are organic extensions of local ones, and one should not be optimized at the cost of the other. Global climate change is the result of the lopsided pattern of development in the world. Emissions of CO_2 are largely from a few economic 'growth poles' of the world. Action to mitigate climate change has to come from these growth poles. At the same time, it is important to ensure that today's developing countries do not repeat the mistake of the developed world in promoting unsustainable growth patterns. For this to happen, it is important that low-carbon technologies that do not adversely affect economic development are made available to developing countries. Currently, there are many barriers to the realization of this possibility.

Similarly, in the fields of biodiversity conservation, the strategic importance of ensuring the success of local conservation efforts has to be recognized by the global community. Since local conservation efforts undertaken by local institutions aim to link livelihoods with the conserved, it is important that they are supported and promoted by the global community through appropriate incentives, including benefit sharing.

Similarly, the market control functions of global commodity agreements such as the International Coffee Agreement were dismantled at the turn of this century. As a result, price fluctuations have become the order of the day, prompting small peasants to invest less in their landholdings. This, in turn, has been one of the potent causes of land degradation in agro-commodity exporting countries of the developing world. Institutions, which ameliorate the lot of farmers in developing countries should focus on diversifying the income of farmers by promoting, revenue-yielding biodiversity products and services in conventional monocropped farms.

To this extent, it is important that investments in projects that have a bearing on global public goods is carefully carried out. A process of publicly advertising the global and local environmental consequences of projects funded through Foreign Direct Investment (FDI) can promote informed decision making.[18] Currently in India, FDI-funded projects are subject to environmental assessment and clearances. While decision making on FDIs are getting streamlined in India in the direction of faster approvals, they do suffer from the inadequacy of not *ab initio* entitling local communities to be informed about the possible environmental and social consequences of the project in a local area. An economically attractive FDI package will sail through despite the fact that it would not be fulfilling the requirements of informing local communities and decision makers about likely environmental impacts. The situation has not changed even after the Bhopal gas tragedy of 1985. The advent of legislations such as the Environment Protection Act 1985 and the extensive regulations on hazardous waste management and GMOs have not altered the bias towards economically attractive, overseas funded ventures. Similarly, there has been no effort on the part of MEAs to look at the impact of international investments. Most of the MEAs have clear provisions for trade and place restrictions on trade between parties to the protocol and non-parties. However, there is a need to prescribe guidelines for flow of investments towards technologies to avoid such flows that may ultimately generate hazardous substances or employ hazardous processes.

Indeed, civil societies can make up for deficiencies that MEAs have in regulating global investments. Paul Wapner has written an article of great interest, on the changing role of civil society in promoting healthy business (Wapner 1995, 525–49). He brings out the point that civil society needs to be seen differently from how they are seen at present. Wapner rejects the notion that activist organizations are just transnational pressure groups. He argues that they are basically political actors in their own right, and they have their distinct identity. He also advances the notion of 'World Civic Politics'. An activist who plays a part in the drama of world civic politics, would, instead of directly trying to pressurize states to change their ways, carve out its own space and locate its activities within the space of what is called 'global civil society' (1995, 526). He also mentions how voluntary associations have a pervasive influence on our culture or religion (1995). By targeting the processes of institutions, activists use the realms of transnational, social, cultural, and economic life to influence world public affairs (1995). Citing Melucci, Habermas, Offe, and other writers, Wapner further suggests that the effort of transnational civil society is to politicize various arenas. Giving the example of Greenpeace activism in various parts of the world, including the organization's super acts like climbing aboard whaling ships and so on, Wapner says that these dramatic aspects are meant to attract journalists and television crews and thus influence governments. More importantly, they help to ensure that the message is directly taken to all the actors from governments to corporations, private organizations, and even individuals to get them to take decisions that respect the 'environment' (1995, 531). Thus, in terms of this idea, the effort of Greenpeace is not only to influence governments to respond with appropriate changes in behaviour and policies, but also to promote other actors to understand the issues of good conduct and thus go beyond their mandate to persuade governments to come out with new policies. This way, Wapner argues that even if Greenpeace finds it difficult to get governments to accept their prescriptions, they still have the satisfaction of having convinced many people about the larger politics or the sensitivities associated with the environment (1995, 533).

Wapner's point is valid even today. Nearly three decades later, after Wapner's work came out, Tuvalu, the tiny Pacific Island country that lost part of its landmass to rising sea levels, announced its intention of building a digital twin of itself in the metaverse (the alternative, digital universe) to highlight the loss of sovereignty it suffered/or was likely to suffer in the real world on account of climate change. Indeed, Simon Kofe, Tuvalu's Foreign Minister, delivered his recorded speech at COP27 against the backdrop of a digital model of a Tuvalu island, which, he said was fasting going under water. Kofe's speech at CoP27, had a chastening impact on delegates from the developed world, who were until then, attempting to stonewall proposals to fund 'loss and damage' suffered by vulnerable countries.

Thus over a period of time, developing country governments too have successfully employed the dramaturgy techniques of civil society movements in MEA forums, with telling effects.

Coming to multinational corporate politics, Wapner has his own analysis. Citing the example of the efforts of the McDonald Corporation to change their businesses in the light of greater corporate environmental responsibility, Wapner says that these are not the result of governments breathing down their necks. He goes on to argue that multinational corporate politics that have beneficial impacts on the environment have created a new corporate culture. Wapner says that the enhanced direct flow of ODA to local NGOs obviously enhances their ability to take a more active and effective role in guiding the economic and environmental destinies of their communities (1995, 538). However, the effects are not limited to a robust civil society. Many of the activities related to investments concern state policies as well. Thus, governments are concerned about who controls foreign resources that come into the country (1995, 538). Wapner points to the fact that where direct flow of funds to environmental NGOs and other NGOs take place, governments of the countries concerned perceive this form of assistance as a pattern of foreign intervention addressed to diminish state power (1995, 539). Finally, addressing the issue of world civil politics, Wapner states that the focus on the civil dimension of world collective life is not meant to obscure the importance of inter-state relations in world affairs. He considers states to be major actors in the international system and hopes that they will continue to be so in future as well. However, the world civil politics has its own role to play. Transnational NGOs have a greater role in keeping the world consciousness at a more generic level; and in this world, civic efforts of non-state actors lives on (1995, 542).

An issue that comes out from the analysis of civil societies is how these sections contribute to the development of civic public spheres that articulate the aspirations of local communities to translocal decision-makers, who do not understand the logic of local communities that practise simple lifestyles. Reference is obviously to the role of civil societies in carving out a public sphere that relays the feelings of local communities, which are threatened by developments 'that can unsettle their peaceful lives. Peter Bunyard (1997) mentions the Gandhian traditions of the Chipko Movement led by Sunderlal Bahuguna and how the same movement transformed into a bitter struggle against the onset of the Tehri Dam in the Himalayas. For Bahuguna, the Chipko leader, the desire to save the environment was to ensure that children acquired a pollution-free and ecologically balanced world (1997, 262). Bunyard goes on to cite an article by Fred Pearce (1991) that eloquently stated what the local communities wanted—that the Tehri Dam be halted; however, for the policy and decision makers who were wedded to modernity, the justification for halting the project had to be reinvented in terms of modernity paradigms such as balance sheets, sanctity of science and seismology. The basic fact is that Bahuguna and the other locals of Uttarakhand do not require any interlocuters. They do not need any scientist or 'enlightened' member of the transnational civil society organizations to come and preach on what is good environmental practice. The local communities of the Himalayas have been rooted in traditions of environmentalism and are imbued with Gandhian ideals that help them teach global environmentalists a word or two on sustainable systems and practices. This rhymes well with our earlier analysis—that transnational global civic communities have to experience a reverse flow of communication from local communities about how important the local commons are to global commons and how best the former are preserved by endogenous societies.

Global civil society movements of the world have to be analysed from the viewpoint of how much of their arguments are situated on the concept of modernity. As already noted, when it comes to MEAs, especially the Basel Convention, the POPs Convention and the Rotterdam Convention, the critical problem is the environmental crisis created by modernity. Such issues need to be debated and deliberated not only in terms of the 'traditional other' but also in terms of the intrinsic perils of modernity products, such as chemicals, pesticides and other hazardous substances. Communication strategies need to be ambidextrous, i.e., they have to embrace the traditionalist and the modernity paradigms to contribute to the cause of sustainable development.

As a matter of fact, the arena of global civil society is dualistic; one which speaks the voice of conservation, articulating the rich traditions of endogenous communities and the other which speaks the language of modernity. The focus of the latter is on pointing out the perils of embracing highly energy-intensive and chemical-driven processes promised by the industrialized world.

It will be interesting to also take a look at how the global civil society is in tune with the reality of nation-states in developing countries. In the case of India, as is well known, the struggle of both the endogenous and local communities has been against the factors of so-called development that have ruined or altered ecosystems habitats. By comparison, the entire struggle for the Basel ban and the ban on POPs seems to be entirely spearheaded by Greenpeace and other transnational actors, which have at times tried to rope in local communities to join their cause. Governments resent the activities of transnational civil society groups as it is seen as an incursion on their space. However, when it comes to the struggle of local and endogenous communities such as the one led by the Narmada Bachao Andolan, there is no such resentment, despite serious disagreements on other scores. Also, when it comes to industrial projects by transnational corporations, states that have liberalized their economies take special interest in ensuring these projects are cleared and made operational, even if confronted with strong protests from both civil society groups and local communities.

Lessons from Mega Water Projects

In India, civil society concerns have been upheld by judicial intervention in a number of instances. Despite this, the Sardar Sarovar Project has come into existence and is going from strength to strength. The roots of the Narmada struggle go back to the Narmada Water Disputes Tribunal of 1969, which in its award of 1979, approved the project that had the potential of affecting nearly 158 villages in Madhya Pradesh and 27 villages in Maharashtra. Though a rehabilitation programme was put in, this did not fructify for long as envisaged by the Tribunal and the Supreme Court. The Apex Court was for a rigorous implementation of a rehabilitation and resettlement programme for those displaced by the Sardar Sarovar Project.

Though it is a fact that the Narmada Bachao Andolan has not got what it wanted over the years, it is nevertheless true that the changing stand of the union government, coupled with judicial interventions, ensured some salvage. The major lesson of mega projects like the Sardar Sarovar is that it has the potential of reviving inter-state differences on rehabilitation and resettlement.

The other basic truth is that the dam has not brought benefits to small farmers in Vadodara and other districts. This demolishes the standard refrain of development protagonists that environmental movements have only sought to disrupt ambitious development projects that would have provided basic infrastructure and life support systems for agriculturalists. The fact that the dam authorities have been criticized on two counts, namely the failure to rehabilitate and resettle the ousted communities and for creating an alternative that has not helped the ordinary farmers, is not palatable to the 'development school' of policy makers. The Narmada Bachao Andolan has succeeded in putting the World Bank on the defensive, forcing it to recant. In the past few years, the World Bank seems to have completely disassociated itself from the project, and it is now left to the state government to take up the cause of not only promoting the dam but also of confronting environmental groups.

Examples of similarly promoted large water projects abound. In Mizoram, a state in India's north-east, well-known for its immense forest and bamboo wealth, the capital city of Aizawl has been suffering from a serious water shortage. Srinivasan (2006) states that Aizawl's history of water scarcity commenced with the decline of traditional water conservation systems. Though two water reservoirs of 8,000 kL capacity were constructed way back in 1953 and 1954, they proved to be totally inadequate. The operation and maintenance costs of these reservoirs were such that they far outweighed the benefits. The unsustainability of the high-cost project caused the two water reservoirs to fail in Aizawl. Paradoxically, today the inhabitants of Aizawl are going back to old systems of decentralized water harvesting, having experienced failure of centralized water reservoir projects.

Adding to the problems is the fact that there are many places in India where fresh water supply sources have been rendered unsafe due to disposal of hazardous substances into them. Discharge of hazardous substances into water streams and agricultural lands is common in many parts of India. These problems persist despite awareness among the public about the virtues of safe drinking water and the importance of ensuring that sanitation facilities are fool-proof. Programmes which highlight the role of different natural ecosystems in preserving or contributing to human health and livelihood could ensure that a greater role is played by civil society groups, NGOs and local communities in the conservation of natural resources. Indeed, as per the direction of the Government of India, many state governments have gone in for rainwater-harvesting systems. For instance, the Government of Kerala amended its Kerala Municipality Building Rules Act in 2004 to provide for rooftop rainwater harvesting. As per the amendments to the Act, building owners are required to ensure that rooftop rainwater harvesting arrangements are provided as an integral part of new building constructions, including residential and non-residential buildings such as schools, colleges, and office buildings.

A related initiative on the part of Kerala relates to steps taken to improve the safety of dams. As per the Dam Safety Act of 2000, every state which has a significant number of dams has to constitute a body called, 'Dam Safety Organization', whose work will be to closely monitor the safety aspects of dams in terms of an emergency action plan. These measures go with serious efforts to ensure that indigenous knowledge regarding water management (including rainwater storage and other storage systems) are revived. However, the fact is that indigenous knowledge systems for water resources are dependent for their survival on local community initiatives. Much depends on how these actions can tap their knowledge systems.

The interesting point that comes out in the discussions in the preceding paragraphs is that in countries such as India, while there are major efforts to construct mammoth water projects like the Narmada Sagar Project, there have also been substantial policy initiatives to tap traditional knowledge of local communities in the areas of water conservation and storage. With the growth of local civil society movements, it is to be assumed that traditional water conservation systems will grow from strength to strength, enabling a greater role to be played by decentralized water structures that benefit local communities. A convergence between environmental movements and national bureaucracies can be brought about if there is a progressive realization that large multi-purpose irrigation and power generation projects are extremely unwieldy, socially insensitive, and difficult to maintain in terms of operational and maintenance expenditure. There is also a realization in India that large irrigation systems are intrinsically or inherently unsafe as demonstrated in the case of the Morvi dam disaster in Gujarat a few years ago.

Therefore, a combination of economic efficiency and safety could motivate governments to go for decentralized natural resource systems, at least in the realm of water resources. If civil society and activist groups queer the pitch for the government, the country could move away from large structures to small structures. Though it was true that during the late 1990s, there was an effort to bring about an active programme for river linking in India, the fact that this aroused considerable opposition from water conservationists and environmental groups had virtually led to the grandiose idea being abandoned.

The real purpose of highlighting these examples is to underscore the point that large-scale projects that are introduced to replace small capacity water bodies are not as effective as one would like to believe due to their low social benefits. Instead, they create bureaucracies and control systems that exist for their own sake, irrespective of whether these bodies contribute toward the cause for which they were created. This is instrumentalism in action.

Joint Forest Management

The trend towards instrumentalism that one sees in the realm of water resources extends to other natural resources, such as forests and common lands as well. Despite protests against the forest bureaucracy and state control over forests and common land resources in different parts of India, and in spite of movements against forest bureaucracy in different parts of India, both during the British period and in the post-independence period, ownership rights have not changed for these resources. Here, I would like to bring out the difference between forest movements in the British period compared with those that have taken place in the post-independence phase.

The movements against the forest establishment in the British period arose due to the state abrogating the customary rights over forests enjoyed by the tribal and local communities. Once the process of state takeover was complete, the focus of local community struggles was not to get back ownership rights, but to prevent transfer of forest lands for industrial and infrastructural projects, which entailed displacement of local communities from forests. This has, therefore, been the situation in the post-independence period.

The decentralization processes in forestry that were inspired by local movements was formalized by the Government of India. The government took the lead in bringing about the JFM Initiative in 1990. The Scheduled Tribes and Other Traditional Forest Dwellers (Recognition of Forest Rights) Act 2006, which was passed by Parliament for providing tribal communities with rights over forest lands, has been another effort at the 'inclusiveness' initiated by the central/federal government of India. It is likely that in the future, the process of decentralized management of forests may proceed on regional lines, enabling an autonomous course of forest development in the different regions and locations of India powered by local communities.

The JFM Programme, which began in India in 1990, was conceived in a top-down fashion. Guidelines and resources on JFM trickled down from the central/federal government to the state governments and finally to the local levels. In terms of the PEER criteria (Policy intent, Efficiency, Effectiveness and Ramifications) developed by Damodaran and Engel (2003), it is seen that the functioning of this programme in different states of India had suffered from the absence of a policy intent of promoting active community rights over forests. When it came to the efficiency dimension, namely the efficiency of JFM in translating the idea of community involvement in forests into tangible ground-level realities, it was seen that the process was deficient in many states. Evidence of the slack on the efficiency front was the high transaction costs incurred in managing degraded forest with community support (Damodaran and Engel 2003). Coming to the 'effectiveness' dimension of the PEER paradigm, it was noted that the impact of JFM in promoting community empowerment was suspect in many parts of the country. However, when it came to the ramification dimension, that is, the larger policy and sub-national programme effect of JFM, the study noted that many states had almost made it a habit to introduce the term 'community involvement' in forestry projects that were externally aided and funded by different donor agencies.

In terms of the PEER criteria, the major drawback of the JFM lay in the philosophical and effectiveness dimension. It was indeed one of the striking observations of the study by Damodaran and Engel (2003) that states such as Kerala, which had implemented the ambitious programme of People's Planning Process, fell far behind when it came to implementing the JFM concept in its true spirit. This questions the notion that political decentralization automatically promotes decentralization in the management of natural resources. This is not to state that the Government of Kerala had not taken steps to implement the JFM. The Kerala government set up about 323 participatory forest management committees, involving 1.71 lakh hectares of forest area and also involved nearly 41,000 families including nearly 4,000 scheduled castes and 11,371 scheduled tribes. Ground-level studies on afforestation, eco-development programmes, and tree plantation programmes in the state conducted by the authors show that the participative approach entailed involvement of village communities by way of providing labour for forestry operations. This is a far cry from the notion of peoples' planning programme of the state government, which had empowered local communities in the design, formulation, and implementation of development plans.

Moving to another state in India, famous for its relatively high social development indicators and political decentralization traditions, namely Karnataka, an interesting scenario emerges. A rapid assessment of the Joint Forest Planning Process in the eastern plains of Karnataka done by Lélé et al. (2005) mentions the existence of a big divergence between what are considered to be technical objectives of the process, namely achieving physical targets in terms of tree planting and so on, and what is considered to be the social or institutional dimension, namely involvement of people in the management of forest projects. The study notes that the stiff loans taken by the Karnataka Forest Department through the Japan Bank for International Co-operation at 12 per cent interest prompted the Karnataka Forest Department to utilize the services of village forest committees set up under the JFM process in order to bring a very large area of degraded land under plantations. The large loans and interest payments entailed by it required them to take to commercially valuable softwood species. The authors proceed to note that the key challenge of the JFM process in Karnataka is to bring about an attitudinal change on the part of the forest department. Findings in the study about the Karnataka Forest Department's JFM initiatives go well with the findings by Damodaran and Engel (2003) about the philosophical infirmities of the JFM process in India. It is clear that the Karnataka Forest Department did not focus on the policy intent behind the JFM process, which was to empower local communities to run the assigned forest lands. Rather, the forest department got itself entangled in procedural matters and instrumental issues connected to performance monitoring in terms of the parameters set up from above.

The Scheduled Tribes and Other Traditional Forest Dwellers (Recognition of Forest Rights) Act 2006 could get into a similar problem if officials in charge of its implementation get lost in instrumentalities connected with grant of tenancy rights over assigned forest lands, rather than ensuring the basic policy intent of conferring property rights for deserving tribals. Since this Act has been formulated within the framework of the Forest Conservation Act of 1980, grant of land to tribal communities is considered to be 'non-forestry' purpose, requiring prior permission of the Ministry of Environment, Forest and Climate Change.

Issues such as determining the settlement date of a tribal household will mean the play of the state machinery in operational details, thus deflecting the government from the larger task of ensuring that deserving tribal households are conferred with tenancy rights.

Thus, the deficiency with policies for empowerment of local communities in the management of natural resources is that they lose their intended focus and get lost in technicalities and procedures. Instead of viewing empowerment as ethically desirable and justice driven, efforts are made to associate communities in the management of natural resources in order to utilize them for policing and protecting the resource. The assumption is that community help will contribute to reduced destruction of forests. Such an instrumental view that seeks community involvement for a narrow functional purpose obfuscates the larger ethical dimensions of empowerment that underlies community welfare projects.

In the context of the priorities identified by the CBD, the UNEP had taken up assessments of biodiversity wealth all over the world with a view to documenting or detailing proximate and non-proximate causes for the decline of biodiversity. In conjunction with the introduction of the MDGs, there was a major effort to undertake a comprehensive survey of different ecosystems in the world through the millennium ecosystem assessment. The millennium ecosystem assessment has gone beyond the ambit of the global biodiversity assessments conducted by the UNEP in the 1990s. For one, it goes beyond biodiversity to embrace total ecosystems and conceivably includes both natural and non-constructed ecosystems in the world. In the second place, the major emphasis of the millennium ecosystem assessment was on its relationship with the MDGs, which, as we have noted earlier, tries to concentrate on extremes of poverty and underdevelopment.

Global efforts like the millennium ecosystem assessment should focus on linking assessment exercises with detailed diagnosis of the causes of biodiversity and ecosystem degradation. The next step is to prescribe, on the basis of the diagnosis, as to what could be possible modes of improving the functioning of the ecosystems. Prescriptions laid down in global assessment exercises should not try to be specific in terms of localities and regions. They should avoid viewing ecosystems from a strictly utilitarian or a functional point of view, i.e., in terms of how they could make ecosystems look better. These exercises ought to look at the ethical prerequisite of situating community needs and aspirations in their solutions.

Indeed, as Swanson (2005) argues, the main factor that has caused the decline of biodiversity has been the failure on the part of all concerned to appreciate and appropriate the values of biological diversity (2005, 42). Biodiversity is endangered when human communities are selective in exploiting biological resources for their economic needs. What Swanson seems to be alluding to is a pattern of development that creates over-dependence on certain natural resources to the exclusion of certain others. He relates the case of the African elephant and its rapid depletion, which, according to him, has been due to the apathy of the owners of wildlife. A large mammal like an elephant requires a large land habitat along with voluminous feed. The unsustainability of maintaining the African elephant in its true habitat and the attraction of populating the elephant habitat with easy-to-manage species set the stage to grant liberal access regime to poachers, who in turn used their might to obtain as much ivory as possible to feed ivory-greedy consumers in the developed world. In the process, the elephant population rapidly declined paving the way for an alternative land use pattern that might not be conducive to biodiversity conservation. If assessments of biodiversity loss had been properly carried out, it would have attributed the biodiversity loss in elephant habitats to ivory trade. This would, in turn, have led to policy solutions that aimed to increase anti-poaching or anti-hunting squads in national parks and sanctuaries.

Most of the policy prescriptions for managing forest in India have been based on the diagnosis of what constitutes the proximate causes for the decline of forest cover in the country. Shifting cultivation has been considered as one of the potent sources of deforestation in India. The discourse was so strong that during the colonial period, the practice of shifting cultivation was banned in forest lands. This brought considerable hardships to the tribal communities of North-East India, who practised shifting cultivation. The thinking did not change even after independence. However, in the 1970s, studies by P.S. Ramakrishnan and a few others questioned the very basis of considering shifting cultivation to be the source of all problems. By pointing to the benign influence of shifting cultivation on nutrient cycles, these scientists criticized earlier theories which had deplored shifting cultivation and related practices in a technically narrow way without going into the ultimate issue of 'when' and 'why' shifting cultivation becomes unsustainable.

Likewise, it has been common to attribute deforestation in India to the increasing dependence of forest dependent villages on small timber and non-timber forest produce. This diagnosis, which had dominated forestry literature during the 1950s to the 1970s, led to two policy prescriptions which were inimical to the age-old rights that India's village communities enjoyed over forests. The first prescription aimed to extinguish the few rights that local communities enjoyed over forest areas, which caused considerable hardship to forest-dependent villages. The second prescription led to the promotion of social forestry enclaves in non-cultivated village lands. The idea behind social forestry was that the small timber, firewood and other non-timber forest produce from these enclaves would serve to reduce the dependence of local communities on natural forests. The tragedy of India's social forestry schemes was that it was often executed in grazing lands that formed the fodder base of village livestock. This, in turn, disturbed the traditional man livestock relations underlying the subsistence agriculture systems in these villages.

Societal Risks

The fundamental principle underlying all environmental agreements in the world, signed prior to and after the Rio Summit, is that environmental protection should go with development. The conventions also carry with them the underlying point that the concepts of environment protection and economic development need to take into account the dimension of societal risks or risks faced by a social group or community, either due to the depletion of global public goods or due to the influx of substances that harm global goods. There has been, for quite some time, a fair amount of research on societal risks, particularly on the significance of societal risks in decision-making. Most of the concepts that relate societal risk and risk assessment to remediation emerged in the 1980s and 1990s. Their evolution has gone hand in hand with the evolution of MEAs. More specifically, all global environmental agreements that were signed in the 1980s and 1990s, namely the Vienna convention on Ozone Depleting Substances, the Montreal Protocol, the Basel Convention on Transboundary Movement of Hazardous Wastes, the Rio Conventions of Climate Change, Biodiversity and Desertification, and POPS and the related Chemicals Conventions, have a common point in that they are squarely premised on an implicit notion of risks that confront human society; and so have been the cases of the Cartagena Protocol and the WTO Agreements on Sanitary and Phytosanitary Agreement.

National legislations in countries such as India have also been premised on implicit notions or principles on what constitutes social or societal risks. Thus, the Environment Protection Act of 1986 and its associated rules provide guidelines for chemical accidents, emergency planning preparedness and associated public liability insurance regimes. In recent times, the Ministry of Environment, Forest and Climate Change of the Government of India, has gone a step further and adopted a system of good practices in environment and regulations with a strategic view to codifying standardized methods of dealing with the societal risks.

Excess codification can, in turn, be related to a progressive tendency to treat societal risks as an instrumentalist concept. Of the two streams of research on societal risks, the first one looks at conceptual issues relating to societal risks and the second one at the technique of measurement and assessment of risks. The first category has not received close attention (Damodaran 2006). In the second category, where the focus has been on measuring societal risks, one of the favourite techniques has been to work out the cumulative distribution of the number of fatalities in relation to the consequences. Clearly, this kind of approach that tries to measure frequencies of fatalities is an effort at perfecting the concept of societal risks in instrumentalist terms. Indeed, there have been a number of studies which deal with conceptual issues relating to societal risks from the angles of equity and justice. One of the key approaches in this category has been to view risks from an 'individual-society interface' paradigm (2006). Following J.K. Brijling and P.H.A.J.M. van Gelder, the individual-society paradigm can be tackled at two levels. The first level entails efforts on the part of an individual to evaluate risks by weighing them against direct and indirect personal benefits. Here, the individual's ability to absorb risks may be co-related to her ability to withstand harm from hazards. The specified level of harm is narrowed down to loss of life in many practical cases (2006). Another method of looking at social risks is to undertake the assessment of an activity in terms of what are the acceptable risks to society. The focus is not on an individual but on a collection of individuals who make up the total population of the society. Nevertheless, here again, societal risks are sought to be traced to the number of casualties, which is once again an instrumentalist notion.

However, when it comes to risk perception of communities, we enter a new terrain. Risk perception of communities is mapped on issues such as recombinant DNA products, pesticides use in agriculture, genetically modified crops, hazardous chemicals, and nuclear materials management (Sandquist 2004). Another interesting mapping exercise relates to the aspect of risk bias. Studies by Slavic (1999) analyses the role of psychological variables, such as an individual's background traits in colouring individual perception (Damodaran 2006).

Instrumentalist approaches to societal risks lose out, on the cognitive dimension of risks. If studies on societal risks were conducted in non-instrumental terms, the results would be different and better. For instance, an anthropological perception of what constitutes risks would cast an issue in a different mould. Thus, the crisis management measures adopted in the wake of the Bhopal gas tragedy in India placed importance on a system of safeguards and emergency preparedness rather than on regulations, which prevent hazardous technologies from being employed. What is more, the 'safeguards approach' did not incorporate the dimension of anthropological perception of risks. While experts have underscored the importance of undertaking risk analysis and assessment at the points of individual-society interaction, it is important to ensure that such approaches are not simply reduced to measurement tools such as fatalities or the measurement of frequencies of fatalities. These measures ought to be supplemented by tools that can assess the resilience of social institutions and local self-governments to withstand risks based on the risk perceptions of the affected human communities.

Therefore, when a policy maker carries out risk assessment exercises in relation to an industrial project that makes use of hazardous substances, it is important to ensure that the perception of the local community is mapped through a process of perception mapping (Damodaran 2006). The mapping needs to be done at the local self-government levels so that a decision that is specific to the project locale is adopted. The offshoot of such an approach would be that a risk communication system would not be a vertical process based on a top-down approach, but one which is horizontal. Translated in simple terms, it means that local mapping of risk perceptions should be independent of 'top-down approaches' that communicate risks in an instrumentalist manner.

The absence of such an approach was felt when the tsunami hit the Indian and Sri Lankan coast lines, devastating human and material life along the coastal lines, with attendant consequences in terms of deprivation, loss of human life and destruction of natural resources. The rehabilitation process for the tsunami aftermath was initiated by a shell-shocked state machinery comprising both the central and state governments (which were clearly not prepared for such an eventuality). The crisis management operations were executed in a haphazard manner. In the wake of the tsunami, a frantic state machinery sent in a series of communications to local administrations and local communities hinting at the possibility of more devastating waves like the tsunami hitting the coastal areas and requesting local communities to evacuate people from the shorelines. A day or two later, when the tsunami waves did not hit as predicted by the state machinery, the faith of the local communities in the state machinery was lost. Likewise, though rehabilitation packages were introduced over a period of time to help the victims, this was not to their satisfaction.

Indeed, in the tsunami-hit areas of southern India, there has been a wealth of new local knowledge generated after the calamity. This was sought to be explored by the author a few years after the havoc through a field survey (2006). The survey sought to understand from the victims about the types of risks that they had to face on account of the calamity. The survey yielded the result that local communities were badly hit by loss of assets (boats, agricultural implements, and land degradation). Their sufferings were compounded by delays in asset reconstruction. Local communities who had a better understanding of their losses came up with solutions to minimize damage to their assets. Their suggestions on how to design rehabilitation packages were an eye-opener to me. For the victims, the best way of speeding up asset reconstruction was to streamline the flow of finances. Clearly, risk perception of local communities cannot be dismissed as unscientific. Further ignoring these perceptions would be fatal because people who experience calamities could have their own unique ways of looking at both the probability of risks as well as the ability to meet or cope with these risks if appropriately supported by the state.

It is here that the importance of horizontally mapping risks is vital. Unfortunately, societal risk analysis does not perceive the importance of this step and gets lost in instrumentalities of the 'probability of cyclone', the 'intensity of cyclone', the probability of seismic activities, and the best methods by which tsunami waves could be kept under check based on top-down studies. Indeed, as we noted elsewhere, many coastal protection policies reduced amelioration measures to a choice between seawalls and bio-shields. However, very few policies have sought to elicit the preferences of local communities regarding amelioration measures.

The instrumentalist notion of societal risks has influenced the evolution of the MEAs as well as national plans that have been framed to tackle these risks. The lessons that we learn from the instrumental upstaging of the paradigm of societal risks are many. For instance, in the case of UNFCCC, the issue of catastrophic impacts of sea level rise had been a major point of contention amongst scientists. The problem with the climate change discourse is that it seeks to handle multiple variables. However, the correlation between increase in temperature and rise in sea levels or between increase in temperature and CO_2 emissions by industries in developed countries is not readily understood by potential victims. A technically-driven risk assessment system that seeks to correlate the rise of ambient temperature with rise in sea level is bound to be neglected by a number of coastal communities. For many local coastal communities, 'shoreland erosion' causes the sea to inundate shorelands. It has nothing to do with the abstraction of global warming. The solution of constructing seawalls is likewise perceived differently by local communities. Sea walls are viewed by local fisherman communities as obstructing their access to shorelands or to fishing and other activities (2006). They do not see any benefits from such walls. Besides, there are too many technicalities with the coastal zone regulations that the local communities do not understand. Rather, it can be surmised that the maze of technicality and instrumentalism associated with the Climate Change Convention and the IPCC reports has resulted in a substantially poor appreciation of the climate change issue amongst the local communities.

Coming to the CBD, the aspect of societal risks is highlighted in portions of the convention that deal with protection and conservation of biological diversity. The importance of safety measures to ward threats to biological diversity is understood by all the stakeholders. The relevance of societal risks is more explicit in the case of the Cartagena Protocol on Biosafety, which specifies the likely adverse impacts of GMOs on ecological habitats. As mentioned, the principle of AIA is designed to prevent possible risks to the environment. It is clear that a system that lays down *de minimis* limits on the presence of GMOs for pronouncing the safety of GM product is instrumentalism at its best. Where technical protocols dominate biosafety tests of genetically modified crops, instrumentalist perspectives tend to dominate assessment of projects. Such instrumental approaches gloss over economic and social impacts of such projects.

A case in point is the story of *Bacillus thurengensis* (Bt) cotton in India, which was imported in 1996 and took nearly six years of lab and field testing before getting approved for commercial release in 2002. Although in terms of the technical parameters, Bt cotton was found to be less risky to the environment, the larger issue of possible economic risks arising from the cultivation of the plant was ignored in the pre-commercial release phase.

A number of NGOs, including Greenpeace and the Centre for Science and Environment (CSE) have documented that the performance of Bt cotton has fallen short of expectations. What is important is the fact that the perception of risks seems to vary from region to region. While studies on farmers who had taken to Bt cotton through the Navbharat route indicate a high degree of acceptance for Bt cotton on account of its economic performance (Shah 2005), reports from the states of Andhra Pradesh and Karnataka suggest the opposite. Thus, varying assessments about economic risks involving Bt cotton do not facilitate decisions by decision-making authorities. An instrumentalist position, which keeps out the ticklish economic and social variations from its ambit, is convenient for policy makers but not an objective one as it ignores social and economic risks.

When it comes to the Basel Convention, the issue of societal risks is shrouded in a maze of technical details and instrumentalist regulations. The same holds true for the Stockholm Convention on POPs and the Rotterdam Convention. These Conventions have also bypassed social and anthropological assessment of risks. While assessing the economic benefits of recycling and reprocessing, these conventions could have also worked out the larger social costs created by systems that reuse and recycle hazardous wastes.

In the preceding discussions about the different global environmental conventions, it was noted that the aspect of instrumentality has obfuscated or obliterated the fairness and equity concepts that characterize the intent of the conventions. It is also explained as to how the instrumentality notion had overridden the concepts of equity and justice. The real issue is why this has happened. The answer needs to be provided at a broader philosophical level.

Instrumentalism: What Does It Deny?

We now take a look at the broad philosophical position that emerges from our preceding discussions regarding MEAs. The constant battle between the forces of instrumentality and the forces that seek to uphold the fairness and equity of dimensions of these conventions throws up interesting philosophical issues.

As Hannah Arendt states, 'Unless a concept is intrinsic, it is vulnerable to instrumentalism'. Arendt's philosopher/teacher, Martin Heidegger, views 'equity' and 'justice' as related to 'authenticity' or in being authentic, which in turn is related to freedom. In the context of a technology, it means the right to redesign and re-function received knowledge, the right to access every product for refinement, or the right to possess the freedom to reject a technology and thus be free from instrumentality and standardization processes. A technology, in Heidegger's words, has to be emancipatory in nature, otherwise the risk is that it will not hold any promise of freedom required to ensure equity and fairness. A technology that does not promise freedom for social groups and communities for which it is intended cannot be considered authentic and, therefore, as promising equity or fairness. The real problem is that instrumentalism tends to deny freedom and authenticity, which in turn affects equity and fairness. As Heidegger and Herbert Marcuse argue, technology is not just an artefact—it is a way of thinking and style of practice (Feenberg 2005).

Feenberg goes on to examine the cultural horizon of a technology, which typically embodies design and carries within it the elements of beliefs, values, and norms. Thus, in terms of this paradigm, it is not difficult to see that even a process of instrumentality, which reifies technism, is basically a social construction and has undertones of the social and cultural elements involved in the process. It is because social and cultural factors are embedded in technology that we tend to argue that an instrumental position is something which could act as a negation of equity and fairness. Feenberg (2005, 49–50) himself uses the concept of instrumentalism and considers instrumentalism as occurring at two levels, namely:

1. An original function and its relation to reality; and
2. Level of design of implementation.

The notion of instrumentalism involves an obsession or preoccupation with technical details, which completely displaces the basic concern of freedom and 'authenticity' that MEAs or conventions are supposed to ensure. What is required is to look at the scope of conventions in terms of their emancipatory power. Environmentally sound technologies (ESTs) that handle climate change, biodiversity conservation or biosafety in a manner that optimizes freedom for the communities is what is required to get the local communities to commit themselves to the cause of sustainable development. Where local communities refashion and redesign technologies, such technologies get to be emancipatory in nature as they free these communities from environmental threats as perceived by the latter.

If one goes through the literature on UNFCCC, the Basel Convention and the Stockholm Convention on POPs, we see that there is scope for transferring technology and tailoring them to suit local circumstances through public-private partnerships. Public-private partnerships for developing EST, which are GHG reducing, backstopping or involve sound environmental management practices in the use of hazardous wastes are desirable, provided the term 'public' seeks to involve local communities. There is a potential case for effecting transfer of technology to local groups and re-infusing IPRs on tailored products. The debates related to the Montreal Protocol, the Basel Convention and the UNFCCC revolve around the relative willingness of private parties to transfer their proprietary technologies protected by IP to countries/communities on fair and equitable terms. However, the literature on EST addresses solutions like joint ventures and related business models that respect IPRs and propose ways by which the inventor can continue to have control over these technologies. Most of the proprietary technologies are licensed or are brought into the fold of joint venture-collaborative projects to ensure that they remain with the proprietor in their unalloyed form without getting reconfigured and readjusted by recipient countries or entities. Non-customized technologies may be inappropriate to local contexts and costly to transplant. Indeed, this is the point that India has been speaking about in climate change forums.

When it comes to the CBD, the situation is no different. Though it is a fact that many modern drugs and pharmaceuticals and nutraceuticals are based on biomaterials and traditional knowledge of the local communities in developing countries, the accent is still very much on a system of benefit sharing which, while recognizing the importance of IPRs over proprietary technologies and products, also seeks to provide incentives to local communities for parting with their traditional knowledge or bio-resources. This has been the spirit of the Nagoya Protocol.

There have been many initiatives by way of participatory plant breeding in various parts of the world. These trends have democratized plant breeding. Even when advanced plant biotechnology products based on Bt were customized to local conditions, the political control over the technology development had been with multi-stakeholders' platforms (Rodriguez, Ruirenkamp, and Jongerden 2006). Of late, the trend in India has been for institutions such as the Indian Council of Agricultural Research (ICAR) and the Indian Agriculture Research Institute (IARI) to conduct research on transgenic crops based on a participatory plant-breeding process that involves local farmers. Here efforts are made to ascertain farmers' requirements and to tailor technologies and products to suit the local environment. It can be anticipated that a similar process of readjusted technologies that seeks to incorporate local culture and local norms could be initiated for the implementation of the Stockholm/POPs Convention. It is quite possible to implement the phase-out of POPS by reviving certain traditional practices that rely on plant-based biochemicals for plant protection measures.

To recapitulate, the main problem with the UNFCCC, the Montreal Protocol, and the Basel Convention is that they deal with technology or products that are based on modernity principles and are driven by exclusiveness that is reinforced by IPRs. These conventions find it impossible to communicate their agenda. Under such circumstances, it is quite likely that instrumentalism, which is implicit in these conventions, will dominate and displace equity and natural justice concerns. The plant biotechnology industry appears to be in the throes of change. There is a greater appetite for local customization. As mentioned earlier, this has been mainly due to the fact that the primary stakeholders who use the plant biotechnology products are small farmers and local communities.

While it is true that the UNFCCC, the Basel Convention, and the Montreal Protocol rely on industries to accept new clean technologies, the emancipatory potential of these technologies can be realized only if there is a process of vertical and horizontal communication systems amongst local communities and the governments. This requires moving away from national communications or nationally determined contributions to local communications and locally determined contributions on climate change even if it is felt that these communities do not in any manner contribute to the basic processes. Manual Castells (2000) once remarked about the annihilation of space in a globalized world that is brought about when the world transitions to a digital space for its functioning.

To sum up, the peril of instrumentalism that has affected global environmental management regimes cannot be overlooked. As we have noted, the UNFCCC, the Basel Convention, and Biodiversity Convention, highlight the importance of instituting elaborate systems of monitoring, verifying, and collating information. Extensive focus on these systems causes these conventions to lose sight of their the basic mission of ensuring conservation of public goods. Instrumentalism that displaces the ideals of equity and fairness and focusses on process and procedures cannot foster sustainable development and community welfare in nation-states. This undermines their efforts to save the global commons from destruction.

12

Civil Society, Environment, and Trade

The Role of Stakeholders

The role of civil society and NGOs in the evolution of international environmental conventions has been phenomenal. This is creditable given the fact that these stakeholders do not enjoy any official *locus standi* in the negotiations associated with these Conventions. In the previous chapters we discussed a few issues concerning the role of civil society groups in the governance of nation-states, their influence on globalization and in securing global accords in the fields of trade and human rights. We have also seen how the civil society has coped with the instrumentalism inherent in MEAs.

Though in the initial stages of the environment and trade debate, civil societies and NGOs were not effective participants, this changed with the efflux of time. Article 71 of the UN Charter requires that the UN Economic and Social Council (ECOSOC) makes suitable arrangements for holding consultations with NGOs on matters falling within its competence (Mori 2004). In the year 1948, in pursuance of Article 71 of the UN Charter, the ECOSOC adopted resolutions providing NGOs with consultative status.[1] Simultaneously, other UN agencies such as the United Nations Children's Fund (UNICEF), the United Nations High Commission of the Refugees (UNHCR), and the United Nations Development Programme (UNDP) introduced their own accreditation system procedures to co-opt NGOs in deliberations (Mori 2004, 159). The idea behind these efforts was to provide legitimacy and intensity to UN deliberations. Following the Rio Summit of 1992 (the UNCED), NGOs and civil society groups really got involved in the process of negotiations by participating in global environmental agreements as observers (Mori 2004, 159). The World Summit for Social Development held in Copenhagen in 1995 accredited 1,299 NGOs, of which 811 participated.

India, Climate Change, and The Global Commons. A. Damodaran, Oxford University Press. © A. Damodaran 2024.
DOI: 10.1093/oso/9780192899828.003.0012

Civil Society participation in world conferences on human rights caused these groups to influence the manner in which the human rights agenda evolved in the international arena. Over a period, NGOs have also realized that they need to go beyond their passive consultative roles (2004, 160). These groups have campaigned to be granted active consultative rights in the UN General Assembly and the Security Council. The Commission on Sustainable Development has proactively sought to involve NGOs in the implementation of Agenda 21 (2004, 161). The establishment of an NGO Steering Committee for the Commission on Sustainable Development (CSD) and the setting of the Sustainable Development Issues Network (SDIN) in 2001 represented further progress in the involvement of NGOs in the international environment process (2004, 162). Many prominent NGOs, which have participated in international environmental deliberations have not been supportive of the stand taken by countries of the North in these forums. The list of such NGOs includes, the Northern Alliance for Sustainability (ANPED), The Third World Network (TWN), and the Environmental License Center International (ELCI). These organizations have played an important part by bringing out position papers and circulating them, thereby mobilizing public opinion and civil society opinion on a variety of issues of concern to sustainable development at the global level. Indeed, according to Mori, the CSD went ahead to organize multi-stakeholder dialogues, based on open participatory approaches. This created enthusiasm on the part of many NGOs to get actively involved in the CSD process. In terms of their role in MEAs, the author notes that NGOs have played an important role in the enforcement of the CITES, while in the case of the Climate Change and the Kyoto Protocol, they presented a picture of confusion. Similarly, involvement of NGOs with other multilateral organizations such as the World Bank and the WTO has been by way of interventions in matters connected to high-profile projects/issues. After the Sardar Sarovar project drew flak from the NGOs and civil society movement, the World Bank initiated an active process of consultations with NGOs on development projects implemented by it in different countries. This included consultations regarding environmental guidelines followed by the Bank for development projects. The World Bank has also been consulting NGOs and civil society groups on global environmental issues such as biodiversity and climate change. Mori notes that NGO involvement in policies has increased and they have substantially transcended the project-based approach. One salient point which emerges in Mori's seminal paper is that NGOs or civil society groups have been expounded alternative viewpoints that differed from official policy lines. In the context of MEAs, organizations such as the TWN and Greenpeace have highlighted the importance of incorporating the principles of equity and natural justice in interventions involving global public goods. The Basel Ban was brought in due to intense pressures mounted by these organizations. Organizations such as TWN, Greenpeace, Pesticides Action Network, and a host of other organizations were in the forefront, demanding hard changes to unfair international regimes. Indeed, on issues relating to GMOs and biodiversity conservation, civil society and NGO groups contributed to an in-depth understanding of the key issues, by getting actively involved with topics related to traditional knowledge, benefit sharing, and biosafety. These organizations have also tried to facilitate policy change, not only at the level of Convention Secretariats, but also at national government levels.

However, NGOs and civil society groups have not been able to secure substantive changes to the CBD, particularly on the issue of interface between traditional knowledge and TRIPS. Part of the reason for this has been their relative failure to intervene in the same matter in the WTO forum. In the case of the climate change convention, NGOs did not, despite their best intentions, produce a very coherent position on implementation issues until 2015. While many NGOs based in Europe and North America were in favour of the United States joining the Kyoto Protocol and had strongly condemned the continuing tendency of countries of the North for using flexible instruments in the climate change convention to avoid or postpone quantitative restrictions on CO2 emissions, a clearer position on the issues of technology transfer and carbon sequestration projects (under the CDM) took longer to emerge.

In the run up to the COP 21 of the UNFCCC at Paris in December 2015, international NGOs like Christian Aid, Green Alliance, Greenpeace, the Royal Society for the Protection of Birds (RSPB), and World Wide Fund For Nature (WWF) vociferously argued that the proposed Agreement on climate change needed to (a) include ambitious action before and after 2020, (b) carry a strong legal framework with clear rules, (c) highlight equity, (d) adopt long-term approaches to mitigation, (e) actively mobilize public finance for adaptation, (f) draft a comprehensive framework for action on deforestation and land use, and (g) adopt action that had close linkages to the Sustainable Development Goals (SDGs).[2]

The kind of articulation that the NGOs and Civil Society groups attempted in the case of the Basel Convention was missing when it came to the Biodiversity Convention proceedings. Part of the reason for this could be the widespread perception in developing countries, especially among the academia, intellectuals, and local activists that NGOs which focus on global environmental issues such as climate change and biodiversity are elitists and are concerned with issues which are not of pressing priority to developing countries. It is also a perception amongst developing countries that climate change is an agenda imposed by the North on the South and that it needs to be seen more as an effort on the part of corporate undertakings in the developed world to re-colonize developing countries to carry out projects that enable them to get away from hard obligations of having to reduce emissions by themselves. Both climate change and biodiversity conservation are viewed as relics of ecological imperialism whereby private industries in developed countries seek to coax developing countries to open their natural resource base in return for capital investments. NGOs in the developed world which espouse the causes of sustainable agriculture and organic foods are viewed by some of their counterparts in the South as tacitly aligned with the policy makers of the North who support causes that, in effect, add to trade barriers on conventional agricultural and horticultural crops emanating from the South. In the case of India, several NGOs have been active at the national level, and many more at the regional and local levels. A few of them, like the Centre for Science and Environment (CSE), function at all three levels. While organizations such as Kalpavriksh have been in the forefront in trying to influence national policies, others like the Consumer Unity and Trust Society (CUTS) articulate positions on world trade matters in the WTO. International NGOs such as the World Wildlife Fund advocate sustainable development agendas with focus on market-based instruments. Organizations led by Vandana Shiva and Suman Sahai (representing the New Delhi-based Research Institute for Science, Technology, and Ecology and Gene Campaign, respectively) are noted for their activism against genetically modified products and related IP issues. The Energy Research Institute (TERI) has been in the forefront of global environmental issues, notably climate change and have also been involved with renewable and energy efficiency projects.

There are NGOs and academic institutions which are consulted by the Government of India and state governments on matters relating to sustainable development and natural resources management. The presumption behind these consultations is that technical and academic institutions approach issues from a scientific perspective rather than getting into ideological positions. Given the philosophical dimensions of the MEAs, it is impossible not to be ideological. There is nothing like a value-free approach to issues of conservation related to global public goods. There is no science that is free from philosophical values, and no technology that defies political and social construction.

India has not been forthcoming when it comes to inclusion of NGOs in official delegations that go for Convention deliberations. Though, for all major summits, like the Rio Summit of 1992, the Indian delegations included NGO representatives, this is not the case with negotiations involving the MEAs.

It will be interesting to look at how NGOs and civil society groups have intervened in the WTO forum. At the WTO ministerial conference held in Seattle in 1999, civil society and NGOs held vociferous protests against the draconian rules of globalization brought in by the WTO. Since Seattle, despite the shift of the next ministerial meeting to a more politically placid place (Doha in 2001), activism by NGOs and civil society groups has been evident by way of demonstrations and holding of parallel forums to draw the attention of the public to the 'voice of the unheard'. The protest patterns that one sees in the WTO conference venues are more acrimonious than what one gets to see in high-level meetings related to MEAs. This is because the WTO is largely viewed as a symbol of unrequited or unmitigated globalization, which carries adverse consequences for the livelihoods of the poor in different parts of the world. As a matter of fact, WTO-related protests have the tacit support of left-wing parties as well as civil society groups that are wedded to welfare causes. Indeed, NGO protests involving movements of other trade agreements in the world have even involved radical left-leaning leaders. The protests against the America Summit at Mar del Plata in Argentina in November 2005 were galvanized by Hugo Chavez and Fidel Castro. The specific street protests against President George W. Bush (for reviving the free trade area of the United States) stood in marked contrast to the ovation received by Chavez and Castro at the same venue.

Let us now take a closer look at why NGOs and civil society groups are against the WTO. The problems that NGOs and the civil society groups have with the WTO have been summed up in a book written by Houthart and Polet (2001). The authors cite Bernard Crick's definition of sovereignty as 'policies that require every government to have within it a source of absolute power on final decisions and the ability to enforce its decisions'. The thesis advanced by the authors is that the WTO undermines the sovereignty of nation-states. The WTO places severe limitations on the ability of developing countries to pursue independent trade and fiscal policies. These countries are not only under pressure to deregulate and liberalize imports but are also pressurized to pare down export subsidies as well as to reduce sops that enable domestic industries to ward off import competition. Nation-states not comfortable with the WTO are those which feel that their identity arises not only from their political sovereignty but also from the 'space' they enjoy in formulating their economic and trade policies in a manner that is conducive to the interests of their domestic constituencies. The interesting part here is that the WTO does not resemble a world state when it comes to framing its policies. All decisions in the WTO are arrived by consensus. Yet the WTO is seen as a mammoth incursion on the freedom of nation-states to pursue their independent policies, which in turn is assumed to endanger their sovereignty and political freedom.

Taking a cue from the successful experience of the WTO in getting some of the nation-states to cede their powers, there have been demands from certain quarters for a super national organization which could look at all issues that the WTO handles, but in a manner that permits better approaches (Jones 2004).

We go back to WTO's Seattle Summit in 1999. The way the WTO was confronted by NGOs and civil society groups at Seattle is best explained in an article[4] entitled 'Flash Point Trade: WTO under Fire'. Analysing the Seattle Summit, the article mentions that civil society groups which protested against the WTO at the Summit comprised various groups with different ideological persuasions. The damages that they brought to the Summit premises were considerable, amounting to $3 million.

The main point made here is that the people who have been protesting against the WTO at Seattle were also those who were against globalization. These people were predominantly from the developed world. Faced by the threat of global movement of capital outside developed countries, many sections which had been adversely affected by the process also joined the ranks of civil society groups to protest against the WTO in Seattle. Sensitive issues for developing countries (like child labour) were attempted to be pushed through at Seattle, both within and outside the Summit premises, with the Clinton Administration tacitly supporting these proposals. Despite the Clinton–Gore efforts to push the labour standards agenda in the WTO, it never got onto the table mainly because of the collective opposition from developing countries, which felt that this issue would threaten their exports in a big way. Other issues that came up from NGOs assembled at Seattle included genetically modified foods, destruction of the Amazon rainforests, and ecological sensitivity of trade-related activities (2004, 20).

There is another point of view on the WTO which states that it seeks to undermine the operations of MNCs as well as the sovereignty of developed countries like the United States. Thus, Paul Krugman (2000) described the 'Seattle Man' as the archetypal person or organization which protests against MNCs for their exploitation of the world's economic and environmental resources. As Krugman goes on to state, somebody like the ace Republican Pat Buchanan has also been a strong opponent of the WTO on the grounds that the organization has eroded even the sovereignty of the United States in the matter of economic rights, the economic policy, and so on. Thus, it is not just the developing countries which have been affected in this manner. This thinking has been pervasive even during the Trump Presidency.

Much of this ire against the WTO comes from the difficult time that the United States had with the WTO dispute settlement body on the issue of use of environmental standards in gasoline imports.

Faced with the criticism by a WTO panel that the United States breached the global trading rules by imposing levies on more than $200bn of Chinese goods, Donald Trump's Trade representative, Robert Lighthizer, said: 'This panel report confirms what the Trump administration has been saying for four years: the WTO is completely inadequate to stop China's harmful technology practices.'[3]

The interesting part of the stand taken by the United States on the trade issue is that it is sectoral and case-to-case based. The more fundamental and philosophical approach to environment and trade is not visible. This leads to inconsistencies in approach. For instance, the US environmental standard that was applied to block gasoline imports, was a stellar example of the resolve to enforce tough environmental standards to block imports. However, the United States did not attempt to have a tight dispensation when it came to CO_2 emissions from fossil fuel combustion. When it comes to trade policy, while the United States would like all subsidies and trade-distorting measures to be removed from imported goods, it does not follow the same by itself. The United States has also been a close supporter of the Cairns group in the WTO forum, which advocated 'freer' trade in agricultural goods. However, agriculture continues to be a protected sector in the United States. Therefore, in an atmosphere where issues are taken on a case-by-case basis, relative economic advantages are assessed on a case-to-case basis, and where trade instruments are applied to block movement of goods, the greatest casualty will be sustainable development.

There are a few NGOs and civil society groups which look at the entire gamut of the North-South dynamics while firming up their position on global environmental issues. However, as with some of the developed member countries of the WTO, a few NGOs also fall into the loop of fragmented or sectoral approaches when it comes to environmental issues. There are technical NGOs which specialize in preparing scientific and technical assessment reports, while there exist others called 'advocacy groups' which are active in mobilizing opinions on various issues connected with a subject. The problem with sectoral approaches is that they overlook broader economic and environmental concerns including cross-cutting issues. Issues such as climate change, desertification, and biodiversity, besides relating to each other, also straddle economic and other environmental concerns. In practical terms, a sectoral approach would cause an NGO, that focuses exclusively on, say, energy-efficiency dimensions of climate change, to avoid taking a comprehensive look at the overall impact of their sectoral policies on other environmental resources such as forests and biodiversity. What causes such tunnel vision is the truncation and fragmentation of environmental themes at the global level.

The real task in the days to come is to find out how far the NGOs themselves try to avoid a narrow sectoral approach and move closer to perspectives which comprehensively look at environmental policy dynamics at country level. The result of such an approach would be creative interventions leading to the adoption of strategies that are integrated.

Interestingly, those NGOs which have been advocating a world government do not realize that the world government could get into the same problems as nation-states when it comes to inter-linking different sectors. In some respects, the Agenda 21 adopted at the Rio Summit by the world community had tried to link global environmental problems with national environmental issues by prescribing a set of guidelines in terms of concrete actions that integrates global and national concerns. When it came to international facilitation, the mammoth agenda was squarely placed at the doors of the Commission on Sustainable Development (CSD), which unfortunately did not have the financial and organizational bandwidth to take up the ambitious task. At the national level, Agenda 21 had practically deteriorated to compartmentalized reading of different chapters by different government departments for possible action points. This has undermined the possibility of integrated approaches to implementation.

In the context of Agenda 21, implementation of different action points mentioned in different chapters does not suffice. It is important that the principles of equity, fairness, and justice are observed for the various action points. It is this strategic focus, which has been lost, and this has been mainly because of the serious capacity barriers organizations have in digesting the maze of facts contained within Agenda 21, and in coming out with workable programmes based on well-integrated approaches.

In other words, to have an ambitious programme of sustainable development and to dream of decentralization of project execution at the same time, does not make much sense, when serious capacity barriers exist at the grassroots. Thus organizational centralization is inevitable when it comes to implementing operational projects that seek to combine multiple elements. However, the problem with organizational centralization in project implementation is that it breeds incompetence. Unfortunately, there has been little capacity amongst large sections of civil society sectors to deal with programmes and actions in an integrated manner. A cross-cutting project that deals with biodiversity and climate change requires the help of project planners and designers who can appreciate the trade-offs between the two concerns and resolve the issue in a manner that advances the maxims of equity and fairness. This is a tall order for the civil society.

The critical challenge confronting civil society groups lies in their ability to appreciate cross-cutting issues involving global conventions on the one hand, and national and local development priorities on the other. Many of these organizations do not have the capacity to visualize such projects. This impedes their ability to monitor their implementation in an efficient manner. Digital literacy on the part of NGOs and civil society groups can facilitate improved monitoring and evaluation of such projects at the local level.

Capacity building of civil society groups is a priority that needs to be taken up in right earnest.

13

COVID-19 as Global Commons

Issues of Equity, Sustainability, and Instrumentalism

The deadly coronavirus of 2019 popularly referred to as COVID-19 was caused by the SARS-CoV-2 virus. COVID-19 was declared by the World Health Organization (WHO) as a Public Health Emergency of International Concern on 30 January 2020, and later on as a pandemic on 11 March 2020. COVID-19 is the successor of a series of severe acute respiratory syndrome coronavirus (SARS-CoV) diseases, commencing with SARS-CoV-1 during 2002–03, which was followed by the H1N1 influenza of 2009, and the Middle East Respiratory Syndrome coronavirus (MERS-CoV) in 2012. However, none of the three precedents to COVID-19 assumed 'pandemic' proportions.

As of 1 December 2021, human lives lost on account of the pandemic stood at a mammoth 5.2 million,[1] thus proving that COVID-19 is the most calamitous pandemic after the infamous Spanish influenza pandemic of 1918–20.[2] But unlike the Spanish flu which ebbed after two years, COVID-19 does not look like vanishing even two years after its inception, primarily due to the high rate of mutations of the original virus that alters its transmission patterns and its degree of virulence. Indeed COVID-19 has undergone as many as five mutations between 2020 and 2022. Thus the Alpha (B.1.1.7) variant which spread to 170 countries, was succeeded by the Beta (B.1.351) variant which was reported in 119 countries and the Gamma (P.1) variant that covered 71 countries. This was followed by the Delta variant (B.1.617.2), which originated in India and spread to nearly 85 other countries. During late November 2021, there emerged the new strain termed as 'omicron', which was first noticed in South Africa. Omicron marked a 'major jump in the evolution' of COVID-19 by way of high-speed transmission, though its adverse impact on human lives was limited.

India, Climate Change, and The Global Commons. A. Damodaran, Oxford University Press. © A. Damodaran 2024.
DOI: 10.1093/oso/9780192899828.003.0013

Unlike the Spanish flu which originated in the West and travelled East, primarily aided by troop movements across the world on account of the First World War, COVID-19 has travelled from the East to the West in a highly globalized world. COVID-19's global spread was aided by the high density of inter-country and inter-continental travel. As a matter of fact, travel and tourism, which was as high as 10.4 per cent of global GDP in 2019, declined sharply to 5.5 per cent[3] in 2020 due to restrictions in mobility imposed by Governments, following the WHO's declaration of the disease as a pandemic.[4]

Sustainability Issues

The epicentre of COVID-19 is widely considered to be the wet markets of the city of Wuhan in China where, in early December 2019, the first case of infection was detected. Wet markets are places where live animals kept in cages, are slaughtered 'live' and sold to customers.[5] While the early versions of SARS and MERS owed their origins to civet cats and camels, the primary source of SARS-CoV-2 is considered to be horseshoe bats with the secondary source of infection being the pangolin. It is conjectured that the coronavirus jumped to human beings from pangolins that were stocked in the Wuhan wet market in dingy cages. The other theory about the origin of COVID-19 is that it occurred due to an accidental leak from a lab of the Wuhan Institute of Virology (WIV). However this is not yet supported by robust evidence.[6] A variant of the latter theory is that the SARS-CoV-2 was bioengineered in the Wuhan Lab. This theory is also not borne out by clinching evidence.

Despite differences of opinion on the sources of origin of SARS-CoV-2, a common point that emerges is all SARS viruses have their origin in animals and are, therefore, zoonotic in nature. Thus the pandemic raises critical issues relating to biodiversity conservation and biosafety. It makes eminent sense to address these issues in the interest of avoiding future pandemics.

The really critical issue about wet markets is not that they trade in live animals but that they deal with species of wild origin which are captively bred in farms. In countries which freely permit captive breeding of wild animals like tigers, leopards, bears, pangolins, there is a strong chance of such animals being more prone to virus diseases that have zoonotic impacts, as compared to regular domesticated animals that are traded in these markets. More serious, is the high probability of illegally trafficked wild species from forests and protected areas, entering the supply chain of wet markets, which besides being a violation of the CITES, also serves to enhance the risk of the outbreak of zoonotic diseases. More basically, captive breeding of wild species for commercial ends and illegal trafficking of endangered and threatened species seriously violate the UN's Convention on Biological Diversity (CBD).

It is noteworthy that both horseshoe bats and civet cats (considered to be the primary source of the SARS epidemic of 2004) are not listed in the Convention on International Trade in Endangered Species of Wild Fauna and Flora (CITES). But then these two species are not trafficked across nation-state borders as much as the animal species listed in Appendices 1 and 2 of the Convention.[7] However 'pangolins' (colloquially referred to as 'ant eaters'), the intermediate species, from which the SARS-COVID 2 virus is supposed to have jumped to human beings, is considered to be one of the most trafficked mammals in the world. While the meat of a pangolin is considered to be a delicacy, its scales are used in traditional medicine and folk remedies to treat a range of ailments from asthma to rheumatism and arthritis.[8] Between 2011 and 2013, an estimated 116,990 to 233,980 pangolins were supposed to have been slaughtered. Experts believe that seizures of pangolin contraband represent only 10 per cent of the actual volume of pangolins figuring in illegal wildlife trade.[9]

Despite deciding to transfer all species of pangolins in the endangered category in 2016, the CITES was not able to prevent trafficking of the species to the wet markets in Asia. When the WHO declared the COVID-19 as a pandemic in March 2020, the world looked towards the CITES for intervention. However, the CITES authorities were not forthcoming with a remediation plan, since they felt that the Convention did not have a mandate to deal with zoonotic diseases. In other words, the argument of the CITES Secretariat was that there were no provisions in the Convention to prevent transboundary movement of species that had the potential to spread diseases amongst other animal and human beings, unless they happened to fall in Appendix 1 or Appendix 2 of the Convention.

Similarly the hygiene of wet markets and the resultant outbreak of zoonotic diseases do not figure in the mandate either of the CITES or the CBD. Rather this aspect has a closer bearing on the WTO Agreement on Sanitary and Phytosanitary Measures (WTO-SPS) which requires governments to apply food safety and animal and plant health measures (sanitary and phytosanitary or SPS measures) to both 'domestically produced food or local animal and plant diseases, as well as to products coming from other countries.'[10] The WTO- SPS requires all countries to maintain measures to ensure that food is safe for consumers, and seeks to prevent the spread of pests or diseases among animals and plants. These sanitary and phytosanitary measures include provisions that require products to come from disease-free areas. In fact, the ambit of sanitary and phytosanitary measures also extends to inspection of imported products and consignments which can be extended to domestically produced food through facilitating national legislations, in case the same is vital in the larger interests of protecting human life and health from zoonotic diseases.[11]

Finally comes the issue of pandemics that are induced by accidental transmission of bioengineered organisms across borders. This issue could possibly come under the ambit of the Cartagena Protocol on Biosafety. As mentioned earlier, the Cartagena Protocol on Biosafety is an international agreement which aims to ensure the safe handling, transport, and use of living modified organisms (LMOs) resulting from modern biotechnology, which may adversely affect biological diversity, besides posing risks to human health. As also described earlier, Living Modified Organism (LMO) is defined by the Cartagena Protocol, as any living organism that possesses a novel combination of genetic material obtained through the use of modern biotechnology. Furthermore under Article 17(1) of the Protocol, any accidental leakage of any genetically modified organism and its unintentional transboundary movement needs to be notified to affected countries by the party concerned as soon as the Party comes to know of the release.

However, the case of fixing the source of COVID-19 ran into political sensitivities. In the first place, the host country denied that the organism had been biotechnologically engineered. The host country government has also denied the allegation that the virus was accidentally released into the environment. Further, international bodies that were deputed to investigate into the causal factors underlying COVID-19, also have failed to establish that the crisis has been engendered by the accidental release and transboundary movement of bioengineered organisms into the environment.

Thus the WHO, which deputed an international team to Wuhan during January–February 2021, could not come to any conclusion about the source of the virus.[12] However, irrespective of this disappointing outcome, there can be no denying that the pandemic has raised important issues regarding the importance of conservation and bio-safety and the need to regulate the insanitary conditions under which live animals of wild origin are housed and slaughtered in wet markets. One of the important lessons arising from the rapid transboundary transmission of the COVID-19 virus across countries, is the importance of conducting risk assessment exercises (as required under the Cartagena Protocol) to determine the source of the problem.

Equity

The equity dimension of COVID-19 centres on the issue of the distribution of vaccines across the world, based on the principle of 'allocation according to needs' rather than free market maxim of 'allocation according to the capacity to pay'. The ultimate organizational vehicle that upholds the equity dimension of COVID-19 is the COVAX facility. COVAX is a partnership venture of GAVI, the Vaccine Alliance, the Coalition for Epidemic Preparedness Innovations (CEPI), and the WHO. Following the outbreak of COVID-19, COVAX took upon itself the task of facilitating research, development, and manufacture of a wide range of COVID-19 vaccine candidates, and also put in place procurement mechanisms which were based on negotiated prices and its distribution amongst needy low-income countries.

COVAX sought to provide a few other benefits as well. Indeed, one of the fundamental successes of COVAX during the 2020–21 lay in its ability to screen and identify promising vaccine candidates and have support systems to help identified companies to manufacture them. In the wake of COVID-19, COVAX instituted schemes to provide incentives to credible manufacturers to enable them to commence vaccine production operations as soon as their vaccine was approved by national authorities. Second, the Facility sought to negotiate competitive prices from vaccine manufacturers to help poor countries to access the vaccines at affordable prices. Finally, the facility enabled well-to-do countries with self-financing capacities to access vaccines in time.

Thus COVAX attempted to help two categories of countries, viz those who are unable to afford COVID-19 vaccines and higher-income, self-financing countries which have not succeeded in working out bilateral deals to procure the requisite quantum of vaccines that have been approved for use by the WHO.[13]

The COVAX facility attempted to mobilize financial resources to enable funding of vaccine procurement operations for distribution to 92 low- and middle-income countries. The Facility also supported procurement of vaccines for upper middle-income and high-income nations that can self-finance their vaccine purchases. The self-financing countries were provided with two options for receiving vaccines through the Facility, viz, committed purchase arrangements and an optional purchase arrangement. Under the former track, self-financing countries could opt to make Committed Purchases of vaccines through the COVAX Facility by providing a lower upfront payment of US$ 1.60 per dose which is 15 per cent of the total cost per dose.[14] Under the optional purchase agreement, these countries were granted the freedom to opt out of any particular vaccine without giving up their entitlement to receive their full share of doses of other candidates, subject to supply becoming available. This facility thus sought to prevent these countries from overcrowding for particular vaccines which they have arranged to procure from manufacturers concerned through direct, bilateral arrangements.

The manner in which the COVAX facility provides special access to lower and middle-income countries (which are neither able to procure nor able to pay for vaccines), is through the COVAX-Advance Market Commitment (COVAX-AMC) which, in turn, is entirely funded through Official Development Assistance (ODA).

The strategic success of COVAX lies in its ability to have in place systems that could provide poorer countries with access to vaccines at affordable prices, thus reducing their vulnerability to COVID-19 or to the different variants of COVID-19 (Gleeson 2021[15]).

Despite its immense potential and well-conceived systems, COVAX failed to deliver on its mandate on more than one count. The Facility's AMC scheme could not raise financial resources on the scale planned. This can be gauged from the fact that as against a seed capital target of US$2 billion by the end 2020, the resources raised by the AMC window was only of the order of US$70 billion.[16]

The other limitation faced by COVAX in relation to the COVID-19 pandemic, was that the higher-income countries (that had signed in to join the facility's efforts) did not really brace up to sign legally binding agreements that would have obliged them to financially contribute to the COVAX facility.[17]

The third limitation of the COVAX facility was that it failed on the vaccine procurement front due to the non-availability of vaccines which, in turn, is attributed to stockpiling and cornering of vaccine stocks by developed countries. It is reported that 13 of the 48 firms engaged in COVID-19 vaccine development had made advance sales mostly to advanced countries, even before emergency-use authorization were granted for these vaccines.[18] Canada ordered vaccines 10 times its population's requirement, while the United States accumulated stocks which was 4 times more than its population needed.[19] Patents and related IPRs have also contributed to lower production of vaccines and largely explains why vaccine technologies have not been smoothly transferred to developing country firms with the requisite capabilities to manufacture them according to the laid-down quality specifications.[20]

Though by the end of November 2021, around 54.2 per cent of the global population had received at least one COVID-19 vaccine dose, for low-income countries, the rate was just around 5.8 per cent (Gleeson 2021). Nearly 40 countries in Africa had only less than 10 per cent of their populations fully vaccinated (Gleeson 2021).

The origin of the Omicron variant in South Africa in late November 2021 and its subsequent spread across the world, has been a matter of concern, partly on account of the high transmission rates associated with the variant and partly due to its high transmission record which threatened to infect people who had undergone vaccination (Gleeson 2021).

These factors explain why there is considerable merit in the proposal brought in by India and South Africa before the WTO-TRIPS Council during October 2020, for the waiver of IPRs (Patents, Copyrights,

Industrial Designs and Trade Secrets) over COVID-19 products and technologies for a period of three years. The proposal gradually gained traction with more than 100 countries signing up and the United States itself joining forces in May 2021. However the proposal is locked up in tough negotiations, with the European Union coming up with an alternative proposal which calls for tweaking the Agreement on Trade-Related Aspects of Intellectual Property Rights (TRIPS) to provide for a regime of compulsory licensing over vaccines and other COVID-19 related products and technologies. As Gleeson (2021) argues, the EU proposal does not extend to trade secrets and hence will act as a severe setback to the transfer of vaccine manufacturing technologies covered by trade secrets.

At a more fundamental level, compulsory licensing regimes requires country-specific action, besides being cumbersome and dilatory in view of the elaborate procedures and extensive negotiations required for signing the requisite agreements with the IPR holder concerned.

In short, the proposal for waiver does not look like going through the WTO in a smooth or timely manner.

The Social Costs of Vaccine Wastage

The macro picture of vaccine shortages and cornering of vaccine stocks by affluent countries does not bring out the social costs associated with the transport and distribution of allocated vaccines in receiving countries. The central problem of social costs incurred by COVID-19 logistics and wastages arises from the geographical and economic divide between producers of COVID-19 vaccines and its consumers (developing and least developed countries). What compounds the problem is the need to dispense with vaccines within a short period of time, due to their limited shelf life. Logistical delays aggravate the crisis by creating wastages of vaccines that are allocated to countries or communities. These wastages arise from poor transportation systems that damage the transported vaccines. In addition, inept handling of vaccines at the entry and exit points at the country level also adds to the social costs. What further compounded the problems were delays in the clearance of imported vaccines by regulatory agencies in receiving countries and the precautionary stocking of vaccines in receiving countries in anticipation of future needs. In the vaccine-receiving countries panic diversion of vaccines to zones which experience a sudden spurt in infections led to denial of vaccines in areas which were scheduled to receive them. These ad hoc measures led to either 'excess stocking' at zones of flare up and understocking at the jab centres in zones which were scheduled to receive them.

Wastages of vaccines in receiving countries constitute wastage of global vaccine production capacities. This aggravates the social costs associated with the production, distribution, and dispensation of vaccines.

Figures 13.1 and 13.2 illustrate the locus of social costs associated with COVID-19 vaccines in producing countries at the global rollout phase. Figure 13.3 summarizes the global social costs chain in receiving countries in terms of primary, secondary, and tertiary wastages and its adverse consequences in straining the limited global production capacities.

As the three figures bring out, the core problems associated with the supply chains of COVID-19 vaccines are (a) shortfall in actual supply of committed vaccine doses from overseas and domestic companies; and (b) stochastic surges in supply flows to distribution centres at the provincial level, followed by choked 'jab points'. The problem was exacerbated

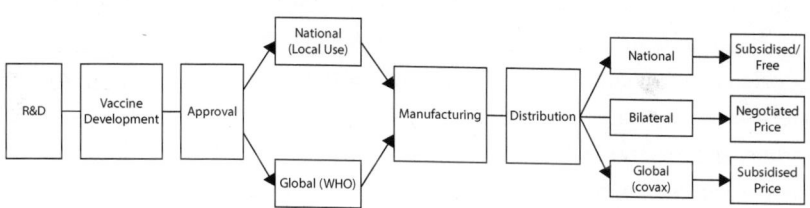

Figure 13.1 Life Cycle of a Vaccine: The Global Rollout Phase

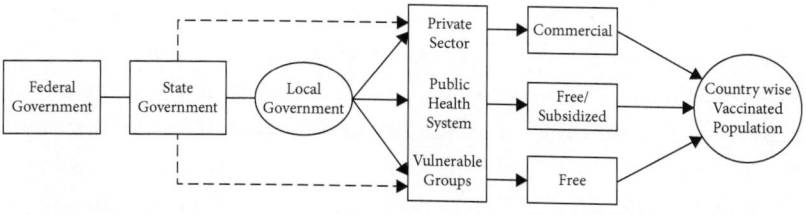

Figure 13.2 Life Cycle of a Vaccine: National Rollout in Vaccine Importing Country

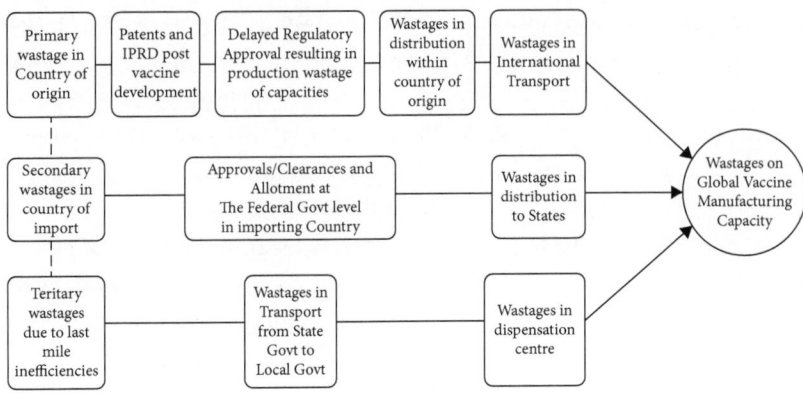

Figure 13.3 The Global Social Costs Cycle for COVID-19 Vaccine

by many unconventional jab centres with insufficient facilities being opened up to increase the pace of vaccine jabs.

Remove Instrumentalism

The WHO has the mandate of (a) coordinating the world's response to health emergencies; (b) promoting the well-being of citizens across the world; (c) preventing disease; and (d) expanding access to health care across the world. As a part of its assigned functions relating to health emergencies, the WHO is required to alert the world about threats arising from pandemics well in advance and provide advice to authorities to handle pandemics by providing requisite tool kits. In addition, as discussed earlier, WHO also partners with governments and international agencies like the GAVI Vaccine Alliance (set up by the Gates Foundation) to save the lives of vulnerable people by ensuring equitable and sustainable use of vaccines through the COVAX Facility. Though the WHO has many successes to its credit, particularly in the realms of the Child Vaccination Program, smallpox immunization, and the management of SARS CoV 1 of 2003, its leadership was found deficient when it came to handling the COVID-19 pandemic. One major criticism against the WHO was its ineffectiveness in alerting various countries regarding COVID-19 in January 2020. The cause of the failure is attributed to the instrumentalism associated with 'scientific semantics'. Thus the first set of alerts by the WHO about COVID-19 was ignored by member countries as it was couched in technical language, viz, 'public health emergency of international concern' (abbreviated as PHEIC). The seriousness of the situation conveyed by the term/acronym was not grasped by many countries. This is said to have led to the rapid spread of the coronavirus across the globe.[21] Had the WHO employed the term 'pandemic', it would have attracted the due attention of the member countries and this could have perhaps minimized the havoc (Maxmen, A. 2021). The other criticism against the WHO has been that it depended on reports and data from national authorities to assess the situation of the pandemic in the country concerned. Since countries fell short on their national reporting obligations, the WHO's ability to effectively intervene in the affected countries was impaired. The fact that the WHO is not mandated to look at non-official data to assess the situation in different countries, is symbolic of a serious instrumental constraint.

Though, in the wake of COVID-19 the WHO has taken up the idea of a separate global treaty on pandemics, this has not so far taken off. What remains clear is that for the organization to be more decisive and effective during pandemics, it is vital that it sheds its instrumentalist approaches of the kind mentioned. Similarly the weak financial situation of the organization has precluded its effectiveness in times of grave emergencies arising from pandemics. The system of assessed contributions has not worked well for the organization as it has proved to be ineffective in ensuring that countries actually contribute to the organization on a sustained basis on the basis of its performance and strategic importance.

The Way Out

For the pandemics of the future to be managed more effectively, it is essential that national governments concerned treat them as a global commons issue based on the criteria of non-excludability and equitable access to relevant health products, services, and technologies. The first pre-condition for such an approach is to set up a 'Global Pandemic Management Fund' based on annual contributions by the member states of the WHO. These efforts could be supplemented by corporates and private international funding organizations. Contributions to this fund need to be additional to the assessed contributions of the member countries to the WHO. The proposed Global Fund may be provided with a 'ring fenced corpus' or endowment fund, that may be utilized for providing emergency services in poor countries in the event of future pandemics. The proceeds of the endowment fund could be utilized to support the COVAX facility during pandemics. In addition to the endowment fund, a revolving fund could also be part of the propose 'Global Pandemic Management Fund'. Money mobilized by the revolving fund could be utilized to (a) carry out R&D work on advanced early warning systems, (b) facilitate the upgrading of health delivery systems in developing countries with a view to overcoming wastages and reducing the social costs of vaccination, (c) assess the progress of R&D work in new generations of vaccines, and (d) facilitate equitable transfer of pandemic related technologies.

The last plank of the alternative strategy is to ensure that the proposed 'Treaty on Pandemics' eschews instrumentalism in its communications and evaluation systems relating to pandemics. More fundamentally, the proposed treaty should facilitate the creation and sustenance of the 'Global Pandemics Management Fund', by having suitable provisos concerning the Fund incorporated in the Treaty. This will confer the proposed fund with legal sanctity.

14

Restructuring Regimes
for Sustainable Development

The central thesis advanced in this book is that international environmental regimes as exemplified by MEAs suffer from the scourge of instrumentalism. Instrumentalism can be viewed as an overwhelming
focus on the instruments and tools of assessing the magnitude of a
problem and the economic efficiency by which laid-down procedures
are followed. The problem with instrumentalism is that the larger ramifications and outcomes of activities get ignored. Instrumentalism is a
political construction and its dominance is a hard reality that cannot
be ignored in discussions and debates centring on environmental
governance.

Many scholars have taken a hard look at how international environmental governance regimes could be changed for the better. Some
of them have gone into these issues in greater depth and looked for
solutions to ensure that equity and justice reign supreme in the international scheme of things, particularly in relation to sustainable development issues. A case in point is an interesting article written by Yesako
Kameyama (2004) on the genesis of the Intergovernmental Panel on
Climate Change (IPCC). Kameyama states that in the initial stages,
IPCC was basically a group of scientific experts to support policy makers
by reviewing relevant scientific activities around the globe of relevance
to climate change. IPCC's three assessment reports (of 1990, 1996, and
2001) carried startling findings. The finding of the 2001 report that the
global mean temperature is expected to increase from 1.4 degrees centigrade to 5.8 degrees centigrade between 1990 and 2100, was perhaps the
most striking one.

However, in spite of its composition and its role in advancing scientific knowledge and its inputs, IPCC reports have been acrimoniously

India, Climate Change, and The Global Commons. A. Damodaran, Oxford University Press. © A. Damodaran 2024.
DOI: 10.1093/oso/9780192899828.003.0014

debated and disputed. He notes that the IPCC had changed by the turn of the century from what it used to be in the 1990s. Kameyama notes that the role of the IPCC has expanded by the turn of the present century and gone beyond the simple or straightforward activity of writing assessment reports on scientific studies relevant to climate change. He notes that while in the 1980s, the role of the IPCC was to flag climate change as a global issue, in the wake of the adoption of the UNFCCC and the Kyoto Protocol by the majority of nations, the IPCC had to take into account additional demands made by its stakeholders (2004, 138). Many stakeholders argued that if IPCC were to be relevant and legitimate, it had to reflect political imperatives rather than getting bogged down by pushing for technically sound but economically infeasible agenda for action on climate change. Thus Kameyama argues for a complete restructuring of the IPCC process through more inclusive approaches that tap the expertise of developing countries rather than confine their inputs to those offered by experts. He is also for instituting peer review of reports, in order to give IPCC reports greater legitimacy, thereby providing the climate change agenda with a realist touch. Kameyama supports the two-track system of the IPCC, namely producing assessment reports and providing summaries for policy makers (2004, 139). Presumably, Kameyama supposes that such a two-track method is the surest way of ensuring that IPCC reports would not only have scientific quality but also political acceptability. Of course, Kameyama, like many others, believed that a World Environment Organization (WEO) should be established. He views the IPCC as a scientific organization that can be strengthened with objectively crafted studies. Despite its limitations, Kameyama notices that a number of national governments do use IPCC reports to sell to their domestic constituencies about the imminence of climate change. However, despite these arguments, Kameyama concludes that the presence of too many government officials in a scientific body, would shackle its functioning (2004, 151).

The problem with Kameyama's analysis is that he is unduly sanguine about the prospect of a supranational entity being able to govern environmental affairs in the world. The emergence of a supranational entity in the sphere of environment is definitely likely to cast a shadow on the autonomy that nation-states have enjoyed in pursuing sustainable development goals in accordance to the aspirations and needs of their people. Further such supranational bodies would not be sensitive to the political complexions associated with the implementation of MEA programmes on the ground. The main point we have made in earlier discussions on climate change and related conventions is that a politicized system of instrumentalism will promote its own logic of control, which may not go with the fundamental ideals of equity and justice that are necessary to ensure the whole-hearted involvement of developing countries in global environmental affairs. The dimension of equity and justice in the case of the Climate Convention entitles developing countries that are situated on the lower rungs of economic growth to be treated differently from countries that are economically prosperous. Developing countries view themselves as victims of history and see the present climate change regimes as denying them the opportunity to advance economically.

For low carbon pathways of growth to be achieved, developing countries need to be in a position where they can mobilize capital resources that are necessary to deploy advanced clean technologies. This will not easily materialize since capital flows from the developed to the developing world has been sparse. The key issue is whether the IPCC can suggest steps to rectify this situation.

The Kyoto Protocol was a strategic step towards ensuring justice and equity by not requiring any developing country to adopt any quantitative restriction on emissions. More importantly by incorporating the Clean Development Mechanism (CDM) as a flexible instrument that can incentivize developing countries to voluntarily contribute to greenhouse gas (GHG) mitigation, the Protocol got a few developing countries to pay attention to voluntary mitigation. Unfortunately, despite all its merits, the Protocol has been affected by a high degree of instrumentalism on the twin issues of emission trading and evaluation of CDM projects. As mentioned earlier, the manner in which CDM projects are monitored and verified smacks of instrumentalism. The Sustainable Development Mechanism (SDM) that replaces the Kyoto Protocol in the Paris Agreement, will also fall into the same vortex of instrumentalism unless we pay closer attention to the rules of the game.

The key question is whether the IPCC can come up with a science-based, politically acceptable solution to these ticklish issues.

Is the GEF as 'Just' as ODA?

Jake Werksman (2004, 35–49), in his study of the Global Environmental Facility (GEF), explains how the facility is based on the notion of functional clustering. As Werksman argues, the problem with the GEF is that its proponents want it to be a single monolithic financial mechanism that would meet the financial requirements of all the key MEAs. As Werksman proceeds, most of the developing countries in the world were inherently not in favour of the GEF, as they feared that the facility would adopt clustered approaches of bunching different MEA objectives in operational projects which would neither provide justice to individual MEAs nor confer benefits to local communities. Werksman goes on to consider the differences between the governance structures of MEAs (the COP) and the GEF Council. After going through the nuts and bolts of the legal instrument of the GEF, Werksman comes to the conclusion that GEF governance is fundamentally different from those that of MEAs. Werksman argues that the GEF is not an autonomous institution and hence cannot enter into formal legal relationships with other autonomous institutions (2004, 39). Werksman also goes on to note that there is no clearly identified procedure for resolving disputes arising between GEF and the COPs of Conventions or between GEF and its implementing agencies, notably the World Bank, the United Nations Development Programme (UNDP), the United Nations Environment Programme (UNEP), Asian Development Bank (ADB), and the International Fund for Agriculture Development. He points to the tensions that exist between the GEF and the CoPs of MEAs on matters related to financing, which mirror similar tensions that exist at the national level, say, between Ministries of Finance and Environment on matters relating to environmental financing (2004, 41).

Developing countries like India have always been concerned that the GEF should not grow at the expense of ODA funds. They argue that contributions made by donors to the GEF have to be additional to their ODA commitments. In fact, the concept of 'additionality' has been one of the major premises on which the GEF has been designed. However, faced with limited funds at its disposal, the GEF had to embrace the concept of 'incremental costs', which in effect meant that the Facility's funds had to be used to upscale national projects for environmental protection into global ones to yield global benefits. Over time, the principle of cost-effectiveness and co-financing was added to define the GEF financing system which further reflected the funding constraints associated with the Facility. During the Fifth GEF Council Meeting held in 1995 in Washington DC, the operational guidelines of the GEF were adopted in a manner which highlighted the importance of cross-cutting projects. This explains why GEF projects were designed to yield multiple benefits. While it is true that Werksman considers carbon sequestration forestry activities to be potentially in conflict with biodiversity concerns, the GEF was able to steer clear of the problem in a large number of cases, where it tried out a harmoniously blend climate change, biodiversity, and desertification outcomes.

The problems with GEF projects lay elsewhere as discussed in Chapter 5.

Similarly, GEF's concern for cost-effectiveness caused the Facility to refine the concept of incremental costs to mean 'agreed and full incremental costs'. The concept of agreed and full incremental costs became central for ensuring that projects supported by the GEF have been truly equitable and do not in any manner cause developing countries to sacrifice resources meant for development to secure global environmental benefits. To this extent, the GEF has succeeded in imparting the much-needed dimensions of equity and justice in its financing operations. However, the entire emphasis on the technicality of incremental costs and the contentious issues surrounding determination of incremental costs and benefits in biodiversity conservation projects got the Facility into a major instrumentalist jam. What is more, GEF projects with their complex method of measurements and calculation of incremental costs, have not been successful in bringing about neat convergences between national and global environment projects.

The concept of incremental costs implied that the Facility advocated supporting projects which generated global environmental benefits over a pre-existing stack of national benefits. In essence, this also meant that any nationally developed project which was only desired to improve national environmental benefits, would not qualify for any form of assistance from the GEF. The Facility ideally looked for qualitative add-ons to national-level activities, by taking up conservation projects in a given area that national governments would not have otherwise taken up. In other words, the fundamental philosophy of GEF is that global environmental benefits have to be discrete and separated from national environmental benefits. The problem with this philosophy is that it goes against the concepts of equity and fairness that host countries desire. Thus developing countries, would like to see GEF projects to be compliant with national priorities and development goals, which includes poverty alleviation and fulfilment of SDG goals,

This situation has led to a large number of developing countries considering global environmental projects as something which is alien to their priorities. Even least developing countries, which face serious shortage of domestic resources for funding national development programmes, do not stand to benefit from the GEF because of its incremental cost concept and the instrumentalism associated with this concept. This prevents global environmental issues from taking roots amongst local communities, as noted earlier. Clearly, the GEF process needs rebalancing.

Faced with difficulties on the incremental costs front, the Facility moved over to embrace the idea of incremental reasoning in the post-2005 period for biodiversity projects that defied valuation on account of their intangible features. The concept of incremental reasoning aimed to ensure that GEF projects enjoyed intrinsic global environmental benefits than being merely mechanical overlays of national environmental projects. In some ways the application of the idea of incremental reasoning marked an attempt on the part of the GEF to de-instrumentalize its assessment parameters.

The UNEP and the WEO

For quite some time, the failure of global institutions in addressing key environmental issues have led to the demand for restructuring the world environmental system as it exists today. Since 1999, the United Nations University, in collaboration with 15 other UN organizations, agencies, and entities has been looking at possibilities of synergies amongst different Conventions by seeking to bring in greater coordination amongst them (Haas and Kanie 2004, 1–12). One major recommendation, which came up at a workshop organized by the United Nations University on synergies and coordination amongst MEAs, was about the creation of a United Nations Environment Organization (UNEO). Indeed, the earlier proposal for setting up the WEO had received support from certain prominent personalities such as former Director General WTO Renato Ruggiro, former French President Jacques Chirac and Mikhail Gorbachev, the former President of the Soviet Union. Jacques Chirac conveyed his support for the concept in his speech at the 2002 World Summit on Sustainable Development. Following his speech, the French Government went ahead and submitted a formal proposal for a UNEO in 2003. However, the proposal did not receive any enthusiastic consideration on the part of developing countries for various reasons. As Maria Ivanova argues, the idea of opposing the UNEO, and the espousal of the principle of universal membership in the UNEP by developing countries, was designed to ensure that the Programme did not turn into a specialized agency of the UN.[1] Esty and Ivanova (2002) propose the establishment of a Global Environmental Mechanism (GEM), which according to the authors, would integrate liberalism with environmentalism rather than being a marginal improvement over the UNEP.

The reason for the idea of a WEO/UNEO coming up in a big way in the late 1990s was the general dissatisfaction of the developed world with the UNEP. The UNEP which was set up in 1973 as a 'programme' rather than as a specialized agency of the UN, did try to address environmental issues. The UNEP was responsible for spurring national governments to come up with environment legislations, standards, and regulations (Haas et al. 2004, 263–81). However, its ability to influence nation-states was limited and did not go beyond facilitating the passage of a few laws and Conventions (2004, 269). The major constraint with the UNEP was its relatively poor financial muscle, which was compounded by the entry of the GEF and the World Bank in the environment sector in the 1990s. Even the UNDP was able to command more funds than the UNEP when it came to environmental funding and financing.

There were many efforts to give the UNEP a facelift. The Task Force on Environment and Human Settlement of 1997, which was triggered by former UN Secretary General Kofi Annan, proposed strengthening the organization by elevating it to a specialized agency, thus entitling it to a regular and fixed budget, besides enhancing its ability to discharge its various functions (2004, 271). However, this proposal did not get the support of any developed country and hence did not take off. In 1997, the

UNEP brought out the Nairobi Declaration on the 'Role and Mandate of the United Nations Environment Programme', which again called for a revitalized UNEP.

Haas et al. (2004) consider the failure of the UNEP as having triggered the movement for a 'world' or 'global' environment organization. According to the authors, if the WEO were to be a strong organization, it needed to have a supranational focus that aimed at articulating environment and sustainable development policies for the international community. This focus should be backed by resources to verify complaints and enforce sanctions (2004, 272). It is also envisaged that such an organization would act as an effective forum that could negotiate with the WTO on trade and environment matters (2004, 272).

However, the problem with the WEO has been that it has not met with support from the developing world. The UNU study, after considering all viewpoints, stated that the UNEP's initial responsibility was overloaded and that it would have been better for the organization to confine itself to scientific and technical assessments, coordination of scientific activities, monitoring of environmental progress, and setting up reporting systems that benefitted the international community. Going a step further, the United Nations University study called for setting up of a Global Environmental Organization (GEO) to fulfil the policy and technology-based functions that provide institutional support for multilateral environmental governance (2004, 277). The GEO would consolidate environmental policy research, install and utilize technology databases in clearing processes, besides focussing on capacity building. It was recommended that the GEO maintain a close link with civil society groups and promote a system of tripartite representation involving governments, civil society groups, and the industry, which could facilitate the implementation of global environmental accords (Haas et al. 2004, 278). Indeed, there are many scholars such as Najam (2003) who believe that international environmental governance can be strengthened only by revitalizing the existing units. There could be roadblocks here. Ivanova, for instance, observes that despite emphasis on strengthening the UNEP, efforts in this direction did not pay off because of the parallel position that the Commission on Sustainable Development (CSD) held when it came to implementing the Agenda 21. Ivanova cites the concrete instance of the UN General Assembly 1999 resolution, which empowered the CSD to be the high-level policy debate forum on sustainable development. There are scholars like Calestous Juma (2000) who argue that the greater challenge for international organizations (like UNEP) is to strengthen domestic environmental capacity. Coming to trade and environment issues, Bernstein and Ivanova, suggest that it would be a better option to restructure the WTO so that it becomes more environmentally sustainable.

Nevertheless, despite its not-so-impressive performance, developing countries continue to support the UNEP. Their basic argument is that if the UNEP were fully supported and made financially viable, it would have performed much better as an organization and could have met with all the requirements for which it was created. Indeed, the Cartagena meeting held in February 2002 issued a 'Declaration on International Environmental Governance', which clearly outlines that the UNEP had to be the nodal point of governance on environmental issues (Haas et al. 2004). The Cartagena Declaration also laid down that the process of institutional reforms should be evolutionary in nature and that existing structures be strategically utilized. The Cartagena Declaration stated that measures that make better use of existing structures meant for sustainable development, require coordination between the ministries at the national level. This was because environmental issues are complex and the nature of environmental problems called for enhanced capacity in the areas of scientific assessment and monitoring. Further it was argued that NGOs, civil society groups, and the private sector needed to be involved in all areas of decision making in the environment sector. Further, the Declaration exhorted that the UNEP be elevated to the level of a specialized programme of the UN backed by predictable funding. The Cartagena Declaration also called for a clustered approach to MEAs (Haas et al. 2004).

The Cartagena Declaration was noted for another important suggestion, viz, the setting up of the Global Ministerial Environmental Forum (GMEF). Though much has not been discussed about the terms of reference of the GMEF, it was felt that such a forum could establish a sound implementation system for MEAs. Indeed, the Warning Decision Support System (WSSD) has also stressed on the importance of MEAs and the need to ensure that the WTO did not erode them (Haas et al. 2004).

The UNEP has not functioned as a model of efficiency in terms of the transaction cost criterion. It is largely seen as a body which has failed to achieve the very purpose for which it was created. Most of the proposals on international environmental governance restructuring, especially the radical ones that emanated from developed countries, placed a lot of emphasis on technological information generation, clearing houses, and dissemination, which were instrumentalist ways of looking at the basic livelihood issues in developing countries. This is plainly not rational given the essential nature of transaction cost economics. Going by Oliver Williamson's analysis (Williamson 1996), a firm or an organization which is the epicentre of a governance structure in economics has to have the qualities of 'fiat and forbearance' as its necessary characteristic. By 'fiat' is meant a symmetrical organization, while by 'forbearance' is meant that a firm can act as its own Court of Ultimate Appeal, which calls for self-control (Groenewegen 1996, 5). While in the case of a firm, fiat and forbearance are taken for granted, in the case of an international supra-state governing body, adoption of these parameters could lead to problems. For one thing, a 'fiat' assumes the existence of a asymmetrical organization. This has not been the guiding principle of global governance presided over by UN organizations. The second aspect of forbearance is simply not acceptable in a world where subordination is not a way of ensuring order. Also in a world where dictator-driven regimes brazenly violate human rights or indulge in wanton violence over ethnic groups, the concept of self control does not operate. Violations of the UN Charter on Human Rights cannot be adjudged by its perpetrators. Though most nation-states have signed and acceded to the Human Rights Charter, we have noted that there are various interpretations of what constitutes human rights, depending on cultural and political contexts. Either way, for an organization that promotes sustainability, fiat and forbearance are not desirable values. The more crucial requirement is the ability of such organizations to develop a consensual set of environmental values that are founded on equity.

An organization like the WTO cannot also be run on 'fiat or forbearance' either. The WTO, as has been pointed out, is clearly functional on a consensus-based approach to resolution of its disputes, though outwardly it is seen as an organization which has a strong will to impose its agenda of trade liberalization. On the other hand, the Williamsonian notion of fiat and forbearance obtains in a large number of nation-states, particularly those which have non-democratic political systems. Therefore, any talk of a supragovernmental organization to manage international environment governance is bound to be problematic even from the point of view of efficiency or transaction costs economics. Here, there is considerable merit in Young's viewpoint that lessons drawn from the study of local institutions could be valuable for the study of global institutions and vice versa (Young 2002a, 2002b). The dynamics of collective action and adaptability that one sees in local communities is not something that one witnesses in higher formations (Ostrom 2002).

Even otherwise, there are reasons to suppose that standard precepts of institutional economics and transaction costs cannot be applied to global governance issues. It is stated that transaction costs can also be approached from the viewpoint of bounded rationality. There is a school of thought in economics, which refers to privatization of common property resources as the best method of ensuring efficient use of these resources and avoiding the problem of bounded rationality. Milton Freidman (1953) stated long ago that 'the best way out is to individualize property rights so that markets maximize such performance by ruling out inefficient options' (Marshall 2005, 30). Developing countries in the world, with their huge capacity gaps, cannot afford to follow the criteria of competitive selection and efficiency, or, in other words, 'Pareto Optimum'. Further, the path dependencies associated with underdevelopment preclude the probability of institutions in developing countries adopting new ideas. As North (1990) stated a few years ago, these path dependencies cannot be regimented and brought under a supranational international organization, whatever be its mandate and whatever be its rules and regulations.

There are two other issues, which are generally discussed in environmental economics but do not find a place of prominence in debates involving global environmental problems and global governance of international environment agreements. The first one relates to the standard argument that privatization of commons can solve market inefficiencies associated with externalities and the consequent rise in transaction costs. At this point of time, while considerable discussions have been going on about the relative merits of privatization of common property resources versus collective action, a similar kind of argument is not visible in the case of global commons, which is the point of focus here. No one argues that both global climate and global biodiversity be privatized. No one says that global climate management and biodiversity conservation should be subjected to unified governance either. The problem is that when we discuss global environmental issues, the focus of reference is nation-state boundaries and identities. As it has been noted earlier, global commons are nebulous assets. The CBD declares it to be a common concern of humankind rather than its common heritage. In other words, global environmental problems and global commons need to be seen as everybody's property, to which everyone has to equally contribute without fail. And as we have seen, it cannot be subjected to the institutionalist norms of fiat and forbearance either. What is required is a nuanced approach to management that is based on delicate consensus that strategically respects equity and eschews instrumentalism.

Alternatively, one can look at global environmental organizations from the viewpoints of institutional economics and international relations theories discussed in the previous chapters, namely Westphalianism and cosmopolitanism. Cosmopolitanism would prescribe universal ideas about sustainable development and methods of operationalizing the same. For this school of thought, the idea of global/world environmental organizations is acceptable. The opposite school of thought, which believes in the primacy of nation-states, namely the Westphalian system of environmental governance in particular, would resist creation of a supra-national organization like the GEO. The Cartagena Declaration on Environment adopted in 2002, about which reference has been made in the previous chapters, clearly indicates that nation-states are to be given priority in the interests of securing synergies and efficacious implementation of global environmental agreements and that the same can be achieved by UNEP if backed by enhanced funding. A similar view is echoed by Calestous Juma. The realism school in international relations considers that it will be foolish to assume that states will willingly cede their powers to an international agency. If one reads these theories in the light of what green campaigners like Vandana Shiva argue, it is obvious that social injustice at the global and local levels causes environmental degradation. In terms of this paradigm, even global institutions are extremely unjust and any supposition that problems will be obviated by creating super-state structures is far-fetched.

But there are more ingenious explanations offered by the suprastate organization protagonists who would go with those who advocate cosmopolitanism. Abbott and Snidel (1998) state that the roles prescribed for formal international institutions such as the UN Security Council, the WTO, and the International Atomic Energy Agency (IAEA) had the objective of providing for order and efficiency. International organizations of these types have two distinctive qualities, namely centralization and independence. They enhance efficiency and live true to the Coasion theorem that international organizations are only relevant when costs of state actions are high. The authors use a combination of international relations theory and institutional economics to analyse the relevance of international organizations. A similar kind of thesis is advanced by Keohane (1984) when he argues that inter-government bargaining can be facilitated by international regimes which reduce transaction costs, improve information, and raise the cost of violations. The problem with this theory is that it does not, per se discuss the operational significance of international organizations. Further, it is a moot point whether the UNEP or the WTO can be made more efficacious by reducing their transaction costs. Even if it is assumed for a moment that this is not the kind of picture that the protagonists of WEO or UNEO had in mind, there is very little point in counterbalancing a 'Global Injustice Institution' such as the WTO with another suprastate entity, precisely because every institution is structured politically and has structural dimensions to it. If it is argued that the main rationale for the existence of a supernational body is that transboundary issues and global environmental issues are better managed at the international level than at the inter-state level, then what prevents one from stating that a global/world environmental organization is necessary to ensure sound implementation of sustainable development programmes at the regional, national, and local levels in the larger interest of coordination and harmony.

Indeed, the United Nations University study adverted to earlier argues that a GEO can be useful in fulfilling policy and technology based functions apart from providing institutional support for multilateral environmental governance (Haas et al. 2004, 277). Apart from advocating instrumentalism, the other problem with this perspective is that it attributes the inadequacies of scientific work as the underlying cause of poor environmental governance. Further, this theory also assumes that scientific inputs can, to a large extent, be made more valid and meaningful, if freed from political compulsions.

As mentioned earlier, it is the instrumentality associated with the UN Framework Convention of Climate Change had caused developing countries to feel that the Convention does not belong to them. It is this aspect that needs to be addressed in the discussions on global environmental restructuring. Instrumentalism has been very clearly shown as a major malaise in the functioning of most MEAs including the Rio agreements. What has been lost in the process of instrumentalization, however, is the overall vision and the ability of the Conventions to bring the world closer to equity and justice. This kind of reasoning is implicit in the United Nations University proposals on the GEO, when it clearly says that scientists should be encouraged to develop concerns without political oversight (2004, 278). But then, every process of instrumentality and technicality associated with science and scientific evidence is itself culturally and politically constructed. Protagonists of the realism school, while opposing suprastate entities, also do not advocate diversity-based approaches at the national level.

Translated into simple terms, none of the proposals on creating a supranational structure talks about how such a structure would ensure that diversity is captured. The proposal for GEO does not appear to be focused on philosophical values. The GEO's stated mandate confines the organization's role to the dissemination of ideas, information, and knowledge. The GEO's mandate does not embrace realization of the maxims of diversity, equity, and justice. Similarly, the demand for converting the UNEP into a specialized UN agency to look at environmental issues as well as the recommendation for the establishment of a WEO that delves into science and technology assessments and provides political scope for action on sustainable development by nation-states, are flawed for the reason that it creates a kind of hierarchy where instrumentalism gets to be employed as a political technology at the nation-state level.

Likewise, the instrumentalism associated with the UNFCCC and the Kyoto Protocol's CDM have obfuscated the fundamental right of developing countries to achieve cleaner development paths, in an autonomously driven manner. Despite its bottom up nature, the Paris Agreement on Climate Change also does not eschew instrumentalism since it emphasizes the importance of robust monitoring and verification mechanisms in order to ensure the compliance of a country's NDC with the Agreement's Goals of limiting the global rise in temperature to 1.5 degrees centigrade above the pre-industrial levels.

In the case of the CBD, the absence of a technically satisfactory valuation system for biological resources has paradoxically prevented instrumentalism from acquiring an upper hand. The concept of 'total economic values' propounded by environmental economists in the 1980s and the early 1990s was based on an additive approach. By contrast, when it comes to intangible IPRs like trademarks and patents, valuation tools have been perfected. Despite its intangible features, a company can determine the value of IPRs or the costs and benefits of protecting and defending it. However valuation tools for traditional knowledge are imperfectly developed. This acts to handicap local communities who are approached by overseas prospectors for traditional knowledge held by them. Thus, the task of computing values for bio-resources in terms of conservation costs as well as the task of valuing traditional knowledge is fraught with difficulties. As a result local communities are not able to quote a price for the traditional knowledge they possess.

The Basel Convention on transboundary movement of hazardous wastes is also fraught with difficulties on the valuation side. For instance, while the cause of implementing environmental management programmes for managing imported wastes has been elaborately worked out through various exercises, the cost of denying the opportunity of importing wastes has not been systematically assessed. To this extent, the significance of the Basel Ban is lost on many developing countries. Similarly, imperfections exist when it comes to valuation of the damages inflicted by imported hazardous wastes. This explains why the Basel Convention's liability protocol on damages and accidents has not received the kind of attention it should have from economists and experts.

Thus there are differing views on the state of environmental governance in the world. The limitations of the GEF and similar financing facilities are obvious. They do not have roots at the local levels due to their high levels of instrumental abstraction. What is obvious is that standard norms of efficiency associated with transaction costs do not apply to international organizations that seek to deal with global public goods. Likewise, proposals for setting up new global environmental organizations suffer from the deficiency of instrumentalism. The same is true of proposals that seek to restructure the UNEP.

The same holds for global efforts to manage the fallout of COVID-19. The absence of Leadership Summits to address the issue of poor allocation and distributional inequities associated with COVID-19 vaccines is surprising. The failure of COVAX represents the failure of multilateralism in addressing the needs of developing countries for vaccines. This is brought out in Chapter 13.

To sum up, instrumentalism, which has drawn global environmental processes far away from its mandate of conservation of global public goods, is the scourge of global environmental governance. It has securitized issues and removed the scope of diversity.

The key priority is to establish global governance systems for the management of global commons that are free from the scourge of instrumentalism. Such systems, while focussing on global public goods, should have due regard to national and local aspirations and identities with a view to ensuring that the cause of conserving global commons becomes everybody's concern.

15

The Diversity Principle, Digital Technologies, and the Future of Global Commons

Alexander Solzhenitsyn (1991), in his acclaimed book *The Cancer Ward*, describes the wired world of a totalitarian society, where every individual is monitored and kept under watchful eyes for his potential deviation from the norms of the political order. A citizen of such a state is required to fill up myriads of questionnaires about various facets of his life. Instead of rebelling against this kind of regimentation, citizens coming under a totalitarian order tend to respect their enslavers. The real point made by Solzhenitsyn, the wired world continues to be a reality even in a globalized world.

As far as I see, the supraterritorial wired system of the 1990s, which emerged from the ruins of the Cold War, was guided by the need to establish order in a world which was thrown into uncertainty following the demise of bipolarity. When the iron curtains of the communist bloc were torn down, there opened a great opportunity to 'reach the unreached'. However, it did not take long for ICT-powered networks to engender their own systems of wired surveillance. With cyber crimes and terrorism rocking the real and virtual worlds, instruments of control were required to maintain order in a seamless world. More importantly, such instruments were utilized to enforce norms of optimal behaviour in matters that concerned security and order. Alternatives that popped up had to be put out. The casualties of the new wired world of today are diversity in opinions, feelings, perspectives, and practices. Diversity of thinking and opinion is important, as no system which eschews pluralism in processes, thoughts, and ideas, can last. The implosions that wrecked the Soviet system in 1991 were caused by regimentation of thought and action on

India, Climate Change, and The Global Commons. A. Damodaran, Oxford University Press. © A. Damodaran 2024.
DOI: 10.1093/oso/9780192899828.003.0015

an instrumental mode which, in turn, was facilitated by the surveillance society that Solzhenitsyn refers to. Unlike in a communist society, where instrumentalism was enforced with an iron hand by a totalitarian state in the name of the socialist utopia, in today's globalized world there does not exist any formal or visible centre of control to enforce order. In such a system, the method adopted to normalize behaviour was to 'securitize' an agenda that could facilitate instrumentalism and control. The process of securitization of the agenda of global order got a fillip following the 9/11 attacks. The agenda of securitization and instrumentality ensured that controls were legitimate, effective, and desirable. The assumption was that the higher the degree of instrumentalism, the greater would be the 'control' achieved over a process. An agenda which is driven by a high degree of instrumentalism can be pushed to the forefront as has been the case with climate change. The dimmer the local perception of an issue, the greater is the probability of it getting to be instrumentalized and securitized. Today, there is a great obsession to securitize key welfare and development issues. The concepts of energy security, bio-security, climate change, and food security compete with national security for securitization by the State.

However, issues such as food security are intimately connected to the development agenda. They capture the local imagination and, therefore, are not amenable to instrumentalism as much as one would desire. The preceding chapters have listed many ideas, instances, and examples of diversity. Commencing from Mahatma Gandhi's 'village', we waded through imbalanced growth strategies, decentralized management of natural resources, conflicts over global trade regimes and the efforts made by the traditional, modern, and postmodern trends to co-exist. More specific facets of diversity that were mentioned in the previous chapters included the movement against Coca Cola by a local self-government unit in Kerala, the Ralegan Siddhi process in Ahmednagar, Maharashtra, and the Machakos experiment in Kenya, all of which were driven by locally-generated social capital. The facets of diversity mentioned in the previous chapters include Westphalian resistance to globalization as exemplified by Russia and China, the postmodern adaptation of Darjeeling tea since the 1990s, the civil society movements that espouse traditional livelihood systems, and espousal of the principle of common but differentiated responsibility in MEAs and its inclusion as the principle underlying the Conventions of Climate Change, Biodiversity and Desertification.

Standing in contrast are the faces of instrumentalism discussed in the preceding chapters. This includes the advent of the third-generation derivative instruments which are considered to be responsible for the world economic crisis of 2008–9, the hierarchical monitoring and verification systems associated with climate change, the ecosystem valuation systems that mechanically attempt to work out values for services provided by nature and the tools laid down for enabling payments for ecological services. Indeed, while the Climate Change Convention and the Montreal Protocol have adjusted well to the instrumentalist order through an effective securitization agenda, the Conventions of Biodiversity and Desertification have not been able to take to this course. This explains why, unlike Climate Change, the Biodiversity and Desertification agendas have not caught the imagination of the world. Rather, the diversity and pluralistic premises of these Conventions render it difficult for them to be part of the wired world of instrumentalism afforded by the securitization agenda. Now, there are some enablers that display both faces, that is, of instrumentalism and its opposite, namely diversity. The unique trait of ICT in the pre-2010 period in India was that it could be used to promote both instrumentality and diversity. The second enclosure movement—the expanded trade networks ensured by ICT, enabled an e-localized community of silk, coffee, and tea farmers of India to access wider markets. Such developments have the potential to promote non-instrumental approaches in a globalized world. All the same, the use of ICT for surveillance and information gathering in the virtual and real worlds substantially heralds its instrumentalist potential.

By 'diversity' is meant a global order that promotes diversity of stakes and stakeholders. Diversity, if attained in its true sense, would help to promote equity and justice. The argument here is that existing efforts at global environmental governance have failed mainly because of the agenda of securitization that requires gigantic apparatuses of instrumentalism administered by multiple organizations, to monitor and benchmark norms of performance. What is more, the maze of technical and scientific information that emanates from international environmental agreements has completely shifted the focus of decision makers to the technical and instrumental aspects of data handling, data management, and so on. To neutralize this kind of instrumentality bias, one needs to start afresh and look at an international governance system which promotes a new charter of environment and environmental values, and evaluates environmental resources and services for their potential to contribute to the causes of equity and justice. There is the obvious need to re-look at the norms for valuing environmental resources in a more objective manner. As we have noted, environmental economics has drastically expanded and deepened its research agenda in the preceding two decades, with substantial efforts going into the valuation of environment resources. Apart from the specific limitations pointed out earlier, the problem with the environmental valuation exercises has been its excessive focus on techniques and methods rather than on the philosophical objective of situating valuation of environmental services within the framework of the norms of diversity, equity, and justice.

The important point about proposals on restructuring environmental governance in the world is their relationship with the concept of diversity and its concomitants, namely equity and justice. In the context of my earlier discussions about various Multilateral Environmental Agreements (MEAs), I defined equity as the right to social and economic development as well as to enhanced and equitable access to environmental resources and services. There can be finer nuances to this concept depending on the nature of the resource focussed upon. In the context of the Biodiversity Convention, equity means that a country endowed with biodiversity has every right to regulate access to its natural and biological resources and demand benefits arising from its utilization. If biodiversity was viewed as a common heritage of humankind, the canons of equity would have been disturbed. It would have been difficult for a local community to assert its property rights over natural resources (including biodiversity), demand a price for parting with it, by way of benefit sharing. In the case of the Basel Convention and the Cartagena Protocol, by 'equity' is meant the right not only to a clean environment but also to clean technologies in the event of the environment getting spoiled. The same holds for the Stockholm Convention and the Climate Change Convention, where the idea of equity is related to realizing a safe environment which does not compromise the objective of ensuring the socioeconomic well-being of the poorer sections of society. The element of justice here involves application of the rule of law.

The public liability clauses and liability protocols of the Basel Convention, adopt a narrow notion of environmental damage. Applying the principles underlying 'rule of law' to the CBD is complicated. In terms of the biodiversity law, justice would mean the right to demand share in benefits derived by the agencies which have obtained knowledge resources from local communities. The principle of justice also requires that biodiversity wealth which is conserved by local communities are not undermined by companies/corporates or other agencies. In the context of the Biosafety Protocol, the key 'justice issue' is about the possibility of Genetically Modified Organisms (GMOs) or Living Modified Organisms (LMOs) undermining traditional agricultural systems in developing countries. Only an alternative environmental governance system that is federalized and democratic in nature will be able to uphold the equity and justice dimensions of MEAs. Such a governance order needs to be supported by enabling socioeconomic and scientific information so that recommendations are based on scientific data and information.

Crafting alternative governance systems raises interesting issues of how sovereignty can be refashioned as a concept to bring in a non-hierarchical world governance system.

A truly federalized world of environment governance is not easy to realize. This is because world governance systems run into insurmountable problems when it comes to dealing with sovereign countries. Bernard Crick, in the 'Encyclopaedia of the Social Science', defines sovereignty as part of the theory of politics that requires every government to have within it, a source of absolute power to take decisions and the ability to enforce it efficiently.[1] This definition is no doubt based on a juridico-legal understanding of sovereignty in the Westphalian sense. There are a number of arguments which state that the world trade systems do not entail loss of sovereignty. Krasner even goes to the extent of saying that globalization has not compromised on the Westphalian notion of sovereignty (Krasner 2001). Indeed global trade has, in some respects, facilitated sovereignty instead of undermining it (2001). However, from a strict anti-globalization point of view, this argument is not necessarily right, because by entering into a multilateral trade regime like the WTO, states are compelled to restrict their sovereignty in law-making in the overall interest of securing global welfare through trade. A case in point is the manner in which India had to amend its IPR laws in order to comply with the requirements of WTO's Trade Related Intellectual Property Rights (TRIPS).

Indeed, in the post-WTO world, sovereignty has assumed a different connotation. Civil society groups and NGOs which have been in the forefront of raising issues connected to human rights, environment, and labour standards, are deemed as questioning the notion of state sovereignty. When one talks about global trade, one has to grapple with multiple sovereignties, namely consumer sovereignty, 'civil society' sovereignty, and state sovereignty. There is also the larger question as to whether the WTO has succeeded in fusing these multiple manifestations of sovereignty unto itself. The answer is in the negative. In reality, the WTO is not a supranational body to which nation-states have surrendered their 'trade policy making' powers. It is an international body that seeks to promote voluntary abnegation of policy space by its member states in order to facilitate 'freer' multilateral trade. This is the case with MEAs as well. Then what gives? The real problem is that despite its seemingly consensual framework, both the WTO and MEAs have not incorporated the principle of 'diversity' in their operations.

In its most direct sense, diversity can be defined to mean 'representation of stakes and interests of local communities, ethnic groups, and regional economies'. At a deeper philosophical sense, diversity is related to the concept of sovereignty as strategically defined in a post-structuralist sense. Since the 1960s, there has been a serious effort to look at the philosophical underpinnings of the concept of sovereignty. For Aristotle, sovereignty existed as a unified concept and any multiple or diffused concept of sovereignty is no sovereignty at all. In terms of the Aristotelian notion, sovereignty is singular and non-contestable. It is in this sense that sovereignty is defined as an 'unmoved mover' by philosophers such as Derrida. As Emanuelle Levinas states singular' sovereignty persists in its violent image of truth of being instrumentalist (Burke 2002). Indeed, instrumentalism, apart from being a weapon in the hands of the singular sovereign, acquires sovereignty on its own. Jacques Derrida employs a spherical notion of sovereignty whereby the sovereign gets tossed from one entity to another and keeps circulating between one entity and the other.[2] He goes on to question the notion of rogue states and asks the fundamental question as to who has the right to determine or identify certain states as rogue states and threaten them with measures that include military force (2002). As Derrida states, an entity which intervenes to correct a rogue state has itself to be one, because consciously or unconsciously it is seeking to violate the fundamental canon of 'coexistence' which underlies the fabric of international relations. In more fundamental terms, a rogue state could be defined as one which does not fulfil the canons of peace, equity, and justice, and the dominance of the rule of law in the world. In the context of the Basel Convention, a rogue state would be one which contributes to the export of hazardous wastes without the Prior Informed Consent (PIC) of the importing state.

Other issues, not addressed by Derrida, concern the issue of the inter-relationship between sovereignty and state power and about situations where state power does not monopolize 'sovereignty'. Michael Foucault states that a juridical political concept of sovereignty which centres on the state (in the classical Westphalian sense of the term) is erroneous. As Michael Hardt and Antonio Negri, in their book *Empire* (2000), state: sovereignty does not vanish with the demise or weakening of the nation-state. The authors go a step further and say that sovereignty and nation-state need not go together. As Burke proceeds to state, sovereignty is a political technology that tries to reach every nook and corner and is closely associated with Foucault's concept of 'governmentality', a concept that is based on the notion of bio-politics that rests on desire, discipline, and self-government. Thus, the issues posed by Foucault, Negri, and Hardt, and Burke and Levinas, make it clear that the notion of sovereignty and its connection to state power needs to be re-examined. It is also clear that, much against the wishes of Aristotle, the concept of 'sovereignty' has been de-centred from the State and that it needs to be located elsewhere. Thus, the juridico-political concept of sovereignty, as described and defined by Bernard Crick, has been effectively questioned by these philosophers. It is clear from the preceding discussions that instrumentalization has been the central feature of the manner in which multilateral environmental agreements have been implemented or are sought to be implemented in different parts of the world. The concept of sovereignty has worked in a perverse way in the case of MEAs. While these agreements function through multiple secretariats and multiple power centres in the world, a nation-state must combine or capsule within it, the multifariousness of international environmental issues, with associated complexities. In other words, it must successfully 'encircle the seamless'! The instrumentalism of MEAs has been painful to nation-states since they do not have an overall vision of the basic nature of MEAs. As a result, nation-states are not able to appreciate the importance of seeing global environmental problems as their own problem.

Additionally, nation-states do not bear the brunt of the adversities posed by global environmental problems. It is the local communities that directly suffer from climate change, biodiversity loss, desertification, and the adverse effects of toxic chemicals.

The way out is to descuritize the global environment by eschewing instrumentalism. This also means that the 'diversity' principle needs to be brought in, which recognizes, the multi-layered nature of sovereignty in global environmental governance frameworks.

It is here that the advent of distributed digital networks holds promise for the governance of global commons.

The advent of distributed digital networks in the shape of blockchains can be traced to the world economic crisis of 2008. The crisis was a severe challenge to the global economic order that owes its origin to the Bretton Woods Agreement. The delinking of the US Dollar from gold and the subsequent free float of the global reserve currency led to the rapid expansion of the monetary base in various economies of the world. The resultant environment of 'moral hazard' behaviour by the world's financial institutions led to periodic economic crisis which reached an unprecedented level in 2008. The subsequent bail out of the 'too big to fail' institutions like the AIG provoked resentment and rebellion amongst a community of 'technocrats' belonging to the ICT industry, who came out with an alternative solution to the world's financial systems through the concept of 'blockchains' or digital ledgers in 2008.[3] The blockchains sought to distribute and diffuse financial powers to a larger community of 'digital ledger programmers and verifiers', thus seeking to usher in an era of distributed networks based on the principle of 'open access' by all those who desired to participate in the system. The community of verifiers and computation specialists that appeared were employed to validate financial transactions constructed by individuals, without the agency of banking and financial institutions.[4] As digital ledgers, blockchains recorded and firmly secured data on financial transactions undertaken by individuals and companies, besides ensuring that the transactions were efficient, streamlined and quicker than conventional payment settlement systems.

Blockchain operations were carried by a community of 'miners', or computation specialists who not only captured individual transactions, but also sealed the ledger by solving a complex cryptographic/mathematical puzzle in order to ensure that the ledger was securely closed and not rendered vulnerable to mutilation. The entries (data) in a blockchain are immutable and cannot be erased. Even where an entry is found to be wrong, it cannot be deleted. Instead, the correct entry can be made in the same or a different ledger. Since different blockchains are chained, it is impossible for any individual blockchain to be hacked or mutilated without alerting the other blockchains in the chain.

The test of the robustness of a 'closed blockchain' is conducted by a team of verifiers drawn from the community at large. In return for the service of 'mining', the miners were provided crypto coins as an incentive which they could as alternative means of payment to meet their needs. The birth of the cryptocurrency, Bitcoin,[5] is owed to the Blockchain technology. Bitcoin was a challenge to the Central Bank's fiat money since it offered an alternative means of payment.[6] Since crypto coins, like Bitcoin, are programmed to be inelastic in supply, their value has consistently gone up in comparison to that of fiat money currencies which (barring a few exceptions) are lax on the supply side, which, in turn, abets moral hazard behaviour on the part of formal financial institutions. Paradoxically, the supply-side constraints of the Bitcoin led to the failure of Bitcoin as a means of payment. However, the evolution of smart contracts-based blockchains in 2014, notably the Ethereum has led to the widespread application of the idea to public governance. Smart contracts are computer-programmed digital contracts that are 'performance contingent'.[7]

Blockchains were originally conceived as open access system which was open to participation by anyone desiring to access them. The problem with such blockchains was that they obfuscated the identity of participants, thereby allowing the entry of even those who did not believe in the objectives for which the blockchain was brought into operation. However, over a period of time, closed blockchains evolved, which were less open. Such blockchains are referred to as permissive blockchains, where the process of writing and verifying smart contracts vests with a few people in an identified group. Governments and corporate undertakings have adopted permissive blockchains as they enable them to have open access to a set of authentic participants.

Permissive blockchains can be employed by MEAs to have real time information and data. These blockchains will provide scope for participation by a large community of authentic verifiers, which are drawn from local communities of programmers and verifiers, thus rendering their operations true to the cause for which the blockchains were developed.

Smart contracts-based blockchain platforms, which do not involve energy-intensive mining operations are not only climate friendly, but also provide a robust and unalterable record of MEA-related commitments and their fulfilment on a real time basis. Blockchains based on smart contracts can be deployed to keep an unalterable digital record of commitments made by countries on the climate financing front. Blockchains can also provide similar services for the CBD, the UNCCD,

Coming to pandemics, blockchains can be useful in tracking the performance of vaccine donors and recipients and can be utilized as an authentic record of global social costs arising from inefficiencies in vaccine logistics. In turn, blockchain-related data can be helpful in informing forums outside COP about the state of performance of various global commons conventions, which, in turn, can be useful to non-state actors to mount pressure on official negotiators to work towards more effective agreements.

By virtue of being transparent and efficient, blockchains can be turned into valuable tools for de-instrumentalize MEAs. By enlisting voluntary groups and NGOs, Blockchains ensure that the causes of equity, fairness, and justice are sharply brought out. More significantly, blockchains, with their inherent inclusiveness, would enable local communities to have a say in MEA or GEF-assisted projects. This can be helpful in overcoming the communication barriers that have prevented MEAs from taking local roots.

Indeed, international forums that are creatively crafted can serve as platforms and can play a vital role in resolving global environmental problems. For instance, Barack Obama's 'Major Economies Forum' (MEF) on Energy and Climate, which was convened on 28 March 2009, provided a qualitatively different approach to climate change as compared to the earlier initiative taken up by the G-8 forum to address the issue. The MEF sought to create a global partnership on climate change involving the countries of the 'North' and the emerging economies of the South. Diversity was the bedrock principle of the 'Major Economies

Forum (MEF). The MEF sought to build a broad-based approach to climate change issues without compromising on the responsibility of developed countries for historical emissions. Indeed forums like the MEF have the potential for providing valuable inputs to CoP meetings.

Forums like the MEF system have continued to be active even after the entry into force of the Paris Agreement on Climate Change in 2016. President Joe Biden convened 'The Leaders Summit on Climate' during April 2021 to set the tone for negotiations at the Glasgow Climate Summit. The pre-COP 26 summit held in Milan (Italy) during early October 2021, which involved leaders from more than forty countries, discussed key political aspects concerning the agenda listed for discussion at Glasgow. These pre-COP apex level meetings had their desired effects, as evidenced by India's Prime Minister announcing his country's commitment to achieving net zero emission targets by 2070 at the Glasgow Summit, an announcement that India had held back for nearly four years after joining the Paris Agreement.

The experience of managing COVID-19, also offers valuable lessons. As we mentioned in Chapter 13, creative approaches are required to solve the problems arising from inequitable distribution of vaccines.

To sum up, the concept of a new environmental order is not about the creation of new supra-world structures that tower over nation-states. It is about contesting sovereign regimes that de-securitize and de-instrumentalize the agenda of global commons. Such an approach calls for strengthening the involvement of local communities in global commons projects. In addition, the new world order should influence policy makers to actively consider the larger issues of equity and justice while dealing with global environmental issues. The instrument of distributed digital networks based on blockchain technologies could accelerate the pace of such initiatives by acting as dispassionate data holding points on different types of global commons. More importantly, they could ensure more inclusive approaches to the implementation of operational projects that seek to resolve global environmental problems.

The best approach to the sustainable development of the global commons is one which embraces diversity and removes the veil of instrumentalism that obfuscates the pursuit of equity, fairness, and justice. There are indeed many valuable lessons in global commons management that India can offer.

Notes

Chapter 2

1. Government of India 2015. India's Intended Nationally Determined Contribution: Working Towards Climate Justice, https://www4.unfccc.int/sites/ndcstaging/PublishedDocuments/India%20First/INDIA%20INDC%20TO%20UNFCCC.pdf

Chapter 4

1. See Cooper (2003). Cooper, a British diplomat, was Tony Blair's advisor and is considered to have influenced Blair's political thinking.
2. See Said (1978) for the roots of 'oriental' thinking that viewed traditional as irrational and backward.
3. Golwalker (1966) has a hybrid approach which extols 'modernity' and 'traditional' in the same breath. His essay 'Meeting the Challenge' (pp. 313–25) exhorts India's scientists to bring forth such discoveries and inventions that would 'unnerve enemies' (p. 314). Elsewhere, in 'Live Positive Dynamic Hinduism', he speaks of the need for keeping up India's traditions of samskars (pp. 46–60). At the same time, his emphasis on the village as the unit of national morale and vigilance betrays a postmodern streak (p. 319).

Chapter 5

1. Geethanjali Nataraj and Daljeet Kaur.2015. How Achieving Millennium Development Goals will make or break India, July 9, https://www.dailyo.in /politics/millennium-development-goals-un-population-standard-of-living-poverty-line-agriculture/story/1/4870.html, accessed on 18 November 2020.
2. https://www.undp.org/content/undp/en/home/sustainable-development-goals/backgroundhtml#:~:text = Background%20on%20the%20goals& text = The%20objective%20was%20to%20produce,tackle%20the%20indignity%20of%20poverty, accessed on 18 November 2020.
3. https://unstats.un.org/sdgs/report/2016/, accessed on 18 November 2020.

4. https://www.undp.org/content/undp/en/home/sustainable-development-goals/background.html#:~:text=Background%20on%20the%20goals&text=The%20objective%20was%20to%20produce,tackle%20the%20indignity%20of%20poverty, accessed on Oct 7,2020

5. Sustainable Development Goals. A Guidepost Report https://www.guidepost.es/rainbow-of-u-n-sustainable-goals-reflected-in-spanish-social-media-fpr-a-future-we-want/, accessed on 18 November 2020.

6. Sustainable Development Goals. A Guidepost Report https://www.guidepost.es/rainbow-of-u-n-sustainable-goals-reflected-in-spanish-social-media-fpr-a-future-we-want/, accessed on 18 November 2020.

Chapter 6

1. Clark (1977; as also cited by Sachs [1997]).
2. Brundtland Commission.
3. Refer Rishab Iyer Ghosh (2005, 259–86).

Chapter 7

1. http://www.un-documents.net/wced-ocf.htm accessed on 10 December 2021.
2. http://www.unccd.int/, accessed on 10 December 2021.
3. https://www.unccd.int/sites/default/files/relevant-links/2018-08/cop21add1_SF_EN.pdf, accessed on 10 December 2021.
4. IISD Reporting Services, through its ENB meeting coverage, https://enb.iisd.org/desert/cop14/, accessed on 18 November 2020.
5. See Gopal Krishna.2006. 'The Scrapping of Riky', March 23, https://indiatogether.org/riky-environment accessed on 10 December 2021.
6. 'Stockholm POPS Convention: Overview and Status of US Ratification and Implementing Legislation', WWF, http://www.wwf.or.jp/activity/toxics/ lib/POPSbackgrounder.pdf, accessed on 10 December 2021.
7. http://chm.pops.int/Default.aspx?tabid=3016, accessed on 10 December 2021.
8. Separating Signal from Noise at COP26, Interview with Robert Stavins https://www.belfercenter.org/publication/separating-signal-noise-cop26 accessed on 2 December 2021.
9. Damodaran A 2021. 'Why global commodity supercycles are not good for Paris climate targets', Forbes India, https://www.forbesindia.com/article/iim-bangalore/why-global-commodity-supercycles-are-not-good-for-paris-climate-targets/67945/1, accessed on 4 December 2021.
10. https://www.climatebonds.net/, accessed on 15 December 2021.
11. Martin Wolf (2005), article titled 'Traumatized By Trade' in his book *Why Globalization Works*, pp. 173–219.

Chapter 10

1. World Bank (2006).
2. https://www.worldbank.org/en/country/costarica/overview#1, accessed on 10 December 2021.

Chapter 11

1. https://www.cbd.int/intro/, accessed on 19 November 2020.
2. Equity and fairness in this case are not related to the freedom to access resources. It is basically related to the right to demand benefits flowing from appropriation of resources through access, including traditional knowledge.
3. https://www.cbd.int/sp/targets/ accessed on 19 November 2020.
4. Damodaran, A. 2012. 'India's Biodiversity Financing Assessment Exercise', Dialogue Seminar Scaling Up Biodiversity Finance 6–9 March 2012. Quito, Ecuador, https://www.cbd.int/doc/meetings/fin/ds-fb-01/other/ds-fb-01-ppt-c07-in-iim-damodaran-en.pdf, accessed on 18 November 2020.
5. https://www.biodiversityfinance.net/index.php/history,accessedon19November 2020.
6. Anonymous. Ud. 'Resourcing the Aichi Biodiversity Targets: An Assessment of Benefits, Investments and Resource needs for Implementing the Strategic Plan for Biodiversity 2011–2020', Second Report of the High-Level Panel on Global Assessment of Resources for Implementing the Strategic Plan for Biodiversity 2011–2020. Montreal, Canada.
7. Convention on Biological Diversity.2020. Open-Ended Working Group on the Post-2020 Global Biodiversity Framework Second meeting. Kunming, China, 24-29 February 2020,CBD/WG2020/2/3 dated 6 January 2020, https://www.cbd.int/doc/c/efb0/1f84/a892b98d2982a829962b6371/wg2020-02-03-en.pdf, accessed on 4 August 2020. The draft framework prepared by a working group of the CBD co-chaired by Canada and Uganda provides for five long-term goals slated to be achieved by 2050 and 20 near-time targets to be achieved by 2030. The draft was the major agenda before COP 15, which was planned to be held in Kunming in 2020, but got postponed to 2021 on account of COVID-19.
8. https://www.indiatimes.com/explainers/news/kunming-declaration-biodivers ity-551631.html#highlight_68105, accessed on 15 November 2021.
9. https://enb.iisd.org/UN-Biodiversity-Conference-CBD-COP15-15Oct2021, ac-cessed on 15 November 2021.
10. https://www.indiatimes.com/explainers/news/kunming-declaration-biodivers ity-551631.html#highlight_68105, accessed on 15 November 2021.
11. https://unfccc.int/process/conferences/the-big-picture/milestones/outcomes-of-the-durban-conference, accessed on 18 November 2020.

12. https://unfccc.int/process-and-meetings/the-paris-agreement/the-paris-agreement, accessed on 18 November 2020.

13. See Kelly Levin and Mandy Rambharos (2019). 'What you Need to know about Article 6 of the Paris Agreement', World Resources Institute, Dec 2, https://www.wri.org/blog/2019/12/article-6-paris-agreement-what-you-need-to-know, accessed on 18 November 2020.

14. Kelly Levin and Mandy Rambharos.2019.'What you Need to know about Article 6 of the Paris Agreement', World Resources Institute, Dec 2, https://www.wri.org/blog/2019/12/article-6-paris-agreement-what-you-need-to-know, accessed on 18 November 2020.

15. https://www.futurebridge.com/industry/perspectives-energy/why-did-cop-25-fail/, accessed on 18 November 2020.

16. https://www.futurebridge.com/industry/perspectives-energy/why-did-cop-25-fail/, accessed on 18 November 2020.

17. UNEP/CHW.6/23, 8 August 2002, entitled 'Consideration of Implementation of the Basel Convention Technical Matters: Preparation of Technical Guidelines', Sixth Meeting of the Conference of Parties, Geneva, item 6 (e) (II) of the Provisional Agenda, UNEP.

18. Most of the FDI proposals in India are initially processed by the FIPB.

Chapter 12

1. Resolutions 1 to 96, https://www.un.org/ecosoc/en/ngo/consultative-status accessed on 10 December 10 2021.

2. Anonymous. 2014. 'NGOs Outline Position on Paris Agreement', Sep 11, http://sdg.iisd.org/news/ngos-outline-position-on-paris-agreement/, accessed on 4 December 2020.

3. Anonymous. 2020. 'Trump attacks WTO after it says US tariffs on China broke global trade rules', September, https://www.theguardian.com/world/2020/sep/16/trump-attacks-wto-after-it-says-us-tariffs-on-china-broke-global-trade-rules, accessed on 4 December 2020.

Chapter 13

1. https://www.worldometers.info/coronavirus/, accessed on 1 December 2021.

2. Marco Cascella; Michael Rajnik; Abdul Aleem; Scott C. Dulebohn; Raffaela Di Napoli. 'Features, Evaluation, and Treatment of Coronavirus (COVID-19)'. 2 September 2021. https://www.ncbi.nlm.nih.gov/books/NBK554776, accessed on 29 November 2021.

3. http://ieg-ego.eu/en/threads/europe-on-the-road/the-history-of-tourism accessed on 1 December 2021.

4. WTTC, Economic Impact Reports, https://wttc.org/Research/Economic-Imp act, accessed on 1 December 2021.

5. Mohan BS* and Vinod Nambiar, *J Infect Dis Epidemiol* 6:146.doi.org/10.23937/2474-3658/1510146. https://clinmedjournals.org/articles/jide/journal-of-infectious-diseases-and-epidemiology-jide-6-146.php?jid=jide, accessed on 1 December 2021.

6. Maxmen, Amy, and Mallapaty, Smriti. 2021. 'The COVID lab-leak hypothesis: what scientists do and don't know', *Nature*, https://www.nature.com/articles/d41586-021-01529-3, 8 June, accessed on 1 December 2021.

7. Appendix 1 and 2 of the CITES include animal and plant species that fall in the categories of 'critically endangered' and 'risk of extinction' species, respectively.

8. https://www.worldwildlife.org/stories/what-is-a-pangolin accessed on 1 December 2021.

9. There are eight species of Pangolins in the world of which four are in Africa and four in Asia. All the eight are vulnerable to trafficking, Kapil, Shubhta. 2019. 'Pangolin: Adorable but Endangered'. *Science Reporter*, pp. 29–31, http://nopr.niscair.res.in/bitstream/123456789/45900/1/SR%2056%283%29%2029-31.pdf accessed on 1 December 2021.

10. 'Understanding the WTO Agreement on Sanitary and Phytosanitary Measures', https://www.wto.org/english/tratop_e/sps_e/spsund_e.htm, accessed on 1 December 2021.

11. https://www.wto.org/english/tratop_e/sps_e/spsund_e.htm, accessed on 1 December 2021.

12. https://www.who.int/news/item/30-03-2021-who-calls-for-further-studies-data-on-origin-of-sars-cov-2-virus-reiterates-that-all-hypotheses-remain-open, accessed on 1 December 2021.

13. https://www.gavi.org/vaccineswork/covax-explained, accessed on 4 December 2021.

14. https://www.gavi.org/vaccineswork/covax-explained, accessed on 1 December 2021.

15. Deborah Gleeson.2021. 'Omicron variant is proof of the high cost of rich countries' greed for Covid-19 vaccines' The Conversation, 1 December 2021, https://theconversation.com/wealthy-nations-starved-the-developing-world-of-vaccines-omicron-shows-the-cost-of-this-greed-172763, accessed on 1 December 2021.

16. https://www.gavi.org/vaccineswork/covax-explained, accessed on 1 December 2021.

17. 'Coronavirus (COVID-19) vaccines for developing countries: An equal shot at recovery', OECD Policy Responses to Coronavirus (COVID-19), OECD, 4 February 2021 https://www.oecd.org/coronavirus/policy-responses/coronavirus-covid-19-vaccines-for-developing-countries-an-equal-shot-at-recovery-6b0771e6/

18. 'The political economy of COVID-19 vaccines', Third World Resurgence, Third World Network Berhad, https://twn.my/title2/resurgence/2021/347/health1. htm, accessed on 4 December 2021.

19. The political economy of COVID-19 vaccines', Third World Resurgence, Third World Network Berhad, https://twn.my/title2/resurgence/2021/347/health1. htm, accessed on 4 December 2021.

20. The political economy of COVID-19 vaccines', Third World Resurgence, Third World Network Berhad, https://twn.my/title2/resurgence/2021/347/health1. htm, accessed on 4 December 2021.

21. Maxmen, Amy. 2021. 'Why did the world's pandemic warning system fail when COVID hit?', Nature, 23 January 2021, https://www.nature.com/articles/d41586-021-00162-4, accessed on 4 December 2021.

Chapter 15

1. Crick, as cited by Houthart and Francois (2001, 93).

2. See Jacques Derrida's Schurken Rouges (2005, 34–5) in French.

3. The progenitor of the blockchain idea was Satoshi Nakamoto, a pseudonymous name, who expounded the theory of blockchains through a white paper in 2008.

4. Damodaran A. 2018. 'When Gandhi met Spinoza', Forbes India, 12 February, https://www.forbesindia.com/article/iim-bangalore/when-gandhi-met-spinoza/49413/1, accessed on 8 December 2021.

5. A cryptocurrency is a digital or virtual currency, comprising of a set of binary data, which is secured by cryptography and is invulnerable to counterfeiting and to the malaise of 'double-spend'.

6. Damodaran A.N. 2018. 'The bitcoin innovation, crypto currencies and the Leviathan', Innovation and Development, 9(1), 85–103, 27 July.

7. Damodaran, A. 2021. 'Towards a Sui generis Crypto money Regulation System for India', Forbes India, 3 December 2021, https://www.forbesindia.com/article/iim-bangalore/towards-a-sui-generis-cryptomoney-regulation-system-for-india/71969/1, accessed on 8 December 2021.

Bibliography

Abbott, K.W., and Snidal, D. 1998. 'Why states act through formal international organizations', *Journal of Conflict Resolution*, 42, 1, 3–32.

Agarwal, A., and Narain, S. 1989. 'Towards green villages', in *Global Ecology*, ZED Books, Fernwood Publishing, London, pp. 242–56.

Agarwal, A., and Narain, S. 1991. *Global Warming in an Unequal World: A Case Study of Environmental Colonialism*, Centre for Science and Environment, Delhi.

Allison, G. 2000. 'The impact of globalization on national and international security', in S.J. Nye and J.D. Donahue (Eds.), *Governance in a Globalizing World*, Brookings Institution Press and Visions of Governance for the 21st Century, Washington, pp. 72–85.

Annan, K. 2002. *Towards a Sustainable Future*, The American Museum of Natural History's Annual Environmental Lecture, United Nations, New York.

Appadurai, A. 2000. 'The grounds and the nation-state: Identity, violence and territory', in K. Goldmann, U. Hannerz, and C. Westin (Eds.), *Nationalism and Internationalism in the Post–Cold War Era*, Routledge Publications, London, pp. 127–42.

Applbaum, A.I. 2000. 'Culture, identity, and legitimacy', in S.J. Nye and J.D. Donahue (Eds.), *Governance in a Globalizing World*, Brookings Institution Press and Visions of Governance for the 21st Century, Washington, pp. 319–29.

Archer, C.I. 2002. *Cassell's World History of Warfare*, Nebraska Press, Great Britain.

Arendt, H. 1958. *The Human Condition*, University of Chicago Press, Chicago, IL.

Arrow, K.J. 1951. *Social Choice and Individual Values*, John Wiley and Sons, Yale University Press, New Haven, CT.

Arrow, K.J. 1974. *The Limits of Organization*, Norton, New York.

Arthur, W.B. 1994. 'Inductive reasoning and bounded rationality', *American Economic Review*, 84, 2, 406–11.

Axelrod, R. 1984. *The Evolution of Cooperation*, Basic Books, New York.

Ayre, G., and Callway, R. (Eds.) 2005. *Governance for Sustainable Development: A Foundation for the Future*, Earthscan Publications Limited, London.

Ban Ki-Moon. 2008. *The United Nations and Security in a Nuclear Weapon-Free World*, Address to the East-West Institute, 24 October, UN News Centre.

Barbier, E.B. 1987. 'The concept of sustainable economic development', *Environmental Conservation*, 14, 101–10.

Bauer, P. 1956. 'Lewis theory of economic growth: A review article', *American Economic Review*, 46, 4, 632–41.

Bell, C. 2005. 'The twilight of the unipolar world', *The American Interest*, 1, 2.

Berkes, F. 2002. 'Cross-scale institutional linkages: perspectives from the bottom up', in E. Ostrom, T. Dietz, N. Dolsak, P.C. Stern, S. Stonich and E.U. Weber (Eds.), *The Drama of the Commons*, National Academy Press, Washington, pp. 293–321.

Bhagawati, J., Panagariya, A., and Srinivasan, T.N. 2004. 'The muddles over outsourcing', *Journal of Economic Perspectives*, 18, 4, 93–114.

Bogason, P. 2000. *Public Policy and Local Governance: Institutions in Post-modern Society*, Edward Elgar Publishing, UK.

Bollier, D. 2003. 'Rise of netpolitik: How the internet is changing international politics and diplomacy', Report of the Eleventh Annual Aspen Institute, Aspen Inst Human Studies (Feb. 28).

Boserup, E. 2005. *The Conditions of Agricultural Growth: The Economics of Agrarian Change*, Transactions Publishers, New Jersey.

Botkin, D.B. 1990. *Discordant Harmonies: A New Ecology for the Twenty-first Century*, Oxford University Press, New York.

Boyle, J. 2002. 'Fencing off ideas: Enclosure and the disappearance of the public domain', *Daedalus*, 131, New York.

Bromley, D.W. 1989. *Economic Interests and Institutions: The Conceptual Foundations of Public Policy*, Basil Blackwell, New York.

Brown, L.R. 2003. *Plan B: Rescuing a Planet Under Stress and a Civilization in Trouble*, Earth Policy Institute, USA.

Brown, L.D., Khagram, S., Moore, M.H., and Frumkin, P. 2000. 'Globalization, NGOs, and multisectoral relations', in S.J. Nye and J.D. Donahue (Eds.), *Governance in a Globalizing World*, Brookings Institution Press and Visions of Governance for the 21st Century, Washington, pp. 271–96.

Buchanan, J.M. 1954. 'Social choice, democracy, and free markets', *Journal of Political Economy*, 62, 114–23.

Bunyard, P. 1997. 'Tehri: A catastrophic dam in the Himalayas', in M. Rehnema and V. Bawtree (Eds.), *The Post-Development Reader*, ZED Books, London, pp. 252–62.

Burke, A. 2002. 'The perverse perseverance of sovereignty', *Borderlands*, 1, 2, 1–15.

Cascella, M., Rajnik, M., Aleem, A., Dulebohn, S.C., and Di Napoli, R. 2021. *Features, Evaluation, and Treatment of Coronavirus (COVID-19)*, 2 September 2021 [Online]. Available at: https://www.ncbi.nlm.nih.gov/books/NBK554776 [Accessed 29 November 2021].

Castells, M. 2000. *The Rise of the Network Society*, Blackwell, Oxford.

CBD High-Level Panel. 2014. *Resourcing the Aichi Biodiversity Targets: An Assessment of Benefits, Investments and Resource Needs for Implementing the Strategic Plan for Biodiversity 2011–2020*, Second Report of the High-Level Panel on Global Assessment of Resources for Implementing the Strategic Plan for Biodiversity 2011–2020. Montreal, Canada.

Challen, R. 2000. *Institutions, Transaction Costs and Environmental Policy: Institutional Reform for Water Resources*, Edward Elgar Publishing, Cheltenham.

Chang, H.-J. (ed.) 2003. *The Market, the State, and Institutions in Economic Development*, Anthem Press, London, pp. 41–60.

Chawla, R. 2005. 'The bhoomi project', in E.V. Anand (Ed.), *Learn from Them: A Compilation of Best Practices*, Department of Administrative Reforms and Public Grievances, Government of India, Penguin Enterprises.

Ciriacy-Wantrup, S.V. 1971. 'The economics of environmental policy', *Land Economics*, 47, 36–45.

Clapp, J., and Dauvergne, P. 2005. *Paths to a Green World: The Political Economy of the Global Environment*, MIT Press, England.

Clark, D. 1977. *Basic Communities: Towards an Alternative Society*, SPCK, London.

Clark, W.C. 2000. 'Environmental globalization', in J.S. Nye and J.D. Donahue (Eds.), *Governance in a Globalizing World*, Brookings Institution Press and Visions of Governance for the 21st Century, Washington, pp. 86–108.

Clippinger, J., and Bollier, D. 2005. 'A renaissance of the commons: How the new sciences and internet are framing a new global identity and order', in R.A. Ghosh (Ed.), *Code: Collaborative Ownership and the Digital Economy*, MIT Press.

Coase, R.H., 1937. 'The nature of the firm', *Economica*, 4, 386–405.

Colander, D. 2000. 'New millennium economics: How did it get this way, and what way is it?', *Journal of Economic Perspectives*, 14, 121–32.

Coleman, W.D. 2006 *Globalization and Co-operatives*, Centre for the Study of Co-operatives, University of Saskatchewan, Canada.

Convention on Biological Diversity. 2020. *Open-Ended Working Group on the Post-2020 Global Biodiversity Framework Second meeting Kunming*, China, 24–29 February 2020, CBD/WG2020/2/3 dated 6 January 2020, [Online]. Available at: https://www.cbd.int/doc/c/efb0/1f84/a892b98d2982a829962b6371/wg2020-02-03-en.pdf [Accessed 4 August 2020].

Cooper, R.N. 2000. 'International approaches to global climate change', *The World Research Observer*, 15, 2, August 2000, pp. 145–72.

Cooper, R. 2003. *The Breaking of Nations—Order and Chaos in the 21st Century*, Atlantic Monthly Press, New York.

Cox, R.W. 1996. 'A perspective on globalization', in J.H. Mittelman (Ed.), *Globalization: Critical Reflections*, Lynne Rienner, Boulder, CO, pp. 21–113.

Dalton, R.J., and Kuechler, M. 1990. *Challenging the Political Order: New Social and Political Movements in Western Democracies*, Oxford University Press, New York, p. 526.

Damodaran, A. 1992. 'Local self-governments and the geometry of bio-diversity conservation: roots of the incompatibility', *Economic and Political Weekly*, February 1992.

Damodaran, A. 1997. 'Disengaging for sustainable development: On the art of the possible in India', in A. Agarwal (Ed.), *The Challenge of the Balance, Environmental Economics in India*, Proceedings of the National Environment and Economics Meeting, January 1994, Centre for Science and Environment, New Delhi, pp. 81–8 and 371.

Damodaran, A. 1998. 'Stakeholder management policies for sustainable bio-diversity services', *Decision*, January–December, 25, 1–4, 63–78.

Damodaran, A. 2001a. *Towards an Agroecosystem Policy for India–Lessons from Two Case Studies*, Centre for Environment Education, Tata McGraw Hill, New Delhi.

Damodaran, A. 2001b. *Strategies for Restructuring Mulberry Silk Sector for Sustainable Competitive Advantage*, Central Silk Board of India, Government of India.

Damodaran, A. 2002. *Ecosystem Multifunctionality, a Proposal for Special and Differentiated Treatment for Developing Country Agriculture in Doha Round of Negotiations*, DP 60-2003, RIS, New Delhi.

Damodaran, A. 2003. 'Economics and policy implications: India's national biodiversity legislation', *Economic and Political Weekly*, December 2003.

Damodaran, A. 2004. 'Agricultural biotechnology sector in India: issues impacting innovations', *Asian Biotechnology and Development Review*, 6, 2, 41–51.

Damodaran, A. 2006. 'Coastal resource complexes of south India: Options for sustainable management', *Journal of Environmental Management*, 79, 1, 64–73.

Damodaran, A. 2007. *Coconut-copra Complex in Karnataka, Andhra Pradesh and Kerala: Streamlining Structure, Functioning and Inter-market Price Transmission Systems*, Coconut Development Board, Ministry of Agriculture, Government of India.

Damodaran, A. 2009. *Climate Financing Approaches and Systems: An Emerging Country Perspective, Working Paper 8(E)*, Graduate School of Management, St Petersburg University, Russia.

Damodaran, A. 2012. 'India's Biodiversity Financing Assessment Exercise', Dialogue Seminar Scaling Up Biodiversity Finance 6–9 March 2012 Quito, Ecuador [Online]. Available at: https://www.cbd.int/doc/meetings/fin/ds-fb-01/other/ds-fb-01-ppt-c07-in-iim-damodaran-en.pdf [Accessed 18 November 2020].

Damodaran, A. 2018. *When Gandhi Met Spinoza*, Forbes India, 12 February [Online]. Available at: https://www.forbesindia.com/article/iim-bangalore/when-gandhi-met-spinoza/49413/1 [Accessed 8 December 2021].

Damodaran, A.N. 2018. 'The bitcoin innovation, crypto currencies and the Leviathan', *Innovation and Development*, 9, 1, 85–103.

Damodaran, A. 2021. *Towards a sui generis Crypto Money Regulation System for India*, Forbes India, 3 December 2021 [Online]. Available at: https://www.forbesindia.com/article/iim-bangalore/towards-a-sui-generis-cryptomoney-regulation-system-for-india/71969/1 [Accessed 8 December 2021].

Damodaran, A. 2022a. Challenges of realising a global carbon price, Forbes India, 6 October 6. Available at: https://www.forbesindia.com/article/iim-bangalore/challenges-of-realising-a-global-carbon-price/8033 [Accessed 1 November 2022].

Damodaran, A. 2022b. Will private investments in climate action projects become a game changer?, Forbes India, 28 October, Available at https://www.forbesindia.com/article/iim-bangalore/will-private-investments-in-climate-action-projects-become-a-game-changer/80815/1 [Accessed 7th March 2023]..

Damodaran, A., and Engel, S. 2003. *Joint Forest Management in India: Assessment of Performance and Evaluation of Impacts*, ZEF-Discussion Papers on Development Policy: 77, University of Bonn, Germany.

Damodaran A., and Suneetha, M.S. 2007. *Emerging Issues in Global Governance: Multilateral Environment Agreements and the WTO: Are Synergies Desirable?* Monograph 2, Centre for Public Policy, Indian Institute of Management, Bengaluru.

Dasgupta, P. 2008. 'Discounting climate change', *Journal of Risk and Uncertainty*, 37, Cambridge University, pp. 141–69.

Demsetz, H. 1967. 'Toward a theory of property rights', *American Economic Review*, 57, 347–59.

Demsetz, H. 1969. 'Information and efficiency: Another viewpoint', *Journal of Law and Economics*, 12, 1–22.

Derrida, J. 2005. *Rogues: Two Essays on Reason*, Stanford University Press, Stanford, CA.

Dhanani, S., and Iyantul I. 2002. 'Poverty, vulnerability and social protection in a period of crisis: The case of Indonesia', *World Development*, 30, 7, 1211–31.

Dittmar, T., Hertkorn, N., Kattner, G., and Lara, R.J. 2006. 'Mangroves: A major source of dissolved organic carbon to the oceans', *Global Biogeochemical Cycles*, 20, GB1012.

Dixit, A.K. 1996. *The Making of Economic Policy: A Transaction-Cost Politics Perspective*, MIT Press, Cambridge.

Dobson, A. 2003. 'Ecological citizenship', in J.S. Dryzek and D. Schlosberg (Eds.), *Debating the Earth: The Environmental Politics Reader*, Oxford University Press, New York, pp. 596–607.

Dorosh, P. 2004. 'Trade, food aid and food security: Evolving rice and wheat markets', *Economic and Political Weekly*, 29, 4033–42.

Dryzek, J.S., and Schlosberg, D. 2005. *Debating the Earth: The Environmental Politics Reader*, Oxford University Press, Second edition, New York.

Earth Report [Online]. Available at: http://www.tve.org/mp7/details.cfm?1=eandfid= 2720 [Accessed 2001].

Economic Review, 2005. State Planning Board, Thiruvananthapuram, February, pp. 124–6.

Escobar, A. 1997. 'The making and unmaking of the third world through development' in M. Rehnema and V. Bawtree (Eds.), *The Post-Development Reader*, ZED Books, London, pp. 85–93.

Esteva, G. and Prakash, M. 1997. 'From global thinking to local thinking', in M. Rehnema and V. Bawtree (Eds.), *The Post-Development Reader*, ZED Books, London, pp. 277–89.

Esty, D.C., and Ivanova, M.H. 2002. 'Revitalizing global governance: A function-driven approach', in D. Esty and M.H. Ivanova (Eds.), *Global Environmental Governance—Options and Opportunities*, Yale School of Centre for Environmental Law and Policy.

Fay, Robert. 2019. 'The Long-simmering Economic Issues Behind Brexit', Centre for International Governance Innovation, 22 January. Available at: https://www.cig ionline.org/articles/long-simmering-economic-issues-behind-brexit?utm_sou rce=google_ads&utm_medium=grant&gclid=CjwKCAiA8Jf-BRB-EiwAWDtE GgH8zIjKaO4VMxP-SDmgA9ZJpLawVZZzNgtu0oP_dDhRJow_Sj9-2RoC2zoQ AvD_BwE [Accessed on 1 December 2020].

Feenberg, A. 2005. *Heidegger and Marcuse: The Catastrophe and Redemption of History*, Routledge, New York.

Fernand, B. 1992. *The Mediterranean and the Mediterranean World in the Age of Philip II*, translated from the French by S. Reynolds, HarperCollins, London.

Frankel, J. 2000. 'Globalization of the economy', in J.S. Nye and J.D. Donahue (Eds.), *Governance in a Globalizing World*, Brookings Institution Press and Visions of Governance for the 21st Century, Washington, pp. 45–71.

Freidman, T.L. 2005. *The World Is Flat: A Brief History of the Twenty-First Century*, Farrar, Straus and Giroux, New York.

Freidman, M. 1953. *Essays in Positive Economics*, Chicago University Press, Chicago, IL.

Frey, B.S., and Eichenberger, R. 1999. *The New Democratic Federalism for Europe: Functional, Overlapping and Competing Jurisdictions*, Edward Elgar Publishing, Cheltenham.

Fuglestvedt, J., Hanisch, T., Isaksen, I., Selrod, R., Strand, J., and Torvanger, A. 1994. *Review of Country Case Studies on Climate Change*, Number 7, Global Environment Facility, Washington DC.

Fukuyama, F. 2005. 'AI Symposium: The sources of American conduct', *The American Interest*, 1, Autumn.

Gadgil, M., and Iyer, P. 1987. 'On the diversification of common property resource use by the Indian society', in B. Fikret (Ed.), *Common Property Resources: Ecology and Community-Based Sustainable Development*, Belhaven Press, London.

Gandhi, M.K. 1997. 'The quest for simplicity: My idea of swaraj', in M. Rehnema and V. Bawtree (Eds.), *The Post-Development Reader*, ZED Books, London, pp. 306–7.

Garfinkle, A. 2005. 'A conversation with Condoleezza Rice', *The American Interest*, Autumn.

Geethanjali, N., and Kaur, D. 2015. *How Achieving Millennium Development Goals Will Make or Break India*, 9 July, [Online]. Available at: https://www.dailyo.in /politics/millennium-development-goals-un-population-standard-of-living-poverty-line-agriculture/story/1/4870.html [Accessed 18 November 2020].

Ghosh, A.K. 1989. 'Rural poverty and relative prices in India', *Cambridge Journal of Economics*, 13, 2, 307–31.

Ghosh, R.I. (Ed.) 2005. 'A renaissance of the commerce: How the new sciences and the internet are framing a new global identity and order', in *Code: Collaborative Ownership and the Digital Economy*, MIT Press, England, pp. 259–86.

Ghoshal, S. 2005. 'Towards a good theory of management', in J. Birkinshaw and G. Piramal (Eds.), *Sumantra Ghoshal on Management*, Prentice Education Limited, Great Britain, pp. 1–27.

Giddens, A. 1990. *The Consequences of Modernity*, Polity, Cambridge.

Gleeson, D. 2021. 'Omicron variant is proof of the high cost of rich countries' greed for Covid-19 vaccines', *The Conversation*, December 1, 2021 [Online]. Available at: https://theconversation.com/wealthy-nations-starved-the-developing-world-of-vaccines-omicron-shows-the-cost-of-this-greed-172763 [Accessed 1 December 2021].

Gopal Krishna. 2006. 'The Scrapping of Riky', March 23 [Online]. Available at: https://indiatogether.org/riky-environment [Accessed 10 December 2021].

Golwalker, M.S. 1966. *Bunch of Thoughts*, Vikrama Prakasham, Bengaluru.

Gopichandran, R., and Praveen, P. 2006. 'Resolving conflicts and facilitating cooperation in preventive management of large scale mobile common resource: Lessons from Montreal protocol', Paper presented at Asia regional workshop on compensation for ecosystem services, Institute for Social and Economic Change, Bangalore, India.

Gordon, H.S. 1954. 'The economic theory of a common property resource: The fishery', *The Journal of Political Economy*, 62, 124–42.

Governance in a Globalizing World. Brookings Institution Press and Visions of Governance for the 21st Century, Washington, pp. 72–85.

Government of India. 2005. *Demystifying WTO and Development: Frequently Asked Questions*, UNCTAD-Ministry of Commerce, Government of India–DFID Project on 'Strategies and preparedness for trade and globalization', CENTAD, New Delhi.

Government of India. 2015. India's intended nationally determined contribution: working towards climate, justice [Online]. Available at: https://www4.unfccc.int/sites/ndcstaging/PublishedDocuments/India%20First/INDIA%20INDC%20TO%20UNFCCC.pdf [Accessed 20 December 2021].

Grindle, M.S. 2000. 'Ready or not: The developing world and globalization', in J.S. Nye and J.D. Donahue (Eds.), *Governance in a Globalizing World*, Brookings Institution Press and Visions of Governance for the 21st Century, Washington, pp. 178–206.

Groenewegen, J. 1996. *Transaction Cost Economics and Beyond*, Kluwer Academic Publishers, London, pp. 1–10.

Gupta, R. 2006. 'Business as usual—ITC's CDM project', *Down to Earth*, 14, 23, 16.

Haas, P.M. 1992. 'Introduction: Epistemic communities and international policy co-ordination', *International Organization*, 46, 1.

Haas, P.M., and Kanie, N. (Eds.). 2004. *Emerging Forces in Environmental Governance*, United Nations University Press, Tokyo, pp. 263–81.

Haas, P.M., Kanie, N., and Murphy, C.N. 2004. 'Conclusion: Institutional design and institutional development for sustainable development', in P.M. Haas and N. Kanie (Eds.), *Emerging Forces in Environmental Governance*, United Nations University Press, Tokyo, pp. 263–81.

Hajer, M.A. 1997. *The Politics of Environmental Discourse: Ecological Modernization and the Policy Process*, Oxford University Press, USA.

Hanley, N., Shogren, J.F., and White, B. 2001. *Introduction to Environmental Economics*, Oxford University Press.

Hardt, M., and Negri, A. 2000. *Empire*, Harvard University Press, USA.

Harris, O. 2003. *Benign or Imperial? Reflections on American Hegemony*, Boyer Lectures, Computer Publications, http://www.abc.net.ac/rn/boyers/stones/s 987632.html

Harriss-White, B. 2003. 'On understanding markets as social and political institutions in developing economics', in H.-J. Chang (ed.), *Re-Thinking Development Economics*, Anthem Press, London, pp. 481–97.

Havel, V. 1990. *Disturbing the Peace*, Faber and Faber, London, UK.

Hayami, Y., and Ruttan, V.W. 1985. *Agricultural Development—An International Perspective: Revised and Expanded*, The Johns Hopkins University Press, Baltimore, MD, USA.

Hayek, F.A. 1945. 'The use of knowledge in society', *American Economic Review*, 35, 519–20.

Hayward, J.W., and Varela, F.J. (Eds.) 2001. *Gentle Bridges: Conversations with the Dalai Lama on the Sciences of Mind*, Shambhala Publications, Boston, MA, pp. 6–24.

Heita, K. 2004. 'Japanese civilization (Part 14): Japan and the transfer of economic hegemony', *Japan Spotlight*, May/June, pp. 37–41.

Held, D. 2000. *A Globalizing World? Culture, Economics, Politics*, Routledge Publications, London.

Helvarg, D. 1994. *The War Against the Greens: The Wise-Use Movement, the New Rights and Anti-Environmental Violence*, Sierra Club Books, San Francisco.

Hildyard, N., Hegde, P., Wolvekamp, P. and Reddy, S. 1997, *Same Platform Different Train: Pluralism, Participation and Power*, Corner House Document, http://www.thecornerhouse.org.uk/document/partfao.html

Hirst, P.Q., and Thompson, G.F. 1999. *Globalization in Question: The International Economy and the Possibilities of Governance*, Polity Press, Cambridge.

Houthart, F., and Polet, F. (Eds.) 2001. *The Other Davos: The Globalization of Resistance to the World Economic System*, ZED Books, New York.

https://www.biodiversityfinance.net/index.php/history [Accessed 19 November 2020].
https://www.cbd.int/intro/ [Accessed 19 November 2020].
https://www.cbd.int/sp/targets/ [Accessed 19 November 2020].
https://enb.iisd.org/UN-Biodiversity-Conference-CBD-COP15-15Oct2021 [Accessed 15 November 2021].
https://www.futurebridge.com/industry/perspectives-energy/why-did-cop-25-fail/ [Accessed 18 November 2020].
https://www.gavi.org/vaccineswork/covax-explained [Accessed 1 December 2021].
http://ieg-ego.eu/en/threads/europe-on-the-road/the-history-of-tourism [Accessed 1 December 2021].
https://www.indiatimes.com/explainers/news/kunming-declaration-biodiversity-551631.html# highlight_68105 [Accessed 15 November 2021].
http://www.unccd.int/ [Accessed 10 December 2021].
https://www.unccd.int/sites/default/files/relevant-links/2018-08/cop21add1_SF_EN.pdf [Accessed 10 December 2021].
http://www.un-documents.net/wced-ocf.htm [Accessed 10 December 2021].
https://www.undp.org/content/undp/en/home/sustainable-development-goals/bac kgroundhtml#:~:text=Background%20on%20the%20goalsandtext=The%20ob jective%20was%20to%20produce,tackle%20the%20indignity%20of%20poverty [Accessed 18 November 2020].
https://www.undp.org/content/undp/en/home/sustainable-development-goals/bac kground.html#:~:text=Background%20on%20the%20goalsandtext=The%20ob jective%20was%20to%20produce,tackle%20the%20indignity%20of%20poverty [Accessed 7 October 2020].
https://unfccc.int/process/conferences/the-big-picture/milestones/outcomes-of-the-durban-conference [Accessed 18 November 2020].
https://unfccc.int/process-and-meetings/the-paris-agreement/the-paris-agreement [Accessed 18 November 2020].
https://unstats.un.org/sdgs/report/2016/ [Accessed 18 November 2020].
https://www.who.int/news/item/30-03-2021-who-calls-for-further-studies-data-on-origin-of-sars-cov-2-virus-reiterates-that-all-hypotheses-remain-open [Accessed 1 December 2021].
https://www.worldbank.org/en/country/costarica/overview#1 [Accessed 10 December 2021].
https://www.worldometers.info/coronavirus/ [Accessed 1 December 2021].
https://www.worldwildlife.org/stories/what-is-a-pangolin [Accessed 1 December 2021].
AHurley, D., and Mayer-Schonberger, V. 2000. 'Information policy and governance', in J.S. Nye and J.D. Donahue (eds), *Governance in a Globalizing World*, Brookings Institution Press and Visions of Governance for the 21st Century, Washington, pp. 330–46.
IISD Reporting Services, Through Its ENB Meeting Coverage [Online], Available at: https://enb.iisd.org/desert/cop14/ [Accessed 18 November 2020].
Illich, I. 1997. 'Development as planned poverty', in M. Rehnema and V. Bawtree (Eds.), *The Post-Development Reader*, ZED Books, London.
India: Sustainable Development. 1998. *Ministry of Environment and Forests*, Government of India, New Delhi.

International Centre for Trade and Sustainable Development, ICTSD. 2008. *Liberalization of Trade in Environmental Goods for Climate Change Mitigation: The Sustainable Development Context*, Background Paper, Trade and Climate Change Seminar, Copenhagen, 18–20 June 2008, http://www.ictsd.org/

Jones, K.A. 2004. *Who Is Afraid of WTO*, Oxford University Press, New York.

Juma, C. 2000. 'The perils of centralizing global environmental governance', *Environment*, 42, 9, 44–5.

Kameyama, Y. 2004. 'IPCC: Its role in international negotiations and domestic decision making on climate change policies', in N. Kanie and P.M. Haas (Eds.), *Emerging Forces in Environmental Governance*, United Nations University Press, Tokyo.

Kanie, N. 2004. 'Global environmental governance in terms of vertical linkages', in N. Kanie and P.M. Haas (Eds.), *Emerging Forces in Environmental Governance*, United Nations University Press, Tokyo, pp. 86–114.

Kapil, S. 2019. 'Pangolin: Adorable but endangered'. *Science Reporter*, pp. 29–31, [Online]. Available at: http://nopr.niscair.res.in/bitstream/123456789/45900/1/SR%2056%283%29%2029-31.pdf [Accessed 1 December 2021].

Kelly L., and Rambharos, M. 2019. *What You Need to Know About Article 6 of the Paris Agreement*, World Resources Institute, Dec 2, [Online]. Available at: https://www.wri.org/blog/2019/12/article-6-paris-agreement-what-you-need-to-know [Accessed 18 November 2020].

Keohane, R.O. 1984. *After Hegemony: Cooperation and Discord in the World Political Economy*, Princeton University Press, Princeton, NJ.

Keohane, R.O., and Nye, J.S. 2000. 'Introduction', in J.S. Nye and J.D. Donahue (Eds.), *Governance in a Globalizing World*, Brookings Institution Press and Visions of Governance for the 21st Century, Washington, pp. 1–41.

Keohane, R.O., and Nye, J.S. 1972. *Transnational Relations and World Politics*, Harvard University Press, Centre for International Affairs.

Kiely, R. 2005. *The Clash of Globalisation: Neo-Liberalism, The Third Way and Anti-Globalisation*, Brill Academic Publishers, Boston.

Kindersley, N. 2005. 'Nature's fury in Europe', *Down to Earth*, 14, 9, 13–4.

Knight, F.H. 1947. *Freedom and Reform: Essays in Economic and Social Philosophy*, Harper, New York.

Krasner, S.D. (ed.) 2001. *Problematic Sovereignty*, Columbia University Press, New York.

Krugman, P. 2000. 'Reckonings: The magic mountains', in *New York Times*, 23 January.

Krugman, P. 2009. 'Decade at Bernie's', *New York Times*, 15 February.

Kulkarni, P. 2005. *Non-tariff Barriers and NAMA Negotiations: Developing India's Negotiating Position*, Hong Kong Series, Centre for Trade and Development (CENTAD), New Delhi.

Kumar, S. 2006. 'Slow to share: Biodiversity convention makes tardy progress', *Down to Earth*, 14, 23, 18–9.

Leblang, D. 2003. 'To devalue or to defend? The political economy of exchange rate policy', *International Studies Quarterly*, 47, 4, 533–59.

Lélé, S.M., Kiran Kumar, A.K., and Shivashankar, P. 2005. *Joint Forest Planning and Management in the Eastern Plains Region of Karnataka: A Rapid Assessment*, Technical Report, CISED, Bangalore, September.

Levy, D.L., and Newell, P.J. (Eds.) 2005. *Introduction in the Business of Global Environmental Governance*, MIT Press, Cambridge.

Margerum, R.D. 1999. 'Getting past yes: From capital creation to action', *Journal of the American Planning Association*, 65, 181–92.

Markandya, A. 1993. *Environmental Economics: A Reader*, Macmillan, Palgrave.

Marshall, G. 2005. *Economics for Collaborative Environmental Management: Renegotiating The Commons*, Earthscan Ltd., London.

Marx, K. 1974. *Capital*, 3, Progress Publishers, Moscow.

Maxmen, A. 2021. 'Why did the world's pandemic warning system fail when COVID hit?', *Nature*, 23 January 2021, [Online]. Available at: https://www.nature.com/artic les/d41586-021-00162-4 [Accessed 4 December 2021].

Maxmen, A., and Smriti, M. 2021. The COVID lab-leak hypothesis: what scientists do and don't know, *Nature* [Online]. Available at: https://www.nature.com/articles/ d41586-021-01529-3 [Accessed 1 December 2021].

Mayer-Schonberger, V., and Hurley, D. 2000, 'Globalization of communication' in J.S. Nye and J.D. Donahue (Eds.), *Governance in a Globalizing World*, Brookings Institution Press and Visions of Governance for the 21st Century, Washington, pp. 135–51.

Mehta, R. 2005. *Non-tariff Barriers Affecting India's Exports*, RIS Discussion paper 97, India.

Menon, K.P.S. 1972. *Many Worlds: An Autobiography*, Pearl Edition, Oxford University Press, Bombay.

Meyer-Abich K.M. 2004. 'Winners and losers in climate change', in *Global Ecology*, ZED Books, Fernwood Publishing, London, pp. 68–87.

Mishra, A., Nayak, T., and Ghate, R. 2005. *Dependency on Common Property Resources: A Case Study of Water*, Indo-Dutch Programme on Alternatives in Development (IDPAD) Newsletter, III, 2, July–December, pp. 21–5.

Mohan, B.S., and Nambiar, V. [Online]. *J Infect Dis Epidemiol* 6:146. doi.org/10.23937/ 2474-3658/1510146. Available at: https://clinmedjournals.org/articles/jide/jour nal-of-infectious-diseases-and-epidemiology-jide-6-146.php?jid=jide [Accessed 1 December 2021].

Mori, S. 2004. 'Institutionalization of NGO involvement in policy functions for global environmental governance' in N. Kanie and P.M. Haas (Eds.), *Emerging Forces in Environmental Governance*, United Nations University Press, Tokyo, pp. 157–75.

Nairn, T. 1997. *Faces of Nationalism: Janus Revisited*, Verso, London (2nd edition 2005).

Najam, A. 2003. 'Towards better multilateral environmental agreements: filling the knowledge gaps', in T. Bigy (Ed.) *Survival for Small Planet: Issues Addressed at the World Summit on Sustainable Development*, Earthscan, London, pp. 74–84.

Nandy, A. 2007. *Time Treks: The Uncertain Future of Old and New Despotisms*, Seagull Books, London and New York.

Nash, J. 1951. 'Non-co-operative games', *Annals of Mathematics*, 54, 286–95.

National Action Plan on Climate Change, 2008, *Prime Minister's Council on Climate Change*, Prime Minister's Office, New Delhi.

Nehru, J. 2004. *The Discovery of India*, Penguin Books, New Delhi.

Nelson, R. 1994. *An Agenda for Formal Growth Theory*, Working Paper, International Institute for Applied Systems Analysis, Luxembourg, Austria.

Newell, P. 2000. 'Managing multinationals: the governance of investment for the environment', *Journal of International Development*, Special Conference Issue, 13, 7, 907–19.

NGOs Outline Position on Paris Agreement. 2014. September 11, [Online]. Available at: http://sdg.iisd.org/news/ngos-outline-position-on-paris-agreement/ [Accessed 4 December 2020].

Nilekani, N. 2008. *Imagining India: Ideas for the New Century*, Penguin Books, India.

Nolan, P. 2003. *Industrial Policy in the Early 21st century: The Challenge of the Global Business Revolution*, Anthem Press, London, pp. 299–321.

Nordhaus, W.D. 2007. *The Stern Review of the Economics of Climate Change*, Department of Economics, Yale University.

Norris, P. 1999a. 'Conclusions: The growth of critical citizens and its consequences', in P Norris (Ed.), *Critical Citizens: Global Support for Democratic Governance*, Oxford University Press, New York, pp. 257–72.

North, D.C. 1990. *Institutions, Institutional Change and Economic Performance*, Cambridge University Press, Cambridge.

O'Brien, R. 2000. *Contesting Global Governance: Multilateral Economic Institutions and Global Social Movements*, Cambridge University Press, Cambridge.

Obama, B. 2007. *The Audacity of Hope: Thoughts on Reclaiming the American Dream*, Crown Publishers, New York.

Ocampo, J.A. 2003. 'Development of the global order' in H.-J. Chang, *Re-thinking Development Economics*, Anthem Press, London, p. 91.

OECD Newsletter, Coronavirus (COVID-19) Vaccines for Developing Countries: An Equal Shot at Recovery, OECD Policy Responses to Coronavirus (COVID 19), OECD, 4 February 2021, [Online]. Available at: https://www.oecd.org/coronavirus/policy-responses/coronavirus-covid-19-vaccines-for-developing-countries-an-equal-shot-at-recovery-6b0771e6/ [Accessed 1 December 2021].

Oloka-Onyango, J., and Udagama, D. 2000, 'The realization of economic, social and cultural rights: globalization and its impact on the full enjoyment of human rights,' Preliminary Report, Geneva: United Nations Sub-Commission on the Promotion and Protection of Human Rights, http://www.unhchr.ch/huridocda/huridoca. nsf/2848af408d01ec0ac1256609004e770b/21a92d3d0425a0cec125693500484 d2f?OpenDocumentandHighlight=2,Oloka-Onyango

Ophuls, W.P., and Boyan, A.S. 2005. 'The American political economy II: The non-politics of laissez faire', in J.S. Dryzek and D. Schlosberg (Eds.), *Debating the Earth: The Environmental Politics Reader*, Oxford University Press, New York, pp. 191–206.

Ostrom, E. 1990. *Governing the Commons: The Evolution of Institutions for Collective Action*, Cambridge University Press, Cambridge.

Ostrom, E. 2000. 'Collective action and the evolution of social norms', *Journal of Economic Perspectives*, 14, pp. 137–58.

Ostrom, V., Bish, R., and Ostrom, E. 1988. *Local Government in the United States*, San Francisco, Institute for Contemporary Studies.

Ostrom, E., Dietz, T., Dolsak, N., Stern, P.C., Stonich, S., and Weber, E.U. (Eds.) 2002. *The Drama of the Commons*, National Academy Press, Washington.

Our Common Future. 1987. Oxford University Press, Oxford.

Pareto, V. (Ed.) 1935. *The Mind and Society*, Translated from the Italian/Latin by A. Livingston/A. Bongiomo, Harcourt, Brace, and Co., New York.

Paterson, M., D. Humphreys, and L. Pettiford. 1998. 'Conceptualizing global environmental governance: From interstate regimes to counter-hegemonic struggles', *Global Environmental Politics*, 3, 2, 1–10.

Payne, C. 2005. 'UN commission awards compensation for environmental and public health damages from 1990–1 Gulf war', *ASIL Insights*, http://www.asil.org/insight s050810.cfm, 10 August.

Pearce, F. 1991. 'Building a disaster: The monumental folly of India's Tehri Dam', *The Ecologist*, 21, 3, May/June.

Pirenne, H. 2001. *Mohammed and Charlemagne*, Courier Dover Publications, USA.

Polanyi, K. 1957. *The Great Transformation: The Political and Economic Origins of Our Time*, Beacon Press, Boston.

The Prototype Carbon Fund–The World Bank's Commitment to Climate Change, 2002, ECOAL, 33, pp. 6.

Puente-Rodriguez, D., Ruivenkamp, G.T.P. and Jongerden, J.P. 2006. *Redesigning the Production of the Bacillus Thuringiensis Bio-Pesticides: An Analysis of an Experience in Andhra Pradesh, India*, Paper submitted to the Innogen Annual Conference 2006: Genomics for Development, The Life Sciences and Poverty Reduction, Regentis College, London.

Rajasthan Human Development Report. 2002, Government of Rajasthan, Jaipur.

Ranjan, P. 2006. *NAMA Tariff Negotiation: What Are South Asia's Best Options?*, Working Paper, CENTAD, New Delhi.

Rehnema, M., and Bawtree, V. (Eds.) 1997. *The Post-Development Reader*, Zed Books, London.

Report of the World Commission on Environment and Development: Our Common Future, [Online]. Available at: https://sustainabledevelopment.un.org/content/documents/5987our-common-future.pdf [Accessed 10 December 2021].

Resolutions 1 to 96 [Online]. Available at: https://www.un.org/ecosoc/en/ngo/consultative-status [Accessed 10 December 2021].

Risse-Kappen, T. 1995. *Cooperation Among Democracies*. Princeton University Press, Princeton.

Rodgers, N. 2004. *The History and Conquest of Ancient Rome*, Anness Publishing Limited, Hermes House, London.

Rodrik, D. 2000. 'Governance of economic globalization', in J.S. Nye and J.D. Donahue (Eds.), *Governance in a Globalizing World*, Brookings Institution Press and Visions of Governance for the 21st Century, Washington, pp. 347–66.

Rosendorf, N.M. 2000. 'Social and cultural globalization: Concepts, history, and America's role', in J.S. Nye and J.D. Donahue (Eds.), *Governance in a Globalizing World*, Brookings Institution Press and Visions of Governance for the 21st Century, Washington, pp. 109–134.

Rowell, A. 1996. *Green Backlash: Global Subversion of the Environment*, Routledge Publications, London.

Sachs, J.D. 2005. *The End of Poverty: Economic Possibilities for Our Time*, Penguin Press, USA.

Sachs, W. (ed.) 2004. 'Global ecology and the shadow of development', in *Global Ecology*, ZED books, Fernwood Publishing, London, pp. 3–22.

Sachs, W. 1997. 'The need for the home perspective', in M. Rehnema and V. Bawtree (Eds.), *The Post-Development Reader*, Zed Books, London, pp. 290–301.

Saich, T. 2000. 'Globalization, governance, and the authoritarian state: China', in J.S. Nye and J.D. Donahue (Eds.), *Governance in a Globalizing World*, Brookings Institution Press and Visions of Governance for the 21st Century, Washington, pp. 208–28.

Said, E.W. 1978. *Orientalism*, Vintage Books, USA.

Sainath, P. 1996. 'The house that Laurie built-1', in *Everybody Loves a Good Drought: Stories from India's Poorest Districts*, Penguin Books Ltd., Canada.

Sandquist, G.M. 2004. 'Quantifying the perceived risks associated with nuclear energy issues', *International Journal of Nuclear Energy Science and Technology*, 1, 1, 61–8.

Sassen, S. 2001. *The Global City: New York, London, and Tokyo*, Princeton University Press, Princeton.

Saul, J.R. 2005. *The Collapse of Globalism: The Reinvention of the World*, Penguin Books, India.

Schama, S. 2009. *The American Future: A History from the Founding Fathers to Barack Obama*, Vintage Books, London.

Schelling, T.C. 2006. 'What makes greenhouse sense', in T.C. Shelling (Ed.), *Strategies of Commitment and Other Essays*, Harvard University Press, USA.

Schneider, L. 2021. '#COP26 in Glasgow delivered rules for international carbon markets—how good or bad are they?'. Available at: https://blog.oeko.de/glasgow-delivered-rules-for-international-carbon-markets-how-good-or-bad-are-they-cop26/ [Accessed 1 November 2022].

Scholte, J.A. 2000. *Globalization: A Critical Introduction*, Palgrave, London, pp. 15–7.

Scott, J.C. 1997. 'The infra-politics of subordinate groups', in M. Rehnema and V. Bawtree (Eds.), *The Post-Development Reader*, Zed Books, London, pp. 311–28.

Sen, A.K. 1995. 'Rationality and social choice', in *American Economic Review*, 85, 1–24.

Sen, A.K. 1983. *Poverty and Famines: An Essay on Entitlement and Deprivation*, Oxford University Press, New Delhi.

Sender, J. 2003. 'Rural poverty and gender: Analytical frameworks and policy proposals', in H.-J.-Chang (Ed.), *Re-Thinking Development Economics*, Anthem Press, London, pp. 405–22.

Sethi, N. 2006. 'Worldly wise: India hard sells its troubled protected areas abroad', *Down To Earth*, 14, 21, 31 March, p. 30.

Shah, E. 2005. 'Local and global elites join hands: development and diffusion of Bt technology in Gujarat', *Economic and Political Weekly*, October 22.

Shanin, T. 1997. 'The idea of progress', in M. Rehnema and V. Bawtree (Eds.), *The Post-Development Reader*, ZED Books, London, pp. 65–72.

Shiller, R.J. 2008. *The Subprime Solution: How Today's Global Financial Crisis Happened, and What to Do About It*, Princeton University Press, Princeton, USA.

Shiva, V. 1995. 'The greening of the global reach', in W. Sachs (Ed.), *Global Ecology and the Shadow of Development*, ZED Books, Fernwood Publishing, London, pp. 149–56.

Simon, H.A. 1946. 'The proverbs of administration', *Public Administration Review*, 6, 53–67.

Simon, H.A. 1955. 'A behavioral model of rational choice', *Quarterly Journal of Economics*, 69, 99–118.

Simon, H.A. 1991. 'Organizations and markets', *Journal of Economic Perspectives*, American Economic Association, 5, 2, 25–44, Spring.

Simon, J. and Kahn, H. 1986. 'Introduction to the resourceful earth', in *Debating the Earth*, Oxford University Press, New York, pp. 51–73.

Sinai, A., and Merrill, P. 2005. 'Debating the future of the US economy', *The American Interest*, 1, 2, Winter.

Snow, E. 1970. *Red China Today: The Other Side of the River*, Penguin Books, London.

Solzhenitsyn, A. 1991. *The Cancer Ward*, Farrar, Straus, and Giroux. New York.

Spash, C. 2007. 'Changing climates, changing values, changing editors all change', *Environmental Values*, 16, 2, DOI:10.3197/096327107780474537, http://www.erica.demon.co.uk/EV/EditEV162.html

Spretnak, C., and Capra, F. 1986. *Green Politics*, Bear and Co. Rochester, USA.

Srinivasan, R.K. 2006. 'Catching rain', *Down to Earth*, 14, 24, 15 May; pp. 42–5.

Stavins, R. 2008. 'Addressing climate change with a comprehensive US cap-and-trade system', *Oxford Review of Economic Policy*, 24, 2, 298–321.

Steiner, A. 2009. *Speech at the Fourth Meeting of the Conference of Parties to the Stockholm Convention on Persistent Organic Pollutants*, 7 May 2009, http://chm.pops.int/Convention/Media/Speeches/tabid/538/language/en-US/Default.aspx

Stern, N. 2008. *Key Elements of a Global Deal on Climate Change*, London School of Economics and Political Science, Stern_Papers/key%20Elements%20of%20%20Global%20Deal%20Final01may.pdf

Stern, N. 2006. *The Stern Review of the Economics of Climate Change*, Cambridge University Press, Cambridge.

Stiglitz, J.E. 2002. *Globalization and Its Discontents*, Norton, New York.

Stockholm POPS Convention: Overview and Status of US Ratification and Implementing Legislation, WWF, [Online]. Available at: http://www.wwf.or.jp/activity/toxics/lib/POPSbackgrounder.pdf [Accessed 10 December 2021].

Sustainable Development Goals. A Guidepost Report [Online]. Available at: https://www.guidepost.es/rainbow-of-u-n-sustainable-goals-reflected-in-spanish-social-media-fpr-a-future-we-want/ [Accessed 18 November 2020].

Swanson, T. 2005. *Global Action for Biodiversity: An International Framework for Implementing the Convention on Biological Diversity*, Earthscan Publications Limited, London.

Takashi, I. 2004. 'Social capital in 10 Asian societies: is social capital a good concept for gauging democratic, developmental, and regionalizing trends in Asia?' *Japanese Journal of Political Science*, 5, 197–212.

Taleb, N.N. 2005. *Fooled by Randomness: The Hidden Role of Chance in the Markets and Life*, Penguin Books, London.

Thompson, D.B. 1999. 'Beyond benefit-cost analysis: institutional transaction costs and regulation of water quality', *Natural Resources Journal*, 39, 517–41.

Thorstein, V. 1994. *The Theory of the Leisure Class*, Dover Publications Inc., New York.

Tiffen, M, Mortimore, M., and Gichuki, F. 1994. *More People, Less Erosion: Environmental Recovery in Kenya*, John Valley Publication, Chichester.

Torgerson, D. 1999. *The Promise of Green Politics: Environmentalism and the Public Sphere*, Duke University Press, Durham.

Torgerson, D. 2005. 'Farewell to the green movement? Political action and the green public sphere', in J.S. Dryzek and D. Schlosberg (Eds.), *Debating the Earth: The Environmental Politics Reader*, Oxford University Press, New York, pp. 509–24.

Touraine, A. 1983. *Anti-nuclear Protest: The Opposition to Nuclear Energy in France*, Cambridge University Press.

Toye, J. 2003. 'Changing perspectives in development economics', in H.-J.-Chang (ed.), *Re-Thinking Development Economics*, Anthem Press, London, pp. 21–40.

Trump attacks WTO after it says US tariffs on China broke global trade rules, 2020, September, [Online]. Available at: https://www.theguardian.com/world/2020/sep/16/trump-attacks-wto-after-it-says-us-tariffs-on-china-broke-global-trade-rules [Accessed 4 December 2020].

UNEP 200, UNEP/CHW.6/23, 8 August 2002, *Consideration of Implementation of the Basel Convention Technical Matters: Preparation of Technical Guidelines*, Sixth Meeting of the Conference of Parties, Geneva, item 6 (e) (II) of the Provisional Agenda, UNEP (hard copy).

Vasavi, A.R., and Upadhya, C. 2005. 'New global workforces and virtual workplaces: connections, culture, and control', *Indo-Dutch programme on alternatives in development (IDPAD) Newsletter*, 3, 2, July–December, pp. 37–41.

von Weizsacker, C. 2004. 'Competing notions of biodiversity', in N. Kanie and P.M. Haas (Eds.), *Emerging Forces in Environmental Governance*, United Nations University Press, Tokyo.

Wapner, P. 1996. 'Politics beyond the state: environmental activism and world civic politics', in J.S. Dryzek and D. Schlosberg (Eds.), *Debating the Earth: The Environmental Politics Reader*, Oxford University Press, New York, pp. 525–49.

Werksman, J. 2004. 'Consolidating global environmental governance: new lessons from the GEF?', in N. Kanie and P.M. Haas (Eds.), *Emerging Forces in Environmental Governance*, United Nations University Press, Paris, pp. 35–49.

Williamson, O.E. 1975. *Markets and Hierarchies: Analysis and Anti-Trust Implications*, Free Press, New York.

Williamson, O.E. 1996. *The Mechanisms of Governance*, Oxford University Press, New York.

Wolf, M. 2005. *Why Globalisation Works (Yale Nota Bene)*, Yale University Press, USA.

World Bank. 2002. *Evaluating the World Bank's Approach to Global Programs: Addressing the Challenges of Globalization*, Independent Evaluation Group, World Bank, Washington, DC.

World Bank. 2006. *Equity and Development*, The World Development Report, The World Bank, Washington, DC.

World Development Report (WDR). 2006. *Equity and Development*, The World Bank, Washington, DC.

Worster, D. 2004. 'The shaky ground of sustainability', in W. Sachs (Ed.), *Global Ecology and the Shadow of Development*, ZED Books, Fernwood Publishing, London, pp. 132–45.

WTO. 1998. *Understanding the WTO Agreement on Sanitary and Phytosanitary Measures*, [Online]. Available at: https://www.wto.org/english/tratop_e/sps_e/spsund_e.htm [Accessed 1 December 2021].

WTTC, Economic Impact Reports, [Online]. Available at: https://wttc.org/Research/ Economic-Impact, [Accessed 1 December 2021].

Young, O.R. 2002a. *The Institutional Dimensions of Environmental Change: Fit, Interplay, and Scale*, MIT Press, Cambridge.

Young, O.R. 2002b. 'Institutional interplay: The environmental consequences of cross-scale interactions', in E. Ostrom, T. Dietz, N. Dolsak, P.C. Stern, S. Stonich, and E.U. Weber (Eds.), *The Drama of the Commons*, National Academy Press, Washington, pp. 263–91.

Index